A Mind

Patient and Untamed

Published in association with the
Institute of Mennonite Studies

A Mind
Patient and Untamed

Assessing
John
Howard
Yoder's
Contributions
to Theology, Ethics,
and Peacemaking

Edited by
Ben C. Ollenburger and Gayle Gerber Koontz

Introduction by Stanley Hauerwas

Cascadia
Publishing House
the new name of Pandora Press U.S.
Telford, Pennsylvania

copublished with
Herald Press
Scottdale, Pennsylvania

Cascadia Publishing House orders, information, reprint permissions:
contact@CascadiaPublishingHouse.com
1-215-723-9125
126 Klingerman Road, Telford PA 18969
www.CascadiaPublishingHouse.com

A Mind Patient and Untamed
Copyright © 2004 by Cascadia Publishing House,
Telford, PA 18969
All rights reserved.
Copublished with Herald Press, Scottdale, PA
Library of Congress Catalog Number: 2003055662
ISBN: 1-931038-20-1
Printed in the United States by Evangel Press, Nappanee, Indiana
Book design by Cascadia Publishing House
Cover design byJim Butti

Library of Congress Cataloguing-in-Publication Data
A mind patient and untamed : assessing John Howard Yoder's contribu-
tions to theology, ethics, and peacemaking / [edited by] Ben C. Ollen-
burger and Gayle Gerber Koontz ; introduction by Stanley Hauerwas.
     p. cm.
Includes bibliographical references and index.
 ISBN 1-931038-20-1 (alk. paper)
 1. Yoder, John Howard. I. Ollenburger, Ben C. II. Koontz, Gayle
Gerber. III. Title.
 BX8143.Y59M56 2004
 230'.97'092--dc22

                                                      2003055662

12 11 10 09 08 07 06 05 04   10 9 8 7 6 5 4 3 2 1

"Be patient, therefore, beloved, until the coming of the Lord."
—James 5:7 (NRSV)

"Let the same mind be in you that was in Christ Jesus."
—Philippians 2:5 (NRSV)

Contents

Introduction: Lingering with Yoder's Wild Work   11
  Stanley Hauerwas, Duke University

FIRMLY GROUNDED WITHOUT FOUNDATIONS: YODER'S PATIENT (NON-)METHOD

1 The Christian Life as Gift and Patience: • 23
  Why Yoder Has Trouble with Method
  Harry Huebner, Canadian Mennonite University

2 The Radical Christological Rhetoric of John Howard Yoder   • 39
  Gerald Biesecker-Mast, Bluffton College

3 Patience, Witness, and the Scattered Body of Christ:
  Yoder and Virilio on Knowledge, Politics, and Speed   • 56
  *Chris K. Huebner, Canadian Mennonite University/Duke University
  (Ph.D. candidate)*

4 Yoder's Patience and/with Derrida's *Differance*   • 75
  Peter C. Blum, Hillsdale College

THE CHURCH, POWER, AND EXILE: YODER'S (NON-)CONSTANTINIANISM

5 Yoder's Idea of Constantinianism:
  An Analytical Framework Toward Conversation   • 89
  Thomas Heilke, University of Kansas

6 Constantinianism Before and After Nicea:
  Issues in Restitutionist Historiography   • 126
  J. Alexander Sider, Duke University (Ph.D. candidate)

7 Yoder and the Jews:
   Cosmopolitan Homelessness as Ecclesial Model • 145
   Duane K. Friesen, Bethel College

8 On Exile:
   Yoder, Said, and a Theology of Land and Return • 161
   Alain Epp Weaver, Mennonite Central Committee (West Bank)

THE CHURCH, ETHICS, AND THE NATIONS:
YODER AND HAUERWAS

9 Share the House:
   Yoder and Hauerwas Among the Nations • 187
   Paul Doerksen, Mennonite Brethren Collegiate Institute

10 The Public Ethics of John Howard Yoder and Stanley Hauerwas:
   Difference or Disagreement? • 205
   Craig R. Hovey, Fuller Theological Seminary

ENGAGING SOCIETY:
YODER, THE STATE, AND INSTITUTIONS

11 The Christian Witness in the Earthly City:
   John H. Yoder as Augustinian Interlocutor • 221
   Gerald W. Schlabach, University of St. Thomas

12 "I came not to abolish the law but to fulfill it":
   A Positive Theology of Law and Civil Institutions • 245
   *A. James Reimer, Conrad Grebel University College/Toronto
   School of Theology*

THEOLOGY, ETHICS, AND THE BIBLE:
YODER READING SCRIPTURE AND TRADITION

13 The Anabaptist and the Apostle:
   John Howard Yoder as a Pauline Theologian • 274
   Douglas Harink, The King's University College, Edmonton

14 Smelting for Gold:
   Jesus and Jubilee in John H. Yoder's *Politics of Jesus* • 288
   Willard M. Swartley, Associated Mennonite Biblical Seminary

15 Yoder's Mischievous Contribution
       to Mennonite Views on Anselmian Atonement • 303
       Rachel Reesor Taylor, Bluffton College

16 Did Yoder Reduce Theology to Ethics? • 318
       Thomas Finger, Center for the Study of Anabaptist Groups

Select Bibliography of the Writings of John Howard Yoder   340

The Index   343

The Contributors   353

The Editors   356

Editors' Preface

A MIND PATIENT AND UNTAMED. That ascription would be mistaken if it suggested Yoder's mind was either indifferent or undisciplined. Anyone who engaged him in conversation or has read anything he wrote would recognize that Yoder possessed a mind and heart deeply committed, fiercely engaged, and severely disciplined. At the University of Basel, he studied (1954-57) with Walter Baumgartner, Walther Eichrodt, Oscar Cullmann, Karl Jaspers, Ernst Stahelin, and Karl Barth, arguably the strongest theological faculty in Europe or anywhere else at the time. His doctorate from Basel was in historical theology, and he devoted numerous studies to Reformation history, theology, and historiography—in German, English, French, and Spanish. Yoder respected the academic disciplines, including his own, and the disciplined expertise each required. But no single academic discipline could tame his mind, nor could the academy itself.

Today, John Howard Yoder may be known most widely as a Christian (social) ethicist and proponent of pacifism. Contributing to that reputation was his *The Politics of Jesus*. Three points regarding that book: First, its focus is neither church history nor social ethics, but the New Testament's witness to Jesus. Second, Yoder's "method" comprises serious exegesis of the text and critical conversation with then-prevailing interpretations of the New Testament. Third, in *Politics* as elsewhere, Yoder takes seriously the views he challenges: He assesses them not by the degree to which they depart from his views but by the criteria they claim for themselves. The first two points suggest the untamed quality of Yoder's mind, the third its patience.

Yoder's was predominantly a minority witness voice. Because of this, and because he declined to relativize the particularities of Israel, Jesus, and the church to higher orders of abstraction or more general foundations, some dismissed him as sectarian. Yet few Christian theologians of the past century were more genuinely ecumenical. Not only did he participate, over four decades, in ecumenical and inter-religious dialogues both formal and informal, he undertook with patience what Hans-Georg Gadamer called the "art of strengthening"— stating in their strongest form convictions and arguments in conflict with his own. He exercised with patience his role as a Mennonite theologian in the University of Notre Dame's theology department and as a member of its Joan B. Kroc Institute for International Peace Studies. For many years he conducted a friendship and voluminous correspondence with Rabbi Steven Schwarzchild, to whom Yoder's most recent (posthumous) work, *The Jewish-Christian Schism Revisited*, is dedicated. His replies to questions posed by Notre Dame Law professor Thomas L. Shaffer form the substance of a 121-page book, *Moral Memoranda from John Howard Yoder*. On a concluding page, Yoder explains one reason for his patience: "Part of what it means to be a believers church is to believe that there are answers that we don't have yet." This also helps to explain his untamed mind.

The chapters in this book derive from papers delivered at the "Assessing the Theological Legacy of John Howard Yoder" conference, March 2002. The conference, which took place on the University of Notre Dame campus, was one in the series of Believers Church Conferences. Sponsors were the Department of Theology, University of Notre Dame; Goshen College; the Institute of Mennonite Studies, Associated Mennonite Biblical Seminary; the Joan B. Kroc Institute for International Peace Studies, University of Notre Dame; and the Continuing Conversations Committee for the Believers Church Conference. Faculty from these institutions and organizations formed the conference planning committee.

We thank the conference sponsors, members of the planning committee, and Karl Koop (Canadian Mennonite University), conference coordinator; Mary H. Schertz and Barbara Nelson Gingerich, respectively Director and Administrative Assistant of the Institute of Mennonite Studies; and Amy L. Barker (Bethel College, Kan.), conference assistant. We are grateful to the scholars who have permitted publication of their good work. And we offer special thanks to individuals and organizations whose support helped make possible both conference and book, including The Schowalter Foundation, Shalom Communications Inc., Stanley Hauerwas, Hiram R. and Mary Jane Hershey, Jane and Henry Landes, Phillip and Betsy Moyer.

—Ben C. Ollenburger and Gayle Gerber Koontz, Editors

Introduction:
Lingering with
Yoder's Wild Work

"THE VALUE OF YODER'S WORK IS THAT IT LINGERS." I can think of no better reason for this book of essays on the work of John Howard Yoder than Chris Huebner's observation that Yoder's work "lingers."[1] "Lingering" describes the effect that Yoder's work has or should have on anyone that takes the time required to read John's work. He "lingers" because Yoder is not easily received. He forces you to see the world differently. He lingers because after you have read Yoder, you are not asking the same questions you asked before you read Yoder. For example, you no longer think questions like "What is the relation between Christ and culture?" to be helpful.[2] Of course that is also the reason reading Yoder is difficult. Who wants to be forced into new habits of speech?

The acquisition of new habits, particularly when we are possessed by habits that seem to be working well enough, is never easy. Gaining new habits can be and usually is very painful. I do not believe John Howard Yoder meant to inflict pain on anyone, but he realized that what he cared about could not be considered just "another position." I often think there was an appropriate correspondence between John's personality and his account of Christian nonviolence. Personally and intellectually Yoder took and continues to take some getting used to. John often seemed as personally austere as his prose. He was never tempted to win an argument by being "charming." You had and have to work if you want to understand him. John was a theologian all the way down, but he was one with the analytical skills of the most demanding philosopher. Advocate of nonviolence he certainly was, but that did not make Yoder "soft." Rather, it made him one of the most vigorous minds I have encountered.

Yet just as he insisted that the gospel was not the gospel until it had been received, he worked hard to help us understand that such reception is never finished. That is why I believe this book is so important. This is not just a book of essays about the work of John Howard Yoder; this book represents the kind of work necessary if we are to receive the work of John Howard Yoder. That most of the essays in this book have been written by Mennonites is appropriate. But the Mennonite character of this book could give the impression that Mennonites are more likely to understand Yoder than those outside that community. As Mennonites know, however, Yoder is no less a challenge to Mennonites than he is to non-Mennonites. Because Yoder is equally challenging to everyone, non-Mennonites should not let the Mennonite "ownership" of Yoder deter them from reading this book.

The significance of Yoder's work is beginning to be acknowledged by those who do not come from the Mennonite world. Romand Coles' recent article, "The Wild Patience of John Howard Yoder: 'Outsiders' and the 'Otherness of the Church,'" is a wonderful example of the kind of attention John's work is beginning to receive from those who are not Mennonite or professing Christians.[3] That someone like Coles, a political theorist, can write so insightfully about Yoder makes clear that Yoder is beginning to have an effect in the "wider world."[4] That "effect," as these essays exemplify, is to show that Yoder cannot be understood as a "representative Mennonite" because the politics of Jesus is not something peculiar to Mennonites or even Christians.

This is a reminder that while it is quite appropriate to describe Yoder's work as a "legacy" (as an early subtitle of this book did), such a description can suggest an attempt to domesticate what Yoder was trying to teach us. As I suggested above, Yoder was a "wild thing," not easily tamed. To engage Yoder forces us to learn to live out of control. We cannot, for example, fit him into our normal disciplinary categories. As the essays in this book suggest, he was at the very least an extraordinary reader of Scripture, a historical theologian, an ethicist, as well as a social commentator. Yet even these categories fail to do him justice because he brought a mental power to everything he did that made it impossible to label him.

For example, recently I taught the first seminar on John Howard Yoder I have ever offered. The next year I taught a seminar on Ludwig Wittgenstein. Students who participated in both seminars were convinced that somewhere along the way Yoder must have read Wittgenstein. I assured them that Yoder rarely saw the need to read philosophy and, I suspect, he never read Wittgenstein. That he did not see the need to read philosophy (or Wittgenstein) could well be understood as one of the lessons you could learn from Wittgenstein, who was intent on helping us unlearn mistakes made all the more powerful by being given philosophical legitimation. The operative word for Wittgenstein and Yoder is "need." Yoder was not anti-philosophical, but he saw no reason to pursue philosophy in the interest of theory. Rather he read what he thought crucial to meet the task at hand.

Even though I am sure Yoder never read Wittgenstein, I do think they are in many ways quite similar. Both are what I call "big-brained people." They simply possessed extraordinary intellectual powers. Yet their intellectual power was not what made Wittgenstein and Yoder different. More important was their equal determination to focus their lives and their work on the "important stuff." They were "severe," refusing to be distracted by issues they thought less than serious. As a result anyone encountering them now cannot help but find the clarity of their thought frightening just to the extent that they force us to challenge our cherished sentiments and conventions. Wittgenstein has been dead for fifty years, but the significance of his work is only beginning to be received. I suspect it will take us at least that long to understand what John Howard Yoder has to teach us.

But this book is surely a good start for anyone who desires to understand what Yoder was up to. We will need to return time and again to what John wrote. We will need to do so because as with any significant thinker, changing circumstances help future generations to see what may well have been hidden to those who first encounter the kind of work Yoder produced. The "unsystematic" or occasional character of Yoder's thought, moreover, will invite continuing attempts to see how it is all connected. A Yoder sentence—like a Wittgensteinian epigram—is an invitation to think further and harder than any one person may be able to do. To think "after Yoder" cannot be done alone; rather, just as nonviolence is not an ethic for heroes, so reading Yoder is best done in conversation with others.

We are, therefore, fortunate that so many of the essays in this book put Yoder into conversation with interlocutors that he did not specifically engage. For example, Peter Blum explores how there may be some quite unexpected similarities between Yoder and Derrida. It must surely be the case that the significance of patience for Derrida is not readily apparent unless he is read through Yoder's eyes. Blum rightly does not argue that Derrida and Yoder are in fundamental agreement, particularly about nonviolence, but he does help us see why recognition of *difference* can be understood as a form of patience.

Equally interesting is Chris Huebner's use of Paul Virilio's work for helping us understand Yoder. Some years ago I was directing David Toole's dissertation, *Waiting for Godot in Sarajevo: Theological Reflections on Nihilism, Tragedy, and Apocalypse.*[5] David had read Michel Foucault long before he encountered Yoder. I was insistent, however, that he read Yoder. After reading Yoder, particularly reading Yoder after Foucault, David reported that he was unsure if there was anything in Foucault you could not learn from Yoder. It may be the case, however, that the significance of Yoder's work is best appreciated after having read Foucault. Huebner read Yoder before reading Virilio but as his essay wonderfully exhibits, Virilio's understanding of the "violent logic of speed" helps us see the significance of how Yoder forces us to understand the violence that grips our lives.

Particularly important is Huebner's contention that Yoder's commitment to pacifism can be obscured by those who assume we already know what peace is. Too often the order that shapes our fundamental habits, an order that may appear "peaceful," is an order that successfully hides from us the violence constituting the everyday. Because those committed to nonviolence must expose the violence called peace, they at times cannot help but appear as "disturbers of the peace." Exposure of the invisibility of the violence that grips our lives requires first and foremost that truth be said. That's a "saying" that may appear, particularly to those who benefit from the hidden violence, to be anything but "passive."

Alain Epp Weaver therefore rightly draws our attention to the similarities and differences between Yoder and (another disturber of the "peace") Edward Said. Reading Epp Weaver's essay, you cannot help but have the sense that this was a comparison waiting to happen. Epp Weaver's suggestion that Said's appropriation of exile can be understood as a "distant analogy" to Yoder's vision of exile in Jeremiah hopefully will be the beginning of an ongoing exploration of these themes.[6] Never far from the surface of Epp Weaver's essay is how John Howard Yoder's work forces Christians to explore how we are and are not similar to Judaism. I think no aspect of Yoder's work more important than the ongoing discussion of how he forces Christians to reconnect with the people of the promise.

The question of how Yoder's work repositions Christian understanding of Judaism cannot be separated from how he provides different reading strategies for the interpretation of Scripture. We are, therefore, very fortunate to have the essays by Harink and Swartley in this volume. Harink proposed that a reading of Paul in the light of Yoder's stress on discipleship hopefully will invite others to explore Yoder's significance for interpreting other biblical sources. Of course, Harink's essay also is important for questions raised in Epp Weaver's and Duane Friesen's essays concerning the implications of Yoder's work for helping Christians understand our relation to Judaism.

Swartley's suggestion that Yoder's reading of the Jubilee be understood as a "performance" strikes me as particularly suggestive. The importance of the notion of performance is currently being explored in a number of disciplines.[7] Swartley's essay may even entice some who do not know Yoder to begin to read Yoder readings of Scripture not as "just another opinion" but as an invitation to enter into another world.

Anyone who engages Yoder cannot avoid historiographical questions. Yoder not only forces us to consider what we mean when we say "history" but also how history is to be done. The essays by Sider and Heilke are particularly important not only because they raise serious questions about Yoder's characterization of "Constantinianism," but because they also help us see—if we are to think "with" or "after" Yoder—that the hard and detailed historical work is unavoidable. Heilke and Sider remind us that questions about how history is done are inseparable from what politics that history is to serve. James Reimer's attempt to provide a more positive theology of civil institutions, and in particular the law, is the kind of investigation Sider's and Heilke's questions about Constantinianism necessarily open up. I think Yoder would have found these attempts to provide a more nuanced understanding of Constantinianism promising as a first step to spell out how the church is to serve the nations.

The essays by Sider and Heilke build on Gerald Schlabach's important paper, "Deuteronomic or Constantinian: What is the Most Basic Problem for Christian Social Ethics?" that appeared in *The Wisdom of the Cross: Essays in Honor of John Howard Yoder*.[8] Schlabach's essay in the present volume continues his exploration of the theological politics necessary to sustain the exilic community that seems so central to Yoder's account of the church. To suggest, as Schlabach does, that Augustine can be a crucial conversation partner in that task will no doubt appear to be counter-intuitive to many Anabaptists. Yet Schlabach's reading of Augustine indicates an important direction that those persuaded by Yoder must go—that is, to read again the

Catholic tradition in the hope of discovering that it holds resources there we need if we are to sustain the kind of commitments so central to Yoder's work.[9]

I am not suggesting, of course, that Yoder can be characterized as having anything so grand as a "position." Harry Huebner's essay is a wonderful reminder that we cannot separate the occasional character of Yoder's work from the material convictions that shaped his work. Recent developments associated with postmodernism may make the way Yoder worked seem less odd; but as Huebner rightly argues, the way Yoder worked was first and foremost determined by his understanding of the gospel. Therefore the kind of questions Finger asks about Yoder's work are perfectly appropriate, even as we need to be careful to acknowledge that Yoder's hesitancy to "do" theology "straight" was not accidental.

Rachel Reesor-Taylor is quite right to suggest that there was a mischievous side to John when he dealt with some of the standard Christian theological loci. Yoder's mischievousness, however, did not derive from a cavalier attitude about doctrine. It is true Yoder seldom asked himself if his views on this or that doctrine were "orthodox." To ask if you are or are not orthodox from Yoder's perspective would only reproduce the assumption that doctrines are sets of propositions. In contrast, Yoder was concerned whether the doctrine or motif did work that needed to be done if we were to be faithful witnesses. His "mischievousness," therefore, reflected his desire not to say more than needs to be said. Biesecker-Mast may well be right that for Yoder the desire for Christian unity cannot begin by privileging "orthodoxy," but neither can it be assumed on Yoder-like grounds that the resources God has made available to the church in the past do not remain significant resources for the challenges that currently face the church.

I began this quick run through of these essays by observing how useful they are for putting Yoder into conversation with figures he did not explicitly engage in his work. The essays by Biesecker-Mast, Doerksen, and Hovey explore the relationship between Yoder and someone that he clearly at times engaged at least implicitly and sometimes quite explicitly: me. I am of course grateful that these authors find it useful to analyze the similarities and differences between myself and Yoder. Yet I find such comparisons embarrassing because I simply do not think my work has the scholarly status or conceptual power of Yoder's extraordinary work. I certainly do not think it appropriate for me to use this introduction to respond to Biesecker-

Mast's, Doerksen's, and Hovey's extremely informative, at least for me, account of my appropriation of Yoder. But I do hope readers will find, as I did, that their accounts are helpful for raising issues that are more important than trying to understand in what way Yoder and I may differ.

I hate introductions to collections of essays that summarize what each essay is alleged to be about. If such summaries are any good, you always wonder why you need to read the essays. So I have not tried to summarize the essays in this book, but rather to whet the reader's appetite for discovering the interconnections between these essays and ways those connections suggest how fruitful John Howard Yoder's work is for helping us think well "after Yoder." I believe these essays help us understand why Yoder's work "lingers."

And why is that? Because this most unsystematic of theologians pulls you into a network of connections that force you to rethink what you thought you had settled. To read one essay by Yoder usually means finding you need to read another essay, and before you know it, you discover that Yoder has taken over your life. Of course, John would say he has not taken over your life. Rather, if his work is helpful, it means that Jesus, not John Howard Yoder, has taken over your life.

The lessons Yoder has to teach are hardwon because they so challenge our endemic laziness—a laziness that too easily accepts the assumption that the way things are is the way things have to be. The excellence of these essays, written largely by Mennonites, is a witness to the community that made Yoder's work possible, a community that at least has a memory that its members can never rest easy with the way things are. John Howard Yoder cannot be understood without the background of the faithful witness of his Anabaptist forebears. It is, therefore, appropriate that these essays representing the beginning of the hard work of receiving John Howard Yoder are by "his people." Hopefully, however, these chapters are only the beginning of the many we will need to help us understand the what and how John Howard Yoder has to teach us. Only a beginning—but what a wonderful one.[10]

—*Stanley Hauerwas*
  Duke University

NOTES

1. Huebner not only makes this observation in his paper in this volume, but this description of Yoder's work is the heart of Huebner's dissertation, *No Handles on History* (Durham, N.C.: Duke University, 2002, Ph.D. dissertation).

2. I am, of course, alluding to Yoder's now famous critique of H. Richard Niebuhr's book, *Christ and Culture*. Yoder's essays circulated for years in mimeographed form. That essay, "How H. Richard Niebuhr Reasoned: A Critique of *Christ and Culture*," is now published in *Authentic Transformation: A New Vision of Christ and Culture* (Nashville: Abingdon, 1996), 31-90. This book also has essays by Glen Stassen and Diane Yeager. James Gustafson has responded to Yoder's critique, characterizing it as "laced with more *ad hominem* arguments and fortified with more gratuitous footnotes than anything I ever read by scholars in the field of Christian ethics." Gustafson acknowledges that he has not read the published form of the article, but I suspect that even if he had, he would not change his opinion. I call attention to Gustafson's reaction to indicate the challenge Yoder presents to those who do not want to change the way questions are asked. Gustafson's characterization of Yoder can be found in his "Preface: An Appreciative Interpretation," in H. Richard Niebuhr, *Christ and Culture* (San Francisco: Harper/San Francisco, 2001), xxiii.

3. Romand Coles, "The Wild Patience of John Howard Yoder: 'Outsiders' and the 'Otherness of the Church,'" *Modern Theology* 18:3 (July 2002): 305-332.

4. I think, however, it is not accidental that Coles and Thomas Heilke are both political theorists. They are able to see the significance of Yoder's work because they have been trained to explore what political practices are required if we are to be able not only to survive but to flourish. Heilke earned his Ph.D. at Duke and Coles is in the Political Science Department at Duke, so some may think their interest in Yoder to be a "happy accident." Of course Heilke's and Coles' fascination with Yoder is a "happy accident," but an "accident" that would not have happened without their training as political theorists.

5. David Toole, *Waiting for Godot in Savajevo: Theological Reflections on Nihilism, Tragedy, and Apocalypse* (London: SCM, 2001). Toole's book was originally published by Westview Press in 1998.

6. Yoder's essays on Christianity and Judaism have been published in a volume ed. Michael Cartwright and Peter Ochs entitled *The Jewish-Christian Schism Revisited* (Grand Rapids: Eerdmans, 2003). This book also contains fascinating critiques of Yoder by Cartwright and Ochs. Rosalee Velloso Ewell's dissertation, *The Politics of Scripture: Jewish and Christian Interpretations of Jeremiah* (Duke University, 2003, Ph.D. dissertation) is a very important study of this aspect of Yoder's work.

7. See, for example, James Fodor and Stanley Hauerwas, "Performing Faith: The Peaceable Rhetoric of God's Church," in *Rhetorical Invention and*

Religious Inquiry: New Perspectives, ed. Walter Jost and Wendy Olmsted (New Haven, Conn.: Yale University Press, 2000), 381-414.

8. Gerald Schlabach, "Deuteronomic or Constantinian: What is the Most Basic Problem for Christian Social Ethics?" in *The Wisdom Of The Cross: Essays in Honor of John Howard Yoder*, ed. Stanley Hauerwas, Chris K. Huebner, Harry J. Huebner, and Mark Thiessen Nation (Grand Rapids: Eerdmans, 1999), 449-471.

9. Schlabach, of course, had begun exploring this reading of Augustine in his *For the Joy Set Before Us: Augustine and Self-Denying Love* (Notre Dame, Ind.: University of Notre Dame Press, 2001).

10. I am indebted to Alex Sider for his critical comments of an earlier draft of this introduction.

A Mind
Patient and Untamed

Chapter 1

The Christian Life as Gift and Patience: Why Yoder Has Trouble with Method

Harry Huebner

"When the Spirit of truth comes, he will guide you into all the truth . . . he will take what is mine and declare it to you" —John 16:13-14

JOHN HOWARD YODER WRITES ONLY A FEW ARTICLES focusing explicitly on method.[1] In them he identifies why it is a problem to conceive of method as is typical among scholars—namely, as universal form housing particular content. Yoder offers an alternative to this understanding, something one might call an epistemology of peace or a methodology of patience. For Yoder, discipleship is not the deduction of a method properly applied; rather, discipleship informs the method appropriate to knowing Jesus Christ. Alternatively, the legitimation of violence is not the conclusion of a neutral way of thinking about the world as it is, but rather it is the outworking and inevitable result of controlling and manipulative epistemologies.

It is not immediately evident how method and discipleship are within the same domain of discourse, or how communion can be an epistemology, yet these are Yoder's claims. One might well conclude from this Macluhanesque "medium is the message" language that his claims ought not to be taken seriously and that they are merely meant as clever rhetoric to extend his pacifist logic all the way down. But this would be a mistake. After all, Yoder is himself fiercely analytical and precise in making explicit the logic of arguments, both those of others and his own. He is a master at definition, clarification, and enumeration. Reading his work often exposes one to an inventory of possibilities on a subject.

However, Yoder neither affirms a particular method nor does he depreciate the importance of method. To do either would extend credence to methodological commitment way beyond his comfort zone. More than anything else he seeks to develop an alternative to the standards set by guilds of theoretical inquiry. Why? Because he worries that the standard approaches will preclude the very affirmations he holds to be part of the Christian narrative. Not only does he worry, he observes it happening. Hence he seeks to avoid the pitfalls of methodological straight-jacketing. To put it simply, Yoder refuses to believe that there is only one method or one kind of language capable of disclosing the power of the gospel to us.

The inspiration for this chapter comes from an observation that the temptation to misread Yoder often has its roots exactly at the point of his teaching on method. The seduction of classical modern methodology is so strong that readers are often unable to believe that Christian pacifism can itself be a method rather than a conclusion of right (or not so right) thinking. This then leads to efforts to repair Yoder's approach in a variety of ways to either make him more convincing or to supply needed missing links to complete his thought. Efforts of this kind abound but they rarely succeed.

There are those who cannot believe that Yoder's epistemology is fragmentary by intent and hence attribute to him a kind of methodological sloppiness. In response these sympathetic readers of Yoder offer to make him more coherent and systematic by imposing on him a kind of methodological narrowing.

There are those who cannot believe that one should adhere to more than one moral theory, and observing in Yoder a multiplicity of moral metaphors and languages, seek to mould him into a particular moral theory like virtue ethics, character ethics, command-obedience ethics, or even a kind of deontology.

There are those who attempt to squeeze him tightly into a specific theological theory like a particular eschatology, an atonement theory, or even a particular ecclesiology. These efforts usually end up over-concluding by under-questioning, resulting in a kind of "violence" to Yoder's convictions, rather than a clarification of his thought. This in no way makes the work of such scholars worthless, but it might make them less Yoderian than they claimed.

Attempting to itemize all the ways in which Yoder seeks to critique method, or as he sometimes says, methodologism, is not possible in a brief essay. Instead I will, in typical Yoderian fashion, list some things Yoder does and does not mean when he critiques methodologism and affirms in its place the interconnectedness of gospel and method, or of epistemology and peace. Admittedly, this is a partial list.

WHAT YODER DOES NOT MEAN!

Yoder does not mean that method doesn't matter

Method does matter! In fact it is precisely because it matters that we must examine and critique the way it gets cast in Enlightenment foundationalist epistemologies. In other words, the debate about method should not be a separate debate as if it can be settled by appeal to abstract concepts alone while the debate about everything else is settled by applying neutral method to empirical data. It is because of the interdependence of method and content that method must be commensurate with content. In other words, to argue nonviolence with a "violent" epistemology is problematic. And yes, epistemologies too can be violent!

Yoder does not mean that therefore all is relative[2]

It is a bit ironic that one would need to make the point that Yoder is not a relativist, since he is more often accused of being an absolutist, especially since he holds to the authority of Jesus. But his denial of the absolutist appellation (he says that "it is always inaccurate when the view I represent is called "absolutist"[3]) might lead those unable to see beyond the absolute/relative dichotomy to make the counterclaim, namely that he is a relativist. After all, Yoder admits that he has no where to ground the authority of Jesus accept within the Jesus tradition itself. "The dean of modern ditchdiggers," Gotthold Lessing, was wrong to set up the problem in terms of an ugly ditch between the necessary truths of reason and the accidental truths of history. All attempts to ground contingency in necessity fail. "None of them can find *beyond the ditch* a place to stand which would be less particular, more credible, less the product of one's own social location."[4] Or as

Yoder says elsewhere, "The particularity of incarnation is the universality of the good. There is no road but the low road. The truth has come to our side of the ditch."[5]

Yoder does not mean we must choose history over dogmatics

Ernst Troeltsch's essay on "Historical and Dogmatic Method in Theology" attempts to force a choice of history over dogmatics not altogether unlike the ditch of Lessing. And while Yoder can say that "reality always was pluralistic and relativistic, that is, historical"[6] he nevertheless can embrace the dogmatics of his teacher Karl Barth. This is possible because of his embrace of the Jesus of history as the Jesus of dogma.[7]

Yoder does not mean that all we need to do is read the Bible to settle debates

Yoder is not saying that if we just read the Bible as it is, we need no method. Granted Yoder has great respect for the "plain person's" reading of the Bible and even the empirical world, yet he does not assume we have simple access to ancient texts. Hermeneutical assumptions are at work in every reading of the Bible, but if these are not commensurate with the *message* of the Bible, then there is a problem. If this is so, then proper method cannot be independently determined.

WHAT YODER DOES MEAN!

There is no scratch to start from

Yoder takes a clear stand on the "first principles" debate. The starting point of knowledge is not abstract first principles but the real experience of valuing communities.[8] He speaks in avowedly unambiguous language regarding what he wishes to deny but in much less clear terms on what he wishes to affirm in its stead. He sometimes calls it the "phenomenology of the moral life" (79). What he means is that even before any first principles get formulated, as the cases of such attempts always bear witness, there is already something going on. Hence he can say that "the life of the community is before all possible methodological distillations" (82). This is perhaps why the intellectual worlds that get built on the basis of first principles often look so much like the worlds assumed before the first principles approach gets embarked on to begin with (To wit, Descartes).

Yet the ambiguity of the language of "phenomenology" appears to be deliberate. It is simply to admit that there is no "avoiding the pitfalls of particular identity" (79) and foundationalism does not succeed in "sheltering itself against the challenges of the relativists" (79). In other words, the answer to relativism is not to be found in first principles, but somewhere else. He puts it in the living, valuing community called church. After all, for Yoder the church precedes the world both epistemologically as well as axiologically.[9]

There is no total perspective[10]

Just as Yoder rejects the notion of a fundamental starting point derived from the work of abstract reasoning, so he rejects the ultimate unification of all knowledge. There is no fundamental rational starting point and there is no ultimate rational ending point either. We could say that Yoder rejects both the rationalism of Descartes and the idealism of Hegel. In its place he affirms something that looks a lot more like Kierkegaard, who repudiates system and affirms fragmentary knowledge and paradox.

Yet unlike his friend Vernard Eller, who sees Kierkegaard as the model of radical discipleship, Yoder does not.[11] For him Kierkegaard is at most half right. He is right only in what he rejects, namely Enlightenment foundationalism on the one hand and Hegelian rational eschatology on the other. For Kierkegaard remained locked in a methodologism still far too akin to his adversaries. His approach, for example, for all his references to the story of Abraham, disallows learning anything of content from Abraham—only form (method). In other words, *what* God taught Abraham, according to Kierkegaard,[12] could not be what God teaches us. *How* God teaches us is exactly like God taught Abraham. In other words, don't learn anything from history. Each generation must begin from the beginning in terms of knowing what God asks of us.

Here Yoder is far too Jewish to accept such anti-tradition logic. Kierkegaard's existentialist epistemology cannot successfully replace Enlightenment rationalism. After all, according to Yoder, if Abraham is our father,[13] we can know from the Abraham story that God no longer requires of the faithful to sacrifice children, rather than the merely formal notion that God is able to paradoxically call us to do something awful. In other words, if Abraham is our father then, according to Yoder, we can learn something about faithfulness from Abraham, while, according to Kierkegaard, we must like Abraham learn faithfulness from scratch. In this way Kierkegaard still remains too much within the Enlightenment and by implication within the Constantinian paradigm. Nevertheless, Kierkegaard is right in his critique of Hegel in that there is no total perspective.

He affirms methodological non-Constantinianism[14]

Yoder argues that methodologism is a form of idolatry. He puts it this way: "The worst form of idolatry is not carving an image; it is the presumption that one has—or that a society has, or a culture has—the right to set the terms under which God can be recognized."[15] Yoder observes that humans, especially theologians, are beset by the temptation to develop intellectual systems that reduce moral and theological language to a single structure of meaning or framework of understanding. Such totalizing tendencies characterise much of Western theology. Already in 1971 he put it this way:

> One way to characterize thinking about social ethics in our time is to say that Christians in our age are obsessed with the meaning and direction of history. Social ethical concern is moved by a deep desire to make things move in the right direction. Whether a given action is right or not seems to be inseparable from the question of what effects it will cause. Thus part if not all of social concern has to do with looking for the right "handle" by which one can "get a hold on" history and move it in the right direction.[16]

Yoder's worries are premised on the conviction that underlying the tendencies to move history in the right direction is a tacit commitment to a methodology itself at odds with the very message of gift and patience that characterize the gospel story, a method deeply rooted in a desire to master, dominate, or control outcome. He calls this approach methodological Constantinianism and relates it explicitly to the Constantinian shift. The fundamental ecclesiological shift that took place in the fourth century domesticated the church in the hands of the state. When the state took over the church, the church became complicit in being in charge of the world. The church was coerced into giving up its otherness, its counter politics. Its reassigned role was to another realm within standard politics, which was not its own choosing but a relegation by a superior power. It was given a role as caretaker of the spiritual dimensions of all of humanity, believers and unbelievers. Its task was now to give God's blessing to those charged with ensuring history was moving in the right direction.

This meant that the church was no longer seen as a sign of a future which God was bringing into being and which the world was to be ultimately,[17] but it was now together with the world in charge of bringing about the kingdom. There was now only one politic, no counter politic. The agent of history was the emperor, and the locus of salvation[18] the cosmos, not the church. Hence faith became interiorized and the faithful church became socially invisible.

But not only was the role of the church usurped, the very agency of God was also appropriated by and to the emperor. This is idolatry and legitimates violence. When we are in charge, when the movement from present injustice to future justice is wholly in our hands, whether the state's or the church's or both, not in the hands of a gracious God who wills to give us a just future, then whatever means are at our disposal are what we must use to move forward. Then violence is inevitable and the call to nonviolence, whether by Jesus or anyone else, is seen as unrealistic. Moreover, on this model the practice of vulnerability inherent in bearing witness to a future we believe is breaking into the present through divine agency, is sheer stupidity. What has made it so? The method of inquiry!

According to Yoder the Constantinian consciousness underwrites the efforts to master history with a methodology of control. The latter is brought to full bloom in the Enlightenment. The idolatry of which Yoder speaks, namely the setting of the terms under which God is to be recognised, takes several forms: First, it comes in the form of a language that seeks to speak for everyone. He says, "Language as an autonomous power is not to be trusted."[19] A universalist language is abstract and hence ignores particular difference. Yoder's epistemology of peace is intentionally particularist—Christian ethics is for Christians and therefore remains confessional, not categorical and hence not impositional. The abstract language of peace found in Kant's "Perpetual Peace," for example, is coercive because it seeks to subordinate particular witness to universal conceptualisation.

Second, this idolatry silences minority voices. Yoder claims there has never been a homogeneous language, moral or theological,[20] but the dominant language has intentionally exercised power and control so that minority voices have not been heard. And when they did speak they were shunted aside, called names like sectarian, and thereby made irrelevant to the mainstream. It grows out of a Constantinian controlling consciousness to assume that there must be one dominant idiom into which all difference dissolves. In Yoder's epistemology of peace, language functions not to control but to open up, to make visible what cannot be seen by the old idioms. This is why alternative languages through which faithfulness can be expressed should not be seen as lists one must choose from. For example, it is not a matter of deciding which of several moral theories is right—deontology, teleology, virtue ethics, and so forth. Each opens up what the other on its own conceals. Each has its place.[21] After all, as Yoder claims, "Augustine was deontological about lying and teleological about killing."[22]

Third, the temptations of idolatry are mitigated when the community's discourse is at least as broad (no narrower) and varied as the biblical story on which it is based.[23] People reading texts shape communities. But the Christian text is diverse, not uniform. Even the Jesus story is given to us in multiple form. In order for us to be true to our calling it is therefore just as important that we resist being herded into narrow conformity as it is to read the text through a single metaphor.

Yoder sees methodologism as a form of Constantinianism—another way of controlling outcome, mastering contingency and in its worst form as a reductionistic mastery of divine agency. From his perspective the church's task is not to develop theoretical structures or an abstract logic to explain faithful human existence. In the first place he has no interest in explaining it for everyone, only for followers of Christ. And second, he resists beginning with the arrogance of theory imposed on ordinary moral discourse. Yoder sees nothing wrong with beginning with the language of ordinary people. He puts it as follows: "Instead of standing in judgment of the ordinary people who use now the language of virtue, now that of command, now that of ends, to press their praise and blame on one another, it is rather the methodologists who ought to bear the burden of proof" (82).

Methodological non-Constantinianism therefore seeks to let the word be the walk. Its stance is witness, giving testimony and proclaiming the word. It begins not with a theory but with the language of the ordinary people and seeks from there to embody the truth of the gospel. It ends not with eschewing variance or even with the taming of conflict but with a celebration of divine inbreaking which promises to make new what was old. That is, it begins and ends with openness toward transformation.

Yoder affirms resurrection logic

Yoder is often charged with an excessive fixation on the cross. Yet it is the resurrection that plays a key role in his methodological discourse. He describes the Christian pacifism which is rooted in the biblical apocalyptic image of the lamb as follows:

That Christian pacifism which has its theological basis in the character of God and the work of Jesus Christ is one in which the calculating link between our obedience and ultimate efficacy has been broken, since the triumph of God comes through resurrection and not through effective sovereignty or assured survival.[24]

It is interesting that what is being affirmed here is not just a new version of a social theory which promises everything that we have come to expect from such theories, i.e. a social strategy that advances a plan for ensuring outcome. Yoder's approach is significantly different. Where a Constantinian methodology insists on control and being in charge his approach suggests that control be sacrificed for vulnerability. A "not being in charge" approach to peacemaking has vulnerability as a by-product. In other words this approach advocates commensurability between method and outcome. An imposed peace may well be better than wanton violence, but it is not yet peace. Peace is a gift of acceptance of another given by the other. Hence it cannot be imposed. Since we are not in charge we cannot marry our efforts with wanted outcome. The calculating link has been broken.

This does not mean that we cannot have strategies, but since God is in charge, our strategies may well be wrongheaded. Nor does it mean we cannot have theories, but since we are not in charge our theories should not assume that we are. They may in any event not let us see all there is to see. In other words, the logic of resurrection builds on both an openness that governs our strategies and an openness that protects our theories from overfunctioning. What Yoder is advocating is not just another method designed to deliver the same goods but an approach that refuses the separation of the goods from their delivery. If peace is the goal, then peace is the way. It should not be surprising that God saves us *by* grace, since God saves us *for* grace. A violent methodology cannot produce peace; a dominant mastering method cannot produce a vulnerable people open to God's leading.

In what ways does Yoder's logic of resurrection inform our understanding of method? I suggest four ways:

(1) The guarantee of our rightness lies not in the theories that we produce but in our obedience to the one who is in charge. This statement has significant implications. It does not deny the importance of being thinking people, or theory producing people, but it does suggest that our thinking is not lord. Moreover, it suggests that in the process of getting our theories right we reflect on more than our theo-

ries. This is partly why Yoder is troubled by "liberal" ethicists "whose arguments can be carried out without reference to cases."[25] It is wrong to think that only theory informs life; life also informs theory.

(2) Yoder's resurrection logic suggests that God blesses faithfulness. While the "calculating link between our obedience and ultimate efficacy" may in fact have been broken as attested by the death and resurrection of Christ, nevertheless, the triumph of God still comes and is still assured. How? One can, of course, not give formulaic answers since it is in God's hands. All theories are here inadequate by definition. God's free acts cannot be subordinated to theory. However, one way that has been repeatedly demonstrated throughout the biblical story and certainly also in the life of Jesus and in the history of the church is that God blesses the actions of the faithful. It is therefore our honor to be involved in God's work, not as primary agents of change but as bearers of witness to what God is doing in the world.

(3) Resurrection logic sacrifices effectiveness. The question is sometimes asked why Yoder is opposed to effectiveness. He is not. But the failure to understand the significance of his critique of effectiveness is testimony to the difficulty the Western mind has with thinking outside of the Constantinian box. Yoder's claim is simply that when Constantine married piety with power, the Christian life ceased making sense for minority Christians, that is, for believers who are few and powerless.[26] And since that was all that there were at the time, it made minority Christianity unfaithful. To say this differently, effectiveness language is language of the powerful and already assumes the future of the world is in our hands. Yet this is what Yoder sees as unbiblical. Hence he gives the following advice: "Instead of asking about one's actions, 'If I do this how will it tip the scales . . . ?', one rather asks, 'In a situation where I cannot tip the scales, on what other grounds might I decide what to do?'"[27]

(4) Resurrection logic gives rise to a doxological view of history and indeed all of life. Yoder contrasts doxology with engineering. He points out that what was different for Jesus was not the goal but the "mode of implementation."[28] To give up handles on history is to give up seeing ourselves as agents charged with moving the "messed up world" from here to there. Rather we are to train ourselves to see where the sick are being healed, where the prisoners are being set free. Indeed we need to participate in the healing and the setting free. With respect to the salvation of the world, "We do not achieve it so much as we accept it. It is not as basic to engineer it as it is to proclaim it" (211). Yoder suggests that for followers of Jesus the world is the on-

tological locus of God's sovereign intentions and the believing community is its epistemological locus. It follows from this that the church is "charged with the task of insight" (215), insight that requires many agents within the community: agents of memory, of perception, of teaching, of doxology, and so forth But our chief stance is our witness to and our praise of what God is doing around us.

Resurrection logic begins not with correct theory or proper method but with the conviction that God is at work through us and in other ways. Resurrection logic admits of no mastery of contingency and no single final method, and hence what is not yet can still be. We praise God for the transformations, including of our minds; transformations we see and ones we know are taking place which we cannot yet see. After all, we know that Christ, the one who has already come is also the one who is to come.

Yoder affirms "straightforwardness" and "serendipitous induction" as ways of reading and understanding texts

Yoder places the discerning community at the center of his epistemology. But it is more than a community in radical openness to God. It is a community whose identity is shaped by the texts it reads. Yet how can texts, especially ones in the Bible that do not all appear to be saying the same thing, shape us and guide us? Here Yoder makes the case for a type of quasi-structuralist hermeneutic described as "validation by induction"[29] or "serendipitous induction." He says,

> Induction is the logician's label for what occurs when separate components of a body of data (in our case a body of texts), and when interpreted each in its own terms, turn out to be parallel in their underlying thought structure, even though quite different in setting, vocabulary, and superficial propositional content.[30]

It is this process that allows the reader of texts to find ways of saying "that the several texts in question belong to the same story" (115). It is important for Yoder that this form of induction be "serendipitous" or "straightforward" because precisely its unsolicited "falling into place" ensures that it is not the product of some outside criterion imposed on it. Hence the reading he is proposing is narratalogical and not conceptual. As Yoder puts it, "'straightforwardness' in recourse to the biblical heritage is 'anti-foundationalist' . . ." (118) since foundationalists, he argues, are beholden to a prior value system by which both the reading of the text and its content are adjudicated. Hence Yoder concludes his argument with these words:

The reason it is hard for critics from within those foundationalist games (in the Wittgensteinian sense) to be fair to "straightforwardness" is that they assume, as it does not, the need to justify one's recourse to Scripture by appeal to some other criterion outside it. For my "straightforward" posture (here he cites George Lindbeck, Brevard Childs and Alasdair MacIntyre) the presence of the text within the community is an inseparable part of the community's act of being itself. It would be a denial of the community's being itself if it were to grant a need for appeal beyond itself to some archimedean point to justify it.[31]

In his "The Hermeneutics of Peoplehood" Yoder advances the prototype of the free church as a place where the people engage in the process of opening themselves to the truth of the spirit. He advances several key movements: First, it is an *open* process. It begins not with a theory or a structure, but with ordinary people and speaking and listening with "dialogical liberty."

Second, it is a reconciling process. The word becomes the walk that binds and looses. He calls the community's work of binding and loosing "practical moral reasoning."

Third, the community's "conversation" is aided by agents of direction, of memory, of linguistic self-consciousness, and of order and due process. This "coming to know" is in the process itself, it is the text becoming live again, it is a walk guided by the spirit.

DOES IT MAKE A DIFFERENCE?

It makes a difference for how to read Yoder

Yoder is sometimes read as a traditional theologian with radically new conclusions. He is seen as reaching non-mainline conclusions from reading common biblical texts. But this is only half right. The more radical reading of Yoder suggests that he draws different conclusions from reading the same texts because he reads them differently. Yoder believes that the message of the gospel, that is, the message that all of life is deeply rooted in gift and patience, informs methodology itself. Hence variety is not to be spurned, for God grants us different gifts, and patience is to be cultivated, for human finitude guarantees the perpetual fragmented character of our knowledge. Incompleteness is not a temporary human state while we engage in figuring out how to do theology and ethics; incompleteness is the human condition. That is why it does not matter where we begin, or what language we use provided we do not exclude other languages, but it does matter whom we listen to and whether we are able to learn to walk the word.

It makes a difference for the integrity of the gospel

The Christian gospel is replete with imagery of being on the way, or *being* the truth and the light, or of seeing through a glass dimly. These metaphors are hard to grasp and even harder to embrace on the basis of either the Constantinian or modern enslavement to an epistemology of mastery and control—as are the admonitions to sell what we have and give it to the poor, or to turn the other cheek, or to not resist evil. But this does not mean that they do not make sense or cannot be lived. Yet to do so, one must give up the very way of seeing one is accustomed to. The gospel message is best grasped by an epistemology of peace because its content is a way of peace. Learning and coming to know Christ is a journey that begins with openness to God and ends with openness to God. In between it is best lived doxologically.

It makes a difference for understanding the Christian life

Yoder sees discipleship as rooted in both gift and patience, and as understood not through analysis of the mind but by becoming skilled in following another person. This approach is also a "coming to know" but it is such by revelation of one life to another life. In imitating one who himself imitates the Truth, we can come to know the Truth. Hence knowing the truth is less a product of careful intellectual analysis or certainty accrued from satisfaction that an indubitable method has been followed than a matter of learning to see the world differently in ways that can only happen when we walk in the shoes of another. To say it differently, the Christian life is not first of all about whether a particular approach or language or metaphor can do it justice; rather, it is about how we can become the kind of people who are able to be contemporary disciples of an ancient lord. And for that a variety of images are required.

CONCLUSION

Yoder's critique of method did not emerge late in his life when it became fashionable to make the postmodern anti-theory turn. Yoder was not a trendy theologian. But it may well be that his way of doing theology only became intelligible to many after such a postmodern critique became popular. Yoder refused to accept most approaches not because they had a method and he did not, but because the method of many theologians eclipsed aspects of the Christian life that he thought were simply part of what it means to follow Jesus. So the adequacy of a method should be tested against how well it is able to disclose the truth of the story embodied in the text that shapes communities.

In other words, "form follows function."[32] For example, Yoder could not simply reject liberation theology because it disclosed aspects of the faith which other approaches neglected, nor could he simply accept it either because as a methodology it largely ignored nonviolence and divine agency which were gifts that the biblical text tells us exiles (the unliberated) were able to grasp. Similarly, he was leery of deontology, teleology, responsibility ethics, and characterological ethics because, while the Christian faith must be able to talk about rules, goodness and outcome, response, and virtues, it should do so without reducing all of life to any one of these.

In the final analysis it was his understanding of the Christian life as gift and patience that made Yoder suspicious of the modern preoccupation with method. Gift involved the acknowledgement that we are not in charge; patience had to do with allowing for the Spirit and the believing community to make whatever accommodations are necessary to meet challenges as they arise. As Yoder says it, "the only way to see how this will work will be to see how it will work."[33]

"For now we see in a mirror dimly, but then we will see face to face. Now I know in part; then I will know fully, even as I have been fully known" (1 Cor. 13:12).

NOTES

1. I am referring especially to two articles: "'Patience' as Method in Moral Reasoning: Is an Ethic of Discipleship 'Absolute'?" in *Wisdom of the Cross: Essays in Honor of John Howard Yoder*, ed. Stanley Hauerwas, et. al. (Grand Rapids: Eerdmans, 1999), and "Walk and Word: The Alternatives to Methodologism" in *Theology Without Foundations: Religious Practice and the Future of Theological Truth*, ed. Stanley Hauerwas, et. al. (Nashville: Abingdon, 1994).

2. In other words the absolute/relative debate is itself a misplaced debate since it suggests that the only way to talk about absolutism is to adopt a particular version of the method/content, or theory/practice dichotomy. It is these ways of cutting up the epistemological pie that Yoder objects to.

3. Yoder, "'Patience' as Method," 24.

4. John Howard Yoder "But We Do See Jesus," *The Priestly Kingdom* (Notre Dame, Ind.: University of Notre Dame, 1984), 46.

5. Ibid., 62.

6. Ibid., 59.

7. John Howard Yoder *Politics of Jesus: Vicit Agnus Noster,* 2nd. ed. (Grand Rapids: Eerdmans, 1994), 103.

8. Yoder, "Walk and Word," 78. (Other citations are in text.)

9. Yoder, *The Priestly Kingdom*, 11.

10. I borrow this language from Rowan Williams. See his, *On Christian Theology* (Malden, Mass.: Blackwell Publishers, 2000), e.g., comments like, "In other words, religious and theological integrity is possible as and when discourse about God *declines the attempt to take God's point of view* (i.e., a 'total perspective')," 6 (emphasis his).

11. See *The Politics of Jesus*, 130.

12. See esp. his *Fear and Trembling*.

13. See "If Abraham is our Father" in *The Original Revolution: Essays on Christian Pacifism* (Scottdale, Pa.: Herald Press, 1971), 85-104.

14. I owe some of the key ideas in this section to Chris Huebner. See his *Unhandling History: Anti-theory, Ethics and Practice of Witness,* unpublished Ph.D. dissertation, Duke University 2002, especially the chapter on "Methodological Non-Constantinianism, Epistemological Peace, and the Otherness of the Church: John Howard Yoder's Hermeneutics of Peoplehood."

15. Yoder, "Walk and Word," 89.

16. Yoder, *The Politics of Jesus*, 228.

17. Yoder, "The Church Is Called to be Now What the World is Called to be Ultimately," *Body Politics*, ix.

18. Yoder, "Christ the hope for the World," *The Royal Priesthood: Essays Ecclesiological and Ecumenical* (Grand Rapids: Eerdmans, 1994), 198.

19. Yoder, "Walk and Word," 85.

20. Yoder, "Meaning After Babble: With Jeffrey Stout Beyond Relativism," *Journal of Religious Ethics* 24 (1996), 135.

21. Yoder, "Walk and Word," 86.

22. Ibid., 84.

23. Ibid., 90.

24. Yoder, *Politics of Jesus*, 239.

25. Yoder, "Walk and Word," 84.

26. Yoder, "Constantinian Sources of Western Social Ethics," *The Priestly Kingdom*, 140.

27. Yoder, "The Kingdom as Social Ethics," *The Priestly Kingdom*, 101.

28. John Howard Yoder, "Are You the One Who Is to Come," *For the Nations: Essays Public and Evangelical* (Grand Rapids: Eerdmans, 1997), 211.

29. See John Howard Yoder, "Validation by Induction," in *To Hear the Word* (Eugene, Ore.: Wipf and Stock Publishers, 2001), 114-119.

30. Ibid., 114.
31. Ibid., 118-119.
32. Yoder, "Walk and Word," 87.
33. Yoder, "The Hermeneutics of Peoplehood," *The Priestly Kingdom*, 45.

Chapter 2

The Radical
Christological Rhetoric of
John Howard Yoder

Gerald Biesecker-Mast

YODER, THE POPE, AND CHRISTIAN UNITY

In his 2001 Gifford Lectures, recently published under the title *With the Grain of the Universe*, Stanley Hauerwas offers a challenging account of modern theology's fate in the hands of those who presumed that knowledge about the world and its human inhabitants precedes and grounds knowledge of God and of God's creation. Against a pragmatist like William James and a realist like Reinhold Niebuhr, Hauerwas asserts with Karl Barth that the God revealed in Jesus Christ and witnessed by the communion of saints is the only proper starting point for any Christian theology, indeed, for any thought about or action in the world by Christians. Such a particular Christian theology should also be seen as a most natural theology, according to Hauerwas, since knowledge of the God who was incarnate in Jesus Christ would shape our very recognition of the "natural" world in which we find ourselves.[1]

Among the characteristics of Hauerwas's effort to rescue theology from the clutches of modernity are two clear commitments: the articulation of Christian theology, above all else as a habit of speech that constitutes a witness, on the one hand; and the retrieval of a Catholic ecclesial and intellectual tradition shaped by the Fathers and Aquinas, on the other hand. From these dual commitments emerges a problematic tension in Hauerwas's work exemplified best perhaps by the contrasting examples of Christian witness he names in the concluding chapter of his book: John Howard Yoder and John Paul II. From Yoder he gains an appreciation for the vulnerable and non-coercive witness to the gospel by the church, whereas from John Paul II he receives a vision for the unity of faith and reason in the elaboration of Divine Truth.

That Yoder and the Pope illustrate a problematic tension is clearly not the wish of Hauerwas himself, who in his account stresses their common opposition to the violence and inhumanity of the modern world rather than their differing ecclesial and theological commitments.[2] At one register this bringing together of contrasting yet overlapping Christian witnesses is clearly a function of Hauerwas's concern for Christian unity. At another register, however, the appearance of the Pope alongside Yoder recreates a familiar scene in Hauerwas's recent writings: the shoring up of an admirable yet lopsided free church or peace church ethics by the formidable bastion of catholic classical theology (and philosophy).

In other writings, Hauerwas has made this drama more explicit. For example, in defending his own ecclesial eclecticism he writes, "By saying I am a high church Mennonite, I am trying to suggest the Mennonite understanding of the church's position toward the world is possible only if such a church is sustained by the kind of theology found in the church fathers, and in particular in that confession we call the Nicene Creed."[3] In his presentation at the Anabaptists and Postmodernity conference at Bluffton College in 1998, Hauerwas approvingly quotes Gerald Schlabach's characterization of his convictions: "Hauerwas wants Catholics to be more Anabaptist, and Anabaptists to be more Catholic, and Protestants to be both. . . . "[4]

Of course, Hauerwas is not the only theologian writing under Yoder's influence who has expressed such sentiments. Michael Cartwright, whose own work has been deeply shaped by Yoder's texts, expresses two reservations in a recent essay: (1) Yoder's understanding of Christian formation is too rationalistic and realistic (in short, too Zwinglian), not adequately accounting for the significance of sacraments and rituals on the shaping of Christian moral life; and (2) Yoder's understanding of the church was too focused on the community gathered in the spirit around the word and not adequately considerate of the continuity of tradition wherein is found the communion of saints.[5]

Some Mennonite theologians who agree with these critiques have seen perhaps more clearly than Methodists Hauerwas and Cartwright, that matters of tradition and sacrament are not incidental features of Yoder's theological framework. James Reimer, who has sought in his writings to reinstall Mennonite theology into the mainframe grid of classical Christian orthodoxy, explained in a recent essay how Yoder's believers church sacramental theology and his privileging of communal discernment over the authority of tradition is intrinsically connected with what he views as an overly limited nonviolent Christology. Reimer concludes,

> In his effective corrective to the evangelical tendency to interior-ize the gospel and that of the mainline churches to sacramental-ize it, Yoder offers a powerful political reading of the New Testa-ment which unfortunately devalues the existential-sacramental power of Jesus' message—that part having to do with divine grace, the personal forgiveness of sin, the inner renewal of the spirit, and the individual's stance before God.[6]

To be fair to these writers, it must be said that their proposals are shaped both by their qualified identification with the Yoder project and by the hope for a more fruitful Christian unity in face of a secular process of globalization that poses a unique challenge for an all too fragmented and disunited church. I share the desire of these writers and others for a church in which divisions are seen as occasions for reconciliation, rather than as battle lines in denominational struggle.[7] Indeed, for those who are committed to Christian nonviolence such desire for ecumenical fellowship is an intrinsic dimension of the salvation God offers us. As Yoder put it in an early pamphlet on the ecumenical movement, "It will be a good Anabaptist way of thinking, and a good check on whether the answer we find to the ecumenical question is evangelical, if we ask: 'Where would we be if God took that attitude toward us?'"[8]

Such a linkage between the way God acts toward humans and the way we are called to reconciliation with those from whom we have been divided must shape the habits of speech associated with ecu-menical conversation. Yoder, even when he advocated ecumenical conversation, was critical of what are often called the ecumenical creeds precisely because "the procedure in the councils was itself far from the normal process of seeking the leading of the Holy Spirit," shaped as it was by the politics and coercive force of a Christian empire.[9] Thus, as Yoder argued, "especially in our day, when the essentially missionary nature of the church is being rediscovered, we should learn to challenge the method and rethink the results of these councils."[10] In other words, while the ecumenical creeds are often seen as a beginning point for Christian unity, Yoder saw them as a sign for the division brought about by the coercion of doctrine. Yet Yoder engaged with the creeds both because he saw them as problematic for Christian unity and because he sought to have the same attitude toward creedal churches that God had "toward us."

Yoder's highlighting of the violence associated with what is often seen as a basis for ecumenicity provides support for the central argument I want to make here. In my view, it is a mistake to see Yoder's often criticized theology of the church and of the sacraments as unrelated or incidental to the often admired politics of Jesus with which writers like Hauerwas, Cartwright, and Reimer identify. Put differently, Yoder's nonviolent Jesus leads logically to both a nonviolent (arguably voluntary) church and a nonviolent (arguably "low church") sacrament, rather than to any forceful establishment or fetishization of tradition, of creeds, of sacraments, or even of the church itself.

CHRISTOLOGY AS RHETORIC

To elaborate this argument more thoroughly, I return to a statement made by Hauerwas, summarizing Barth's theology of witness: "Revelation . . . alerts us to the fact that our existence is contingent on the One who is revealed as Trinity, that is, on the God whose being is action—and whose action is speech."[11] Here, as in so many places, Hauerwas acknowledges and even celebrates the performative and communicative character of God's action in the world, the most decisive of which was the life, death, and resurrection of Jesus.

In an essay that draws heavily both on the work of John Milbank and on recent performance theory, Hauerwas and James Fodor offer a compelling picture of the Christian witness that derives from such a performatively constitutive God, rightly emphasizing the improvisational and historical nature of any theological performance and stressing the "peculiar mode of difference" exhibited by Christian speech: trinitarian peaceableness.[12] Yet this account of witness as performance seems to me in the final instance to exceed the boundaries of the faithful performative, because it insists with John Milbank that peaceableness is not simply an act of obedience—that is, a response of Christians to God's action in Christ, nor only an eschatological hope—that is, the messianic anticipation of a redeemed world, but also ontological reality—that is, an aspect of the natural or created present order.[13] And here, I think, they are saying more than ought to be said or even can be said by theologians or witnesses.[14] "As it is, we do not yet see everything in subjection to him. But we do see Jesus . . ." to recall a passage from the book of Hebrews featured in a well-known Yoder essay.

Perhaps because of this eagerness to make the messianic hope a realized ontology, Hauerwas and Fodor do not give very much attention to audience, which is what any run-of-the-mill speech teacher like myself knows is the most important aspect of what in my discipline is called the rhetorical situation—a context that calls forth speech intended to persuade.[15] Speech, whether divine or human, is by definition an action that is given over to the other, that is concerned with how it will be received, that seeks to account for differences of opinion, that speaks from a position of particularity and that is vulnerable to criticism and attack. So when it is said that the God of Abraham and of Jesus Christ is a God "whose being is action—and whose action is speech," this public speaking teacher assumes that here we have a Divine Speaker who is most concerned with audience, and who addresses us—as God did in Jesus Christ—from a position of particularity, and who is vulnerable to criticism and attack. It is this God, whose speech is described along with audience feedback throughout the biblical story and especially in the gospel story, to whom Christians witness in word and deed—which is to say in both content and form, in both what we say and in the way we say it.

In other words, God's vulnerable, audience-oriented, reception-focused speech shapes Christian witness that is vulnerable, audience-oriented, and reception-focused, as well. This audience-orientedness, as I understand it, is what Yoder was describing in his essay, "But We Do See Jesus" when he said that in the witness of Jesus, "the truth has come to our side (the historical side) of (Lessing's) ditch" (that is, the ditch between accidental truths of history and the necessary truths of reason).[16] Such audience-orientedness is noted in the abstract of Yoder's article "On Not Being Ashamed of the Gospel: Particularity, Pluralism, and Validation" where in summarizing his argument he writes that the gospel "is a genre of communication which is at once particular and communicable, by virtue of the communicator's uncoerced and noncoercive submission to the host culture."[17]

Perhaps Yoder's insistence on making style of argument a central component of the pacifist Christian witness he sought to bear is most succinctly summarized by Chris Huebner, who writes that "Just as the church is called to peaceableness which includes, among other things, the refusal of state power and its assumptions about the need to secure its territory, so Yoder advocates a pacifist epistemology that assumes that the truth about God is not something that can be possessed or secured through some kind of theory of justification. It can only be witnessed—vulnerably given and received as a contingent gift."[18] Huebner's essay quite convincingly critiques two friendly readings of Yoder, both of which seek to establish his work within more traditional frameworks of theological analysis that either assume continuity across history or a "formal or systematic argument."[19]

Huebner rightly interprets the characterization of Yoder's work either as an answer to "perennial questions" or as a systematic argument to be a kind of Constantinian violence, what he calls "an epistemological attitude of closure."[20] This is a posture that "tended to understand tradition statically, as a kind of deposit, the truth of which is to be protected and secured; it did not read tradition dynamically, as an ongoing and constantly changing argument extended through time."[21] By way of contrast, "Yoder's dynamic conception of tradition . . . highlights the centrality of disagreement, emphasizing the fallibilist sense in which communities and traditions must remain vulnerably open to questioning through ongoing engagement with rival traditions of inquiry."[22]

My extensive use of Chris Huebner's work here is an indication of the high regard I have for his reading of Yoder. It seems to me that he has understood well that for Yoder, his style of engagement is not ethically separable from the content of that engagement, anymore than a means is from an end, if we take the Sermon on the Mount seriously. Those who do not recognize this dimension of Yoder's own practice of obedience will continue to misread him.

Furthermore, as I am arguing here, such misreadings will continue to misunderstand Yoder's relationship to orthodoxy, as Craig Carter does in his otherwise compelling account of Yoder's work in a recent book entitled *The Politics of the Cross*. While Carter is right to argue that the politics Yoder ascribes to Jesus is compatible with classical Christian orthodoxy (and he does this very carefully and convincingly), he goes too far when he argues that Yoder's account of Jesus is "rooted" in or "derived" from, classical Christian orthodoxy.[23] Carter is understandably trying to correct a misperception of Yoder's work as somehow Christologically unorthodox. He wants to call into question, for example, John Miller's attack on Yoder as a Marcionite or James Reimer's claim that Yoder emphasized the historical, eschatological dimension of Christology at the expense of the spiritual, ontological dimension. However, Carter overreaches when he suggests that Yoder's affirmation of the creeds extends beyond a missiological recognition of their rhetorical validity in the struggle to claim Jesus as Lord in specific, historical settings or as an appropriate source of data for contemporary ecumenical conversation.[24]

Alain Epp Weaver, in a thorough analysis of Yoder's statements about the creeds, as well as of the arguments of Yoder's critics on this point, accurately describes Yoder's position on the creeds as follows: "Yoder's approach to Nicea and Chalcedon followed a two-pronged strategy of appealing to the creeds while simultaneously relativizing their centrality."[25] This is just right, I think.

It might be worthwhile to note that Yoder's claims about the historical particularity of the creeds should not be seen as somehow scandalous to orthodox Christians or as problematic for ecumenical conversation. I recently discovered a book published in 1974 by a Jesuit priest now located at Loyola University in Chicago which argues along lines very similar to Yoder that Christology should be understood as a rhetorical, and thus historical and contingent, articulation of the relationship between the life and death of Jesus and Jesus' lordship over our particular lives. In this book entitled *Christ Proclaimed: Rhetoric as Christology*, Franz Josef van Beeck is concerned especially with the specific concerns and limitations that shaped Chalcedonian Christology. He asserts that the Chalcedonian creed is a rhetorical statement. Thus its meaning is best understood not by asserting "the perpetual validity of the concepts" but rather by accounting for the concerns to which the statement is addressed; in this case, the question of the extent to which Jesus accepts all human concerns as his own and the degree to which Jesus took up the full burden of our humanity.[26]

Beeck describes the particular terminology that emerged in Chalcedon to address these concerns as a "rhetoric of inclusion."[27] Yet he acknowledges that missing in Chalcedon is what he calls an adequate "rhetoric of obedience" or statements about what happens to the human concerns taken up by Jesus. An adequate rhetoric of obedience would explain how those concerns are "tested and assayed, humbled and purified . . . called to obedience and converted to the way of Jesus."[28] Such an argument seems to anticipate and also to validate the vigorous critique of the adequacy of the ecumenical creeds for Christian ethics as currently articulated by one of Yoder's students, J. Denny Weaver.[29]

It should be apparent by now that I am convinced that the incarnation of Jesus cannot be characterized successfully or finally through a formula whose meaning simply requires recovery, restatement, or even recrafting.[30] Jesus' availability to humans through the witness of Jesus' post-resurrection body—the church—is via a witness that emerges historically, again and again, amid controversy and contingency. Moreover, this coming is not so much a truth to be protected against corruption as a gift to be received and offered amid the cultural exigencies of our own time and through peaceable and considerate exchanges not only with the past and present communion of saints but also with any available missiological audience, including the stranger, the outsider, even the enemy.[31]

Perhaps today this means, most urgently, not only the Christian brothers and sisters from whom we have been divided but also the children of Mohammed with whom we share the heritage of Abraham. Such an interreligious conversation might be fruitfully engaged with such questions as those raised by Yoder in an essay entitled "Confessing Jesus in Mission" where he asks,

> Would Islam have taken on the belligerent shape it did, if it had not been for the ease with which trinitarian language could be interpreted as forsaking monotheism? Might the missionary encounters with the Hindu world, or with traditional religious cultures, have taken on a different shape if the gospel texts had been the springboard, if the ontological definities of *physei* and *ousia* and *hypostaseis* had not had to be part of the message?[32]

To be willing to ask such questions is to challenge a commonly held assumption about the nature of the witness we are called to make. That commonly held assumption is that our speech is a container for unalterable truths, rather than the performance of culturally bound proclamation.[33] In fact, our misunderstanding of the character of God's speech is perhaps held hostage by a common sense view of communication we inherited from Plato and Augustine, what communication scholar John Durham Peters has called the "dream of communication as the mutual communion of souls."[34] Under the influence of this dream of communication, according to Peters, the inheritors of the Western intellectual tradition have ascribed to the practices and technologies of communication a task for which it is not well suited: the resolution of human conflict and antagonism through the establishment of shared meaning. Peters argues, following Jewish philosopher and ethicist Emmanuel Levinas, that it is not so much the success but the "failure of communication" that "allows precisely for the bursting open of pity, generosity, and love," for finding "ways to discover others besides knowing," and for providing a "salutary check on the hubris of the ego."[35]

Indeed, Peters argues that a distinctive alternative to the understanding of communication as "shared communion" is found in the Gospels and in Jesus' communication practices. By contrast with the dialogical or spiritualist model of communication, Jesus assumes a model based on dissemination or what we might now call broadcasting: a giving of meaning over to the other without expectation of safe return. "Broadly speaking, Christianity calls for a love based not in comradeship (as in Aristotle's notion of *philia*), the desire for beauty (*eros*), or the "natural" ties of clan or city, but in the recognition of the kinship of all God's creatures," Peters writes.[36]

By way of example, Peters turns to the gospel of John—the gospel that provides an account of the word made flesh, as a text that characterizes human communication through the story of "dialogic mishaps" rather than transparent communion: for instance, the woman at the well who doesn't understand what kind of water Jesus is offering and Nicodemus who doesn't understand how he can be born a second time.[37] Not surprisingly, in Peter's account of the communication model portrayed in the Gospels, patience becomes a virtue: patience with misunderstanding, patience with obstacles to unity, patience with human foibles and limitations; in short the patience that can lead Jesus to pray "Father, forgive them for they know not what they do."

Such patience, of course, is the condition of possibility for the nonviolent witness to God's love that our life together in Christ's body is meant to make visible before the watching world. What I have been arguing thus far is that Yoder's method of engagement, his social ethics of speech, is consistent precisely with his Christological orientation: God's speech performance in the life, death, and resurrection of Jesus Christ—the Word made flesh—is also the basis for the Christian witness—in both word and deed, form and content—to the world God is redeeming through Christ. Since God's speech was for

us, located as we were and as we are in the contingency of the historical now—in other words, in the world—so also will our witness be
self-consciously and vulnerably located in such contingency and
given over to the world. In other words, the church, whose witness
we have just been describing, must in its very social and institutional
character make visible the patience and nonviolence intrinsic to the
witness given in Christ.

THE BELIEVERS CHURCH
AS NONVIOLENT ECCLESIOLOGY

In his book, *The Desire of the Nations*, Oliver O'Donavan critiques
Yoder's ecclesiology as overly obsessed with the voluntaristic character of the church. This for O'Donovan is exemplified by Yoder's treatment of such divergent characteristics of "mainstream Reformation
Christianity" as the practice of infant baptism, support and protection by the state, and acceptance of just war theory under the rubric of
"coerced faith."[38] Such an obsession with voluntarism as a signal
characteristic of the faithful church smacks of "late-modern conceptions of civil society" concerned with contractual autonomy: "Is
Yoder, in the name of nonconformity, not championing a great conformism, lining the church up with the sports clubs, friendly societies,
colleges, symphony subscription-guilds, political parties and so on,
just to prove that the church offers late-modern order no serious
threat?"[39] In a critical review of O'Donovan's book, Hauerwas in a
footnote agrees that "O'Donovan is on to something when he criticizes Yoder's 'voluntarism,' which can too easily, particularly in
modernity, underwrite rationalistic accounts of faith."[40]

These criticisms of Yoder's ecclesiology seem connected with
Cartwright's critique of Yoder's sacramental theology noted earlier.
Yoder is characterized in these readings as being too modern, too rationalistic, and too representational in his description of the church.
And in one respect, at least, these writers and others who have made
similar arguments are correct. Yoder's advocacy of a free church or
believers church ecclesiology is shaped by a tradition that, indirectly
at least, is implicated in the disestablishment of religion in the name
of freedom of conscience.

Yet it is a mistake to ascribe to either the believers churches or to
Yoder the political motivations associated with the rise of liberal
democracies. For Yoder, the motivation for such freedom is not personal autonomy or the triumph of reason but rather the faithful prac-

tices of a defenseless church. Yoder is concerned less about the privileges and liberties offered by a democratic state (although he seems to favor them) than he is with the church's disentanglement from the established powers with which the church had so long identified.

Indeed, the focus in the essay cited by O'Donovan is precisely not on the freedom of the individual to join the church or leave it but rather on the church's posture toward those to whom it is a witness; that is, "how the body of believers relates to the powers of the world."[41] In that essay, Yoder notes two dimensions of ethical practice that have characterized the believers churches, stressing that these distinctives are derived from historical controversies over the shape of reform between believers church advocates and the Protestant mainstream, not from some prior self-definition shaped by distinctive doctrine. First, Yoder argues that the insistence on voluntary church-membership was a way of asserting that "we cannot do ethics for everyone" and that "the obedience of faith does not make sense apart from the context of faith."

Second, Yoder notes that the rejection of violence has marked the believers churches. Neither of these features of believers churches (voluntary churches) that have emerged amid reformation controversies originated in a concern for a liberal society or in maximizing individual freedom. Rather, what both share in common in their historical appearance is a concern to reform the church according to the criterion of the Scriptures, not the preservation of established patterns and practices. I would note, however, that both marks also share in the specific kind of witness or Christological speech I have been describing in this presentation: a witness that is given, not required; speech that invites rather than demands; performance that is peaceable, not coercive.

The claim that Yoder is advocating individualism and autonomy through voluntarism seems to be based on the same kind of assumption that enables critics to dismiss Yoder's method and style of engagement as incidental to the content of his argument. This is the assumption that the historical form taken by an act of communication is merely a container that transports without excess or remainder a message or a tradition across culture or history. It is the assumption that the form of Christ was incidental to the nature of Christ. It is the assumption that the shape of Christian witness is incidental to the content of Christian witness. It is, in short, the assumption that God's action in Christ was not in its basic character a rhetorical and thereby an historical act. Because Yoder did not assume such a disconnection between word and deed, he could not imagine any other way for the faithful church to act than in the way God acted toward humanity in Jesus Christ: that is to say, with patience and without violence toward enemies.

THE SACRAMENTS AS SOCIAL WITNESS

I have just argued that Yoder's advocacy of believers church ecclesiology was a function of his understanding of the way God approaches and interacts with humanity—not coercively but by a freely offered and received gift of love. In the remaining space I want to argue that the sacraments for Yoder extend God's love and grace into history by both constituting and making visible those dimensions of human relationships that are being redeemed in Christ. Far from being reduced to Zwinglian representationalism, as Cartwright has suggested, Yoder's sacramental theology is an ecumenical theology that focuses its attention on the eschatological force of the church's practices. The sacraments do not so much recall the sacrifice made by Christ as they inaugurate the coming reign of God that Christ's sacrifice achieved.

Now is not the time to describe in detail the five practices Yoder elaborates in *Body Politics*: binding and loosing, baptism, eucharist, multiplicity of gifts, and open meeting. Suffice it to note that Yoder explains each of these practices as an activity "mandated" by Jesus "in, with, and under" which "God would at the same time be acting."[42] Each of these practices prefigures "the will of God for human socialness as a whole," thus making visible the ways in which "the people of God are called to be today what the world is called to be ultimately.[43]

Not surprisingly, Yoder seeks in his account of these practices to historicize the development of some of them as ceremonies and rituals. At the same time he seeks to provide a better understanding of what the biblical sources suggest was their specific historical meaning as practiced by Jesus and he suggests ways in which these practices might come to perform a specific political and cultural witness in the contemporary situation.

Yoder's account of sacraments is thus quite similar to his account of creeds. In both instances he seeks to understand what dimension of God's action in Jesus these changing statements or practices sought to make visible in a missionary context. Without denying the particular validity of historically contingent and confessionally reified rituals, he relativizes those historical forms to better understand what might be a persuasive form of that practice or statement in our world today.

Thus Yoder's sacramental theology is intrinsically connected with the vulnerable and nonviolent character of God's actions toward humankind as exemplified in the cross of Jesus Christ. The practices Jesus taught are performances in which humans respond to God's grace by acting in such a way that presumes God's reign to be present. When humans respond in such a way to the saving speech of God, God acts "in, with, and under" that activity. This is not simply a memorialistic understanding of the sacraments nor is it a slavish adherence to representational integrity—wherein, for example, the Lord's Supper can only be observed where all human relationships are assumed to have been repaired or baptism can only represent individual choice for salvation. Rather, this view of sacraments assumes that faithful practices such as baptism are a response to what God is already doing on the one hand, and that such practices become the occasion for God to do even more on the other hand.

In an intriguing article in which he tries to imagine a rapprochement between believers churches and pedobaptist churches on the practice of baptism, Yoder argues that the important question about baptism is whether the baptism takes place in a context in which the candidate for baptism is assured of nurturance into faith, whether that person be a child, a teenager, or an adult convert.[44] In other words, Yoder does not understand that the ritual of baptism can coercively accomplish what is not already intrinsic to the commitments and expectations of the gathered church that performs the baptism. Thus he remains opposed to what he calls "indiscriminate baptism." Yet he recognizes that a practice such as baptism is not merely representational but also constitutive; that is, by responding to God in faith, believers (and, he is willing to concede, possibly even parents or mentors of potential believers) can enter into God's economy of love and grace and thus be transformed into agents of God's reign and made witnesses to God's saving acts.

Here, as with his concern for a noncoercive, nonviolent church that reflects God's nonviolent reign, Yoder also seems to be in search of a sacramental practice that does not run ahead of history or remain enslaved to the status quo. The church should not engage in sacramental rituals that short circuit the concrete tasks of faithfulness to which the church is called. Likewise the church should not become so constrained by its own failings and limitations that it can no longer step forward in faith to proclaim and to perform what God has promised will be joined with divine action.

CONCLUSION

What I have tried to show here is that a dimension of the nonviolent politics of Jesus that Yoder advocated and exemplified is his performance of witness in a way that is consistent with the manner in which the witness was given in Jesus Christ. The story of Jesus and of Jesus' salvific work is extended through history in the same way that Jesus first of all appeared to humanity: in a particular place amid conflict and controversy. The tradition of Christian witness is thus best understood not as a kernel of truth that has been protected through the centuries by orthodox containers but rather as contingent, historically situated arguments among the likes of Peter and Paul, Augustine and the Donatists, Aquinas and Eckhart, Erasmus and Luther, Zwingli and Grebel, Hegel and Kierkegaard, and, surely, of both John Paul II and John Howard Yoder.

Likewise the search for Christian unity cannot be advanced by privileging the triumph of orthodoxy as a starting point for ecumenical conversation or as a fortification of witnesses that operate low to the ground; rather the search for unity will best be advanced through discernment that revisits, as Yoder did, the arguments of the past in their human context to understand better how the missionary witness of God's action in Jesus Christ might be given in our own time and might by its very epistemological and cultural vulnerability, subvert overextended powers and make visible the triumph of the Lamb.

NOTES

1. Stanley Hauerwas, *With the Grain of the Universe* (Grand Rapids: Brazos Press, 2001), 205-207.

2. Ibid., 218-241.

3. Stanley Hauerwas, *A Better Hope* (Grand Rapids: Brazos Press, 2000), 169.

4. Stanley Hauerwas, "The Christian Difference: Or Surviving Postmodernism," in *Anabaptists and Postmodernity,* ed. Susan Biesecker-Mast and Gerald Biesecker-Mast (Telford, Pa.: Pandora Press, U.S., 2000), 51.

5. Michael G. Cartwright, "Sharing the House of God: Learning to Read Scripture with the Anabaptists," *Mennonite Quarterly Review* 74:4 (October 2000): 604-5.

6. A. James Reimer, "Mennonites, Christ, and Culture: The Yoder Legacy," *Conrad Grebel Review* 16:2 (Spring 1998): 8.

7. My understanding of reconciliation, however, is not that it should be based on commonly held commitments that render differences secondary. Rather, reconciliation should be based precisely on the gospel proclamation that God was in Christ reconciling all things to himself; therefore, it is precisely at the point of difference that the struggle for reconciliation begins. As Yoder writes in an essay entitled "The Imperative of Christian Unity," "disagreement calls not for dividing but for reconciling people. Undertaking that reconciling process at the point of division is more important than affirming common conviction where that can be taken for granted. The difference is more important because it deals with more important issues, namely the ones people differ about." John Howard Yoder, *The Royal Priesthood* (Grand Rapids: Eerdmans, 1994), 292.

8. John Howard Yoder, *The Ecumenical Movement and the Faithful Church* (Scottdale, Pa.: Mennonite Publishing House, 1958), 18.

9. Ibid., 26.

10. Ibid., 27.

11. Hauerwas, *With the Grain of the Universe*, 188.

12. Stanley Hauerwas and James Fodor, "Performing Faith: The Peaceable Rhetoric of God's Church," in *Rhetorical Invention and Religious Inquiry*, ed. Walter Jost and Wendy Olmsted (New Haven, Conn.: Yale University Press, 2000), 387-388.

13. For John Milbank's well-stated argument against ontological violence and on behalf of ontological charity, see his *Theology and Social Theory* (Oxford, England: Blackwell, 1990), 278-325, esp. 289-90.

14. Stanley Hauerwas usually describes his own methodology and worldview commitments with much of the explicit antifoundational and narrative-based language often used to describe Yoder's work. Yet, it seems to me that too often such an invocation of the contingency and historicity of narrative accounts provides an opportunity for Hauerwas to simply celebrate, recover, and reinvoke the "great" tradition associated with such figures as the church fathers and Aquinas, rather than to revisit these texts as particular sides of historical arguments that did not necessarily have to have been resolved in the way that they did.

This is no doubt because Hauerwas is more influenced by MacIntyre than by Yoder in his actual reading strategies or practiced methodologies. My hypothesis is that Hauerwas has not yet realized how significant is his own critique of MacIntyre's obsessive separation of philosophy from theology (along with an implicit prioritization of philosophy over theology).

What Hauerwas thinks is a bizarre exception to MacIntyre's otherwise commendable approach to the texts of the tradition is in my view simply another symptom of MacIntyre's commitment to a wider world that can govern, overrule, and make orderly the messiness of historical theological arguments carried out within a particular tradition of discourse. See *With the Grain of the Universe*, 22-23, especially the notes.

15. Lloyd Bitzer, "The Rhetorical Situation," *Philosophy and Rhetoric* (1968): 1-14.

16. John Howard Yoder, *The Priestly Kingdom* (Notre Dame, Ind.: University of Notre Dame Press, 1984), 62.

17. John Howard Yoder, "On Not Being Ashamed of the Gospel: Particularity, Pluralism, and Validation," *Faith and Philosophy* 9:3 (July 1992): 285.

18. Chris Huebner, "Globalization, Theory and Dialogical Vulnerability: John Howard Yoder and the Possibility of a Pacifist Epistemology," *Mennonite Quarterly Review* 76:1 (January 2002): 52.

19. Ibid., 56-59.

20. Ibid., 60

21. Ibid.

22. Ibid.

23. Craig Carter, *The Politics of the Cross* (Grand Rapids: Brazos Press, 2001), 93.

24. In a recent conversation with me, Carter clarified that he did not mean to root Yoder's Christology in the creeds so much as to claim that Yoder's Christology is rooted in a reading of the Scriptures constrained by the hermeneutical rules of classical orthodoxy. This moves matters in the right direction; yet, I am convinced Yoder was willing to acknowledge even an extra-orthodox reading of the Scriptures, if such a reading was associated with obedient practices. Yoder wrote, "It is sometimes hard to see what is the use of having a check list requiring people to accept the biblical view of the cross of Christ if that acceptance does not issue in a biblical view of the cross of the Christian." *The Ecumenical Movement and the Faithful Church*, 40.

Such a statement simply expresses a conventional Anabaptist concern for orthopraxis over orthodoxy. Yoder's familiarity with and affection for the various varieties of sixteenth-century Anabaptist beliefs, not all of which were orthodox (including the monophysite Menno himself), also suggests that Yoder was no doubt more extra-orthodox than he was either orthodox or unorthodox.

25. Alain Epp Weaver, "John Howard Yoder and the Creeds," *Mennonite Quarterly Review* 74:3 (July 2000): 425.

26. Frans Josef van Beeck, S.J., *Christ Proclaimed: Christology as Rhetoric* (New York: Paulist Press, 1979), 134.

27. Ibid., 154.

28. Ibid., 162-67.

29. J. Denny Weaver, *The Nonviolent Atonement* (Grand Rapids: Eerdmans, 2001), 92-94.

30. I acknowledge that in seeking the meaning of Jesus' incarnation there

will no doubt be some work of recovery and restatement of ancient concepts and articulations and that to the extent that an ancient formula has resonance and persuasive power today, its validity can be said to have been sustained historically. What I am rejecting is recovery and restatement on the assumption of a necessary perpetual validity rather than on the basis of a potential and contingent validity. Furthermore, even if we accept a creedal statement as valid and authoritative, we must nevertheless face the likelihood that its meaning in our present context is remarkably different than the meaning attached with it in the ancient world. In other words, we cannot help but reinterpret and rethink creedal statements, even when we insist on their transhistorical authority.

31. In saying that Jesus incarnation is "not so much a truth to be protected against corruption as a gift to be offered and received," I leave open the possibility that protection against corruption is a legitimate concern in the reception and offering of the incarnation. Certainly the concern for correct doctrine is a biblical concern that appears frequently in Paul's writings, for example. But the first and final characteristic of the incarnation is that it is good news to be proclaimed, given away, and received with joy.

32. John Howard Yoder, "Confessing Jesus in Mission" (unpublished paper), 3-4.

33. In contrasting "unalterable truths" with "culturally bound proclamation" I am highlighting the way in which a biblically construed gospel proclamation is not limited by an assumption that language simply reflects reality but is rather possessed of the scandalous presumption to remake the world through the power of the Word.

34. John Durham Peters, *Speaking Into the Air: A History of the Idea of Communication* (Chicago: University of Chicago Press, 1999), 1.

35. Ibid., 21.

36. Ibid., 61.

37. Ibid., 66-7.

38. Oliver O'Donovan, *The Desire of the Nations* (Cambridge, England: Cambridge University Press, 1996), 223-24.

39. Ibid., 224.

40. Stanley Hauerwas, *Wilderness Wanderings* (Boulder, Col.: Westview Press, 1997), 224, n15.

41. John Howard Yoder, *The Priestly Kingdom*, 107.

42. John Howard Yoder, *Body Politics* (Scottdale, Pa.: Herald Press, 2001), 1.

43. Ibid., ix.

44. John H. Yoder, "Adjusting to the changing shape of the debate on infant baptism," in *Oecumennisme: Essays in Honor of Dr. Kenk Kossen*, ed. Arie Lambo (Amsterdam: Algemene Doopsgezinde Societeit, 1989), 207-208.

Patience, Witness, and the Scattered Body of Christ: Yoder and Virilio on Knowledge, Politics, and Speed

Chris K. Huebner

The war-machine is not only explosives, it's also communications, vector-ization. It's essentially the speed of delivery. . . . Pure War, not the kind which is declared. —Paul Virilio

THIS CHAPTER IS AN ATTEMPT TO HIGHLIGHT the connection between Yoder's reflections on patience as method and his understanding of the scattered, diasporic body of Christ as two key moments in his un-derstanding of theological nonviolence. I get there by reading Yoder's work against the background of a discussion of the contemporary French war theorist Paul Virilio. Virilio is best know for his penetrat-ing analyses of the proliferation of violence in the contemporary cul-tures of "advanced" Western capitalism. Most significantly, he argues that to understand violence and war we must look beyond mere con-flict. More important than explosions, bunkers, troop deployments, and other instances of overt conflict, Virilio claims that violence involves a distinctive organization of political space and its characteristic modes of knowledge.

We must move beyond war to an examination of what Virilio calls the "war-machine," beyond a focus on violent activities to an understanding of the conditions that make violent activity possible, and the changing conditions that have made it extreme, total, and ubiquitous. In doing so, Virilio highlights the epistemological and political prioritization of speed, as exemplified in related technological developments involving the commodification of knowledge as information and the rapid and wide-ranging developments in the techniques of surveillance. Because of the largely unquestioned triumph of these forms of power, Virilio argues that violence has come to organize the very way we think and act.

In addition to his analysis of the contemporary war-machine, Virilio's work is important because of its implications for envisioning the possibility of a pacifist alternative to war, a nonviolent counter-politics and counter-epistemology. In the most straightforward sense, he argues that it is inappropriate to describe the mere absence of overt violence, whether in terms of the mutual deterrence between nation-states or the development of technologies which are able to minimize destruction and human casualties, in terms of an advance toward peace.

At the same time, he suggests that pacifism must refrain from humanitarian abstractions—such as development or the idea that violence grows out of limits imposed on free access to information. In short, each of these "liberal" construals of peace fails to break sufficiently with the kind of militaristic epistemological and political categories that breed and sustain violence. Accordingly, resistance to violence requires a more radical reconfiguration of both knowledge and politics.

As important as it is for Christian pacifists to engage Virilio's work in its own right, I am drawing on it in an attempt to better understand Yoder's nonviolent theology. In particular, I shall argue that Yoder is best understood as identifying many of the same conditions of violence and attempting to provide the same kind of double-sensed reconfiguration that Virilio calls for. Most important, reading Yoder's work against the background of Virilio helps to explain the significance of Yoder's appeal to the practice of patience as a way of resisting the violent logic of speed.

Such an approach to Yoder is necessary because too many interpretations of his work end up distorting his account of the gospel message of peace by forcing it into political and epistemological categories whose status he calls into question as contributing to the very kind of violence the church is called to resist.[1] More specifically, Yoder's commitment to pacifism is often obscured by those who read him with the assumption that we already know what peace is. This is particularly problematic when peace is taken to name some identifiable state of affairs or some kind of ideal it is up to us to bring about. Too many continue to enlist Yoder's name in support of an apologetic strategy designed to defend the legitimacy of Christian pacifism to those who doubt its contemporary relevance. In doing so, they place undue stress on the potential of the church to transform society.[2] It is suggested that the church can be a "potent force" which has the "power to shape history," claiming that a better future can thus be secured, albeit nonviolently.[3] Among other things, I am proposing that reading Yoder as a conversation partner with Virilio is valuable precisely in that it helps to avoid this kind of misunderstanding.

By way of situating and anticipating the discussion that follows, I offer three claims that guide my interpretation of Yoder's work more generally: First, like Barth, Yoder refused to let the doubters set the agenda for Christian theology.

Second, Yoder consistently rejected the kind of instrumentalist thinking that such an apologetic approach exemplifies as contributing to just the kind of violent operation of power to which the church is called to witness an alternative. Yoder did not seek a nonviolent way of transforming society or securing the future but claimed that the peace of Christ involves a rejection of the possessive logic of security and social transformation. A key part of Yoder's theology is his critique of the Constantinian project of outfitting history with handles designed to move it in the right direction. The pacifism of Christian discipleship thus crucially involves giving up the assumption that it is up to us to make history come out right.[4]

Third, and perhaps most important for the present discussion, Yoder never assumed he finally knew what peace was. His work often proceeded negatively, as an attempt to unthink the necessity of violence. And when he worked in more positive fashion, Yoder did not write a systematic treatise on the nature of Christian pacifism but engaged in an ongoing series of experiments in understanding the peace of Christ. His work is thus necessarily fragmentary and ad hoc. He offered a collage, a series of sketches designed to reveal certain tendencies, not a final or total perspective on the very nature of peace as such.

My attempt to bring Yoder into contact with Virilio is offered in this same spirit, as an experimental sketch that Yoder did not himself provide. It is not an attempt to bring us a step closer to the final word on peace but an effort to reveal further tendencies that too often go unnoticed by readers of Yoder who continue to filter his pacifism through existing political and epistemological categories.

As noted, the basic tendency Virilio identifies is the close relationship between violence and speed. As Virilio himself puts it, "The war-machine is not only explosives, it's also communications, vectorization. It's essentially the speed of delivery. . . . Pure War, not the kind which is declared."[5] Building upon and at the same time calling into question Marxist interpretations of the politicization of wealth, Virilio calls for a recognition of the political character of speed.[6] Indeed, he suggests that it is possible to see violence as primarily a function of speed and only secondarily connected with wealth. That is because wealth is itself the product of the kind of power and mobility speed engenders.

More specifically, Virilio claims that the logic of violence as speed is best understood in terms of the shift from geopolitics to chrono-politics. Violence unfolds and develops in a transformation from a geographical analysis of space to the merging of space-time.[7] This is reflected in the increasing technologization of the war-machine. By way of example, Virilio identifies three stages in the expanding power of weapons systems.[8] The first instruments of the war were those of obstruction: "ramparts, shields, the size of the elephant." The war machine originally hinged on the deployment of bunkers, walls, and other physical fortifications designed to define and manage space and thereby to inhibit the movement of one's enemies. The next stage arrives with instruments of destruction, from the development of artillery to the invention of the nuclear bomb, and reaches its apex in the "false peace" of nuclear deterrence. Finally, Virilio claims that war reaches still a different stage with the deployment of weapons of communication.

Contemporary war is thus best characterized as a kind of virtual "infowar" or "cyberwar," whose primary mechanism is the "information bomb." Infowar involves the widespread participation of the media and the deployment of technologies of mass communication of the kind that make the phenomenon of terrorism possible.[9] Virilio writes, "yesterday's war was a totalitarian war, in which the dominant elements were quantity, mass, and the power of the atomic bomb. Tomorrow's war will be globalitarian, in which, by virtue of the information bomb, the qualitative will be of greater importance than geophysical scale or population size. . . . Not 'clean war' with zero deaths, but 'pure war' with zero births for certain species which have disappeared from the bio-diversity of living matter."[10]

As the logic of violence unfolds and intensifies, war is becoming less and less about territory and more about the management of information. In its earlier stages, war was about the defence and takeover of geographical space. Now the army only moves in once the battle is already over. In each new stage of weapons development, space is compressed by a newfound capacity for speed. This gives rise to what Virilio calls the "aesthetics of disappearance." The merging of technology and violence gives rise to a new gnostic "mortification of the flesh."[11] As violence grows and intensifies, the city and other local forms of geographical and physical space, not to mention the body, are literally disappearing. As Virilio himself puts it, "the world disappears in war, and war as a phenomenon disappears from the eyes of the world."[12]

In a related point of emphasis, Virilio maintains that our visual capacities are themselves transformed by the war-machine insofar as the "visual field" is reduced to the "technical sightline" of a military device.[13] As perception is mediated by the logic of violence as speed, a new vision of the world emerges. With the perfection of near-instantaneous real-time speed of delivery, television is transformed into a "planetary grand-scale optics" or "tele-surveillance," which fosters a preoccupation with security and a kind of universal voyeurism.[14] Local space and time disappear and are replaced by a single, global and virtual "real-time." With the triumph of this sort of "sightless vision" and the arrival of an "age of intensiveness," space is further compressed and power becomes even more total. Unlike Baudrillard, who welcomes the disappearance of politics into a transpolitical age of the "intensity of the instant," Virilio is harshly critical of this development as signalling a totalizing proliferation of violence.[15]

Because the rise of technology and the military-industrial complex, Virilio argues that the logic of violence increasingly comes to dominate the very way we understand knowledge. This claim is further developed by means of the identification of a shift from strategy to logistics. By logistics, Virilio means the triumph of means over intelligence, where "rationality is considered only in terms of its efficiency, whatever the horizon."[16] Whereas violence begins with a strategic conception of quantitative, calculative rationality designed to manoeuver and prepare for attacks in geographical space, it is

transformed by means of the logic of speed into a logistical conception of technological, instrumental rationality dedicated to management and hyper-centralization.[17] With the triumph of effectiveness,
Virilio again claims that war and violence become increasingly total
and omnipresent. The logic of violence tends toward what he calls
"Pure War." From the standpoint of logistical rationality, violence is
no longer "acted out in repetition," but involves an ongoing state of
"infinite preparation."[18] In such a situation of pure war, "all of us are
already civilian soldiers" participating in "acts of war without war."[19]

Virilio suggests that this totalizing logic of war and violence is exemplified in the way states have become no longer interested merely
in the outward colonization of other peoples—what he calls "exo-col-
onization." Rather, Virilio claims that nations are increasingly engaged in projects of endo-colonization—the "inward" colonization of
one's own population by means of systematic underdevelopment
and "pauperization" in the name of a more complete investment in
the economy of war: "In the society of national security . . . the armed
forces turn against their own population: on the one hand to exact the
funds necessary for Pure War, the infinite development of weaponry
. . . and on the other to control society."[20] Echoing Foucault's account
of "surveillance societies" and Deleuze's discussion of "control societies," Virilio claims that logistical rationality justifies a strategy of
policing and managerial control designed to condition people for
more effective participation in the ever-expanding war-machine.

The strength of Virilio's work consists in its incisive and penetrat-
ing analysis of the logic of contemporary war and the proliferation of
violence even in what is claimed to be a state of peace. Most important, Virilio's readings of contemporary culture help to diagnose the
sense in which much discourse about peace is dangerously misguided because it is blinded by its own complicity in the logic of violence and the war-machine. This is precisely the same danger that
lurks in the work of those who enlist Yoder in support of the kind of
transformative social strategy mentioned above. In Virilio's terminology, this is to defend a logistical conception of peace which is bound
to fail because it is thoroughly embedded in the very logic of violence.

My attempt to read Yoder by way of Virilio in this manner is
meant to suggest that Yoder's theology involves many of the same resources and interpretive moves that Virilio deploys in revealing the
totalizing logic of Pure War and the war-machine. Among other
things, I am suggesting that Virilio's analysis of the war-machine can
be read as an updated and more militarily sophisticated version of

what Yoder calls Constantinianism. In other words, the tendencies Virilio identifies can be added to the list of the many neo-Constantinianisms that Yoder insisted on identifying as an unsettling reminder to those who like to claim that we have reached something called post-Christendom which allegedly provides a newfound opportunity for the nonviolent church to articulate its theology on equal ground with the now disestablished established church.[21]

In short, Virilio articulates various tendencies of the logic of violence with which I think Yoder would be largely in agreement. Yoder's resistance to the triumph of effectiveness, his refusal to read Christian pacifism as an instrumentalist project of "putting handles on history in an attempt to move it in the right direction," is an attempt to call into question just the kind of policing of time Virilio identifies as characteristic of the rise of logistics. Indeed, Virilio's claim that "the will to organize time is a questioning of God" would serve nicely as a guiding hermeneutical principle for the interpretation of Yoder's theology as a whole.[22]

At the same time, Yoder's interpretation of Constantinian violence also echoes Virilio's account of the aesthetics of disappearance, as he narrates the slide of the visible, embodied church into a preoccupation with the doctrine of the church's invisibility. On Yoder's reading, the church's complicity with violence is intimately linked to the disappearance of the visible church as an embodied politics of resistance. More recently, Yoder's interest in patience as an attempt to imagine a pacifist counter-epistemology can be read against the background of an appreciation of the logic of violence as speed that Virilio so helpfully articulates.

But not only are these key features of Yoder's work illuminated and enhanced by this kind of positive engagement with Virilio. Even more significant for understanding Yoder's theology is his avoidance of weaknesses associated with Virilio's work. While Virilio is helpful in diagnosing contemporary escalation of violence even in the absence of war, he is noticeably less instructive on the possibility of resistance. When pushed on the question of what it would mean to resist the totalizing violence he outlines, he tends to fall back on typically banal liberal clichés which appeal to education and better understanding. When asked "What strategies can we adopt to fight this exponential growth of destructive power?" Virilio answers, "Today, the target is to try to have an understanding of speed. Understand what's been happening for twenty-five years."[23] There is, of course, some truth to such an appeal for increased understanding, insofar as it can make us aware of our unacknowledged complicity with the war-machine. But if that is all there is to say on the matter, it remains a rather thin account of resistance. The significance of Yoder's work in this context is that it provides the kind of thick descriptions of counter-political and counter-epistemological practices that Virilio calls for but does not finally deliver.

At the same time, I want to suggest that Yoder's theology is better suited to respond to criticisms that have been directed at Virilio's account of the contemporary merging of violence and technology. In particular, William Connolly has argued that Virilio is finally too preoccupied with speed and the crisis of the physical dimension. Connolly claims that Virilio's interpretation of the logic of speed is overdetermined by the "military paradigm," such that he fails to appreciate the possibility of other, less threatening "modalities and experiences of speed."[24] In particular, he suggests that Virilio undervalues the "positive" contribution speed might make in "desanctifying" closed and exclusionary identities.[25]

Connolly also maintains that Virilio's critical analysis of the transition from geo-political space to the chrono-political merging of space-time reveals an underlying commitment to the centered, territorial "memory of the nation" as the place where political deliberation should occur. In other words, Virilio remains committed to a concentric model of identity as a closed and bounded site of power from which identity emerges as a possession to be secured and protected against external threats. Connolly argues that such a spatial orientation is equally part of the logic of violence. Yet it is important to be clear that Connolly does not offer these objections as a complete refutation of Virilio's analysis of the relationship between speed and violence. Rather, he calls for a more ambiguous appreciation of the logic of speed. Connolly writes,

> Speed can be dangerous. At a certain point of acceleration, it jeopardizes freedom and shortens the time in which to engage ecological issues. But the crawl of slow time contains injuries, dangers, and repressive tendencies too. Thus it may be wise to explore speed as an ambiguous medium containing some positive possibilities. Such possibilities are lost to those who experience speed's effects only through nostalgia for a pristine time governed by the compass of the centered nation, the security of stable truth, the idea of nature as a purposive organism or set of timeless laws, or the stolidity of thick universals.[26]

Whether or not Connolly's criticisms of Virilio are entirely on the mark is a question that merits further attention. Though it is misleading to interpret Virilio as if he were recommending a return to concentric and exclusionary identities of possession and control in which there is no room for any recognition of the positive value of speed, it would be easier to avoid such a misreading if he were more articulate about the possibilities of resistance. But that is a debate for another context. What is more important for the purposes of the present discussion is the claim that Yoder's theology is best understood as providing just the kind of ambiguous analysis of the relationship between violence and speed that Connolly calls for Virilio to acknowledge.

In short, I want to argue that the value of Yoder's nonviolent theology is that it provides both an appreciation of the logic of violence as speed that Virilio identifies, but also an appreciation of the kinds of violence Connolly thinks can be overcome with a more positive account of the value of speed. In doing so, he is simultaneously critical of both the logic of violence as speed and the aesthetics of disappearance that Virilio identifies, on the one hand, and the equally violent logic of the bounded, territorial space of possessive identity that Connolly worries about, on the other.

For the remainder of this chapter, I will briefly outline some of the key resources that I take to support such a reading of Yoder's work. Against the background of Connolly's critique of Virilio, I begin with Yoder's discussion of the counter-political nature of the church as the diasporic, scattered body of Christ. From there, I will work backward to the question of violence and speed I began with, but this will now be approached from the standpoint of Yoder's counter-epistemological notion of "patience as method." Finally, it will be instructive to note how these two closely interrelated moments in Yoder's nonviolent theology come together in his understanding of the practice of witness.

Like Virilio, Yoder's theology implies that the logic of violence manifests itself in an aesthetics of disappearance. It is for this reason that his work highlights the importance of the visible otherness of church as the body of Christ. But this is not to recommend a static, concentric conception of space of the kind that Connolly foists onto Virilio. Rather, Yoder's ecclesiology is best read as an ongoing experiment in the possibility of a nonviolent and non-concentric organization of political space. A key aspect of Yoder's ecclesiology in this regard is his account of the diasporic, non-territorial existence of the church. This is in turn best understood against the background of Yoder's claim that the church must cultivate a readiness for radical reformation which consistently rejects the essentially violent temptations toward closure, finality, and purity that haunt so much contemporary theology—including much theology that claims to be oriented toward peace.[27] In other words, Yoder's reading of the scattered body of Christ is most importantly an attempt to articulate an ecclesiology which resists the Constantinian temptation to self-absolutization.

Yoder's resistance to a concentric model of identity is reflected in his appreciation of the significance of Jewish diaspora existence. "Dispersion is mission."[28] Scattering is the grace of God. It is possible to remain Jewish in exile, not because Jewish identity is strong, unbending, and self-sustaining. Rather, because it understands its peoplehood as a gift over which it is not finally "in charge," Jewish identity is fluid in a way that allows it to flourish in many different social settings.[29] Because its life is gift, God is able to "renew the life of faith anywhere."[30]

It is significant that Yoder uses the terminology of renewing. The continued survival of the people of God is crucially not understood in terms of the category of preservation, but rather in terms of its receptivity to God's ongoing generosity. Jewish identity in exile is not to be secured by reproducing and protecting what has been left behind at "home." Instead it is continuously refashioned as it enters into and interacts with different social contexts. In doing so, Jewish identity itself undergoes significant and unpredictable changes, even while it remains in some ways "the same."

On such a reading, the Jeremian call to "seek the peace of the city" names a way of engaging the world that simultaneously refuses both the universalist (chrono-political) temptation to privilege the language of the wider culture and the isolationist (geo-political) temptation to preserve and maintain the language of "home" in a kind of sectarian withdrawal. Diaspora Judaism neither fully renounces its past identity for unqualified citizenship in the new world, nor does it seek merely to preserve and maintain itself as a kind of static given. Both options presume a territorial conception of self-identity which is defined over against otherness.

The significance of the diasporic scattering of the body is that it allows identity to be defined as an ongoing negotiation with the other. Accordingly, Yoder suggests that in becoming resident aliens, Jewish diaspora existence represents a third alternative to the standard options of universalist denial of the body and its existence in space and the isolationist preservation of it through policed boundaries. Yoder's depiction of Jewish identity—and by extension his understanding of the church as the body of Christ—is thus similar to the "non-concentric" model of identity and social existence that Connolly calls for.[31]

The diasporic notion of a scattered body rejects the idea of a closed and bounded space existing within a series of outwardly expanding circles. Identity is instead viewed as a negotiation of exchange, sometimes affirming, sometimes critical. It involves multiple networks of overlap and engagement with other cultural identities, each of which is itself interpreted as a potential gift in the hope that it participates somehow in the unpredictable and excessive economy of God. Because it renounces the temptation to understand its identity as a stable entity to be protected and preserved, one's social existence in space is thus "complicated and compromised by numerous cross-cutting allegiances, connections, and modes of collaboration."[32]

In addition to his nonviolent reconfiguration of political space, Yoder's theology equally involves the development of a nonviolent counter-epistemology. This is at least part of the meaning behind his well-known declaration of the epistemological priority of the church to the world. In other words, the world names a series of violent habits of thought which are dedicated to security and insulation against risk. By contrast, Yoder's nonviolent epistemology is not an attempt to secure or defend the truth of its distinctive claims against all comers. It is not an attempt to make Christianity necessary by developing arguments designed to make others "have to believe."[33] Rather, it assumes that truthfulness is an utterly contingent gift that can only be given and received and that it emerges at the site of vulnerable interchange with the other. Accordingly, it is fundamentally open-ended and radically concrete, refusing any self-legitimating appeal to theoretical abstraction.

Among the most important aspects of such a nonviolent epistemology is Yoder's understanding of "patience as method." Much contemporary critical theory locates the problem of epistemological violence in the existence of totalizing metanarratives. The possibility of a nonviolent epistemology is then said to involve an appreciation of micronarrative particularity in which knowledges are given more fragmentary and ambiguous forms of expression. While Yoder is sympathetic to the kind of violence associated with epistemologies of totalizing metanarrative singularity, his reconfiguration of knowledge moves beyond the tendency to focus on metanarrativity as such to emphasize the significance of speed of delivery. Epistemological violence is associated not only within the scope of narrative, but is also located in the speed with which such narratives, whether macro or micro, unfold. In other words, epistemological non-Constantinianism is not merely opposed to metanarrative but also to hypernarrative. The problem with much contemporary theology is that it features a preoccupation with the epistemological and rhetorical movement of speed. This can be seen in the current preference for developing sweeping historical narratives that are not continuously problematized the way Yoder's reading of non-Constantinianism is. In short, theology operates according to a violent logic of speed whenever it is unwilling to risk the possibility that truthfulness is the outcome of ongoing, timeful "open conversation."

The value of Yoder's work is that it lingers. Not only is it important to appreciate his account of patience as an epistemological virtue in which the church cultivates a readiness for radical reformation as an alternative to manipulative and possessive modes of enquiry. Perhaps even more important than what he actually says about patience is the sense in which Yoder's work practices patience. Yoder's theology proceeds patiently, entering vulnerably into the world of another, rather than employing an accelerated and possessive or logistical hermeneutics of mastery and control. It is also exemplified in the way he keeps coming back to and complicating his understanding of non-Constantinianism, as noted above.In addition to the vision of a non-Constantinian epistemology of peace Yoder offers, patience is instructively exemplified in Yoder's own rhetorical practice in a way lacking in much contemporary theology and ethics. Yoder patiently enters the messy world of concrete social reality, refusing to outfit history with handles for easier, more efficient negotiation, while others remain captured by the temptation to master contingency by deployment of fast-moving hypernarrative strategies. He refuses to short-circuit debate and genuine engagement by moving on too quickly.

And it is because he appreciates the connection between violence and speed in this way that Yoder helps to envision the possibility of the church as counter-political and counter-epistemological interruption of the logic of violence. The Constantinian logic of violence deploys speed as an evasion of risk, as an attempt to make theology necessary and secure. But Yoder appreciates that Christian theology fails when it tries to escape vulnerability because the gospel message of peace is a gift given in Jesus Christ.

One can see such an attempt to practice patience exemplified in Yoder's lifelong engagement with the just war tradition. For the standpoint of the present discussion, what is particularly noteworthy about Yoder's numerous encounters with the just war tradition is the sense in which they embody a spirit of charitable receptivity to the voice of the other. He takes the possibility of a just war more seriously than many of his fellow pacifists. In fact, there is a sense in which he takes the just war tradition more seriously than many defenders of just war themselves. Yoder argues that christological pacifists have a stake in defending "the integrity of just-war thought" as a tradition "with teeth," and proceeds to do so by calling it to be more "honest" than it characteristically has been in articulating and observing the criteria for the discrimination of just and unjust wars.[34] In particular, he calls contemporary defenders of just war to be more honest in recognizing the stringent limits and restraints the tradition imposes on warfare.[35]

Instead of suggesting that the just war tradition is essentially violent, and that it therefore must be rejected *as such*, Yoder seeks charitably to engage the just war tradition on its own terms and calls it to be clearer in articulating its general presumption against violence. In doing so, Yoder sets out to challenge two common and interrelated assumptions which, he claims, inhibit debate about violence and nonviolence in the Christian tradition. He calls into question the claim that the just war tradition is the majority view in the Christian tradition and the idea that pacifism and just war are "diametrically opposed" stances.[36] Rather, he argues that the consistent embodiment of the just war tradition is an historical rarity, and that the majority stance involves a "realistic" or "blank check" endorsement of war in the name of national self-interest. When just war is thus properly situated alongside pacifism as a minority view, Yoder suggests that both pacifists and the defenders of the just war tradition have much to learn from a more serious engagement with one another.

To say that Yoder's engagement with the just war tradition exemplifies a stance of charitable receptivity to his dialogue partners is not to suggest that Yoder is uncritical of the just war position. Indeed, there is a sense in which he is far more critical than many other pacifist approaches because his criticisms are more direct than the more common "theoretical" objections to the idea of just war in general. The value of Yoder's engagement with the just war tradition is that he strives to move beyond the general question of the rightness or wrongness of war as such and proceeds more deeply into the particularities of the debate, such as a discussion of the kinds of christological commitments involved in their various conceptions of charity or an examination of the kind of social formation the rival stances presume. It is also noteworthy that he often preferred to redirect the discussion to more specific questions such as the possibility of Christian participation in police work.[37] Instead of claiming to produce a final adjudication of the debate between pacifists and just warriors, much of Yoder's work is dedicated to making that discussion more complicated by elaborating the subtle differences and varieties these stances have taken.[38] In all of these ways, he seeks to resist a logistical, totalizing, and concentric model of dialogue between pacifists and just warriors which is rooted in a logic of speed.

In Yoder's hands, pacifism and the just war tradition are not presented as two entirely distinct or concentric wholes. Rather, there are numerous strands of overlap and an openness to the possibility of ongoing development and reformation in a way that cannot be predicted in advance. As Yoder himself puts it, "The exposition I have chosen is to let the panorama of diverse theories unfold progressively, from the dialogue already in progress, rather than proceeding 'foundationally' on the ground of what someone might claim as 'first principles'."[39]

Yoder's interest in defending the integrity of the just war tradition is part of a larger attempt to create conditions for productive dialogue and disagreement to take place. He worries that contemporary discussions too often short-circuit the possibility of genuine debate by oversimplifying and failing to engage the detailed complexity of rival stances.

However, what is important to recognize for the purposes of my interpretation of Yoder is that this way of understanding dialogical engagement grows out of his attempt to articulate a pacifist reconfiguration of knowledge. While he aims to make the just war tradition vulnerable to a pacifist interpretation of the Christian tradition, Yoder's work is equally an attempt to make pacifism vulnerable to a just war understanding. This does not occur at the cost of critical engagement, but Yoder shows how criticism does not mean that we must throw out the just war tradition as such in the way that pacifists too often do. Yoder's engagement with the just war tradition differs strikingly from other pacifist critics of just war who, in making their criticism too complete and thorough, embody violence in a different sort of way, namely methodological Constantinianism.

Accordingly, one of Yoder's main contributions is his attempt to cultivate the kind of patience required to keep the debate alive. He does this from the standpoint which unapologetically defends a particular strand of the pacifist tradition. But he also does so in a way that attempts to take seriously the alternative of a just war as a genuine option in the Christian tradition. Whether defenders of the just war tradition respond in kind by treating pacifism as a genuine option is something he cannot guarantee. It can only be hoped that a gift offered in a spirit of vulnerability is received and exchanged as a counter-gift in return.

It is instructive to note that Yoder's joint emphasis on the diasporic, scattered body of Christ and his understanding of patience as method are brought together in his account of the missionary character of the church, and in particular the practice of witness. In short, the category of witness captures both the assumption that the church is called to be *for* the nations, and the recognition that it must remain nonviolent in being so oriented. Witness is rooted in the confession of the lordship of Christ, and the conviction that the model of lordship Christ embodies is the rule of the lamb. Yoder claims that "to confess that Jesus Christ is Lord makes it inconceivable that there should be any realm where his writ would not run. That authority, however, is not coercive but nonviolent; it cannot be imposed, only offered."[40] Because Christians confess that Jesus is lord of the whole cosmos, the church is called to share the gospel message as good news for the world. But because this good news involves a breaking of the cycle of violence which includes the renunciation of logistical effectiveness and possessive sovereignty, it can only be offered as a gift whose reception cannot be guaranteed or enforced.

A non-Constantinian understanding of witness does not begin with a theory of universal validation through which the truth of the gospel message can *then* be justified to all people. Yoder maintains that this is just another manifestation of the Constantinian preoccupation with effectiveness in attempting to make history come out right. He is thus calling into question the sense in which the category of witness itself tends to be understood in terms of the violent logic of speed. Yoder's genealogical analysis of Constantinianism suggests that such an "apologetic" conception of witness is only intelligible against the background of the presumption that humans are responsible for controlling the world. However, witness looks different from the standpoint of the non-Constantinian church's *hope* that God is in control of history.

To say that witness is gift is to say that the gospel message is offered in the absence of any additional handles designed to make it better stick. The "test" of witness is not simply whether or not it is received "in fact," but whether it is received *as gift*. The gift of good news is to be received "as it is" or "in its own right" and not by means of an additional vehicle or medium that might guarantee its successful passage. Because the gospel message is that of a peace which rejects the primacy of effectiveness, the message itself is the only available medium. Accordingly, Yoder claims that "the challenge to the faith community should not be to dilute or filter or translate its witness, so that the 'public' community can handle it without believing, but to so purify and clarify and exemplify it that the world can perceive it to be good news without having to learn a foreign language."[41] While Yoder emphasizes that the good news turns on its being received by the listener, this is not to suggest that it is preoccupied with what people want to hear.[42]

Such an assumption would suggest that there is a sense in which the gift is "known" before its being received in such a way that it ceases to be a genuine gift.[43] Rather than identifying underlying conditions or developing new strategies for the effective deliverance of the "truth," the church is called to embody its otherness in such a way that makes intelligible the truth of Christ for the world. To emphasize the missionary existence of the peace church is to suggest that it lives not as instrument, but as example. The task of the church is thus not to "Christianize" the world, but to *be* the church. As Yoder himself puts it, the primary meaning of witness is "the functional necessity of just being there with a particular identity."[44]

Witness thus names a way of life which participates in the body of Christ, a scattered body whose existence is non-territorial and non-concentric. In so being, the church is called to provide a concrete example of good news to and for the world. The good news is that of an alternative way of life which is not rooted in the violent impulse toward self-preservation, but rather the nonviolent and vulnerable receptivity of the other as gift.

In conclusion, let me renarrate this interpretation of Yoder's political and epistemological reconfigurations of peace in terms of the logic of violence as Virilio articulates it. Like Virilio, Yoder rejects an outlook of split-second responsiveness and technical effectiveness which ultimately turns on the desire to secure power. But at the same time, this is not a complete refusal of movement which might justify an attitude of closure. Yoder's account of the church and its characteristic modes of knowledge is an attempt to develop a conception of timefulness which resists both the absolute prioritization of speed and its ultimate overcoming. A pacifist outlook is constantly moving, sometimes radically, but only because it involves the patience to hear all the relevant sides of the conversation.

This is a crucial lesson to learn not least because it recognizes that the standard alternatives of a static exclusivism which silences the voice of the other and a hyper-accelerated tolerance that allows a space for the other to talk without hearing what it has to say are equally implicated in a totalizing epistemology/politics which is finally violent precisely because it is primarily motivated by an attempt to insulate against risk. The great significance of Yoder's work is how it demonstrates that no such approach is capable of receiving the gracious gift of God in Jesus Christ that is peace itself.

NOTES

1. Elsewhere, I have developed an interpretation of this tendency to misread Yoder as an attempt to provide answers to questions he actually implicates in the legacy of constantinian violence by focussing on Lisa Sowle Cahill and Nancey Murphy. See Chris K. Huebner, "Globalization, Theory and Dialogical Vulnerability: John Howard Yoder and the Possibility of a Pacifist Epistemology," *Mennonite Quarterly Review* 76:1 (2002): 49-62.

2. See, e.g., Duane K. Friesen, *Artists, Citizens, Philosophers: Seeking the Peace of the City* (Scottdale, Pa.: Herald Press, 2000), 33.

3. Ibid., 127, 217, 237.

4. See, e.g., John Howard Yoder, *The Politics of Jesus*, 2nd. ed. (Grand Rapids: Eerdmans, 1994), 228, 232.

5. Paul Virilio and Sylvère Lotringer, *Pure War*, 2nd. ed., trans. Mark Polizzotti (New York: Semiotext(e), 1997), 27.

6. Ibid., 35, 49.

7. Ibid., 13.

8. Ibid., 175.

9. See Paul Virilio, *Ground Zero*, trans. Chris Turner (New York: Verso, 2002).

10. Paul Virilio, *The Information Bomb*, trans. Chris Turner (New York: Verso, 2000), 144-145.

11. Virilio, *Ground Zero*, 12. Among other things, this recent work is an attempt to link the question of violence to the contemporary fascination with the "neo-eugenic" project of the technological self-perfection of human life.

12. Paul Virilio, *War and Cinema: The Logistics of Perception*, trans. Patrick Camiller (New York: Verso, 1984), 66, as quoted in John Armitage, "Beyond Postmodernism? Paul Virilio's Hypermodern Cultural Theory," *Critical Theory* 23:3, accessed on Internet at http://www.tao.ca/writing/archives/ctheory/0132.html

13. Virilio, *War and Cinema*, 13, as quoted by Armitage, "Beyond Postmodernism?"

14. Virilio, *The Information Bomb*, 12-13.

15. See, e.g., Virilio, *Pure War*, 34.

16. Ibid., 26.

17. Ibid., 99.

18. Ibid., 92.

19. Ibid., 26, 32.

20. Ibid., 94.

21. This tendency is perhaps best represented by J. Denny Weaver, *Anabaptist Theology in the Face of Postmodernity: A Proposal for the New Millennium* (Telford, Pa: Pandora Press U.S., 2000).

22. Virilio, *Pure War*, 128.

23. Ibid., 62.

24. William Connolly, "Speed, Concentric Cultures, and Cosmopolitanism," *Political Theory* 28:5 (2000): 596.

25. Ibid., 597.

26. Ibid., 598.

27. I have further developed such a reading of Yoder's notion of radical reformation as an attempt to give expression to the epistemological virtue of vulnerability in "Globalization, Theory and Dialogical Vulnerability," 60.

28. John Howard Yoder, *For the Nations: Essays Public and Evangelical* (Grand Rapids: Eerdmans, 1997), 52.

29. See Yoder, *For the Nations*, 61, 66-70 for a discussion of the "Jewishness of the case against 'taking charge' of the course of history" (68).

30. Yoder, *For the Nations*, 53.

31. Connolly, "Speed, Concentric Cultures, and Cosmopolitanism," 603.

32. Ibid.

33. See John Howard Yoder, "On Not Being Ashamed of the Gospel: Particularity, Pluralism, and Validation," *Faith and Philosophy* 9:3 (1992): 287.

34. John Howard Yoder, *When War is Unjust: Being Honest in Just-War Thinking*, 2nd. ed. (Maryknoll, N.Y.: Orbis Books, 1996), 5. For a further discussion of Yoder's stake in defending the integrity of the just war tradition, see Reinhardt Hütter, "Be Honest in Just War Thinking! Lutherans, the Just War Tradition, and Selective Conscientious Objection," in *The Wisdom of the Cross: Essays in Honor of John Howard Yoder*, ed. Stanley Hauerwas, Chris K. Huebner, Harry J. Huebner, and Mark Thiessen Nation (Grand Rapids: Eerdmans, 1999) 69-83; and Tobias Winwright, "From Police Officers to Peace Officers," in *The Wisdom of the Cross*, 84-114.

35. Yoder, *When War is Unjust*, 50.

36. Ibid., 6, 63.

37. See Winwright, "From Police Officers to Peace Officers," 108-114.

38. See, e.g., Yoder, *When War is Unjust*, 71, where he argues that "the just-

war tradition is not a simple formula ready to be applied in a self-evident and univocal way. It is rather a set of very broad assumptions whose implications demand—if they are to be respected as morally honest—that they be spelled out in some detail and then tested for their ability to throw serious light on real situations and on the decisions of persons and institutions regarding those situations." See also the examination of the many different varieties of religious pacifism in John Howard Yoder, *Nevertheless: the Varieties and Short-comings of Religious Pacifism* (Scottdale, PA./Waterloo, Ont: Herald Press, 1992).

39. John Howard Yoder, "How Many Ways Are There to Think Morally About War?" *Journal of Law and Religion* 11:1 (1994): 84.

40. Yoder, *For the Nations*, 25.

41. Ibid., 24.

42. Yoder, "A People in the World," in *The Royal Priesthood: Essays Ecclesiological and Ecumenical*, ed. Michael G. Cartwright (Grand Rapids: Eerdmans, 1994), 86.

43. See Yoder, *For the Nations*, 24 n.22: "'Good news is a kind of knowledge which is not known until one receives it, but then is received as good."

44. Ibid., 42.

Chapter 4

Yoder's Patience and/with Derrida's *Differance*

Peter C. Blum

"Have patience; have patience; don't be in such a hurry.
When you are impatient, you only start to worry.
Remember, remember, that God is patient too, and
Think of all the times that others have to wait for you!"
—Music Machine, "Patience (Herbert the Snail)"[1]

Is this a test?
It has to be. Otherwise I can't go on.
Draining patience. drain vitality . . .

But I'm still right here, giving blood and keeping faith.
I'm gonna wait it out . . .

If there were no desire to heal
The damaged and broken met along this tedious
path I've chosen here,
I certainly would've walked away by now . . .

And I still may.
Be patient.
—Tool, "The Patient"[2]

INITIAL THOUGHTS

The two sets of song lyrics with which I open these ruminations are separated in time by about a quarter of a century. They are separated in mood—or perhaps we should say "attitude"—by a distance not so easily measurable. One is a children's song that has been sung in countless Bible school sessions since the late 1970s. The other is a recent song by a so-called "alternative" rock band, the sort of band whose compact discs are often decorated with stickers warning parents of "explicit" content, or in some cases have had alternate packaging in plain white to qualify morally for the bins at Wal-Mart. Both songs are about patience, and I call attention to them here because my central theme is patience.

Patience means waiting; being good and waiting your turn. Being patient means lacking, sitting uneasily in some "not-yet." Being patient means being like God. Being patient means waiting for God.

Being a patient means healing, being cared for, being cured. Being a patient means hurting, waiting for treatment, for the antibiotics to kick in, for morning when we can call the doctor again. Being a patient means—to reverse T. S. Eliot's simile—being "etherized upon a table" like the "evening . . . spread out against the sky."[3]

I want to talk about patience, but I am impatient to do so. I am impatient with patience. This is a tension that I would like to focus on. I don't want us to feel it to make it go away. I want us to focus on it precisely so that we can feel it more clearly, more acutely.

That I wish to explore patience with simultaneous reference to John Howard Yoder and to Jacques Derrida could be considered comparable to playing a compact disc on which there are both light-hearted Bible school songs and angry electric thrashing. Even well beyond the boundaries of his own confessional community, Yoder was (and remains, via his work) a respected Christian theologian, known for his life-long insistence that following Jesus Christ in life is a real possibility. Jacques Derrida, though probably the most famous living philosopher, is vilified at least as often as he is lauded. One might say that he is the Marilyn Manson of contemporary Western intellectual life. Yoder and Derrida may not seem to have much in common at first glance. But I suggest it is important for us to trace the way in which the apparent tension between them might give way to tension *within* the thought of each, and that this same tension may serve rather than hinder us if we allow it into our own thinking.

Consider some similarities between Yoder and Derrida. Both make claims that seem wildly incredible from the perspective of the academic orthodoxies that they challenge. As if Yoder's being a *paci-fist* is not sufficient to brand him as an unreasonable extremist, he audaciously claims more generally that Jesus not only *should* be, but in fact *can* be normative for Christian ethics—*pace* academic assumptions about how contemporary biblical scholarship makes this difficult or even impossible.[4] His advocacy for a church that visibly embodies a radical social alternative, when not rejected as morally and politically problematic, seems downright utopian. Derrida similarly irritates his academic colleagues with apparently ludicrous claims that speaking derives from writing rather than vice-versa, or that the meaning of words is "undecidable," and even that there is nothing "outside texts." Because of the apparent extremity of their claims, both Yoder and Derrida have widely elicited academic responses which amount to summary dismissal. Yoder's "sectarian" ethic seems at best irresponsible, and at worst separatist and quietist. Derrida's "deconstructionism" apparently undermines meaning in general, hence undermining our ability to say anything meaningful about morality (among other things), but also (thank goodness!) undermining itself. We may concede that they are brilliant rhetoricians, but inasmuch as they make any specific claims, they need not be taken very seriously.

There is a clear sense, of course, in which these sorts of reactions both to Yoder and to Derrida are waning recently, and that they are both treated with increasing seriousness—not only by such inbred groups as Mennonites and deconstructionists, but by the scholarly mainstream. To those of us more favorably disposed to either or both, this is surely a welcome development. Or is it? Both Yoder and Derrida, despite their own deep distrust of and warnings about systematizing, are increasingly the subjects of scholarly commentary geared toward exposing the implicit systems that presumably bind together their various writings, just waiting for the careful expositor to render them as series of explicit propositions. Nancey Murphy provides a succinct statement of the tendency that I have in mind here:

> Yoder disclaimed being a systematic theologian. He believed (rightly, I think) that theology should be written in the service of the church, addressing issues as they arise, and not driven by any philosophical or systematic motivations. However, this perspective on the nature of theology does not prevent others from looking at Yoder's many writings and perceiving the organization and coherence of the whole.[5]

Murphy's observation here is clearly correct in a broad sense. "Anti-system" thinkers such as Kierkegaard and Nietzsche have been endlessly summarized and presented in very systematic ways. This seems not only natural, but in fact unavoidable. Murphy's own discussion of Yoder using the Lakatosian notion of a "research program" is in fact quite suggestive and useful. I have no doubt that the same heuristic would prove fruitful if applied to Derrida's writings.

I will not argue that systematizing either Yoder or Derrida is simply an *error*. Indeed, insofar as my discussion here involves an attempt somehow to think Yoder and Derrida together, I am quite sure that it will not escape being systematic in some relevant sense. Assuming, however (following Foucault) that "everything is dangerous,"[6] my impulse is to look for the *danger* in systematizing them, which is not the same thing as looking for an *error*. Yoder himself has told us that "once we have learned how the word-spinners mislead us, we must also recognize that their skills are the only ones we have with which to defend ourselves against their temptations."[7] I will employ a bit of system to suggest that we should remain deeply suspicious of system. The bit of system I plan to use is the one with which I began: *patience*. I would like to take up the idea of patience, as it figures in the posthumous essay by Yoder included in his *Festschrift*,[8] and treat it temporarily as if it were a key with which I can systematically unlock some doors into Yoder's distrust of system.

In Derrida's terms, I intend to use the notion of patience *strategically*. Derrida himself characterizes *differance* "as the *strategic* note or connection—relatively or provisionally *privileged*—which indicates the closure of presence. . . . "[9] Strategic use of a "word" or a "concept" (*differance* is neither, for Derrida) does not imply that it is some sort of Archimedean point, either ontologically or epistemologically. It is privileged *provisionally* for the purposes of a specific inquiry.

DERRIDA

If we follow Derrida's lead and recall that his own use of *differance* in the essay so titled is strategic, it will provide us with something of a point of reference from which to consider patience as strategic as well.[10] Derrida's early work focused on a general critique of what he called (following Heidegger) "the metaphysics of presence." This was carried out, first of all, in a careful analysis of Edmund Husserl's phenomenological theory of meaning. "Presence" in that context may be understood roughly as the sort of presence before consciousness that had already been Descartes' ideal, an indubitable clarity and distinctness that could serve as a sure epistemic foundation. Derrida attacked this notion by juxtaposing it with the general understanding of signs that emerged from the work of Ferdinand de Saussure. Regardless of what details of Saussure's views have or have not been taken up by subsequent linguistics or semiotics, Derrida rightly emphasizes the broad-based acceptance of his two central insights, namely, (1) the *arbitrariness* of signs, and (2) the *differential* character of signs. Both insights are nicely captured in Derrida's phrasing: "The elements of signification function not by virtue of the compact force of their cores but by the network of oppositions that distinguish them and relate them to one another."[11] An individual sign does not have meaning all by itself, in isolation from other signs; meaning is in the differences between signs, and the differences between signs in one sign system need not map directly onto those of another sign system.

The reality that signs do not mean anything by themselves individually entails this: Meanings of signs are never simply "present" in the Cartesian/Husserlian sense. "The movement of signs defers the moment of encountering the thing itself, the moment at which we could lay hold of it, consume it or expend it, touch it, see it, have a present intuition of it."[12] This is precisely what leads Derrida to deploy the term *differance*, according to which "the signified concept, "as he puts it,

> is never present in itself, in an adequate presence that would refer only to itself. Every concept is necessarily and essentially inscribed in a chain or a system, within which it refers to another and to other concepts, by the systematic play of differences. Such a play, then—*differance*—is no longer simply a concept, but the possibility of conceptuality, of the conceptual system and process in general.[13]

The differences which constitute meaning in a language, though they are clearly arbitrary, have not simply "fallen from the sky," as Derrida says.[14] They must have a cause, we would assume; they must have come from "somewhere." The problem is that there is no "somewhere" that we can point to from which they might have come but which itself lies beyond or outside of the play of differences. If a meaning could be intuited clearly and distinctly in the way that Descartes or Husserl would like, then according to Saussure's view, *it could not in fact be a meaning*! An "intuition" of meaning would always already have entered into the play of differences. If presence were required to make sense of a cause, "we would therefore have to talk about an effect without a cause, something that would very quickly lead to no longer talking about effects."[15] Derrida's approach here is, by his own admission, a discursive move akin to negative theology.[16] He "defines" *differance* as "the movement by which language, or any code, any system of reference in general, becomes 'historically' constituted as a fabric of differences."[17] *Differance* is emphatically not God, but the non-word *differance* does not denote in basically the same way that 'God' does not denote according to the apophatic tradition. The terms of his "definition" are used not in their traditional metaphysical senses, he tells us, but "out of strategic convenience."

The sense in which all of this remains *provisional* is precisely the sense in which it all remains wedded to a particular beginning. The beginning, stated much too simplistically, is still his juxtaposition of principles drawn from phenomenology and structuralist semiotics. The point is not that Derrida has somehow created a *new* beginning; even less that he has somehow either surpassed all beginnings, or found THE beginning. Derrida's project, rather, is to grab hold of some of the main resources of the scaffolding on which we have arranged our thinking, and to shake them vigorously, to make them rattle. This is my reading of what Derrida generally calls "deconstruction" (though that word has been so thoroughly "terminologized" that it is even less capable of serving as a disruptive "non-word" than *differance*).

Derrida's general approach here (especially under that notorious name) has often been understood as leading directly to some sort of "nihilism"—as undermining our ability successfully to mean anything that we say, or to say anything that we mean, or something equally hideous.[18] Recent work both by and about Derrida has fortunately mitigated such worries to some extent. Unlike some of his more excitable readers, Derrida has never assumed that deconstruction constitutes some sort of straightforward *refutation* of any particular point of view. His concern is apparently that our general way of embracing *any* point of view is problematic, at least insofar as it is haunted by the expectation of *presence*. As long as we expect presence, presence will be deferred; as long as we expect sameness, there will be difference. This is *differance*. To reach for another gross oversimplification, deconstruction is provisional because what is being deconstructed is provisional to begin with.

This is, in fact, one of the main reasons why "deconstruction" is so *deeply* disconcerting to many of us. We simply do not want provisional views. We want *Truth*, in the sense that so exercised Nietzsche. Derrida does *violence* to the very idea of truth, we often think. Consider, however, that from Derrida's perspective the very idea of truth is, in an important sense, already violence. The longing for truth as presence is one way of trying, in terms that Derrida has learned from Emmanuel Levinas, to reduce the Other to the Same.[19] Derrida's first extended reflection on Levinas[20] clearly identified this "reduction" as a form of violence—ultimately a *discursive* form of violence. "Predication is the first violence," he tells us.[21] Indeed, Derrida makes it sound as if violence is *unavoidable*:

> A Being without violence would be a Being which would occur outside the existent: nothing; nonhistory; nonoccurrence; nonphenomenality. A speech produced without the least violence would determine nothing, would say nothing, would offer nothing to the other; it would not be *history*, and it would *show* nothing. . . . [22]

I already do a sort of violence when I speak to the other. If it were not so, I would not be speaking *about* anything; I would not really be *saying* anything. If there were such a thing as a nonviolent language, it "would be a language which would do without the verb *to be*. . . . "[23]

YODER

How tempting it would be at this point to expect relief when we turn from Derrida back to Yoder. Being a believing Christian, Yoder surely insists on *truth* more clearly than Derrida does. Being a much "clearer" thinker and writer than Derrida, Yoder surely has a more clearly discernable project, one which we can thematize or systematize. Being a pacifist, Yoder surely would reject Derrida's suggestion that violence is unavoidable, that we are already being violent when we *speak*.

Rest assured that I am not about to claim that Yoder and Derrida are simply up to the same thing, that Yoder is Derrida in Mennonite clothing. I do want to suggest, however, that there is a reading of Yoder that drastically reduces the apparent distance between them, and that this reading should not be lost amid the proliferation of Yoderian systems. I have already indicated that patience will occupy a central strategic place. Let me be more clear now as to my strategy: By attending to Yoder's reflections on patience, and placing them in the context of (1) his critical stance toward what he called "Constantinianism," and (2) the "epistemological" preoccupations of some of his late essays, I want to suggest that there is at least a deep kinship between Yoder and Derrida in terms of their avoidance of system. A central claim that I wish to advance is that this avoidance has everything to do with violence.

Yoder's "essay" on patience is not really an essay, of course. It originated as a memo in 1982 and has since been distributed in various forms, often under the more apt title, "Methodological Miscellany."[24] It retains something of the feel of a document in process. Nonetheless, its overall tone is one of a general response by Yoder to the charge that his views are, in some undesirable sense, "absolutist." Yoder rejects either "absolutist" or "relativist" as a way of describing his approach, and uses the word *patience* to convey the sense in which he wishes to steer between these two standard options. The clearest indication of how Yoder defines 'patience' is in his equation of "reasons for 'patience'" and "considerations which call for purported 'absolutes' to be mitigated, yet without justifying the dominant constructions [such as "relativism"]."[25] That he writes here of *purported* absolutes is more significant than it may seem at first. Yoder claims that none of the various kinds of patience he discusses is anything but what should be expected of "any kind of decent person taking a position on the grounds of moral conviction on any important subject."[26] But just as Murphy finds system behind Yoder's protests that he is not being systematic, I would suggest that what we find here may be rather less pedestrian than Yoder himself implies.[27]

I have already discussed in another context,[28] in connection with Foucault, how some of Yoder's other "late"[29] essays may be understood as fully consistent with a broadly Nietzschean hesitation regarding claims to possess *Truth*, a hesitation shared by Derrida as well as by Foucault. Here I want to call attention to the light that this might cast on Yoder's understanding of patience. Patience regarding purported absolutes is, I submit, an integral part of Yoder's more general conviction that the sharing of good news—of gospel—must be noncoercive. Note his comments in connection with patience type 6: "My meeting the interlocutor on his own terms is not merely a matter of accepting the minority's conversational handicap although it is that. It is also a spirituality and a lifestyle."[30] He expands on this with a footnote noting that " nonviolence is not only an ethic about power but also an epistemology about how to let truth speak for itself."[31]

Patience is by no means incompatible with the strong conviction that one's views are in fact true, a point that comes across clearly in

Yoder's essay. It may seem that my attempt to identify patience in Yoder's thought with some sort of Nietzschean suspicion is at least overwrought, if not completely misguided. Being patient with others who disagree is quite different, we might think, from adopting an attitude of suspicion that makes us unable ever to say "this is true" without a set of unpleasant qualifiers about the perspective from which it *seems* so to us. Being patient in a discursive situation where one is in the minority—and thus where one is especially aware of the violent potential of discourse—is quite different, we might think, from pronouncing that discourse just *is* violent.

Insofar as it is one of my intentions here to be a sort of champion of difference, I will certainly not deny the validity of this line of thinking. It is especially clear that Yoder stresses the possibility of nonviolent discourse in a way that Derrida apparently disallows. I believe there is still more to be said, however. The question of the *differences* between the two is not the same as the question of the *distance* between the two. A bit of further examination of the "Patience" essay, though it does not reduce the differences, may reduce the distance.

It is most clear in patience type 13 ("the 'modest' patience of sobriety in finitude") that patience is not simply a communicative attitude adopted on the near side of an epistemic certitude, and hence added onto the certitude externally as a supplement. This patience amounts to more than simply a polite fallibilist admission that the probability of my being wrong never reaches zero. Yoder spells it out precisely in terms of the need for one's fallibility to be embodied in discourse, observing that

> the certainty in which we have to act one day at a time must never claim *finality*. Our recognition that we may be wrong must always be *visible*. One way to say this would be to begin every statement one ever makes with "as far as I know" or "until further notice." That I do not begin every paragraph this way does not mean that I do not mean it.[32]

This is not so far, after all, from the suspicion alluded to above. Citing Hubmaier and Denck's openness to correction from their persecutors, Yoder's footnote[33] notably ties this patience to the context in which violence might be done to the one making the truth-claim. Type 12 ("the 'contrite' patience of repentance") alludes to the possibility of the claimant's own complicity in violence toward others. One crucial implication here is not only that I may be wrong, but that my conviction that I am right may be the occasion for violence, quite apart from its truth or falsity. The primary import of truth and falsity is not *intra*personal (the *presence* of truth within the Same), but *inter*personal (truthfulness toward the Other).

When Yoder pursues what he calls a "phenomenology of the moral life," truthfulness (as opposed to Truth) emerges as a primordial requisite for human association:

> There is, as a matter of empirically undeniable fact, a human social fabric characterized by communication. . . . For society to be viable, most of this communication has to be "true" most of the time; i.e., it has to provide a reliable basis for structuring our common life, counting on each other and not being routinely disappointed.[34]

It is in this context that proscriptions against lying develop, with practice pushing them toward solidification as norms. Because they are applied in everyday contexts, they are "probably concretized as sinning against some simple notion of 'correspondence' between words and reality."[35] This process is proceeding apace long before the ethical theorist arrives and tries to decide between utilitarianism, deontology, virtue theory, or other accounts of what makes it True that one should not lie. "The life of the community is before all possible methodological distillations."[36]

The point at which I would like to suggest that the distance between Yoder and Derrida is especially narrow is at the point of their concern for the violence that we would do to the Other. Our impulse is to reduce the Other to the Same, to make the Other an object that fits into the world of which I am the center, to reduce the other to a concept that is intelligible primarily with reference to *me*. Patience is about the primacy of the Other *vis a vis* "the Truth."

This is where patience also shades into the disavowal of Constantine. The reversal of priorities for the church that Constantine represents, for Yoder, is at bottom a trading of noncoercive witness to the Other for a coercive encompassing that we mistake for redemption. Gerald Schlabach has rightly pointed out that Constantinianism in a sociopolitical sense is but one manifestation of a broader phenomenon. He writes: "The Deuteronomic problem is the problem of how to receive and celebrate the blessing, the shalom, the good, or 'the land' that God desires to give, yet to do so without defensively and violently hoarding God's blessing."[37]

So what about the difference that still glares across this divide, even though it may be more narrow than we thought at first? We noted that Derrida seems to envision violence as unavoidable, as endemic to any discourse, to any "saying that. . . . " Yoder, on the other hand, seems confident that there can be nonviolent discourse. The question of who is correct is beyond my present scope, yet I wish to suggest in passing that, in this case too, the difference may not be a matter of great distance. There are hints throughout Yoder's writings that a commitment to nonviolence, though never *less* than a commitment not to kill, is perhaps never *simply* that, is never a commitment that pretends that killing or not killing is the *only* choice. In response to the allegation that his view would imply that he is more "pure" than others, he responds: "The Niebuhrian or the Sartrian has no corner on dirty hands. The question is not whether one can have clean hands but which kind of complicity in which kind of inevitable evil is preferable."[38]

CONCLUDING COMMENTS

If I have been even moderately successful in my strategic deployment of Yoder's notion of "patience," we should now be able better to feel the tension with which I began, between the lighthearted patience that is certain of God's rule (the patience of Herbert the Snail) and the patience that asks "Is this a test?" and that may still walk away rather than waiting (the patient of Tool). Patience itself is something with which we are less than patient. "Lord, grant me patience. And Lord, please grant it to me *now*!"

What if Yoder's patience is supposed to be patience with Derrida's *differance*? What if that for which we patiently wait, though it is "to come," will never be *present*? Patience is all well and good, as long as I am certain that my patience will "pay off." Images of sudden rapture and of the confusion of those "left behind" appeal as widely as they do because they are visions of vindication not only for God, but *for us*. The more certain I am that I am going to win, the more patient I can be. The more probable it becomes that everything will turn out "right" (by my own lights), the less I will be prone to losing my patience.

Here is where we may note what at the outset I referred to as the tension *within* each of the two thinkers we are attending to. Derrida has emphasized that the difference/deferral of *differance* will not go away; we don't get the presence that we long for. But more recently, he has increasingly written in an eschatological vein, of what he calls "the messianic," which is emphatically "to come," even though it will not be present.[39] Yoder has emphasized the unfaithfulness of the Constantinian settlement, the importance of witnessing by letting the church be the church, and by letting God be God. But letting the church be the church is letting the church be *visible*, and how does one do that both faithfully and patiently? How might we find the level of patience that lets God be God by not trying too hard to *make* the church be the church?[40]

Patience is waiting. It is sitting uneasily in a "not-yet," without control of its own fulfillment. Patience knows not the times or the seasons. Patience knows that it waits for what is to come, but it does not know if what is to come will ever be present. If it were not so, it would not be patience. Patience is something that we may not truly have until we are impatient with it. Hence, I cannot conclude by assuring you that your patience—our patience—will be rewarded in the way that we would like it to be. We know that it will be rewarded insofar as we have been promised this by the one in whom we trust.

But in the way that we would like it to be? That is left unanswered, and it remains the more disconcerting question; it remains *unheimlich*; it makes us tremble. As we pray for patience now, perhaps we will tremble. Indeed, we should do both. We should pray, and we should tremble.

NOTES

1. This song is from an album originally released in 1977 entitled *Music Machine: The Fruit of the Spirit* (sound recording, original record label: Candle; compact disc released 1998 by BCI).

2. Tool, "The Patient," on *Lateralus* (sound recording, BMG/Volcano/Pavement/CZ, 2001). The notes credit all songwriting collectively to Tool (Danny Carey, Justin Chancellor, Adam Jones, and Maynard James Keenan).

3. T. S. Eliot, "The Love Song of J. Alfred Prufrock," *Collected Poems 1909-1962* (New York: Harcourt Brace, 1963), 3.

4. This is presented by Yoder as one of the central theses of *The Politics of Jesus* (1st. ed. Grand Rapids: Eerdmans, 1972; 2nd. ed. Grand Rapids: Eerdmans & Carlisle, UK: Paternoster Press, 1994).

5. Nancey Murphy, "John Howard Yoder's Systematic Defense of Christian Pacifism," 45-68 in *The Wisdom of the Cross: Essays in Honor of John Howard Yoder*, ed. Stanley Hauerwas, Chris K. Huebner, Harry J. Huebner, and Mark Thiessen Nation (Grand Rapids: Eerdmans, 1999).

6. Paul Rabinow, ed., *The Foucault Reader* (New York: Pantheon Books,

1984), 343. See my discussion of this in connection with Yoder in Peter C. Blum, "Foucault, Genealogy, Anabaptism: Confessions of an Errant Post-modernist," 60-74 in *Anabaptists and Postmodernity*, ed. Susan Biesecker-Mast and Gerald Biesecker-Mast (Telford, Pa.: Pandora Press U.S., 2000).

7. John Howard Yoder, "Walk and Word: The Alternatives to Methodologism," 77-90 *Theology Without Foundations: Religious Practice and the Future of Theological Truth*, ed. Stanley Hauerwas, Nancey Murphy, and Mark Nation (Nashville: Abingdon Press, 1994), 85.

8. John Howard Yoder, "'Patience' as Method in Moral Reasoning: Is an Ethic of Discipleship 'Absolute'?" in *The Wisdom of the Cross* 24-42.

9. Jacques Derrida, "*Differance,*" 441-449 in *The Continental Philosophy Reader*, ed. Richard Kearney and Mara Rainwater(London: Routledge, 1996), 441 (his emphasis).

10. It is worth noting how difficult it is for us to do so now. Derrida's fame has given rise to what can only be considered an industry in secondary literature, and various terms in Derrida's strategic lexicon have been transformed into static keys for systematic locks, *differance* being one of the most commonly discussed. It may require a considerable effort to think of the use of a term as *provisional* when it has solidified into an established chunk of academic jargon.

11. Derrida, "*Differance,*" 448.

12. Ibid., 447.

13. Ibid., 449.

14. Ibid.

15. Ibid.

16. See Ibid., 444.

17. Ibid., 450.

18. Dismissal of Derrida as a nihilist is most often based, I would argue, on superficial (if any) reading of his work. It must be stated, however, that some careful and even somewhat sympathetic readers of Derrida conclude that a vicious nihilism of some sort lurks in his thought. The most prominent current examples are Catherine Pickstock and John Milbank. I am not persuaded that they are correct, but detailed engagement with their arguments is far beyond my present scope. For some orientation to the issues involved, see Guy Collins, "Defending Derrida: a Response to Milbank and Pickstock," *Scottish Journal of Theology* 54:3 (2001): 344-365.

19. Levinas' term is *meme* (contrasted with *l'autre*).

20. Jacques Derrida, "Violence and Metaphysics: An Essay on the Thought of Emmanuel Levinas," 79-153 in *Writing and Difference*, trans. Alan Bass (Chicago: University of Chicago Press, 1978).

21. Derrida, "Violence and Metaphysics," 147.

22. Ibid.

23. Ibid.

24. Yoder, "'Patience' as Method," 24, note 1.

25. Ibid., 25.

26. Ibid., 35.

27. Though I emphatically *do not* wish to soften the most important ingredient in his disclaimers that his considerations are "radically ecumenical" and not "sectarian." (Ibid.)

28. Blum, "Foucault, Genealogy, Anabaptism." The Yoder essays in question include "But We Do See Jesus: The Particularity of Incarnation and the Universality of Truth," 46-62 in *The Priestly Kingdom: Social Ethics as Gospel* (Notre Dame, Ind.: University of Notre Dame Press, 1984); "On Not Being Ashamed of the Gospel: Particularity, Pluralism, and Validation," *Faith and Philosophy* 9 (July1992): 285-300; and "Walk and Word" in *Theory Without Foundations*.

29. I keep injecting the qualifier "late" because I suspect, based on both his writings and my personal conversations with him, that Yoder's actual *interest* in what I am calling "epistemological" issues (as opposed to the occasional need to discuss them regardless of interest) grew significantly during the last decade and a half of his life.

30. Yoder, "'Patience' as Method," 28.

31. Ibid., note 9.

32. Ibid., 31.

33. Ibid., note 15.

34. Yoder, "Walk and Word" in *Theory Without Foundations*, 80.

35. Ibid.

36. Ibid., 82

37. Gerald W. Schlabach, "Deuteronomic or Constantinian: What is the Most Basic Problem for Christian Social Ethics?" 449-471 in Hauerwas et. al., *The Wisdom of the Cross*.

38. Yoder, "'Patience' as Method," 40.

39. Cf. Derrida, *Specters of Marx* (London: Routledge, 1994), and *The Politics of Friendship*, trans. George Collins (London: Verso, 1997).

40. The latter problem is a main theme of Blum, "Totality, Alterity, and Hospitality: The Openness of Anabaptist Community," forthcoming in *Brethren Life and Thought*.

Chapter 5

Yoder's Idea of Constantinianism: An Analytical Framework Toward Conversation[1]

Thomas Heilke

SUPPOSING CHRISTENDOM WERE AN ERROR.[2] Supposing there were non-Christendom ways of being church in our post-Christendom era that are neither isolationist nor nostalgic for Christendom or pre-Christendom. So begins the political thought of John Howard Yoder, the "bete noire," in one estimation, of contemporary moral theology.[3] Naming the problem of Christendom would be one step toward conversationally engaging those many who continue to hold to one version or another of it and toward articulating a way of being the church in a post-Christendom political and religious world. Yoder's use of the term *Constantinian* was an effort to do exactly that.

Christendom is part of the Western political experience; since its defense and critique are part of the Western tradition of political philosophy, Yoder may be taken to be not only a moral theologian or a church historian, but also a political thinker in the Western tradition. Provisional support for this claim requires no more than to point to the explicitly *political* character of the titles he gave to nearly all his published books. On more solid ground, Yoder himself argued that his writing had "no one subject." Rather, "the themes [he had] been called to treat over the years overlap and interlock, each of them gaining significance from its connection to the others, but . . . they are in several disciplines."[4] Political philosophy is one of these disciplines.

This paper takes up four tasks in connection with Yoder's political thought. First, by means of historical recollection and a review of Yoder's pertinent writings, it outlines briefly the meaning(s) of Constantinianism as Yoder used it. Second, it considers some contemporary uses of the term that have been influenced by Yoder and that more clearly elucidate his meaning. Third, it outlines some of the consequences for Yoder's political thought in using the term. Finally, it considers the adequacy of the term and provisionally offers a possible political outcome of using it.

INTRODUCTION

Politics appears to have first come into self-consiousness as a specific, goal-oriented, moral enterprise, worthy of close analysis and skeptical examination as to its claims, means, and ends in the marketplace conversations of Socrates, the "gadfly"[5] of late fifth-century B.C.E. Athens. That Socrates discovered the soul as the sensorium of rational order and transcendence, and that this discovery was the beginning of political philosophy as an activity of inquiry into the meaning and purposes of political life is generally acknowledged. Particularly in the last two centuries, however, in which ideological forms of thinking and of conceiving of thought itself have emerged nearly victorious, this Socratic discovery has been dogmatized into a "doctrine,"[6] an "ideology,"[7] or a "teaching,"[8] all of which detract from its original meaning as a quest and an inquiry. While Socrates is not known ever to have written a word, his friends and disciples, especially Plato and Xenophon, did write, thereby preserving a form of inquiry that continued in various schools of philosophy through several civilizations into the modern era.

Four centuries after the execution of Socrates, a Jewish rabbi and carpenter's son wandered a backwater province of the Roman Empire, making outrageous claims concerning his divinely anointed ministry and preaching a message of hope and salvation that was to become even more civilizationally profound than the inquiries of Socrates. Like Socrates, Jesus of Nazareth is not known to have written a word, but like the friends of Socrates, the disciples of Jesus eventually recorded much. That messianic message had deep and extensive political implications. However, at least one set of these implications were gradually and largely lost in all but the fringes of the societies that adopted the message of the Jewish carpenter's son and absorbed it into various versions of a civilizational and political power schematic that ruled parts of the Mediterranean and northern European world for approximately fifteen centuries.

There have always been gaps in the several versions of this overarching schematic, usually known as Christendom, but until the eighteenth and nineteenth centuries, it conceptually, politically, and spiritually held the field in one or another of its instantiations. Classical liberalism—exemplified in the thought of John Locke, Thomas Hobbes, Adam Smith, David Hume, Immanuel Kant, Gotthold Lessing, Thomas Paine, and J. S. Mill, among many others—became the chief modern political, ethical, and epistemological critic of this schematic and also became its most important alternative.

Liberalism retained this pre-eminent position until the middle of the nineteenth century. Modified versions of classical liberalism and their efforts to continue to privatize, marginalize, or co-opt religious tradition struggle to retain this pre-eminent position at present. The incursions of late medieval nominalism, Italian Renaissance Humanism, various forms of mysticism and pietism, and the many reform movements within Roman Catholicism and, later, Protestantism, should not be discounted as contenders for the symbolization and representation of socio-political order; none, however, were able to take the field in the way that liberalism and its ideological progeny eventually did.[9]

Alongside either absorbing it into a civilizational schema as in Christendom, or privatizing it in some way as in liberalism, there is yet another way of understanding the politics of Jesus. This alternative has its own genealogy, with appearances that can be traced to a time before Constantine and that continued in marginalized forms all the way through the dominating centuries of Christendom. It has, therefore, not lacked for defenders at various times, and this past century has played host to a growing number of such articulations.

John H. Yoder gives us one of the most interesting and thorough of these. His alternative way of seeing and instantiating the politics of Jesus is as critically powerful as the specifically political insights of Socrates and as politically interesting and politically engaged as any other exemplar from the Western tradition of political thought. Since the first century C.E., this tradition has been a mixture of two idioms—the Jewish and the Greek. Insofar as Yoder's dialogical inten-

tions are *political*, he must, perforce, participate in this "mixed tradition" of inquiry and prescription.[10] Because the politics of Jesus has
been almost completely absorbed by various versions of the Constantinian tradition and either absorbed or deliberately discarded by
Christendom's modern ideological foes, it is to that tradition and its
meaning as Yoder understood it to which we must first turn as a way
of seeing clearly the alternative political-ecclesiological schematic
that Yoder hoped to develop.

Constantinianism is the marriage of church and society under the
auspices of a political authority. As a way of identifying the basis of
Christendom, it has become a standard item in the theological vocabulary of recent years, apparently (re-)introduced there initially by
Yoder's work, but then firmly entrenched by the subsequent work of
many others who have taken the concept as a given that requires little
elucidation or justification. The underlying conceptual constructs
that the term implies are much older than its recent usage, and arguments regarding the merits and demerits of Constantinianism are as
old as or older than its original historical appearance and its eventual
evolution into Christendom. Indeed, Yoder takes the concept from
early Anabaptist usage. Yoder's use of the term, James Reimer argues,
"reflect[s] in good part the historical Radical Protestant position: the
identification of the Fall of the church with the Constantinian synthesis of church and state . . ."[11] Yoder is explicit about the Radical Protestant origin of the term and especially its relation to the Anabaptist
theme of "restitutionism," the "restoration of the church to its original
state from which it had fallen during the time of Constantine."[12]

Constantinianism takes its meaning from a specific historical career that serves as a useful typological marker, namely the supposed
conversion of the Roman Emperor Constantine to Christianity in A.D.
312 and his subsequent efforts to integrate the church into his imperial ambitions. It refers more broadly to a gradual transition, begun
well before the emperor's conversion and continuing many decades
afterward, in which Christianity was transformed from a minority,
disestablished religion to the majority, established religion of the
Roman Empire.[13] The meanings and implications of Constantinianism continued to unfold for centuries after the Empire had vanished
and new social and political forms had taken its place. In the modern
context of formally and de facto disestablished or marginally established churches, we may also usefully speak of "neo-Constantinianism," in which the churches play a supportive socio-political role, but
with attenuated legal recognition.

Let us recall a well-known scene. The Christian churches are riven with a doctrinal disagreement. Church leaders and theologians from all over the Roman ecumene and even beyond agree to meet in an effort to settle the deeply divisive and theologically complex dispute. A relatively young man, himself a recent convert to Christianity and a complete theological novice—the Roman emperor—presides at the council of the wise and learned leaders of the churches. He does so not in the capacity of a young, new convert, but in his capacity as the ruler of a pagan, ecumenical empire who happens to be sympathetic to its Christians.[14] He is seated in a small, gilded chair in the middle of the room, having arrived there in "his full imperial robes of purple decked with gold and precious stones, but without his usual bodyguard, attended only by a few members of his council."[15]

Peace among his subjects is, quite naturally, an important concern to the emperor,[16] and this particular dispute among the Christians threatens to become ugly. The Christians number about ten per cent of the population, which appears to be enough to cause administrative concern.[17] The emperor presides not merely as a modern chairperson or a parliamentary speaker might: he makes substantial and ultimately unsatisfactory submissions to the debate, and he calls the meeting to resolution.[18] He is also responsible for church discipline, deposing and restoring church leaders in connection with the debate.[19]

These new imperial roles in the affairs of the church entail a significant, new relationship between Christians and rulers, church and empire, ecclesiastical rule and political authority. The implications of this scene are, therefore, sociological, political, anthropological, economic, and ecclesiological in scope.

CONSTANTINIANISM: CURRENT USES

Let us begin anew on the far side of the story. While Yoder has invested the concept of Constantinianism with its current critical force, others have given it a wider popular currency, just as James McClendon has moved it past minority debate in his systematic theology.[20] How does this concept function, and what does it unveil for us?

In *Resident Aliens*, the "theological best-seller" of Stanley Hauerwas and William Willimon,[21] Constantinianism is, as for Yoder, a conceptual tool rooted in the historical events of which I have indicated an episode. As a concept, Constantinianism sets off against one another two broad but distinct accounts of the church, including its message, its mission, and its internal workings, especially as these are all related to a non-church or "secular" sociopolitical realm that can be conceived as being "external" to the community of believers that is the church. Constantinianism is an institutional overlapping of the Christian community (church) and its activities, mores, traditions, and practices with the activities, mores, traditions, and practices of the non-Christian society in which the church, at any given historical moment, finds itself. To use the word *Constantinianism* therefore implies that we can make a meaningful distinction between church and society with regard to their constituents, aims, structures, purposes, and activities, even if under Constantine this distinction may be functionally blurred in the actual relationship of the two.

While this claim for making distinctions has rarely if ever been denied outright, it is problematic even within a strictly Constantinian framework. Let us recall Constantinian society at its apogee and be reminded that:

> Once, there was no "secular." And the secular was not latent, waiting to fill more space with the steam of the 'purely human', when the pressure of the sacred was relaxed. Instead there was the single community of Christendom, with its dual aspects of *sacerdotum* and *regnum*. The *saeculum*, in the medieval era, was not a space, a domain, but a time—the interval between fall and *eschaton* where coercive justice, private property and impaired natural reason must make shift to cope with the unredeemed effects of sinful humanity.
>
> The secular as a domain had to be instituted or *imagined*, both in theory and in practice. This institution is not correctly grasped in merely negative terms as desacralization.[22]

Thus, the church-political authority distinction was a *functional* one, overlaid by a sociological identity between church and society. We see this identity in Oliver O'Donovan's effort to problematize eschatologically the distinction between church and not church when he recalls the political vision of John of Patmos:

> Three political communities, ancient Israel, the pagan empire and the eschatological church, are being drawn together in a startling identification. In fact there is only one city, which is at once the Holy City trampled on by the Gentiles and the Great City where Christ was crucified. The community in which God and the Lamb have set their throne is one and the same with the community where Satan and the beast have set their throne.

The reason why John of Patmos will not allow the church a distinct social presence is that its witnesses claim back the Great City to become the Holy City.

Just as there is only one true throne, so there is but one structured human community, and there can never be a second. Its name and aspect changes as the God who claims it wrests its government away from the pretender. The church is not apart from it; it is the sanctuary within its midst, and by its acts of witness it enables its transformation to begin.[23]

The "is" and "not yet" that James McClendon identifies as a key element of eschatologically informed Christian action, however, does not allow O'Donovan—as he himself clearly recognizes—entirely to bridge this gap, leaving the distinction to stand, but problematically. While the two realms of ecclesiological and political authority or church and secular have been consistently distinguished, at least in their functions (the argument has always had to do with their present and future relationship to one another, not with their distinction from one another), the question of identity between society and church is rather more elusive, and it is here, even as it deploys political means,[24] that Constantinianism has its principal effects. The key question of the debate for or against various forms of Constantinianism is, then, how the transformation that is brought about by God's sanctuary community amid the city where "Satan and the beast have set their throne" is to be carried out. Are the two groups one "society" with temporarily but not ultimately distinct characteristics, subordinate to one ruler, or are they eternally distinct?[25] Yoder's use of Constantinianism argues for making clear and abiding distinctions between church, society, and political authority.

The practices of Constantinianism in the United States include the effort to be "culturally significant" by fitting "American values into a loosely Christian framework"[26] and the effort to legislate for a wider society behavior (such as Sunday closings for commercial activities) that seems consistent with Christian ideals and Christian practices. These practices are being abolished and this, argue Hauerwas and Willimon, is to the good.[27] "The decline of the old, Constantinian synthesis between the church and the world means that we American Christians are at last free to be faithful in a way that makes being a Christian today an exciting adventure."[28] Such an evaluation flies in the face of current conventions, according to which the disintegration of this synthesis is either lamented and a new form of it wanted,[29] or in which it is celebrated as an Enlightenment victory over the forces of ignorance, of superstition, and of tenebrous priestly control.

A consequence of modern Constantinian efforts is a form of Christian apologetics in which the gospel is re-translated into the vernacular of the surrounding society, *not* on its own terms, but in such a way as to defend religious belief generally rather than the content of Christian belief specifically.[30] The difference this effort misses, argue Hauerwas and Willimon, is not that between faith and unfaith, but between faith and idolatry. The Constantinian "retranslation" can be effected in terms of nearly any ideology: Marxism, Nazism, socialism, feminism, liberalism, hedonism, and especially nationalism. Constantinianism, as Duane Friesen points out, can recognize a "politically responsible ethic only if the church is closely aligned with the dominant political and economic institutions of society," because it assumes "that the church needs to fit in with society's values in a synthesis with modern culture. . . ."[31]

The church under Constantine is "imperialized," and made "subservient" to the interests of empire.[32] Its "disembodied" Christology undermines any effort to envision an alternative culture to the one presented in the wider society.[33] Accordingly, in "the Christendom model that developed after Constantine, . . . the church became integrally linked with the dominant institutions of society and lost its prophetic alternative cultural vision."[34] Indeed, if the mission of the church includes providing a vision alternate to that of a culture in which violence is presumed, then Constantinianism spells the end of this possibility and of any social mission that might arise from it.

On this account, Christianity has a specific historically rooted content of doctrines and practices that cannot be genericized to mere "religion." If this were an empirical historical claim, it would be suspect: Constantinianism in several guises, especially in its Enlightenment form, shows that Christianity has, in some cases and with limited success, been genericized. If these forms of Constantinian synthesis and the *corpus Christianum* that eventually followed one version of it were such bad ideas, why did anyone ever decide to try it?

CONSTANTINIANISM:
ORIGINS, INCENTIVES, AND MEANINGS

There are, it seems to me, two sets of motivations at work in the development of Constantinianism, with two sets of outcomes. In the first place, there are the pragmatic motivations of church leaders and imperial political leaders alike, before, during, and after the reign of Constantine. Nearly a century after Constantine, Augustine clearly spells out one of the pragmatic motivations of the church leaders in his letters to his Donatist correspondent, Emeritus: being persecuted can become tiresome, and alliances with political authorities that relieve persecuted Christians of ongoing subjection to fear and physical violence at the hands of their enemies seem a welcome respite.

Moreover, the ongoing divisions within the church, some of which have led to violence between Christians, may now also be resolved with the power of the political authority in favor of truth.[35] In making this argument, Augustine echoes in a more direct and articulate fashion the hope that some Christian believers had held during the principate of Constantine several decades earlier. In a claim reminiscent of the post-medieval doctrine of the divine right of kings, for example, Eusebius praises Constantine for his beneficial use of political power, noting that

> invested as he is with a semblance of heavenly sovereignty, he directs his gaze above, and frames his earthly government according to the pattern of that Divine original, feeling strength in its conformity to the monarchy of God. And this conformity is granted by the universal Sovereign to man alone of the creatures on this earth: for he only is the author of sovereign power, who decrees that all should be subject to the rule of one.[36]

Having received "as it were, a transcript of the Divine sovereignty," Constantine "directs in imitation of God himself, the administration of the world's affairs."[37] With his power, therefore, Constantine brings "those whom he rules on earth to the only begotten Word and Saviour, [and] renders them fit subjects of his kingdom." This friend of God, "graced by his heavenly favor with victory over all his foes, subdues and chastens the open adversaries of the truth in accordance with the usages of war."[38]

The pragmatism of the political authorities and leaders is distinctly theo-political. First, the fractious empire of the late fourth century may now find in (a properly formulated) Christianity a "basis for spiritual unity."[39] More interestingly, the "establishment of ecclesial unity" may serve a new expansionism in which "international relationships" with tribes beyond the imperial frontiers can be forged on the basis of evangelization to Christianity or on the basis of connections to populations of Christians already in existence there.[40]

Less expansive and for that reason more directly pragmatic is a third possible motivation: bringing all the gods possible, including the Christian God, into the imperial camp. In the edict of toleration that the emperor Galerius issued in 311 A. D., and in the so-called "Edict of Milan" of the co-emperors Constantine and Licinius in 313 A. D., Christians are given the freedom to worship as they see fit, "provided," in the former edict, "they do nothing contrary to good order."

In return for this imperial "indulgence," Christians are encouraged "to pray to their God for our welfare, and for that of the public, and for their own; that the commonweal may continue safe in every quarter, and that they themselves may live securely in their habitations."[41] Similarly, in the latter edict the emperors "grant to the Christians and others full authority to observe that religion which each preferred; whence any Divinity whatsoever in the seat of the heavens may be favorable and kindly disposed to us and all who are placed under our rule."[42] The edicts both reflect "the good, solid Roman *do-ut-des* [43] principle. . . . This was no conversion to Christianity but rather an inclusion of the Christian God into the imperial system of divinity."[44]

This act of inclusion is a mutual affair. Christianity is not simply co-opted by the imperium through its representatives, the bishops; it also seeks to assert itself. The agenda, as H. A. Drake has argued, is two-sided. The persecutions of Christians under Constantine's predecessor, Diocletian, had failed, and a new policy of non-coercive inclusion was needed to keep the empire from hemorrhaging internally. The vague wording of the Edict of Milan allowed Christians and pagans to tolerate one another alike, and while it protected Christians, it also allowed them, or at least their leaders, to become "players" in the political game of empire.[45]

In the second place, there are what we might call the existential motivations of church and political authority. Christianity is true. Should it not, therefore, be represented in and through the political powers whose pagan expressions are expressions of untruth? The sentiment is well articulated by Lactantius, a Christian apologist and tutor to the son of the Constantine:

> The providence of the supreme deity has elevated you to the dignity of prince, enabling you with true devotion to reverse the evil policy of others, to repair their errors and, in a spirit of fatherly mildness, to take measures for the safety of men, removing from the commonwealth the malefactors whom the Lord has

delivered into your hands, in order that the nature of genuine sovereignty may be manifest to all . . . By an inborn sanctity of character and with a recognition of truth and God, in everything you consummate the works of justice. It was fitting, therefore, that, in the task of ordering human affairs, divine power should have employed you as its agent and minister.[46]

Echoing the panegyrics indicated earlier, we have here not a Pauline description of the ruler who is a "minister" or "servant" [δι–ακονος]of God to "bring wrath" [εις οργην] upon doers of evil (a description that serves not merely as an empirical statement—which it is not always—but also as a standard) and to whom Christians are to remain in subjection, rendering what is due such an "avenger."[47] Rather, we have now a revelation of "genuine sovereignty" and a consummation of justice, a representative of truth whose ways of governing replicate the "pattern of that divine original" so that the earthly rule imitates the heavenly.

We have moved from an agent with a specific role that is in accordance with good social order, to a representative of cosmic order, which order is imitated in the analogous "cosmion" of the political order he establishes. Paul makes no such claim for either an imitation of the divine or a cosmological analogy. Indeed, "the principalities and powers" of the present "domain" of darkness seem,[48] if anything, to be an anti-cosmos.

In the aftermath of the disintegration of the Roman Empire, the church, having maintained its own structures and often adopted and adapted those of the Empire, frequently functioned as a state; at times it was the only viable organization for providing administrative support to fledgling political re-organization after the barbarian invasions. It had, in R. W. Southern's estimation, "all the apparatus of the state: laws and law courts, taxes and tax-collectors, a great administrative machine, power of life and death over the citizens of Christendom and their enemies within and without."[49] Already the legal measures of the Roman emperor Theodosius in the late fourth century were intended "to establish more or less exact coincidence between Catholicism and citizenship."[50]

While very powerful in certain respects, the church also had significant weakness that reflected its non-state origins and were a direct effect of its ecclesial nature: "those who bore authority in the church were agents with very limited powers of initiative," being restrained both by their beliefs in a punishment hereafter for misdeeds (including the cruelties that pure power politics can demand) and by the "practical impotence" of being unable throughout its many centuries to persuade a "sufficient body of powerful men" to be its "army of willing and disciplined collaborators, capable of being reached by a word of command, of moving when commanded, and of coercion when necessary" in the many lands and realms in which the church held spiritual sway.[51]

Moreover, the church did not have at its direct command the policing and military resources that belong to political rulers. Accordingly, while the church played the role of existential or spiritual representative of European civilization, it could never play the role of elemental, power representative, except—and then not competently or consistently—for a brief period of time in the Italian papal territories.[52] The church required the consent and cooperation of the secular, political authorities to make its Europe-wide spiritual and civilizational discipline effective.

While politically coercive means were not within its grasp, thereby making the medieval church "less than a state," it was at the same time "much more than a state," because "it was not and could never be simply, *a* state among many: it had to be *the* state or none at all."[53] Perhaps it is this impulse that leads Martin Marty to suggest that "the idea of a Christian society" was latent in the thought of the early apologists.[54] "As soon as there were other states similarly equipped to rule," however, "the church was on its way to becoming a voluntary association for religious purposes."[55]

Until this development took hold at the other end of the Constantinian dream, the "universal society" of Christendom would be largely the horizon within which a commonwealth could be imagined, whether "directed by Christian emperors, or by the pope, or by the two of them together, or by the Christian community as a whole," and whether Orthodox, Roman Catholic, or Protestant.[56] From the time of Constantine until the eighteenth century, the question was not "whether society could be Christian, but rather how this was to be realized."[57]

The existential motivations of the authorities led to the positive civilizational outcomes of Christendom itself to which its supporters can justifiably point. With the gradual evacuation of the Roman civic religion, the sources for symbolic order in the Roman Empire began to derive from Christianity, mixed with Greek philosophy and some localized pagan elements. As the exclamations of Eusebius and Lactantius show, this role of civilizing spiritual force was not a natural role for the Christian faith: to play it, adaptations were necessary so that the cosmic truths of Christianity could express the order of empire. For example, the church had to compromise the ethics articulated in the so-called "Sermon on the Mount" to accommodate it to "the weakness of human nature" and "the existence of governmental power." The eventual institutional result of this compromise was a remarkable overlapping of church and society in rituals that originated in a quite differently conceived church:

> The compromise with the weakness of man expressed itself in the inclusion of everybody into the mystical body of Christ through the sacraments of baptism and the Lord's Supper; the foundation for membership is laid through the sacramental reception, not through any guarantee that the person is, indeed, a member of the invisible church. The actual status of the soul in salvation or damnation is known to God alone; it cannot be judged by the brethren in the community.[58]

This ethical compromise and reworking of ecclesial order is manifested in a system of ethics derived from Stoic natural law doctrines that are adapted by Christian thinkers for applications "to relations between men who live in the world."[59] Secular rulership, as begins to emerge already in the panegyrics of Eusebius and Lactantius, becomes an explicitly *Christian* function, so that by the ninth century, the "royal function" has been integrated "into the order of the charismata."[60] In this evaluation, the anti-Constantinian criticisms of Hauerwas and Willimon are reversed: the re-translation of the gospel through a synthesis of church with (pagan) social norms is a civilizational achievement of the first order without which Christianity would have remained a negligible Jewish sect of little historical interest.

Key to the success of these adaptations and compromises, moreover, is the "creation of [a] sacramental organization," by means of which grace can be mediated to everyone, thereby making "grace objective." Most important for political order, "the state of grace cannot be obtained through religious enthusiasm or through the efforts of heroic saintliness; it must be obtained through sacramental incorporation into the mystical body of Christ." This incorporation is an objective one, effected through the "sacerdotal office" that administrates grace as a function of the priestly office, independently of the personal worthiness or other attributes of the office-holder. These adaptations create a powerful institutional force for civilization, a "civilizationally magnificent merger":

The compromises, together with the sacramental objectification of grace, are the basis for the civilizing function of the church. Through its compromises the church is enabled to accept the social structure of the people as a whole, with its occupations, habits, and legal and economic institutions, and to inject into the social body the spiritual and ethical values of Christianity with such gradations as are bearable for the average human being at the time.[61]

Church and society are fused. To allow the "injection" to do its proper work and to keep the fusion intact, the eschatological elements of early Christian understanding must be attenuated:

> No revolution is required, no eschatological upheaval that would establish the realm of Christ within the generation of the living. The tension of eschatological expectation is toned down to the atmosphere of a civilizing process that may take its good time; in slow and patient work it may extend over centuries. By virtue of its compromises the church can operate on the masses; it can use the wealth of natural gifts and slowly ennoble them by giving them direction toward spiritual aims.[62]

This civilizational complex is sufficiently powerful, coherent, and long-lived that it may appear as one of "history's inevitable fixtures."[63] Nonetheless, as this laudatory analysis hints, and as Christian schisms, heresies, and renewal movements had already indicated before the advent of Constantinianism, the complex has existing within itself considerable tensions. Even the imperialization of Christianity could not entirely erase its origins and its non-imperialistic impulses. Both reside in the canonical and post-canonical texts that sustain the traditions to which imperialized Christianity, too, wishes to appeal.

Indeed, as Duane Friesen asserts, even the Constantinian church tradition continues to retain "rich resources to use in constructing an alternative cultural vision."[64] The monastic movements of the third, fourth, and later medieval centuries, the renewal movements initiated in the era of Francis of Assisi, and John Wycliff's desire for a translation of the Bible that would be "for the Government of the people, by the people, and for the people," are examples of the continuing prophetic and renewal elements that are an ineluctable and not entirely to be co-opted part of the Christian tradition.[65] So, too, are a manifold variety of millenarian movements that accompany Christianity from the second century to the present.[66]

Finally, there are the negative effects that Yoder, in the believers church tradition, deplores. Yoder's criticisms, however, must be understood against the backdrop of the coherent, civilizational form that is mature Constantinianism and against the backdrop of continuing efforts to re-assert some version of it in what Yoder called "neo-Constantinianism." How does one argue against a civilizational paradigm that *is* the West? After all, Christians and non-Christians, clerics, other classes and rulers alike saw benefits in the Constantinian order with its ethical system, spiritual institutions, and efforts at cosmic analogy. And soon enough, there were few non-Christians.

CONSTANTINIANISM: YODER'S CRITIQUE

For Yoder, the alliance of church and political authority on the basis of the argument that Christian truth should be represented politically is a question-begging exercise, because it assumes that Christian truth is of a kind that *can* be represented politically in the Constantinian manner. Modern evaluations of the evolution of Christendom tend to agree that the enterprise was, at least, problematic. Along with a tendency that Christianity had to de-divinize the cosmos and eschatologize or apocalypticize historical existence, its trinitarian symbolisms worked poorly for analogous political symbolization, and its call to faith was difficult to sustain in a mass society.[67] Yoder's concerns are of a different kind, however.

Yoder's critique begins with the assumption, first made widely known by his *Politics of Jesus*, that Jesus' life and teaching actually matters to the way Christians should do ethics and think about politics. Constantinianism, he argues, hides or denies Jesus' life and teaching. The "total religious-cultural package" that is Christendom originates, even as its friends admit, in "ideas and practices largely of Greek, Roman, and Germanic origin." When the message of the gospel is packaged with the marks of these cultures, its self-proclaimed universal stance is, in fact, attached to a "very specific Mediterranean-plus-Germanic cultural and geographical location."[68] With its Constantinian power structures, it comes to "foreigners" in the form of a Crusade (Arabs) or Inquisition (Jews) or imperialist colonialism (African and American natives).[69]

Dissent within this tradition is either suppressed or externalized. When, for example, Constantine helped to formulate the anti-Arian conclusions of the Council of Nicea, which, although not yet baptized, he convened, his personal interventions "had the effect with time of reinforcing the linkage of Arianism with the people outside the empire to the north." Similarly, the "later imperial-ecumenical councils relegated Nestorianism to Persia and Monophysitism to Abyssinia, thus identifying the concepts of 'heretic' and 'barbarian,' and turning over the expansion of Christianity for a millennium to the heterodox."[70]

Yoder's interests in telling and "disavowing" the story of Constantine, it seems to me, are closely focused on two tasks: drawing the outlines of a non-Constantinian community of faith, and engaging in dialogue with other, mostly Constantinian or neo-Constantinian groups, on that basis. His critique, on the basis of which he outlines the alternative community of faith, is sociological, anthropological, and ecclesiological, with a political critique implied. Let us consider some aspects of these.

Sociology

The first set of characteristics to consider in elaborating a set of pre- and post-Constantinian distinctions are sociological. The pre-Constantinian church was, first, a visible, concrete entity, and Christians were, second, recognizably a minority of the population. Belief, third, was based on individual assent and commitment to a cult, creed, and code that were distinct as a unity from all other cults, creeds, and codes present in the ecumenical society of the Roman Empire. Fourth, God's rule in and of history was therefore invisible, which is to say, it was not visibly represented by city, empire or kingdom, assembly, emperor or king, as it was in all pagan cities, kingdoms, and empires.[71] Fifth, Christianity could be characterized by the outward behavior of its adherents (including, but by no means exclusively, their assembling together with other Christians for fellowship and worship). Sixth, Christianity was explicitly counter-cultural, which is to say that Christians did not take as their standard of behavior or ethical deliberation the standards and behaviors of the surrounding culture.[72] When one professes that "Jesus is Lord," Yoder remarks, then "what is definitional is the ultimate normative claim of the appeal to Jesus."[73] This profession has consequences, and so do its modifications.

In the post-Constantinian world of established Christianity, every one of these six markers, along with the definitional force of Jesus as Lord, is reversed. The church is now everyone, so that the "true" church of committed or genuinely converted believers has become, in the Augustinian formulation, an invisible church. Belief is, accordingly, sociological and politic, and God's rule in and of history is actualized in the reigning authority, a point that is clearly shown in paeans of Eusebius to Constantine himself, which are dubious for their accurate portrayal of the politically opportunistic emperor.[74]

Christianity thus becomes inward, since outwardly everyone is a Christian by virtue of membership in a society, not in consequence of informed assent and commitment. Thus, finally, Christianity has become the culture and is the ethical authority. Once the Christian church and the surrounding pagans have established this new relationship, the new basis of ethical reasoning is nearly unrecognizable from the old.

The various sociological changes wrought by Constantinianism that Yoder lists focus toward a point: the faithful witness of the church in speech and practice. This witness is less severely compromised in the Nicean scene described earlier than in some of its future permutations; it continues to be compromised in various iterations and mutations through the course of Western and Eastern Christendom and beyond.[75] The church begins to lose its independence from imperial prerogatives, and as imperial citizenship and church membership begin to coincide over the next century, it also begins to lose its independent identity.[76]

We may note the difficulty in using cleanly the social-scientific categories available to us: sociological characteristics are intertwined with anthropological and political ones.

Anthropology

Anthropology is the study of what it is or what it means to be human by considering such human phenomena as culture, physiology, language, and social interaction. While it overlaps with several of the other social sciences, anthropologists might argue that their study is more comprehensive, because they consider "the entire human condition over time and space."[77] Be that as it may, if anthropological concerns are specifically about "humaness," then it is useful to separate out such concerns from sociological and political ones and to indicate that Yoder's project has specific anthropological foci. These are most incisively articulated in his *Body Politics*.[78] While the book, as both its title and Yoder's "Introduction" indicate, is clearly and consciously directed at political questions, it also contains within it considerations concerning the nature of expressing humaness, over against the Constantinian forms that remain central to current church practices.

Let us briefly consider two practices of a non-Constantinian "believers church" in which anthropological principles are expressed. In the first, baptism, we see an overt political expression of equality and classlessness. Baptism "*is* the formation of a new people whose newness and togetherness explicitly relativize prior stratifications and classification."[79] This "interethnic inclusiveness," while clearly carrying political features, also indicates that "belonging" is not ethnically, physiologically, linguistically, or economically based, nor is it based on citizenship or birthright in a particular place, being rooted instead in a divine incorporation with individual consent and community support. Baptism, in other words, indicates a new, non-Constantinian culture in which there is "neither Jew nor Greek, there is neither slave nor free man, there is neither male nor female," all being "one in Christ Jesus."[80] Such incorporation is a cultural rarity, expressing a rare conception of humaness.

Second, sacerdotalism was a key element in the civilizational function of Christianity, but "the objectification of the spirit in the sacerdotal and sacramental institution, the adaptation to the exigencies of the world, the gradualism of spiritual realization," was also the focus of a continual line of "sectarian" criticisms. Troeltschian categories aside, a desire for "an uncompromising realization of the evangelical counsels, of renouncing the universalism of the institution, and of concentrating on the realization of the spirit in small communities with high standards of personal religiousness and moral conduct" is an "equally authentic manifestation of Christianity."[81] Accordingly, while the presence of a "professional religionist" assumes that such professionalism "is a part of the fallen nature of things, a universal anthropological constant underlying the great varieties of form" in religious expression,[82] there exists for Yoder an alternative anthropological expression:

> The specialized purveyor of access to the divine is out of work since Pentecost.
>
> Sometimes the early Christians said they were all priests: sometimes they said that the priesthood was done away with. The concrete social meanings of the two statements, though verbally opposite, were the same. All members of the body alike are Spirit-empowered. The monopoly of the sacrificial celebration that enables and delimits human access to the divine is swept away. The priestly person as the primary agent of access to the divine is swept away with the special ceremonies. Jesus was the last sacrifice and thus he was also the last priest. The antipriestly

impact of this change, although expressed emphatically in the Pauline writings and in Hebrews, is one of the dimensions of redemption least noted and least honored in Christian history since then.[83]

The "monopoly of the priestly role" was fully re-established in Constantine's re-formation of church practices, where priest and king, both sacrally understood, became closely allied.[84] This alliance may have begun, as Drake argues, as primarily a political arrangement between bishops and emperor, but it rapidly took on a panoply of clearly theological meanings with anthropological consequences.

Instead of ceding this monopoly, the non-Constantinian church not only "grants" immediate access to the divine to all believers, it also sees in the gathering of the body of believers an opportunity for each of the members to share directly in the functioning of the community through "charismatically empowered roles," and to be recognized for that participation.[85] Here again, we see not only a political expression of community; we see an anthropological expansion of the possibilities of human nature (which, for Yoder, is a theological way of speaking anthropologically[86]).

POLITICS: ASPECTS OF CONSTANTINIANISM AND CONVERSATION

The church of the Constantinian synthesis was, we might say, "a compulsory society in precisely the same way as the modern state is a compulsory society."[87] If that claim is true in each of its particulars, then the most significant issue confronting Christians who live in the West in the post-Constantinian era may not be the claims that the Constantinian tradition makes on them, but rather, the claims that the modern "Leviathan," the universal and homogenous nation-state[88] makes on them and in terms of which Christians, in their turn, make demands on the state. Perhaps it is more accurate, therefore, to speak of "neo-Constantinianism" as the specific form in which these new demands are presented to Christians.

Yoder wants to wean his readers from the notion that the Christian, or, more especially, the assembly of Christians—the church—can or should find a stance from which it speaks to the world that is other than or apart from its usual activities. The Christian's dynamic and varied stance in facing "the powers" or "order of society" or "mandates" ("marriage," "the free market," or "the military," for example) "is already foreshadowed by the complex mission and ministry of Jesus and by Christ's requirement of intelligible obedience from those who follow him."[89] Readers who have been trained to script moral language on a Kantian or a liberal individualist parchment are likely to hear words like "obedience" or even "follow" in an *individualistic*, perhaps decisionistic, perhaps categorical imperative mode. Yoder's emphasis on "Body Politics" or "Kingdom"[90] or "Peoplehood"[91] deflect this individualist tendency toward a more communal vision.

If we take the political to mean that which is public or in common, specifically with regard to such questions as "power relations between ruler and ruled, the nature of authority, the problems posed by social conflict, the status of certain goals or purposes as objectives of political action, and the character of political knowledge," then certainly the seeming "religious" or ecclesiological, or ecumenical, or ethical concerns Yoder has are political. "Power," "authority," and "consent," for example, are all central concepts in Yoder's work, as they are in the Western tradition of inquiry into political matters.[92] If we follow de Jouvenel's definition of politics as "every systematic effort, performed at any place in the social field, to move other men in pursuit of some design cherished by the mover,"[93] then again, Yoder's treatment of ecclesiological concerns is clearly political, as the titles of all his major works indicate.

The ideal of community that the early church expressed is one of the beginning points for Yoder: out of this same ideal developed a "tradition of civility" and a tradition of "political ways of behavior and political modes of thought" that preserved "political ways of thought and action" in the West.[94] Following in the pattern of Socrates, Yoder was intent not merely on analyzing the shape of the Constantinian church and polity in distinction to his own: he was most interested in engaging in conversation with those who represented versions of the Constantinian church form—of any denominational stripe—as a way of recalling them to faithfulness and of being taught himself.

Constantinianism, we have now seen, refers not merely to the Emperor becoming a Christian and entwining and imposing himself in the deliberations and the disciplinary activities of the church. It refers to a complex political, sociological, and ecclesiological phenomenon with wide-ranging practical and theoretical consequences. It describes a patterned set of relationships between two complex entities—the church (broadly understood in Christian terms) and the ruling authorities (broadly understood in classical, premodern, modern, and postmodern terms) of the polity. At the pragmatic level, it refers to a specific relationship between a community of Christian believers and the political authorities. At the theological level, it refers to a specific conception of the way God acts in history and of the instruments he uses to act. At the ethical level, it refers to a particular way of being community, of relating to outsiders, of conducting one's affairs, of displaying moral excellence, of showing what God is like.[95]

Above all, and with reference to each of these three levels of consequences, pre- and post-Constantinianism represent contrasting political and ecclesiological ideas of what it means for Christ to be Lord. They therefore represent different ideas of what the shape and character of Christian witness to that Lordship will be. This difference will shape Christian conduct within the church and in the surrounding world, which is to say, it will shape Christian politics. Within the sphere of the political, let us briefly consider three of many aspects that Yoder introduces as ways of conducting a political conversation.

Jesus as Lord and the rulers

If Jesus is truly Lord, then what will be the relationship between the believers and the secular instruments of power? The question has a form, if not substance, that is familiar to political philosophers: if philosophy supplies a form of knowledge and political wisdom that is superior to what is conventionally supplied through poets, prophets, priests, or politicians, then what will be the relationship of the philosopher to the city (which receives its wisdom from one or more of these prior four sources)? Or, to state the Platonic question: why did the best of cities (Athens) kill the best of men (Socrates)?

For the post-Socratic political philosopher, the answer might imply that one must hide one's work from those who lack understanding.[96] For the pre-Constantinian Christians, the answer might be that one reasons with, witnesses to, or speaks with the statesman from an explicitly minority position of outside weakness without presuming one can become a member of either the ruling clique or the majority. In such a position, Yoder argues, we give up asking "How can we help to move the total social system," because "there are other ways to do Christian ethics."[97] A minority, be it religious, ethnic, or otherwise, need not assume responsibility for what it cannot control. Establishment rulers, on the other hand, do so or even must do so, since their calling is to make history go the way they want it to go.[98]

This position of minority is most certainly a position of weakness, but, contra Reinhold Niebuhr and others, it is neither a position of "irresponsibility" nor an assumption of "ineffectiveness." It is, rather, a position of different response under different premises about how God effects his rule in history and about the priority of obedience over expediency. Yoder points to numerous examples of what minority (not necessarily Christian) groups can do that takes up the initiative and is positive and socially beneficial without having either to take power or assume that one day they will have it.[99]

In one example, "a minority group with no immediate chance of contributing to the ways things go may still by its dissent maintain the wider community's awareness of some issues in such a way that ideas which are unrealistic for the present come to be credible later."[100] It may therefore "exercise pioneering creativity in places where no one is threatened."[101] A minority group may also play the role of being a public conscience; hard-core realism notwithstanding, such a minority may have some purchase on the decisions people make. While two million Germans perished in the realist geopolitical Soviet occupation and relocations of 1945-47, how many of the twelve million who survived were sustained through Red Cross packages donated by church organizations in America—their former enemy. In contrast, what relief did the American geopolitical strategy of the time provide them?

If the specific question is obedience to the commands and examples of Jesus, "It is . . . a misperception when radicals, responding to the way issues have been put by Tolstoy and by Niebuhr, tend to concede that this ethic of "obedience" sacrifices "effectiveness."[102] If the Lordship of Jesus implies actions, but without realist conventions or the violence their underlying assumptions frequently imply, the submission to this peaceable Lordship does not imply "retreat" from the political realm, but engagement in a different key.[103]

Conversational patience under Jesus as Lord

Government involves the use of power to coerce others in the act of ruling over them. Such coercion may be for good or ill, but it *is* coercion. The *libido dominandi* being what it is, "the alliance of church and state for the purpose of government"[104] that constitutes the pragmatic heart of Constantinianism may therefore be described as a temptation, even if that temptation consists in an invitation to pick up the instruments of coercion to bring about some perceived good.[105] A key historical example of such a temptation is illustrated in Augustine's decision to forego principled nonresistance and instead to persecute heretics rather than persuade them. The thrust behind the reversal is utilitarian—persecution works. Augustine asserts that the church has a right forcefully to defend herself against aggression.

This first major step away from his original position is accompanied by a second argument for using force against dissent. Advocates of force could point to "conclusive instances" in which bringing heretics back to orthodoxy by force appeared to work. The forceful, violent interventions of the political ruler get results for the cause of orthodoxy, and that outcome justifies the means used.[106] When it is more effective than the use of persuasive argument for achieving Christian purposes, it is legitimate.[107] Augustine's efforts indicate, moreover, that the instruments of coercion include not only material instruments of force, but intellectual instruments that define and bind.[108]

Consider what this new stance implies for the shape of a politico-ethical conversation. A pacifist stance implies a generosity and patience, according to Yoder, that a Constantinian orthodoxy—enforced by the ecclesiastical use of secular means of violence or by the forceful interference of the secular ruler into ecclesiastical affairs—cannot have. Orthodoxy based on philosophically doctrinal assumptions, moreover, impose an added form of coercion:

> Classical "natural law" or "reason" arguments make (or presuppose tacitly) the claim that the person arguing has the right and the power to dictate what the common language is; a nonviolent epistemology cannot do that. Sometimes the only nonviolent response to a skewed dialogical situation is silence, as a refusal to collaborate in epistemological tyranny.[109]

A desire for closure, reinforced by Constantine's sword, is a kind of impatience that, Yoder argues, flies in the face of Jesus' injunction to love the enemy and accordingly be patient with him. Augustine, one of the first great (even if ambiguous) apologists for Constantinian Christendom, originally thought so too.

Jesus as Lord and the moral agenda

When a minority group plays the role of public conscience, on what terms will the role be played? Who will control the moral agenda? Suppose we granted the Constantinian claim that a Christian church or some such "religious" organization is the spiritual representative and guide of society?[110] What then? It might seem that for the larger society, such guides are necessary and beneficial. Whether or not that is true, such a stance poses great peril for the church, which

ultimately rebounds on society. First, churches that "entrust reformation [of themselves] to government" tend thereby to prevent "reformation on moral matters from being kept within the continuing control and responsibility of ecclesiastically committed Christians."

> Accordingly, the institutionalization of church renewal in the
> hands of civil governments, whether directly through the consis-
> tory as an arm of the state or less directly through synods author-
> ized and protected by the state, had the opposite effect from that
> implied in this slogan [*ecclesia reformata, semper reformanda*]. . . .
> Most strikingly, with regard to our question of moral discern-
> ment, to assign matters of church order, and thereby also matters
> of teaching on morality, to the surveillance of civil government is
> practically to guarantee that some kinds of moral agenda will be
> much more difficult to manage.[111]

Yoder's example is the development of democracy and religious
liberty in Europe, which was brought about in anti-church and even
anti-Christian modes. This anti-Christian characteristic of their development arose not because democracy or religious liberty imply an
anti-Christian stance, but because the state-sponsored churches, as in
seventeenth- and eighteenth-century France and in nineteenth-century Germany, were often rigidly conservative on the basis of a Constantinian theology and therefore strongly supportive of the status
quo. This stance made them the deserving co-targets of the criticism
against the enlightened despots whom they supported.

Second, the interests of the authorities in church unity—because
the church is the spiritual core and validation of civil society—makes
independent intra-church dialogue concerning moral and theological
matters harder and sometimes impossible. If we go about moral reasoning "in an open context, where both parties are free to speak,
where additional witnesses provide objectivity and mediation, where
reconciliation is the intention and the expected outcome is a judgment that God himself can stand behind, then the rest of the practical
moral reasoning process will find its way." When, however, the civil
authorities, "whose concerns were more punitive than unitive," have
stood amid this dialogue, they have "prevented the dynamics of dialogue from functioning in its own right."[112] This intervention raises a
"basic theological issue": is the church "a reality," or is it "the institutional reaction of the good and bad conscience, of the insights, the
self-encouragement—in short, of the religion of a society."[113]

Under this issue, we can raise a related question: who has the authority to speak of the public good?[114] If the church, as a community

of believers, is an entity visibly identified by "baptism, discipline, morality, and martyrdom" that is distinct from the "world," which includes "the 'world' of politics, the 'world' of economics, the 'world' of the theater, the 'world' of sports, the under-'world,' and a host of others—each a demonic blend of order and revolt,"[115] then the authority to speak rests *not* only with the political authorities, but also with the believing community. In the Constantinian order, "the two visible realities, church and world, were fused." Accordingly, "there is no longer anything to call 'world'; state, economy, art, rhetoric, superstition, and war have all been baptized."[116]

In this fusion, the church gives up its voice concerning the moral question—how shall we be responsible for society or "what is the rule of God,"[117]—and delivers this prerogative to the civil authority, with the consequences that the possibilities of reform, dialogue, and calling the "world" in its demonic revolt to a higher standard of performance are severely attenuated.[118] Uniquely Christian political thought and the dialogue that might emerge from it, in other words, are hardly possible.[119] The order of Christendom, established over time, tends to suppress such dialogue.

RESERVATIONS

Tradition, process, and moment: The appearance of Constantinianism was a moment embedded in a longer process of accommodation preceding and following Constantine, and this moment as we have seen, was part of the establishing of a new tradition. But can the concept of Constantinianism do the work that Yoder would have it do? Does it take sufficient notice of the benefits Christendom confers? Does it sufficiently capture the compromises Christendom demands? Does it accurately grasp the political temptations Christendom and its descendant forms of political rule pose to Christians in times of war and of peace?

Two writers within the Anabaptist tradition have suggested that while we should not simply abandon the concept of Constantinianism, it does have serious shortcomings. Gerald Schlabach, for one, argues that use of the term may neglect too much. While Constantinianism "offers a trenchant heuristic device," it tends to make us focus on "the effort to avoid evil and unfaithfulness," deflecting us from "the challenge of embracing the good in a faithful manner."[120]

Insofar as Constantinianism is comprised of both moment and process, "Constantinianism always begins before there is some Constantinian settlement proper . . . some other problems always arise before some emperor presents his tempting offer."[121] This "chronological priority,"which I have already noted, indicates a logical priority, that of "the Deuteronomic juncture ["the problem of how to receive and celebrate the blessing, the *shalom*, the good, or 'the land' that God desires to give, yet to do so without defensively and violently hoarding God's blessing"] over the Constantinian one."[122] The Deuteronomic problem, according to Schlabach, is "more basic" than the Constantinian one. Believing that "a firm renunciation of church-state alliances and use of the sword is *sufficient* to avoid Constantinianism," thereby neglecting the need to love one's neighbor, to "welcome strangers and love enemies," and not to allow the need to sustain the communal worship practices of the church to deflect from the need to love neighbor and enemy, is not enough.[123] Such abuses were apparent in at least some of the bishops' responses to Constantine's political initiatives.

The problem that is before the Constantinian problem, then, is this: how will Christians, who are a Diaspora people, live in the land that God has given them while attending faithfully to questions of: dispossession of others; building settlements and institutions and managing communal life; conserving and protecting (policing) such communities in light of Christian eschatology; maintaining disciplined communities of faith without being either rigidly exclusive or carelessly inclusive.[124]

These questions deserve far more extended treatment than is possible here. Schlabach is surely correct to argue that the extent of Christian sociopolitical engagement is much greater than a narrow use of Constantinianism might indicate. Yoder was aware of this problem and he appears at times to have reached for new terminology.[125] Moreover, we have seen that Yoder's use of Constantinianism is expansive, allowing him to move toward key political themes, including, for example, the problems of time, space, community, and power. Nevertheless, Schlabach provides a needed horizon-stretching corrective to overcome the temptation overly to narrow our focus concerning the requirements of faithful community.

Jim Reimer suggests another serious limitation: use of the term takes away too much. Constantinianism is not a one-way street to ecclesiological and theological perdition, as some in the Anabaptist tradition might seem to assert. Indeed, the so-called "Constantinian" tradition has given Christians rich ecclesiological, theological, and spiritual resources they reject at their peril.[126] Schlabach similarly reminds us that "there is even something right about the vision of Christendom—as that *societas* in which right relationship with God is rightly ordering and reintegrating every relationship and all of life," and that "the Christendom vision is itself a vision of *shalom*."[127]

Constantinianism is an impoverishing concept if it implies a wholesale rejection of the Christian tradition since Constantine. Yoder did not intend such a move. Nevertheless, a continued use of the term would require carefully taking an inventory of which practices should be kept and which should be discarded if we are to avoid the temptations and pitfalls of the Constantinian inheritance while keeping the beneficial treasures that were developed during its aegis.

A PROVISIONAL CONCLUSION

Bearing in mind these limitations of the Constantinian concept, let us consider what would happen if someone were an unbeliever and did not acknowledge Jesus as Lord. What kind of dialogue with a community of Christians that is formed and informed by some kind of non-Constantinian understanding could that person expect? Supposing, moreover, she were a political ruler, whether city council-person, congressional representative, or state governor. The basis of her decision-making might be a version of Enlightenment rationalism, a Millian utilitarianism, a pure Machiavellian power calculus, or something else, or a mixture of several forms of moral reasoning (which is the most likely case). How would the members of Yoder's kind of Christian community be speaking to her? What kind of conversation might be going on?

They would not assume belief on her part. Depending on her previous behavior, they would regard her as anything from a trustworthy but unbelieving decision-maker who has discretion over some aspects of their lives and who deals justly and reasonably with those subject to her decisions, to a violent tyrant who is their avowed enemy and ruler, to whom they are nevertheless called to speak and to witness, for whom they are asked to pray, and to whom they are called to display patient love, even while speaking the truth.[128] In either case, they would recognize that she—along with the rest of the world/cosmos—exists in rebellion. They would accordingly call her peaceably to restraint.[129]

They would not assume they would someday be able to take power from her. They *would* assume themselves and her to be both fallible and blameworthy. Their non-Constantinian arguments regarding the performance of her functions would not present baptized forms of liberalism in which there are two separate, unbreachable spheres, ordained with separate competencies. Nor would they encompass a revised Gelasian "two-powers" doctrine, in which one is subordinate to the other.

Beginning with the assumption that Jesus is Lord of *everything*, they would call her to his obedience. Failing that, they would call her to a better level of moral performance, using her language of moral justification (*every* ruler has one) to do so.[130] The credibility of this call, however, would depend in part on their ability to have navigated the troubled waters of the Constantinian and Deuteronomic temptations.

The truth of existence represented by such a community is the truth of God's *kenotic* love for a world in rebellion.[131] Their conversation would be supportive and critical, repentant and peaceable. How the conversation goes would depend in part and only temporarily on their interlocutor.

NOTES

1. Part of the research and writing of this paper was conducted with the support of an NEH Summer Stipend Grant (#45947-01). Portions were also written with the support of a Sabbatical Leave Grant from the University of Kansas. My sincere thanks to the directors and referees of the former agency, and to the committee members and governing officers of the latter institution, and to the many who, knowingly or unknowingly, support the activities of either or both. Earlier versions of this paper were presented at the Annual Meeting of the American Political Science Association, San Francisco, August 30-September 2, 2001; and at the Believers Church Conference: "Assessing the Theological Legacy of John Howard Yoder," University of Notre Dame, Notre Dame, Ind., March 07-09, 2002.

2. But not in the Nietzschean sense.

3. James Wm. McClendon, Jr., *Systematic Theology: Ethics* (Nashville: Abingdon Press, 1986), 73.

4. John Howard Yoder, *For The Nations: Essays Evangelical and Public* (Grand Rapids: Eerdmans, 1997), 10.

5. This is Socrates' self-description in Plato's *Apology of Socrates*.

6. Sir Ernest Barker, *Greek Political Theory: Plato and his Predecessors*, 4th. ed. (New York: Barnes & Noble, 1951).

7. Karl R. Popper, *The Open Society and its Enemies*, 4th rev. ed. (Princeton, N.J.: Princeton University Press, 1963).

8. Leo Strauss, *The Argument and the Action of Plato's Laws* (Chicago: The University of Chicago Press, 1975).

9. I also set to one side the Eastern Orthodox experience of establishment and disestablishment.

10. We might think of the Christian theological tradition as being a mixture of these two elements as well. Consider Yoder's discussion of Pauline theology in *Preface to Theology: Christology and Theological Method*, ed. Stanley Hauerwas and Alex Sider (Grand Rapids: Brazos Press, 2002), 96-110 (esp. 107-108), in which Yoder explicitly recognizes this mixture and shows no discomfort in working with it. My claim leaves out, of course, *how* Yoder works within that tradition, and *how* he will appropriate its language. See, for example, John Howard Yoder, *The Priestly Kingdom: Social Ethics as Gospel* (Notre Dame: University of Notre Dame Press, 1984), 48-62.

11. A. James Reimer, "Trinitarian Orthodoxy, Constantinianism, and Radical Protestant Theology," in A. James Reimer, *Mennonites and Classical Theology: Dogmatic Foundations for Christian Ethics* (Kitchener, Ont: Pandora Press, 2001), 259.

12. Benjamin Wirt Farley, ed., [John Calvin] *Treatises Against the Anabaptists and Against the Libertines* (Grand Rapids: Baker Book House, 1982), 296, n.15. Cf. John Howard Yoder, "The Prophetic Dissent of the Anabaptists," *The Recovery of the Anabaptist Vision: A Sixtieth Anniversary Tribute to Harold S. Bender*, ed. Guy F. Hershberger (Scottdale, Pa.: Herald Press, 1957), 97; and John Howard Yoder, "If Christ is Truly Lord," in John Howard Yoder, *The Original Revolution: Essays on Christian Pacifism* (Scottdale, Pa.: Herald Press, 1971), 69; reprinted as "Peace Without Eschatology" in John Howard Yoder, *The Royal Priesthood: Essays Ecclesiological and Ecumenical*, Michael G. Cartwright, ed. (Grand Rapids: Eerdmans, 1994), 143-167.

"Restitutionism" or "restorationism" as a central Radical Reformation theme is well-attested in historical analyses of the movement. See George Hunston Williams, *The Radical Reformation* (Philadelphia: The Westminster Press, 1962) 97, 375-378; Franklin Hamlin Littell, *The Anabaptist View of the Church: A Study in the Origins of Sectarian Protestantism*, 2nd. ed. (Boston: Star King Press, 1958), 46-108. Even during that early period, Constantine's initiatives were understood as the beginning point of the "fall" of the church. See James M. Stayer, *Anabaptists and the Sword*, 2nd. ed. (Lawrence, Kansas: Coronado Press, 1976), 171; Williams, *Radical Reformation*, 198; Littell, *Anabaptist View*, 63-64.

13. Concerning this gradual transition: Lietzman claims, for example, that many Christians rejected pacifism (not soldiering) by 250 A. D., because they were becoming "respectable" and "sharing in administration of city or state." (Hans Lietzmann, *A History of the Early Church, Vol 3: From Constantine to Julian*, trans. Bertram Lee Woolf (Cleveland and New York: The World Publishing Company, 1953), 57. Yoder was clear on the process character of the transition: "The term [Constantinianism] refers to the conception of Christianity which took shape in the century between the Edict of Milan and the *City of*

God. The central nature of this change, which Constantine himself did not invent nor force upon the church, is not a matter of doctrine nor of polity; it is the identification of the church and world in the mutual approval and support exchanged by Constantine and the bishops." "If Christ is Truly Lord," 69.

14. In Eusebius' report, Constantine sees himself as both a servant of God and the emperor of Rome who has military power at his disposal. The two seem to harmonize without difficulty. See Eusebius Pamphilus, "The Life of the Blessed Emperor Constantine," ed. and trans. Ernest Cushing Richardson, in *A Select Library of Nicene and Post-Nicene Fathers of the Christian Church, 2nd Series, Vol 1: Eusebius*, ed. Philip Schaff and Henry Wace (Grand Rapids: Eerdmans, 1952), II.46-65.

15. A. H. M. Jones, *Constantine and the Conversion of Europe* 2nd. ed. (New York: Collier Books, 1962), 131.

16. Eusebius, "Life of Constantine," I.65-66.

17. Christianity *really was* a minority religion at the time of Constantine. The estimate is from Donald R. Dudley, *The Civilization of Rome* (New York: New American Library, 1962), 213. While Jones declines to give a figure, his description of this minority population supports Dudley's estimate:

> The Christians were a tiny minority of the population, and they belonged for the most part to the classes of the population who were politically and socially of least importance, the middle and lower classes of the towns. The senatorial aristocracy of Rome were pagan almost to a man; the higher grades of the civil service were mainly pagan; and above all the army officers and men, were predominantly pagan. The goodwill of the Christians was hardly worth gaining, and for what it was worth it could be gained by merely granting them toleration. Jones, *Constantine*, 73.

Constantine, however, appears to have considered this minority capable of sufficient mischief, and also of a sufficiently important supporting role for his policies of imperial unity, so that, spurred by his sympathies for the church, he decided to take the disputatious situation in hand.

18. His most important contribution is the insertion of what Cochrane calls the "sublimely meaningless 'homoousios'" into the credal formulation that emerged from the synod. Cf. Cushmann, "Prolegomena: The Life and Writings of Eusebius of Caesarea," in Schaff and Wace, *Eusebius*, 16-17. For details of the council, see Socrates, "The Ecclesiastical History," ed. and trans. A. C. Zenos, in *A Select Library of Nicene and Post-Nicene Fathers of the Christian Church, 2nd Series, vol 2: Socrates, Sozomen: Church Histories*, ed. Philip Schaff and Henry Wace (Grand Rapids: Eerdmans, 1952), chs. 5-15, pp. 3-20, and Sozomen, "The Ecclesiastical History," ed. and trans. Chester D. Hartranft, in *Socrates, Sozomen: Church Histories*, ed. Schaff and Wace, chs. 17-25, pp. 254-55.

19. Socrates, "Ecclesiastical History,"ch. 14.

20. McClendon, *Ethics*, passim.

21. Stanley Hauerwas and William H. Willimon, *Resident Aliens* (Nashville, Tenn.: Abingdon Press, 1989).

22. John Milbank, *Theology and Social Theory: Beyond Secular Reason*(Oxford: Blackwell Publishers, 1990), 9.

23. Oliver O'Donovan, *The Desire of the Nations: Rediscovering the roots of political theology* (Cambridge, England: Cambridge University Press, 1996), 156; see McClendon, *Ethics*, 251, 253; and McClendon, *Systematic Theology: Doctrine* (Nashville, Tenn.: Abingdon Press, 1994), 69.

24. Consider the advice of Thomas Aquinas to the princely ruler that he concern himself with both the material and moral well-being of his people (*De Regimine Principium*: 1.2.10).

25. Cf. Thomas Aquinas, *Summa Theologica*, Pt. III, Qu. 8, art. 3.

26. Hauerwas and Willimon, *Resident Aliens*, 17.

27. Ibid.; Cf. Stanley Hauerwas, "A Christian Critique of Christian America," in Stanley Hauerwas, *Christian Existence Today: Essays on Church, World, and Living in Between* (Grand Rapids: Brazos Books, 2001), 171-190.

28. Hauerwas and Willimon, *Resident Aliens*, 18.

29. David Walsh, *After Ideology: Recovering the Spiritual Foundations of Freedom* (San Francisco: HarperCollins Publishers, 1990).

30. Hauerwas and Willimon, *Resident Aliens*, 22. For an example of translating the gospel on its own terms, rather than on Constantinian premises, see Yoder, *Priestly Kingdom*, 49-54.

31. Duane Friesen, *Artists, Citizens, Philosophers: Seeking the Peace of the City: An Anabaptist Theology of Culture* (Scottdale, Pa.: Herald Press, 2000), 14, 45.

32. Ibid., 31.

33. Ibid., 16.

34. Ibid., 53.

35. Augustine, *Letters of St. Augustine, Bishop of Hippo*, trans. J. G. Cunningham, (Edinburgh, 1872), vol. 1 in *The Works of Aurelius Augustine, Bishop of Hippo*, ed. Marcus Dods (Edinburgh); vol 6 (Letter LXXXVII), 361-362; (Letter XCIII), 400-412.

36. Eusebius Pamphilus, "The Oration of Eusebius Pamphilus in Praise of the Emperor Constantine," ch. 3, trans. Ernest Cushing Richardson, in *Eusebius*, ed. Schaff and Wace, 584.

37. Eusebius, "Oration," I, 583.

38. Eusebius, "Oration," II, 583.

39. Charles Norris Cochrane, *Christianity and Classical Culture: A Study of Thought and Action From Augustus to Augustine* (New York: Oxford University Press, 1957), 210.

40. Cochrane, *Christianity and Classical Culture*, 210-211.

41. Lactantius, "Of the Manner in Which the Persecutors Died," XXXIV, trans. and ed. William Fletcher, Alexander Roberts and James Donalson,

Ante-Nicene Fathers: The Writings of the Fathers down to A.D. 325, Vol. 7: Lactantius, Venantius, Asterius, Victorinus, Dionysius, Apostolic Teaching and Constitutions, Homily, and Liturgies (Grand Rapids: Eerdmans, 1975 [1886]), 659.

42. Lactantius, "Persecutors," ch. 48. This text is translated in: University of Pennsylvania Department of History: Translations and Reprints from the Original Sources of European History, vol. 4 (Philadelphia, University of Pennsylvania Press [1897?-1907?]), 28-30, retrieved March 4, 2001 at: http://www.fordham.edu/halsall/source/edict-milan.html

43. "I give (to you) that you may give."

44. Eric Voegelin, *The New Science of Politics* (Chicago: The University of Chicago Press, 1952), 99-100.

45. H. A. Drake, *Constantine and the Bishops: The Politics of Intolerance* (Baltimore: Johns Hopkins University Press, 2000), 191-231. An important thrust of Drake's book is to dispel the ideologically motivated premise, held at least since Jacob Burkhardt's biography of Constantine, that Christianity is necessarily coercive, and that Constantine's toleration of pagans (and of competing forms of Christianity) makes his religious commitments suspect. On the contrary, argues Drake, Constantine's religious commitments are not violated by his *political* commitments to toleration. Toleration, a policy that numbers of both Christian and pagan leaders seemed to have advocated for nearly fifty years after Constantine's reign (249-250), is, like intolerance, a *political* matter, not a religious one (17-33).

46. Lactantius, "Divine Institutes," Vii.26, quoted in Cochrane, 186. An alternate translation may be found in Lactantius , "The Divine Institutes," *Lactantius*, trans. Fletcher, ed. Roberts and Donalson, at 456-457.

47. Romans 13:1-5.

48. Ephesians 6:12; Colossians 1:13.

49. R. W. Southern, *Western Society and the Church in the Middle Ages* (Harmondsworth, Middlesex, England: Penguin Books Ltd., 1970), 18.

50. Cochrane, *Christianity and Classical Culture*, 332.

51. Southern, *Western Society*, 18.

52. On elemental and existential representation, see Voegelin, *New Science*, 1-75.

53. Southern, *Western Society*, 21.

54. Martin E. Marty, *A Short History of Christianity* (Cleveland and New York: The World Publishing Company, 1959), 98.

55. Southern, *Western Society*, 21.

56. It is worth quoting at length Southern's cosmic portrait:

> But of course the church was much more than the source of coercive power. It was not just a government, however grandiose its operations. It was the whole of human society subject to the will of God. It was the ark of salvation in a sea of destruction. How far there could be any rational social order outside the ark of the church was a disputed

question, but at the best it could only be very limited. It was membership of the church that gave men a thoroughly intelligible purpose
and place in God's universe. So the church was not only *a* state, it was
the state; it was not only *a* society, it was *the* society—the human *societas perfecta*. Not only all political activity, but all learning and thought
were functions of the church. Besides taking over the political order of
the Roman Empire, the church appropriated the science of Greece and
the literature of Rome, and it turned them into the instruments of
human well-being in this world. To all this it added the gift of salvation—the final and exclusive possession of its members. And so in all
its fullness it was the society of rational and redeemed mankind.

One of the great achievements of the Middle Ages was the detailed development of this idea of universal human society as an integral part of a divinely ordered universe in time and in eternity, in nature and supernature, in practical politics and in the world of spiritual
essences. Nearly everything of importance that was written in the
Middle Ages, until the system began to break up in the fourteenth
century, was written with some consciousness of this cosmic background. (22)

57. Marty, *Short History*, 100.

58. Eric Voegelin, *History of Political Ideas: Vol. 9: Renaissance and Reformation*, ed. David L. Morse and William M. Thompson (Columbia, Mo.: University of Missouri Press, 1998), 140. Thus, while a foe of Constantinianism can
refer to the baptismal ceremony as "an abnormality" and "a mere religious
mining-claim staked out on the territory of babes in arms," that claim and the
practices that confront the non-Constantinian church are nevertheless powerful (McClendon, *Ethics*, 258), 176.

59. Ibid., 141.

60. Ibid., 140.

61. Ibid., 142.

62. Ibid.

63. McClendon, *Ethics*, 192.

64. Friesen, *Artists, Citizens, Philosophers*, 34.

65. Cochrane, *Christianity and Classical Culture*, 268; Voegelin, *New Science*,
107-110; the Wycliffe quote is from Eric Voegelin, "Democracy in the New Europe," in *Eric Voegelin: Published Essays, 1953-1965*, ed. Ellis Sandoz (Columbia, Mo.: University of Missouri Press, 2000), 61.

66. Out of the rich literature on such movements, see especially Norman
Cohn's sweeping, though geographically and temporally circumscribed history, *In Search of the Millennium* (London: Secker and Warburg, 1957).

67. Voegelin, *New Science*, 100-110; 119-126.

68. John Howard Yoder, "The Disavowal of Constantine: An Alternative
Perspective on Interfaith Dialogue," in Yoder, *Royal Priesthood*, 248.

69. Ibid., 250, 251, 255, 259.

70. Ibid., 259.

71. We can include here the Israelite kingdom of David and its two bastard offspring, against whose unfaithfulness and concerning whose questionable status in regard to "representation" of the rule of God the Israelite prophetic tradition is clear.

72. This is a summary, with lacunae, of Yoder, *Priestly Kingdom*, ch. 7 (135-147), and of numerous, scattered comments throughout his work.

73. Yoder, *Priestly Kingdom*, 88.

74. Eusebius, "Life of Constantine," II.1.

75. Yoder's critique on this point is not entirely obvious, since the autonomy of the church over against the political authorities in the cultural context of the late Roman Empire was not altogether obvious, perhaps even to many of the Christians of the time. Consider, for example, Drake's comments:

> Conceivably, Constantine could have adopted a hands-off approach, but to do so not only would he have had to deny three centuries of imperial tradition concerning the religious role of the emperor, but he also—given the common belief of his age in the direct role played by deity in the success or failure of imperial plans and the need to consult deity before the simplest duties could be discharged—would have had to surrender his control over important sectors of government policy. Roman rulers extending back to the earliest days of the republic and beyond had always been responsible for maintaining the pax deorum, the 'peace of the gods,' and it was natural both for Constantine to assume a position of leadership in the Christian organization once it became one of Rome's legally recognized religions and for Christian leaders to accept him in that role. It is anachronistic to see the authority Constantine asserted as either a power grab on his part or as spiritual capitulation by the bishops on theirs. Religious matters in the ancient world were no more clearly defined than secular ones, and in such an environment, participation by the emperor was not only normal and expected, but even demanded. (Drake, *Constantine and the Bishops*, 283)

One might say, however, that this lack of obviousness is another indication of the loss of the church's original (ethical, ecclesiological, and political) vision by the beginning of the fourth century.

76. "If, as Jesus called for it and the apostles practiced it, voluntariness is a constitutive aspect of a valid relation to Christ as Lord and to the church as community, then the shift in the fourth and fifth centuries made the gospel call into its opposite. Theodosius made it a civil offense not to be a Christian. Within a century after Constantine, Augustine was calling for it to be a civil offense to be the wrong kind of Christian. The meaning of the decision to confess Christ was thereby not simply warped or fogged over but structurally reversed, i.e., denied." Yoder, "Disavowal," 245-46.

77. http://www.nmnh.si.edu/anthro/whatisan.htm, retrieved March 5, 2002.

78. John Howard Yoder, *Body Politics: Five Practices of the Christian Community Before the Watching World* (Scottdale, Pa.: Herald Press, 1992).

79. Ibid., 33 (Yoder's emphasis).

80. Galatians 3:28.

81. Voegelin, *Renaissance and Reformation*, 142.

82. Yoder, *Body Politics*, 55.

83. Ibid., 56-57.

84. Ibid., 57.

85. Ibid., 50-55.

86. Ibid., 86, n.64.

87. Southern, *Western Society*, 17.

88. I deliberately and with every respect due, take the sobriquets from Thomas Hobbes and Alexandre Kojève's interpretation of Hegel, in *Introduction to the Reading of Hegel, by Alexandre Kojève. Lectures on the Phenomenology of Spirit Assembled by Raymond Queneau*, ed. Allan Bloom, trans. James H. Nichols Jr. (New York, Basic Books, 1969).

89. McClendon, *Ethics*, 177.

90. Yoder, *Priestly Kingdom*, 80-101.

91. Yoder, *Priestly Kingdom*, 15-45.

92. Sheldon S. Wolin, *Politics and Vision: Continuity and Innovation in Western Political Thought* (Boston: Little Brown and Company, 1960), 5.

93. Bertrand de Jouvenel, *The Pure Theory of Politics* (Cambridge, England: Cambridge University Press, 1963), 30.

94. Wolin, *Politics and Vision*, 97.

95. It is very likely the case that communities of believers other than Christian ones (or individuals apart from such communities) may also describe themselves and their relationship to political authority at least partially in categories that either resemble or explicitly reject "Constantinianism," as the case may be. To claim to speak for or about such communities here, however, would be presumptuous and a misreading of Yoder: he specifically, explicitly, and exclusively uses the term to refer to a historical effort of Christians in relation to political authority, and he rejects any attempt to universalize the characteristics of this effort across cultural or historical lines. Translation at the boundaries of very different communities is possible, and certainly highly desirable. See Yoder, *For the Nations*, 17; John Howard Yoder, *The Politics of Jesus: Vicit Agnus Noster*, 2nd. ed. (Grand Rapids: Eerdmans, 1994), 41, 48-56. However, Constantinianism as a specifically Christian concern is what Yoder knew and about which, being a *Christian* scholar, he was competent to speak.

96. The foremost example of recent interpretation along these lines is, of course, the work of Leo Strauss. See especially *Persecution and the Art of Writ-*

ing (Chicago: The University of Chicago Press, 1952), 7-37.

97. Yoder, *Politics of Jesus*, 96.

98. Ibid., 100.

99. Ibid., 96-99.

100. Ibid., 96.

101. Ibid., 97.

102. Ibid., 99.

103. Cf. John Howard Yoder, *The Christian Witness to the State* (Newton, Kan.: Faith and Life Press, 1964), 85-90.

104. Michael G. Cartwright, "Radical Reform, Radical Catholicity: John Howard Yoder's Vision of the Faithful Church," in Yoder, *Royal Priesthood*, 37.

105. Alain Epp Weaver, "After Politics: John Howard Yoder, Body Politics, and the Witnessing Church," in *The Review of Politics* 4:61 (Fall 1999): 637-73, 649ff.

106. Augustine, *Letters* (Letter XCIII), 409.

107. Augustine, *Letters*, (Letter XCIII), 410-412; cf. (Letter XCII), 395-6. For my further discussion of this problem, see "On Being Ethical Without Moral Sadism: Two Readings of Augustine and the Beginnings of the Anabaptist Revolution," *Political Theory* 24:3 (Summer 1996): 493-517.

108. For a highly useful, even if monolinear, account of such instruments in Augustine, see William E. Connolly, *The Augustinian Imperative: A Reflection on The Politics of Morality* (Newbury Park, Calif.: Sage Publications, Inc., 1993).

109. John Howard Yoder, "'Patience' as Method in Moral Reasoning," in *The Wisdom of the Cross: Essays in Honor of John Howard Yoder,* ed. Stanley Hauerwas et al. (Grand Rapids: Eerdmans,1999), 34; cf. Yoder, *Priestly Kingdom*, 114-116.

110. " . . . the church represents the spiritual ordering of man toward God. That is to say, the German people in politics and the German people in the church are one and the same, and, as people, it is part of their constitution to be oriented transcendentally. The churches are nothing but the representation of the spiritual transcendence of man." Eric Voegelin, "Hitler und die Deutschen" (unpublished transcript, 1964, my translation), 162.

111. Yoder, *Priestly Kingdom*, 23.

112. Ibid., 28.

113. Ibid., 61-62.

114. Yoder, *For the Nations*, 19.

115. Yoder, *Royal Priesthood*, 56.

116. Ibid., 57.

117. Ibid., 54.

118. "Still another variation is the cultural criticism being formulated by the 'theologies of liberation.' The way in which Christians have come to be at home with the powers of the wealthy world and the alliance of the older churches with colonialism and capitalism are denounced as a failure faith-

fully to represent the gospel's liberating impact." Yoder, *Priestly Kingdom*, 68.

119. Yoder, *Royal Priesthood*, 246-248.

120. Gerald Schlabach, "Deuteronomic or Constantinian: What Is the Most Basic Problem for Christian Social Ethics? in *Wisdom of the Cross*, ed. Stanley Hauerwas et al., 449.

121. Schlabach, "Deuteronomic," 454.

122. Ibid., 451, 454.

123. Ibid., 454-455.

124. Ibid., 463-468.

125. See, for example, the essays in *For the Nations*.

126. Reimer, "Trinitarian Orthodoxy," 259-271.

127. Schlabach, "Deuteronomic," 456.

128. "The real test of the accessibility of a common moral language 'out there,' more general than confessional language, must then not be the times we find ourselves agreeing with 'men of good will' (especially not if they be Western humanists); it must be the capacity of this line of argument to illuminate meaningful conversations with Idi Amin or Khomeini or Chairman Mao." Yoder, *Priestly Kingdom*, 42.

129. "The 'world' is neither all nature nor all humanity nor all 'culture'; it is *structured unbelief*, rebellion taking with it a fragment of what should have been the Order of the Kingdom. It is not just an 'attitude,' as is supposed by the shallow interiorization of attempts to locate 'worldliness' in the mind alone. Nor is it to be shallowly exteriorized and equated with certain catalogued, forbidden, leisure-time occupations. There are acts and institutions that are by their nature—and not solely by an accident of context or motivation—denials of faith in Christ." Yoder, *Royal Priesthood*, 62.

"Perhaps the best description of the effect of Christian proclamation on the powers would be to say that it constrains them to be modest. What had been considered an end in itself comes to be seen as a means to promote human welfare. What had been a source of social and cultural stability turns into part of a process of change. As long as the commitment of the Christian community is clear, the powers which have been 'spoiled' can be kept under control." Yoder, "Christ the Hope of the World," in *Original Revolution*, 149 (reprinted in *Royal Priesthood*, 192-218).

130. Yoder, *Christian Witness*, 72-3.

131. See Milbank, *Theology and Social Theory*, 380-438, for one such account, but which, from the perspective of the present argument, requires significant correctives.

Chapter 6

Constantinianism Before and After Nicea: Issues in Restitutionist Historiography

J. Alexander Sider

IN JUNE 2001, I WAS PRIVILEGED TO ATTEND the meeting of the Historic Peace Church Consultation at the Bienenberg, near Liestal, Switzerland. That Consultation was prompted by the World Council of Churches' decision in its assembly in Harare, Zimbabwe, to proclaim the years 2001-2010 an ecumenical Decade to Overcome Violence. Konrad Raiser, general secretary to the WCC, put the matter this way in his remarks to the Consultation:

> The ecumenical community has been struggling with the question of war and peace, violence and nonviolence, and reconciliation in a way ever since the beginnings of the ecumenical movement. The whole history of the World Council of Churches has been inscribed into that context. It is not an additional or external concern that is thrust on the churches seeking unity and rebuilding communion among each other, but it is integral to the emergence of the ecumenical impulse and the ecumenical movement.[1]

Nevertheless, in the course of the week-long consultation it became clear that many of the "mainline" churches associated with the WCC continue, if grudgingly, to tolerate the use of armed force in "humanitarian intervention." The WCC study paper, "The Protection of Endangered Populations in Situations of Armed Violence: Toward an Ecumenical Approach," recognizes both that "The perspectives of Christians on matters of war and the use of armed force differ radically" and that there exists a "moral obligation of the international community to protect the lives of civilian populations that are at risk in situations where their government is unable or unwilling to act."[2] The study document, as Mark Siemens notes, "Thus . . . implicitly recognizes the necessity that at times Christians will need to support armed intervention for humanitarian purposes."[3]

During the Bienenberg Consultation the Historic Peace Churches drafted a response to "The Protection of Endangered Populations," now promulgated as "Just Peacemaking: Towards an Ecumenical Ethical Approach from the Perspective of the Historic Peace Churches—A Study Paper for Dialogue with the Wider Church."[4] While "Just Peacemaking" represents an admirable beginning "attempt further to diminish the objection that pacifism is incompatible with a commitment to justice,"[5] it remains, to my mind at least, curiously silent at one point. I am thinking here of the obstacles presented to ecumenical engagement in peace theology by the "Constantinian captivity" of many if not most contemporary ecclesial communions.[6] Yet, if nothing else, the WCC's "Protection of Endangered Populations" document sounds a clarion call that the burden of proof for demonstrating why the Constantinian settlement remains not only "a strategic mistake" but a "denial of gospel substance" still sits squarely on the shoulders of the Historic Peace Churches.[7]

John Howard Yoder was both a leading diagnostician of Constantinianism and intimately involved in the ecumenical movement of the twentieth century. That the two have something to do with each other should not be overlooked, especially given the Historic Peace Churches' current effort to engage the ecumenical community on issues of nonviolence and reconciliation. This essay moves toward clarifying some of the issues at stake in Yoder's account of Constantinianism as a piece in the framework of conditions for coherent ecumenical dialogue. At least, that is my hope.

My task is twofold. In the first place, it is to give a brief account of Yoder's use of Constantinianism as a trope to describe a certain set of compromised ecclesiologies. In the second place, I wish to begin to address a set of historical problems Yoder's use of Constantinianism provokes, especially as it regards the possibilities for ecumenical discussion. That set of problems can be stated generally as a question: What difference does it make to contemporary theological use of Constantinianism as a descriptive term if and when the period or person whence the description derives its name is the subject of revisionist historiography?[8] Stated slightly differently: Is Yoder's account of Constantinianism sufficient on his own restitutionist historiographical grounds?

To the first part of the task, then: How did Yoder describe Constantinianism, and how did he use it to analyze a certain kind of ecclesiological pitfall? In his essay, "Peace without Eschatology," Yoder put the matter succinctly: Constantinianism "refers to the conception of Christianity that took shape in the century between the Edict of Milan and the *City of God*."[9] Here, Constantinianism emerges as a distinct problem in the fourth and early fifth centuries, notably demarcated by two documents, the first of which grants "freedom of religion" to Christians—the legal right to be a visible and practicing body in the world—and the second of which deals at least in part with the necessary invisibility of the true church.[10] The texts signal that the problem is one of visibility, of the creation during this period of sociopolitical obstacles that inhibit the ability to identify concretely a determinate body of believers as the church.

But the creation of such obstacles is in Yoder's account not solely a fourth-century phenomenon, and is not exclusively to be connected to Constantine. Rather, as Gerald Schlabach observes,

> If Constantine's policies do mark a watershed in church history, his importance is still one that was conferred upon him at the time by bishops and other Christian leaders such as the church historian Eusebius [of Caesarea, also a bishop]. Constantinianism then really consists of all the reasons they did so—trends that were already in place before Constantine and rationalizations that only a minority of Christians have resisted since.[11]

Elsewhere, Yoder confirms Schlabach's view:

> The Roman emperor who began to tolerate, then supported, then administered, then finally joined the church, soon became and has remained until our time the symbol of a sweeping shift in the nature of the empirical church and its relation to the world. Constantine neither initiated that shift nor concluded it, and our present interest is not in the extent to which he knew what he was doing. The shift is what matters. That it took place,

was far-reaching, and changed much of the concrete social meaning of Christianity, all historians agree.[12]

"The shift is what matters." If one refrain throughout Yoder's analysis of Constantinianism remains puzzling, this is it. Constantine is emblematic of "a new era in the history of Christianity,"[13] and "he inaugurated the age of Christianity's being the official religion,"[14] but we are not interested in the man; our business is to attend to the shift. In part, at least, this has to do with Yoder's skepticism—in marked contrast to most other inquiries into the Constantinian era since Jacob Burckhardt's *Die Zeit Constantins des Grossen*—that much can be known about the man. Yoder asks, "Was Constantine sincere or was he only using Christianity as a political tool? What did Christianity mean to him? Why did he postpone his baptism? Why did he convene and control the Council of Nicea? Did he see himself as the savior of the church, i.e., as an eschatological sign? *Are these questions that can fruitfully be posed?*"[15] The implied answer to that last question is, "Probably not." Far too many layers of interpretation and reinterpretation lie between Constantine and us to allow investigation into his life to yield results we could deem veridical.

Moreover, apart from those layers of interpretation and reinterpretation, a process that commenced with Eusebius of Caesarea's *Vita Constantini*, there is no history to which we might turn to get Constantine the man straight. Constantinianism, like the Jeremian turn in the life of ancient Israel or the New Testament itself, demands exposition "in a larger than life way, i.e., as 'legend,' as something having to be recounted, bigger in its meanings than what the historians' questions about documents and causation can contain."[16]

So we must concentrate on the shift. We must do so not only because historians have been telling us for decades not to blame Constantinianism on Constantine, and not only because we lack the resources to investigate the man in any way that would be other than futile, but also because it is the shift and not the man that accounts for the distance of most contemporary ecclesiologies from the New Testament church.[17] In what, then, does the Constantinian shift consist?

Yoder's claim is that at base the Constantinian shift represents the "reorientation of the meaning of history . . . when it became obvious, because of the victory of Constantine that the God of Moses is on the side of the people who come out triumphant in a particular course of events."[18] This is to say that the question, "How does God work in history?" receives a new answer at a systemic level.[19] Before the Constantinian era it remained unclear whether God was governing history, even though one knew "as a fact of lived experience that there was a church" through which God was working in the world. After the Constantinian settlement, however, it is evident that God governs history (through the arm of the empire), but one must "take it on faith that there is a church."[20] This reorientation of the meaning of history is deeper than the changes in church polity and Christian ethics that followed it, and it is more basic than the "more recent turns, which Western Christians call 'the Reformation' and 'the Enlightenment.'"[21]

The shift can first be detected, according to Yoder, during the latter part of the second century, when Christian theologians like Tertullian, Origen, and Cyprian began to address the way the Christian church should comport itself vis-à-vis the empire. Each of these theologians at the same time acknowledged a pendulation in Christian attitudes toward the empire and put "his pacifism within a more global rejection of the Caesar system as a diabolical system as it . . . [was then] encountered."[22] The implication, in Yoder's view, is that, though the theologians continued to argue strongly against Christian involvement with the sword, the imperial cult and oath-taking, nevertheless at the popular level at least two things were in flux. In the first place, the extent to which Christianity in large measure viewed itself as a set of moral rules to be followed was less significant than it had been earlier in the second century. Correlatively, and in the second place, the repercussions on Christians who stepped outside the bounds of Christian doctrine loosened as the century neared its end.[23]

These two factors, taken together, were both symptomatic of and contributed to the church's increasingly acculturated self-perception. Moreover, such acculturation prompted the apologetic concerns that dominated Tertullian's ecclesiological thought and, though to a lesser extent, were noteworthy in Origen's and Cyprian's writing as well.

Yoder's linkage of the apologetic enterprise and nascent Constantinian views of the empire may be true as far as it goes. But it is interesting that Yoder nowhere ties Christian apologetic concerns in the late second and early third centuries to major changes in the imperial stance toward Christianity, such as the dramatic revision of the Roman constitution, which commenced with Caracalla's edict of 212. Elizabeth DePalma Digeser, in *The Making of a Christian Empire*, comments on the unifying effects of the Antonine Constitution:

> From a loose collection of *civitates*, each under the central authority of the emperor but also maintaining its own laws and citizenship, the empire became one great *civitas* under Roman law. In the early empire, religious pluralism survived in the inter-

stices between peregrine and Roman law. But after the passage of the Antonine Constitution, Decius, Valerian, and Diocletian were quite willing to use force against groups whose refusal to worship the gods called into question their loyalty to the laws.[24]

Before the passage of the Antonine Constitution, many if not most Christians were not Roman citizens. But the Constitution granted rights of citizenship to all imperial subjects, Christians included. Consequently, the Antonine Constitution may have created some of the conditions for the increased social mobility of Christians that Yoder cites as a motivating factor in third century apologetic theology. This is not, however, to suggest that the Constitution's effects were an unmixed blessing for Christians, for it initiated, in a way that had never been the case before, imperial policy regarding the cultic affiliation of all citizens of the Roman empire. As Digeser's account intimates, after 212, failure to participate in the imperial cult, which Christians had always refused to do, became a treasonable offense.[25]

The point to be learned in this connection is simply that the Christian apologists of the early third century responded not only to a process of acculturation initiated by, as Yoder put it, "second, third and fourth generation Christians, who . . . never really, deeply suffered for being Christian."[26] Their apologies for Christianity were also prompted by the imposition of the imperial cult on all subjects of the empire, newly defined as citizens—and this latter is the basic polemical context for their theologies.[27]

The problem this example presents to thinking about Yoder's account of the Christian slide into Constantinianism is also evident elsewhere in his work: the "history" he adduces to support his case is surprisingly monological. It is easy to get the impression, reading *Christian Attitudes to War, Peace and Revolution* for instance, that second-and third-century Christianity can be configured as a contest between the martyrs, who represent convicted Christianity, and the apologists, who represent Hellenization and acculturation. The Constantinian settlement then appears as the logical outworking of the apologetic tradition—Tertullian sets the stage for Theodosius.[28] But, inasmuch as legal measures like the Antonine Constitution forced Christians into a context where they had both to legitimate their practice and to begin to make a case for religious toleration in terms recognizable to the *imperium*, the registers in which a contemporary account of Constantinianism must be pitched are modulated, and in ways that Yoder's telling of the story does not take into account. Given this, Yoder's argument for increasing acculturation in the pre-Constantinian church and a slow but perceptible drift into a comfortable relationship with the empire begins to look like an attempt to retell the past to furnish it with a suitable denouement.

As Yoder continues the story of the Constantinian shift other instances emerge that sustain the assessment that his historical work in this period lacks sufficient subtlety to bear his descriptive argument. He writes, "In the fourth century an age of toleration and accommodation begins. There was still, in the early part of the century, some persecution of Christians, but it soon ended."[29] Elsewhere he notes that the "last wave of persecution was not successful. The alternative for the Empire was then: 'if you can't lick 'em, join 'em.' It is that alliance that Constantine represents."[30] In these passages Yoder gives two impressions: (1) that the persecution under Diocletian and Galerius was in fact not terribly consequential for the formation of Christian consciousness in the fourth century; and (2) that the empire conceived of itself as waging an ongoing and losing battle with Christianity.

Both impressions deserve much more careful attention than Yoder gives them. At the least it needs to be said that the persecution of Christians under Diocletian and Galerius was remembered as the "Great Persecution," distinct from its predecessors in both scope and systematic focus. Moreover, at this point Yoder's arguments about the fourth century still focus on the accommodation of the church "to the culture of the surrounding world."[31] He fails to mention that by the end of the third century the "surrounding world" had itself cultivated assumptions regarding the importance of the singular divine mind in human affairs that were increasingly similar to those already held by Christians.

The central figure in Yoder's commentary on the fourth century is undoubtedly the emperor Constantine himself. Yet only slightly less central are Yoder's references to Eusebius of Caesarea, who along with Augustine of Hippo, is Yoder's dominant theological touchstone in the fourth and fifth centuries. Eusebius, who authored the *Ecclesiastical History*, the *Life of Constantine* and the *Oration in Praise of Constantine*, deservedly plays a major role in the history, historiography, and legend that surrounds Constantine's reign. He has himself been the subject of intense inquiry in the nineteenth and twentieth centuries. That inquiry goes back at least to Jakob Burckhardt, who in 1852 denounced Eusebius as "the first thoroughly dishonest historian of antiquity."[32] The twentieth century saw a more refined point put on Eusebius' apparent political propagandism.[33] It is a strand of criticism from which Yoder appears to have learned much. Erik Peterson, in *Der Monotheismus als politisches Problem*, as well as Hendrik Berkhof, in both *Kirche und Kaiser* and *Die Theologie des Eusebius von Caesarea*, detected christological subordinationism in Eusebius' theology, which they then correlated to his panegyrics for the emperor.[34] If Christ was not God in the way that the Father was God, then the emperor and Christ could exercise more or less parallel rules, Christ in heaven over the cosmos and Constantine on earth over the *imperium*. Peterson and Berkhof were followed in large part by George Hunston Williams and Per Beskow.[35]

Williams is especially interesting in counterpoint to Yoder. Whereas on Yoder's account pro-Nicene orthodoxy is ambiguously related to Constantinianism, in Williams' view, "All who have worked through the fourth century have sensed some affinity between Arianism and Caesaropapism on the one hand and on the other between Nicene orthodoxy and the recovery of a measure of ecclesiastical independence."[36] Indeed, Williams takes up Peterson's mantle in terms of arguing that only "a fully understood Trinitarianism proved itself capable of resisting the exploitation of Christian monotheism as a means of sanctioning political unity and securing social cohesion."[37] Williams, as I have indicated, identifies "Arianizing" or subordinationist christologies in the fourth century as contributing to the uncritical linkage of church and state. He writes,

> Over against the Catholic insistence on the consubstantiality of the Son . . . are the various forms of subordination of the Son and the Holy Spirit worked out among the different Arianizing parties of the fourth century. Roughly speaking these two Christologies gave rise to, or are at least associated with, two main views of the Empire and the relationship of the Church thereto. According to one view the emperor is bishop of bishops. According to the other, the emperor is within the church.[38]

The pro-Nicene view, with its insistence that the Son is consubstantial with the Father is in Williams' estimation the view that preserves the New Testament's logic concerning the deity of Jesus. It was therefore easier for "Arians" than for "Catholics" to accommodate themselves "to the assimilation of pagan conceptions of kingship" and to "lavishly compensate the ruler for relinquishing purely pagan attributes and honors."[39] In other words, "Arianizing" theologies contributed to the Constantinian captivity of the church in a way that pro-Nicene theologies did not.

We do not have to agree with Williams that there was in the fourth century an "Arian party" to note the stark contrast between Yoder's assessment of the fourth century and this tradition of inquiry.[40] For Yoder, even if pro-Nicene theology safeguards the Christology of the New Testament in the "hellenized" idiom of the late empire, that does not mean it has been vindicated. Rather,

> It must mean something to us that the Arians and the Nestorians—each in their own age—were less nationalistic, less politically bound to the Roman Empire, more capable of criticizing the emperor, more vital in missionary growth, more ethical and more biblicist than the so-called orthodox churches of the Empire.[41]

As might be expected, Yoder draws attention to the extent to which politics cannot be abstracted from doctrine. Thus he problematizes, in a way unavailable to Williams, any easy reading of doctrine of politics or vice versa. Yet while the point is formally correct, to my mind, Yoder's grounds for these specific claims about "Arian" and "Nestorian" politics remain controversial. This is the case not only because of the extent to which they contrast with the assessment of the political implications of pro-Nicene theology that runs from Peterson to Williams to T. D. Barnes and Gerhard Ruhbach. It is also the case given the attempts by recent historians of Christian doctrine to offer a more complex account of the range of theological positions both leading up to the Council of Nicea and in the years between the Council and its ratification, so to speak, in Constantinople, Ephesus, and Chalcedon.[42]

The point is clear enough, however, and is one we have come to expect from the author *of The Politics of Jesus*: Theology is not merely theology; it is politics, institutional arrangements, and practices as well. It is therefore not credible on Yoder's grounds to defend pro-Nicene theology *despite* the politics associated with it. But if this is to come dangerously close to falling into the genetic fallacy, then Yoder's historicism is the antidote:

> The creeds are part of the only history we have. It is a fallible history and a confused history. A lot of dirty politics were involved in defining the creeds, in explaining their meaning, and still more in applying their authority, but this is the history with which God has chosen to lead a confused people toward at least a degree of understanding of certain dangers and things not to say if we are to remain faithful.[43]

We do not have another history than that which is described as turning out both pro-Nicene and Constantinian to which we can appeal in our theological judgments. Theology is never vindicated despite its history, and history is the only arena in which we have to play the theological game. This is however, not to insist that the way things are is the way they have to be. It is, moreover, not to deny the need for ongoing revisionist historiography. But it is to say that revisionist historiography will itself be but another part of "the only history we have."

It is in this connection that I wish to turn now from describing Yoder's views on Constantinianism to asking whether his arguments live up to his claims about the way Christians need to practice the doing of history. On the one hand, Yoder's theses regarding Constantinianism are historical: A shift in the relation of church and world occurred, such that, although first century Christians were minorities in an hostile world like we are now, nevertheless we do not reason as they did. On the other hand, Yoder repeatedly skirted the historical coordinates of the shift. Yoder's inattention to the effects of Roman law on Christian self-perception and theology, as well as his unnuanced account of the political implications of pro-Nicene theology are only two instances in which I take this to be the case.

Another instance might be cited in brief. Yoder's claim is that Constantinianism creates a "two-tiered ethic," wherein the "evangelical counsels" are reserved only for the "religious and the highly motivated," and the less demanding "precepts" suffice for the baptized laity. Before Constantine, the Christian was "a minority figure, with numerous resources not generally available to all people: personal commitment, regeneration, the guidance of the Holy Spirit, the consolation and encouragement of the brotherhood, training in a discipleship life-style."[44] Christian ethics was for Christians. After Constantine, when "Christian" means everyone, Christian ethics must either be watered down, or if retained, be supererogatory.

Certainly, thought about the nature of Christian discipleship changed during the age of Constantine. But it is less clear than Yoder makes it out to be that the early church had a more rigorous account of Christian ethics than did the church in the post-Constantinian era. Indeed, the situation seems to have been much more complex, as Hal Drake has shown:

> The theological battles triggered by Arius resonated throughout the fourth century, producing ever more careful and sophisticated definitions of Christian belief. In a parallel process, con-

versions prompted new thinking about what it meant to be a Christian and a longing to reconnect with an unspoiled and innocent primitive church. . . . On both levels, the effect was to prompt new thinking about what was essential to Christianity, and the side effect was to raise and tighten the standard by which Christian performance was measured. . . . [A] by-product of this effort to establish ties with an idealized past was a reconstruction of that past as one of fortitude and resistance which resulted in a tightening of criteria, a raising of the threshold of Christian identity.[45]

To at least a certain extent, then, the Constantinian church created the narrative on which Yoder's account of the discipleship ethic of the pre-Constantinian church is based. Again, the point is not to provide grounds for discounting Yoder's use of Constantinianism to describe an ecclesiological pitfall. Nor is the point to claim that the Constantinian settlement did not represent the "fall of Christianity," though I have reservations, which I think are held on Yoderian grounds, about the usefulness of the very notion of a "fall of Christianity."[46] The point is to foreground the extent to which the history Yoder adduces in support of his case is much more complex than his own account suggests.

There is a sense in which all I have said to this point is that the historiography on which Yoder based his research in regard to the genetics of Constantinianism was not very good. That may not be terribly telling, given that Yoder never claimed to be more than an interested amateur in the Patristic era. But if one theme in Yoder's theology is both recurring and commonly overlooked by commentators on his work, it is that "historiography is theologically necessary," or, as he puts it slightly later in the same passage, that theologians committed to a restitutionist view of history accept "the challenge to be critical of history and thereby to take it more seriously than do those for whom some other criterion than the New Testament determines the faithfulness of the church."[47]

In what, precisely, does a restitutionist view of history consist? In "Anabaptism and History," Yoder maintains that

There are a limited number of possible ways to take history seriously. One may do so by arguing against its importance; this is the stance of the Spiritualizer. One may reject the past globally in the name of a present or future takeover: the apocalyptic. One may accept the frame it has produced; so the official churches. In any of these cases one is free to study the data of the past or not; the meaning of truth and obedience goes on from today. The past must however be taken seriously in a very different way if one claims to critique the course of history using as criterion a point within history, namely the incarnation, or the canon.[48]

The restitutionist view of history argues that it is part of the integrity of Christian ecclesiology to evaluate and re-evaluate its past as contributing to the sense in which the present furnishes the church "with the choice between fall and renewal," with the possibility of judging our reception of our past faithful or not on the basis of "the very particular story of the New Testament."[49] The restitutionist argues that the church can and must engage in continuous critique of its own story. It "can" because the norm by which it engages its history is itself historical—"to be found fully within the researchable, debatable particularity which according to the New Testament witness is the meaning of incarnation."[50] It "must" because "the wholesome growth of a tradition is like a vine: a story of constant interruption of organic growth in favor of pruning and a new chance for the roots."[51]

A comparison between Yoder and another prominent thinker might be fruitful at this point for further spelling out Yoder's conception of history and historiography. Yoder's stated commitment to taking history seriously bears significant affinities with the philosophical hermeneutics of Hans-Georg Gadamer, and the former's account of Constantinianism is a point at which to clarify the commonalities. Yoder, as I have said, is clear that Constantine is not the locus of his critique of Constantinianism. And, as I have argued in this essay, it should be equally clear that he is not overly concerned with the specific contours of this or that set of events in the third, fourth, or fifth centuries. Rather, his concern is with an ethos; namely, our way of experiencing the history of the shift for which Constantine stands. To use Gadamer's phrase, Yoder's concern is with how Constantinianism has become "historically effective."

By historically effective, Gadamer means simply that events have histories that determine how we become conscious of them. Those historical consequences include a given event's immediate—many would say "causal"—effects, but also, and perhaps more importantly, the history of interaction with and interpretation of the event, which configures our prejudices for encountering it. "Real historical thinking, " as Gadamer puts it,

> must take account of its own historicity. . . . A hermeneutics adequate to the subject matter would have to demonstrate the reality and efficacy of history within understanding itself. . . . *Understanding is, essentially, a historically effected event.* . . . If we are try-

ing to understand a historical phenomenon from the historical distance that is characteristic of our hermeneutical situation, we are always already affected by history. It determines in advance both what seems to us worth inquiring about and what will appear as an object of investigation, and we more or less forget half of what is really there—in fact, we miss the whole truth of the phenomenon—when we take its immediate appearance as the whole truth.[52]

Historical thought that accounts at least in part for its own historicity seems to me basic to the restitutionist's task.[53] "At least in part," because Gadamer and Yoder agree that there is no stance purified of contingency to which we can retreat to "start from scratch." Alasdair MacIntyre recently made the point in respect to Gadamer; I think it pertains to Yoder as well. MacIntyre wrote that

> One of Gadamer's key theses that I take to be unquestionably true [is] to have become aware of the historically conditioned character of our philosophical enquiries and interpretations is not to have escaped from it. There is no standpoint outside history to which we can move, no way in which we can adopt some presuppositionless stance, exempt from the historical situatedness of all thinking. . . . [But] a certain kind of awareness, while not providing a standpoint outside history, can transform our relationship to that history.[54]

My question is whether Yoder's view of Constantinianism accounts for its own historicity enough to transform our relationship to that history. The answer, I think, must be equivocal. There is after all a "finished" quality to many of Yoder's claims about the Constantinian shift that make one wonder just how necessary he thought the restitutionist imperative always to review history and historiography was to the effort to articulate a non-Constantinian theology. One wonders, that is, whether the assessment of Constantinianism can admit of a "mid-course correction," as he puts it elsewhere, "a rediscovery of something from the past whose pertinence was not seen before, because only a new question or challenge enables us to see it speaking to us."[55] In principle Yoder does affirm the possibility of such "looping back," for he denies the appropriateness of a systematically pessimistic view of Constantinianism as "not only . . . equivalent to denying the rhetoric of Christian belief in Providence, but also the actual lessons of modern social experience, in which there has been at least some progress in the direction of greater humanity and justice."[56]

The question I have attempted to raise, however, is not about principle, but about Yoder's actual textual and historiographical practice. Yoder's account of Constantinianism, I have tried to show, does not always measure up to his own assumptions about how Christians should do history. To the extent that I am correct, ecclesially mainstream theologians and historians will not be compelled to take non-Constantinian theologies seriously.

And this brings us back to the context in which I originally brought up Yoder's account of Constantinianism, namely ecumenical dialogue. What has emerged in this chapter is not an answer to what peace churches should say to the mainstream about how to extricate ourselves from Constantinian social arrangements. Much less has the chapter addressed what a coherent non-Constantinian perspective on the use of armed force in "humanitarian intervention" would look like.

However, the chapter has, I hope, formulated a task: that if the theological voices of the Historic Peace Churches are to begin to discharge the burden of proof that rests on non-Constantinian ecclesiologies, it will have to be within the context of a patient and thorough willingness to reassess the stories we have inherited about Constantine's legacy. It will require a renewed focus on the political and doctrinal history of the Patristic era—a focus that cannot be content with a "take it or leave it" attitude, but which is willing to labor through and tarry with the process of negotiating "the only history we have," the same history "with which God has chosen to lead a confused people toward at least a degree of understanding of certain dangers and things not to say if we are to remain faithful."[57]

NOTES

1. "Remarks to the Bienenberg Consultation," *MCC Peace Office Newsletter* 31:4 (October-December 2001): 3.

2. Quoted in Mark Siemens, "Peace Churches Respond to World Council," *MCC Peace Office Newsletter*: 9.

3. Ibid., 9.

4. For the Bienenberg document text, see www.peacetheology.org/papers/study.html.

5. "Peace Churches Respond," 11.

6. This is not to imply that the Historic Peace Churches remain immune to Constantinian temptations.

7. The language is John Howard Yoder's. See, e.g., "The Constantinian Sources of Western Social Ethics," in *The Priestly Kingdom: Social Ethics as*

Gospel (Notre Dame, Ind.: University of Notre Dame Press, 1984), 145. Cf. "The Disavowal of Constantine: An Alternative Perspective on Interfaith Dialogue," in *The Royal Priesthood: Essays Ecclesiological and Ecumenical,* ed. Michael G. Cartwright (Grand Rapids: Eerdmans, 1994), 245.

8. This is the case today. In the last twenty-five years of the twentieth century historians and theologians alike re-opened the "Pandora's Box" of the fourth century. In much of the investigation Constantine's political program and the role he played in the developing ascendancy of Christianity has come under thoroughgoing scrutiny. Notably diverse accounts include those collected in *Arianism after Arius: Essays on the Development of the Fourth Century Trinitarian Conflicts,* ed. Michel R. Barnes and Daniel H. Williams (Edinburgh, Scotland: T&T Clark, 1993), as well as the monographs by T. D. Barnes, *Constantine and Eusebius* (Cambridge, Mass.: Harvard University Press, 1981), Elizabeth DePalma Digeser, *The Making of a Christian Empire: Lactantius and Rome* (Ithaca, N.Y.: Cornell University Press, 2000), H. A. Drake, *Constantine and the Bishops: The Politics of Intolerance* (Baltimore: Johns Hopkins University Press, 2000), and R. P. C. Hanson, *The Search for the Christian Doctrine of God* (Edinburgh: T&T Clark, 1988).

9. Yoder, "Peace without Eschatology," *The Royal Priesthood,* 153-154.

10. "Freedom of religion" remains a problematically anachronistic way of stating what it was that Constantine extended to Christians in the Edict of Milan. On this, see now Lester R. Fields, Jr., *Liberty, Dominion and the Two Swords: On the Origins of Political Theology in the West,* 180-395 (Notre Dame, Ind.: University of Notre Dame Press, 1998), 65-81.

11. Gerald Schlabach, "Deuteronomic or Constantinian: What Is the Most Basic Problem for Christian Social Ethics?," in *The Wisdom of the Cross: Essays in Honor of John Howard Yoder,* ed. Stanley Hauerwas, Chris K. Huebner, Harry J. Huebner, and Mark Thiessen Nation (Grand Rapids: Eerdmans, 1999), 452. Cf. 449-450 in *idem:* ". . . in Yoder's reading of church history and social ethics, Constantinianism is not simply a fourth-century phenomenon but is emblematic for a thoroughgoing and oft-repeated Christian unfaithfulness."

12. Yoder, "The Disavowal of Constantine," 245. Cf. Yoder, *Christian Attitudes to War, Peace, and Revolution: A Companion to Bainton* (Elkhart, Ind.: Goshen Biblical Seminary, 1983), 39; and *The Priestly Kingdom,* 135 and 209 n.3.

13. Yoder, "Constantinian Sources," 135.

14. Ibid., 209 n.3.

15. Yoder, *Royal Priesthood,* 245 n.3 (emphasis added).

16. Yoder, *For the Nations: Essays Public and Evangelical* (Grand Rapids: Eerdmans, 1997), 8.

17. Yoder, "Constantinian Sources," 144: "The fourth-century shift continues to explain much if not most of the distance between biblical Christianity and ourselves, which is a distance not simply of time and organic development, but of disavowal and apostasy."

18. Yoder, *Christian Attitudes to War, Peace, and Revolution*, 50.

19. Ibid., 42.

20. Ibid., 44.

21. See Ibid., 41 and *For the Nations*, 8, where Constantinianism is placed in parallel to the "other ancient turning point" represented by Jeremiah.

22. Yoder, *Christian Attitudes to War, Peace and Revolution*, 30.

23. Ibid., 34.

24. Digeser, *The Making of a Christian Empire*, 119.

25. Ibid., 50.

26. Yoder, *Christian Attitudes to War, Peace, and Revolution*, 30-31.

27. Yoder's thought on the political theology of the pre-Constantinian church depended in large part upon Hendrik Berkhof, *Kirche und Kaiser: Eine Untersuchung der Entstehung der byzantischen und der theokratischen Staatsaufassung im vierten Jahrhundert*, trans. Gottfried W. Locher (Zürich: Evangelischer Verlag A. G. Zollikon 1947) and Jean-Michel Hornus, *It Is Not Lawful For Me To Fight: Early Christian Attitudes Toward War, Violence, and the State*, rev. ed. and trans. Alan Kreider and Oliver Coburn (Scottdale, Pa.: Herald Press, 1980). Whereas Berkhof dealt mainly with the fourth century and Eusebius of Caesarea, Hornus' account began with the Apostolic Fathers and worked toward Constantine and Eusebius. Neither theologian notes the significant changes in Roman law prior to the Edict of Milan held for Christian self-definition and theological engagement with the empire.

28. Notice that while Tertullian's *Apologia* is dated from around 197, the dates of *De corona militis* and *Contra Marcion* are at least a decade later—possibly, though not certainly, under the edict of 212. Too, the Severan persecution out of which the *Apologia* grew is another instance of a largely external pressure that prompted Christian theologians into apologetic inquiry, which Yoder does not mention.

29. Yoder, *Preface to Theology: Christology and Theological Method* (Grand Rapids: Brazos, 2001), 195.

30. Yoder, *Christian Attitudes to War, Peace, and Revolution*, 39.

31. Yoder, *Preface to Theology*, 195.

32. Jakob Burckhardt, *The Age of Constantine the Great*, trans. Moses Hadas (New York: Pantheon Books, 1949), 283.

33. Michael J. Hollerich, in *Eusebius of Caesarea's Commentary on Isaiah: Christian Exegesis in the Age of Constantine* (Oxford, England: Clarendon Press, 1999), 193, notes that "Much of the work on Eusebius has been done with one eye on the crisis which convulsed Europe in the 1930s and 1940s; the involvement of Christianity in the fate of the Third Reich has left its mark on scholarship." The extent to which Yoder's own analysis of the Constantinian settlement may have been marked by such concerns remains unclear. It is, however, indubitably the case that he was influenced by theologians and historians for whom the cultural accommodation of the *Deutsche Christen* to Nazism

was a major issue (Barth and Berkhof both leap immediately to mind). In terms of clarifying Yoder's assumptions about the nature of Constantinianism, then, more work remains to be done on the extent to which European historiography of the age of Constantine in the second third of the twentieth century projected its own political context onto the fourth century.

Notice, however, that T. D. Barnes, "Constantine, Athanasius and the Christian Church" in *Constantine: History, Historiography and Legen*, ed. Samuel N. C. Lieu and Dominic Montserrat (New York: Routledge, 1998), 7-20, esp. 8-9, locates the projection of modern German politics onto the fourth century in the Germany of Bismarck and Kaiser Wilhelm II. Then, significantly, Yoder's relationship to Troeltsch's historical method might require extended inquiry as regards thinking about Constantinianism.

34. Erik Peterson, *Der Monotheismus als politisches Problem: Ein Beitrag zur Geschichte der politischen Theologie im Imperium Romanum* (Leipzig: Jakob Hegner, 1935), 71ff. (see especially p. 81: "Der *eine* Monarch auf Erden—und das ist für Euseb nur Konstantin—korrespondiert dem *einen* göttlichen Monarchen im Himmel." Hendrik Berkhof, *Kirche und Kaiser*, 100-102 and *Die Theologie des Eusebius von Caesarea* (Amsterdam: Uitgeversmaatschappij Holland, 1939), 53-59, 83-85.

35. G. H. Williams, "Christology and Church-State Relations in the Fourth Century," in *Church History* 20:3, 4 (September-December, 1951): 3-33, 3-26; notably 20:3:18: "The facility with which Eusebius could assimilate the Constantinian with the Messianic peace is connected . . . with the fact that for Eusebius the Logos was a subordinate *deuteros theos*, a mediator primarily in the cosmological rather than in the religious sense. Hence salvation was understood as coming through the might of a godly ruler." cf. Per Beskow, *Rex Gloriae: The Kingship of Christ in the Early Church*, trans. Eric J. Sharpe (Uppsala: Almqvist and Wiksells, 1962), esp. 161-175. See Beskow's negative assessment of Williams at pp. 316-324 and of Berkhof at pp. 325-328.

36. Williams, "Christology and Church-State Relations," 3:10. For Yoder's assessment of the ambiguity surrounding pro-Nicene theology and the Constantinian settlement, see *Preface to Theology*, 204: "If we look back at the politics between 325 and 431 [the ecumenical Councils of Nicea and Ephesus, respectively], at some of the theologians' methods and motives, at the personal quality of Constantine, or if we ask in what sense he was a Christian when he dictated this dogma [the *homoousion*], then we have to be dubious about giving this movement any authority."

37. Williams, "Christology and Church-State Relations," 3:6.

38. Ibid., 3:9.

39. Ibid., 3:5.

40. See, for thorough investigations of the usefulness of the notion of "Arian" as an historical term, the essays collected in Barnes and Williams, *Arianism after Arius*. Cf. Rowan Williams, *Arius: Heresy and Tradition* (London:

Darton, Longman and Todd, 1987) and Rowan Williams, ed., *The Making of Orthodoxy* (Cambridge, England: Cambridge University Press, 1989).

41. Yoder, *Preface to Theology*, 223.

42. See particularly, Lewis Ayres, "Re-thinking Nicaea, Chapter 1: The Emergence of the Christian Doctrine of God, AD 300-360" (unpublished draft), and Michel R. Barnes, "The Fourth Century as Trinitarian Canon," in *Christian Origins: Theology, Rhetoric, and Community*, ed. Lewis Ayres and Gareth Jones (New York: Routledge, 1998), 47-67.

43. Yoder, *Preface to Theology*, 223.

44. Yoder, "Constantinian Sources," 139.

45. Drake, *Constantine and the Bishops*, 432-433. That Yoder might well have objected to Drake's distinction between "definitions of Christian belief" and "thinking about what it meant to be Christian" does not, I think, invalidate the point that the idealized pre-Constantinian church was at least partly a reconstruction.

46. In this respect I disagree with Gerald Schlabach, who claims that "One thing . . . explanations for church-state accommodation have in common is their attempt to trace backwards toward some basic mistake or cluster of mistakes—a point at which early Christians begin to fall into temptation. If the fourth or third centuries do not adequately explain Constantinianism, then developments in the second or first century may do so. . . . Of course it might be hard to conclude such digging without eventually questioning the apostolic wisdom of calling Jesus 'Lord' and thus vindicating the language of dominance" ("Deuteronomic or Constantinian," 452). To the extent that Schlabach takes these reflections to characterize Yoder and to implicate him in a search for a basic problem in Christian ethics, I think he has missed the significance of Yoder's claim that "Any existing church is not only fallible but in fact peccable. That is why there needs to be a constant potential for reformation and in the more dramatic situations a readiness for the reformation even to be 'radical'" *Priestly Kingdom*, 5. In a similar vein, note, "Anabaptism and History," *The Priestly Kingdom*, 129: "It is not claimed that history always goes wrong or always needs to be reversed. A particular fall necessitates a particular restitution."

47. Yoder, "Anabaptism and History," 127.

48. Ibid.

49. Ibid., 128.

50. Ibid.

51. Yoder, "The Authority of Tradition," *The Priestly Kingdom*, 69.

52. Hans-Georg Gadamer, *Truth and Method*, 2nd. rev. ed., trans. Joel Weinsheimer and Donald G. Marshall (New York: Continuum, 1997), 299-300.

53. In a similar connection, Yoder, Gadamer, and possibly Michel Foucault share a set of sensibilities about how to respond to the methodological captivity that plagues contemporary approaches to history. One response, which

each rejects, would be further methodologization. Another more appropriate response would begin to help us reflect about the fragmentary and reified contemporary experience of history—a thinking about thinking wherein we discover that the character of our historicity is most obvious where there is the greatest rupture with thinking historically. The legacy of Constantinianism is one such site; the scientific ideal of objectivity and the linkages between knowledge and power are others.

54. Alasdair MacIntyre, "On Not Having the Last Word: Thoughts on Our Debts to Gadamer," in Jeff Malpas, Ulrich Arnswald, and Jens Kertscher, *Gadamer's Century: Essays in Honor of Hans-Georg Gadamer* (Cambridge, Mass.: MIT Press, 2002), 158.

55. Yoder, "The Authority of Tradition," 69.

56. Yoder, "Constantinian Sources ," 146-147.

57. Yoder, *Preface to Theology*, 223.

Chapter 7

Yoder and the Jews: Cosmopolitan Homelessness as Ecclesial Model

Duane K. Friesen

JOHN HOWARD YODER HAD A DEEP INTEREST IN the theological and ecclesiological connections between Diaspora Judaism[1] and the believers church tradition.[2] Yoder's exploration of the theological and ecclesiological implications of the Diaspora Jewish tradition for believers
church Christianity goes back to a series of five lectures he gave in the
Menno Simons Lectureship at Bethel College in 1982.[3]

The phrase which best captures Yoder's position, "cosmopolitan
homelessness," appears in Yoder's essay. "See How They Go with
Their Face to the Sun," in his book of essays, *For the Nations: Essays
Public & Evangelical*. "See how they go with their face to the sun,"
comes from Stephan Zweig's poem-drama "Jeremiah," written during World War I.

Yoder summarizes Zweig's thesis as follows: "To be scattered is
not an hiatus, after which normalcy will resume. From Jeremiah's
time on, rather, according to the message of the play, dispersion shall
be the calling of the Jewish faith community."[4] "Cosmopolitan homelessness" holds together two dimensions. These minority communities are "exiles," who have a distinctive identity as a pilgrim people
within the dominant cultures where they live. They are also called by

145

God to a cosmopolitan vision and mission to the larger world (not a withdrawn status as an ethnic enclave).

Yoder identifies a number of common features of the Jewish Diaspora and the believers church: the view of history, their peace narrative, a non-Constantinian way of thinking ethically, the logic of mission to the larger culture, and a decentralized view of authority of a community gathered around Scripture.

After elaborating on these common five features, I will take up an issue raised by A. James Reimer, whether a particularistic exilic vision can adequately address how God is at work in the larger cosmos and the nations beyond the exile community. A correlate of this issue is whether Yoder's emphasis upon de-centralized authority can adequately address problems of the larger social order.[5] Do these questions arise from a deeper problem, that Yoder's overall position is premised too much on a negative critique of Constantinianism? Does Yoder adequately develop a normative framework for "living on the land," living as a community, not just in opposition, but one called to seek the peace of the city where we dwell?[6]

COMMON FEATURES OF
DIASPORA JUDAISM AND THE BELIEVERS CHURCH

View of history

Diaspora Judaism and believers churches share a view of history. Israel and the church are called by God to be a people among the nations. The center of history is not empire (Babylon, Rome, Germany, the United States), but a people God has chosen from among the nations to be a light to all. Sociologically this history has been lived by a people who are on the margins, people for whom it is not an option to "be in charge." For Jews in the Diaspora it meant to live as a minority within the Babylonian, Persian, and Roman Empires, and later within Christendom and Islam. Until Constantine, Christians lived with a similar marginal status, and later within Christendom various renewal movements experienced a similar status: minorities who were not only not in charge, but had little or no influence on kings and princes, and what they commanded their armies to do.

The people in these movements, however, have a real historical past, a narrative that defines their identity, a narrative that can be contrasted with the narrative of empire. There is a fundamental continuity in the central story of the Bible beginning with God's call to Abraham to leave country and kindred to be a "blessing to the nations" and the call of God's anointed, Jesus, to be a light to the world. It is not a "mythic" story about cosmic origins, but a real historical story with names, places, and events that define a people's identity.

A peace narrative

Though the Jewish rabbis do not identify themselves as pacifists and are not doctrinaire advocates of nonviolence, they live out an ethic of nonviolence in the Diaspora. Yoder even titles a Menno Simons Lecture at Bethel College "Judaism as a Historic Peace Church." The basis of the rabbis' position, he says, was God's call, since Abraham, to be different amid the world's exercise of power and violent force. "They were committed to reasoning from within a worldview where the inscrutable omnipotence and sovereignty of ADONAI makes it inappropriate, if not blasphemous, to claim to save God's cause for Him."[7] Jews, in fact, practiced more faithfully Jesus' ethic of nonviolence than most Christians within Christendom who after Constantine adopted just war theory as a framework for the shape and control of the political order.[8] The basis for both the Jewish tradition of nonviolence and the believers church commitment to nonviolence is an alternative peace narrative of God's call to Abraham and to the church to be a light to the nations. This narrative stands in contrast, for example, with the story of America which James C. Juhnke and Carol M. Hunter summarize in their recent book:

> Our nation, we all instinctively assume, is a country made by war. In public schools we learn a history of freedom and independence won through war with Britain, land expansion and growth through war with Native Americans and Mexicans, preservation of the union and freedom for slaves through the Civil War, achievement of world power through naval power projected overseas, and deliverance of the world from Nazi and Community totalitarianism through war and threatened war.[9]

Unfortunately, with the development of political Zionism, and with the establishment of the State of Israel, many Jews have "bought into" the same blend of religion and empire that has been characteristic of the church since Constantine.

A non-Constantinian vision

Yoder calls the alternative identity of both the Jewish Diaspora and the believers church "non-Constantinian." By this he means that these communities did not define their primary goal as "making things come out right," or shaping their ethic to fit what was effective for the preservation of the empire. Instead their ethic was shaped by a vision of how God had called them to be an alternative community in the world that marched to the beat of a different drummer.

As we have already said, Yoder also calls this identity, "cosmopolitan homelessness." In the words of the second Century Epistle to Diognetus: "Every homeland is a foreign land, and every foreign land is our homeland." It is a tradition that Yoder says begins with the Letter of Jeremiah to the exiles, his advice to prosper in pagan Babylon and in Babylon to seek the peace of the city where they dwell, but where they are not in charge. This vision is "cosmopolitan," actually a wider worldview than that of Babylon or Rome. Though Rome encompassed a vast territory, it excluded civilizations where Jews had been living for centuries. As Yoder puts it,

> The Jewish world vision was *in lived experience* wider than was the Roman Empire.
>
> This social fact parallels the fundamental notion of monotheism. If there is but one God, then his dignity and power must somehow hold sway over other nations too. Other nations were not merely hypothetically imagined, in the sense that there must be someone out there beyond the confines of the Empire. Jews had cousins living there, worshiping in sister synagogues, and (for the case of Babylon) Jews around the Roman-ruled world received moral guidance from those centers outside Roman control. Likewise the way in which monotheism demanded detachment from civil religion was a safeguard of a wider worldview than the imperial one. We have been thinking so long of Jews as being in the ghetto and of Rome as being the world, that it takes a special mental effort to be able to come to terms with the fact that it was really the other way 'round.[10]

Further, we are so accustomed to using the term *sectarian* to designate Radical Reformation and believers church traditions as a minority group within nations that we have not adequately noticed the transnational identities of these groups. Their identity paradoxically can be more cosmopolitan than those whose Christians whose identification with "America" or some other empire is paramount.[11]

Missionary communities

People in these communities are called by God to a mission to the larger world. "Only the Jew Jesus, by announcing and accomplishing the fulfillment of God's promises to the Jews, could send out into the world a people of peace open to the Gentiles. Only the Jewish claim that the one true God, known to Abraham's children through their history, was also the Creator and sustainer of the other peoples as well, could enable mission without provincialism, cosmopolitan vision without empire."[12] In the words of Jeremiah's letter to the exiles, these communities are called to seek the peace of the city where they dwell. This could mean resistance to the dominant power and the willingness to suffer as martyrs. It could mean living out an alternative vision of life and witnessing to the dominant power about alternative ways to conduct public affairs. It could mean pioneering in areas not being addressed by the larger society. It could even mean, on occasion, to serve within creative niches at the behest of an imperial power (symbolized by Daniel, Esther, and Joseph in the Bible).

In his 1982 Bethel College lecture, "Paul: Jewish Missionary,"[13] Yoder draws on both Christian New Testament scholarship and Jewish scholarship on Christian origins to develop an argument against the standard account that Judaism was bound to a narrow Jewish ethnicity, whereas Paul the Christian extended the vision of God's people to include the Gentiles.[14] Most rabbis did not ask Gentiles to keep the law or to become full Jews, but they developed a theory based on God's covenant with Noah to explain how Gentiles can be accepted by God in the age to come on their own terms. Gentiles could become "God-fearers," free to attend synagogue services without observing Jewish circumcision and dietary laws, and provisions were made to be included as proselytes into the synagogue through baptism and circumcision.

In summary, Judaism in Paul's time was a missionary movement, though the mission to the Gentiles largely died out after the Jewish wars and the Fall of Jerusalem. Paul, a Jew in continuity with the majority of rabbis, believes that since the Messianic Age has dawned with Jesus, Gentiles do not need to become Jews to participate in the Torah of the Messiah.[15] Jews, furthermore, can continue to practice their observant customs, so long as they do not force Gentiles out of the synagogue. Paul argues not against "Judaism" (as if there existed a monolithic "normative" Judaism), but against some Jews who wanted to make of Jewish ceremonial law a requirement for being part of God's people. "Paul is not hardening the Jewish/Christian schism; he is denying or forbidding it. He is combating those who would precipitate schism by forcing believing Gentiles out of their fellowship."[16] In summary, with the birth of the church, when Jews and Gentiles embraced Jesus the Messiah as a light to the nations, they were not breaking from Judaism, but were in continuity with the commitment of mission to the nations that had been an integral part of Jewish Diaspora identity since Jeremiah.

A decentralized authority of a community gathered around Scripture

In the absence of the temple and a central political authority, Jews developed in the Diaspora a form of worship centered in the synagogue. The synagogue was a house of prayer, a gathering of believers around the scrolls of Scripture. A community was created that needed neither priest nor temple. Yoder argues that the "book" represents a form of transcendence, something beyond the community and any contemporary authority. "When the believing community is a beleaguered minority, what matters is rather that the book or the scroll is there, as the inescapable symbol for the axiom that our identity and our marching orders come from before and beyond the society in which we live, and as testimony to the past story which defines the community."[17] Though Yoder acknowledges that often people do not agree about what the book says, and sometimes there is much discontinuity between text and the believing community's practice, what matters is not so just what the book says but the principle of gathering around the book as a point of orientation for a community.

Central to the study of Torah were rabbis, teachers schooled in the interpretation of the Torah, who passed on their wisdom to disciples. Their teaching was passed on orally, then put in writing in the Mishnah about 200 C.E. Further commentary, known as the Gemara, developed to establish the scriptural foundations for the teachings of the different schools of rabbis identified in the Mishnah. Eventually all this commentary became the basis for the Jerusalem and Babylonian Talmud. We see here a highly de-centralized process of ongoing discernment of how the Scripture should be applied to life. It is a process that holds together the firm conviction that God reveals his will for humans in the Torah, while at the same time the interpretation of the Torah is always open, subject to ongoing debate. Jews of the Diaspora did not appeal to a creed, to a person like a pope, or to a special kind of centralized council to resolve arguments once and for all. They became unintentionally communities of a transnational character as they struggled many generations across the boundaries of empires and diverse cultures to consult the interpretations of rabbis about how Torah applies to life.

Yoder argues that "what the Babylonian Talmud does for Jews, the canon of apostolic writings is supposed to do for Christians. It can provide a fulcrum, or a fixed star, outside the Hellenistic-Roman system, morally and philosophically, although within it politically and geographically, whereby to evaluate both acceptable compromises and unacceptable betrayals." This "transcendence" was lost sociologically when the Christian church became imperially provincial. And also, he argues, the church became theologically provincial (paradoxically) when it began to borrow alien thought forms (e.g. Neo-Platonism). Jesus was detached from his Jewish roots, such that the radical ethical claims of Jesus, particularly his call to nonviolence, were watered down to fit the needs of empire.[18]

AN ANALYSIS OF YODER'S VIEW OF THE RELATIONSHIP BETWEEN "PARTICULARITY" AND "UNIVERSALITY"

A. James Reimer argues that Yoder does not show how the particular vision of the exile community is related to the larger world beyond this community. Reimer puts it this way: "For Yoder, because exilic culture is ethically and politically normative, it is not clear whether and how God is at work outside that alien community. If exile and Diaspora are the norm, how is a unified vision ever possible?"[19] Reimer also cites Old Testament scholar John W. Miller, who agrees with Yoder that God calls Israel and the church to be a blessing to the nations, but "where Yoder falls short is in not seeing this blessing in the context of the whole of creation and history."[20]

I agree with Reimer that Yoder does not fully address this question, particularly in his essays on Diaspora Judaism and its correspondence to the believers church tradition. But I do not agree that this failure to address this question is due to a flaw in Yoder's theology as such. For Yoder the particular Jewish Jesus who became flesh *IS* the Logos, the Lord of history, the One in whom all things are united. The ecclesiological implications are that the exilic and Diaspora communities, though particular, are witnesses of a universal vision. The church as Christ's body in the world, witnesses to a vision of shalom, a vision for the nations.

Yoder implicitly provides the grounds with his affirmation of an orthodox doctrine of the Trinity for a unified theory of culture, albeit from within the particularity of a believers church vision grounded in a Jewish Jesus who is both Lord and Logos. Jesus Christ, as one person in the Trinity, reveals the universal God of the cosmos. Though Yoder did not work out his position systematically, he presupposes implicitly an orthodox doctrine of the Trinity. We can see this in *The Politics of Jesus*[21] and his response to H. R. Niebuhr's treatment of the Trinity in *Christ and Culture*.

The intention of the post-Nicene doctrine of the Trinity was precisely *not* that through the Father, Son, and Spirit differing revelations come to us. The entire point of the debate around the nature of the Trinity was the concern of the church to say just the opposite, namely that in the incarnation and in the continuing life of the church under the Spirit there is but one God.[22]

I think John W. Miller's criticism of Yoder is misplaced. Miller is right that Yoder does not place the emphasis upon the God of the whole cosmos. That is because Yoder wants to be sure that we do not evade the importance of Jesus for ethics. However, the God of the covenant and the God of Jesus is the One who also creates the world and who is sovereign Lord of the nations. And because the God in Jesus Christ is the God of the cosmos and the nations, those faithful to the covenant and to their calling to be disciples can "seek the shalom of the city where they dwell."

Though Reimer acknowledges Yoder's Trinitarianism in the above mentioned sources, Yoder's lectures on Judaism raise doubts in Reimer's mind that Yoder presupposes classical orthodoxy.

> He seems more radically restitutionist than ever. He suggests that the Fall occurred not in the fourth century but in the second century with the apologists and the consequent loss of the early Jewish-Christian paradigm. The fall now occurs at the point where the Hebraic-Christian and Greco-Roman worldviews encounter each other in a creative synthesis.[23]

I think here Reimer's criticism of Yoder is misplaced. Yoder is not opposed to "translation" of the gospel into an idiom that is appropriate to different cultural settings. In other words, the problem is not that the gospel was adapted to the Greco-Roman setting. The question is whether a "translation" is faithful to the good news. In the translation of the gospel into the categories of Neo-Platonic thought, the rich particularity of the Jew Jesus and his radical call to discipleship in this world disappears.

Implicit in a believers church missionary vision is the commitment to "translate" the good news into the language of one's neighbor. For Yoder that means we need to be bilingual. It is important that we learn the language, the worldview, and culture of our neighbor. At the same time, it is critical that we be faithful to the good news that we share with our neighbor. The problem with the Neo-Platonic categories is that they are not adequate to convey the earthly embodied, call to discipleship of the Jew, Jesus. In a sense, then, the missionary calling of an exilic community requires both that we "Judaize" the language of the culture into which the good news is translated and that we find the appropriate idiom and categories within that culture to share the good news.

Yoder, as a non-foundationalist accepts the "gift" of particularity represented by Babel. He opposes the post-Enlightenment project to find a "third" foundationalist, objective, universal language beyond the particularity of cultural pluralism. Does this, then, not lead to relativism?

Yoder also objects to "babble," the position of some deconstructionists and postmoderns, the incommensurability of communicating across cultural boundaries. His answer to "babble" is not foundationalism but rather the affirmation of the possibility of translation, that the good news of the gospel can cross cultural barriers and be communicated to a variety of cultural contexts.[24] Translation is also an alternative to sectarianism. A sectarian is one who insists on the exclusive priority of his own language. In order for the "other" to become part of "us" they must adopt "our" language, and if not they are excluded.

The problem with Constantinianism is not the fact of "translation" of the good news into idioms that communicate to the larger culture concerning the peace of the city. Issues of peace, justice, and the order of society are integral to the good news of the gospel. The problem with Constantinianism is analogous to the problem with the categories of Neo-Platonism. The radical ethic of Jesus disappears in the translation. In the case of Constantine, the ethical categories of how to run and preserve the empire (e.g. the justification of war) replace the radical ethic of Jesus to love the enemy and overcome evil with good.

How do we translate the good news into a vision for the peace of the city without falling into the Constantinian mistake of evading Jesus' ethic in order that we might be successful in running the world? What would it mean to "live well on the land" and contribute positively to the peace of the city? Does the Diaspora and believers church model of the church contribute to or does it hinder a positive engagement with the larger culture? At the sociological level Reimer argues that Yoder's position is flawed because of his general suspicion of central organized authority. Reimer believes Yoder "idealizes decentralized diversity, and is suspicious. . . . of all centers of power and authority" (446). I believe Yoder's response to Jeffrey Stout in the article referred to above is the key to understanding Yoder's position. Yoder believes the story of the Tower of Babel reflects God's gift to humans.

> Babel in the myth of Genesis places the multiplicity of cultures under the sign of the divine will. . . . It was rebellious humankind, proud and probably fearful, who wanted to live all in one place, seeking to escape their dependence on divine benevolence by pulling back from the dispersion and reaching heaven on their own. It was JHWH who scattered them, for their own good, restoring his original plan. This scattering is still seen as divine benevolence in the missionary preaching of the Paul of Acts. It appears as "confusion" only when measured pejoratively against the simplicity of imperially enforced uniformity.[25]

The calling into being by God, therefore, of the particular communities of Israel and the church correlates with God's will for the world. Yoder's view of what it means to seek the peace of the nations, therefore, flows from Yoder's vision of the church. The church is not a hierarchal organized monolithic structure, but a transnational network of communities who, living within the diversity of cultural contexts, share and communicate with each other given this cultural diversity to discern together what it means to be faithful as followers of a common story. Yoder's model, therefore, of the good society is by analogy a culturally pluralistic network of communities rather than world government (to state the extreme opposite), or imperial domination by a monolithic power (symbolized by Constantine and by the United States today).[26]

Christian witness among the nations "to seek the peace of the city" entails, therefore, the translation of the good news into appropriate recommendations about how to "order" the city. For some readers of Yoder, this may sound like "Constantinianism." Chris Huebner, in his review of my book, *Artists, Citizens, Philosophers: Seeking the Peace of the City*, believes I follow Yoder when I suggest "that the stance of the church with respect to the world is best understood in terms of witness, by which he means a non-instrumentalist sense of simply 'being the church' as a model of an alternative way of life." However, when I use language about the church engaging the larger culture to change the world he argues that I "would do well to learn more thoroughly from Yoder, for whom non-Constantinianism involves giving up the assumption that it is up to us to ensure that history comes out right."[27]

Huebner's mistake is to assume that all forms of "instrumental reasoning" signal Constantinianism. I also do not read Yoder in quite the same way. In the *Politics of Jesus* Yoder, for example, says that "The primary social structure through which the gospel works *to change other structures* is that of the Christian community."[28] I have emphasized part of Yoder's statement to indicate a dimension of his thought too often overlooked. He does not oppose working in the larger society "to be effective" to bring about social change, so long as that is consistent with Jesus' call to discipleship—not to resort to the use of power and coercive force to "make things come out right." Instrumental reasoning is wrong when it over-rides faithfulness.

There is another kind of instrumental reasoning, however, when one asks what it means to witness faithfully. How do we do that effectively? How do we witness, for example, in behalf of the marginal within the body politic? What policies should the church recommend that can address the needs of the poor? How can we participate with fellow citizens to change a policy to address needs more effectively? To monolithically reject all forms of instrumental reasoning is simply non-sensical. Yoder argues that we do not have to choose between faithful but irrelevant dualism and relevant but unfaithful compromise. Yoder's more subtle and nuanced understanding of ethical reasoning is evident in his chapter, "The Hermeneutics of Peoplehood," in *The Priestly Kingdom: Social Ethics as Gospel*.

> By "practical moral reasoning" is meant that people make particular choices which are illuminated by their general faith commitments, *but which still need to be worked through by means of detailed here-and-now thought processes*. . . . One of the standard lessons any beginning student of religious or philosophical ethics learns is to tell the difference between an argument from duty and an argument from utility.. . . . The academic ethicist still sees it as his contribution to call for relative purity of type to bring the debates more under control. In a more communal and less monolingual context of discernment, the task of the teacher will rather be the opposite: to contribute to the community's awareness that *every decision includes elements of principle, elements of character and of due process, and elements of utility*." (emphasis added) [29]

Yoder's writings are full of references of the implications of a Christian vision for the ordering of society (e.g. nonviolent forms of conflict resolution, democratic decision making processes, restorative systems of justice instead of capital punishment, affirmation of religious liberty and pluralism). There is a clear line of continuity in Yoder's thinking that begins with his first major book, *The Christian Witness to the State*.[30] There he uses "middle axioms" language to designate how Christian social analysis "will usually coincide with the best informed secular analysis." In this book he refers to the following examples of Christian political judgment: international conflict, international government, international law, the ethics of war, the just war, the penalty of death, revolution, nuclear pacifism, civil disobedience, involvement in political responsibility, and the economic order. Though Yoder discontinues using the language of "middle axioms," he continues the practice of the analogical application of Christian moral reflection to the problems of the larger society beyond the church.

Though Yoder constantly warns against the temptation of Constantinianism, he does not in principle exclude Christian participation in the ordering of society. Christians can and should participate in the cities where they dwell to engage particular concrete problems on a case by case basis. Just as the Jewish Diaspora community and a believers church community discern what it means to be faithful in concrete situations in response to Torah and Jesus, so a Christian can and should be a participant in the cities where they dwell as they share with their neighbors how to address complex social and political questions. Yoder is wary of "grand visions" about how to order society because of the temptation to water down or evade Jesus' call to discipleship in the process, but he supports Christian participation in the community in the engagement of concrete issues on a case by case basis.[31] This is the logic of the missionary impetus of the Christian faith.

This dimension in Yoder's writing is hidden because of the overriding negative criticism of Constantinianism. I agree with Gerald W. Schlabach that "to define Constantinianism as the core problem for Christian social ethics is to concentrate our ethical reflection on the effort to avoid evil and unfaithfulness—rather than the challenge of embracing the good in a faithful manner."[32] Yoder's work tends to focus his readers primarily on the "Constantinian" problem, and that leads readers to overlook his emphasis on mission to "seek the peace of the city." Schlabach challenges us to embrace the positive question of how to live faithfully in the land and in the cities where we dwell. Can we approach this task not with the arrogance that we do not need God because we are running the world, but with humility and faithfulness grounded in God's gracious gift and call to follow the One who is Lord?

NOTES

1. By Diaspora Judaism Yoder means the tradition of Judaism that begins with the Babylonian exile. The Diaspora includes Jews who have lived faithfully as Jews within a variety of political and cultural situations without a temple in Jerusalem and without being in political control. After the Jewish Wars with Rome from 66-70 C.E. and the Bar Kokba revolt from 132-135 C.E. Jews lived as minority communities under the leadership of non-Zealot rabbis within empires where others were in charge until the establishment of the State of Israel in 1948. The spirit of this vision is captured in the teaching of Rabbi Yohanan ben Zakkai, who, when confronted with the ruin of the temple and Jerusalem said, "Be not grieved. We have another atonement as effective as this. And what is it? It is acts of loving kindness, as it is said, 'for I desire mercy, not sacrifice' (Hosea 6:6)." Quoted in Jacob Neusner, *Judaism in the Beginning of Christianity*, (Philadelphia: Fortress Press, 1984), 96.

2. Yoder thinks of "believer's church" in a very broad way to include not a specific denomination but rather a position taken by scores of renewal communities to live as an alternative witness to the way of Jesus within other dominant cultures. Sometime these communities have eventually become new denominations, and at other times they have remained renewal movements within established denominations.

3. The five lectures were titled "It Did Not Have to Be: Jewish/Christian Division; Jesus–Jewish Pacifist; Judaism as an Historical Peace Church; Paul–Jewish Missionary; Jewishness of Anabaptism." These lectures were given again at Earlham in 1985, and sometimes they are referred to as the Bethel/Earlham series. A. James Reimer in *The Wisdom of the Cross: Essays in Honor of John Howard Yoder* (Grand Rapids: Eerdmans, 1999), 440.

4. John H. Yoder, "See How They Go With Their Face to the Sun," *For the Nations: Essays Evangelical and Public* (Grand Rapids: Eerdmans, 1997), 51. This essay was first delivered as an address for a conference at Loyola Marymount University in 1995.

5. A. James Reimer, "Theological Orthodoxy and Jewish Christianity: A Personal Tribute to John Howard Yoder," in *The Wisdom of the Cross*, 430-438.

6. Gerald W. Schlabach identifies "living on the land," as the key problem of Christian social ethics. "After all, to define Constantinianism as the core problem for Christian social ethics is to concentrate our ethical reflection on the effort to avoid evil and unfaithfulness—rather than the challenge of em-

bracing the good in a faithful manner." "Deuteronomic or Constantinian: What is the Most Basic Problem for Christian Social Ethics?" in *The Wisdom of the Cross*, 450.

7. Yoder, "Jesus the Jewish Pacifist," 65, the second lecture in a series delivered at Bethel College in 1982 and Earlham in April 1985. The quotation is from the collection of essays titled *The Jewish-Christian Schism Revisited: A Bundle of Old Essays* (Elkhart, Ind.: Shalom Desktop Publications, 1996), 50.

8. "For two millennia Judaism has lived its ages of toleration and its ages of renewed exile or even martyrdom, sometimes within and sometimes outside the 'Christian' empires of East and West, but never have they reached for the sword. Their literature never justified violence, and in fact created a special genre of literature, the rabbinic rhapsodic 'praise of Peace.' Occasionally privileged after the model of Joseph, more often emigrating, frequently suffering martyrdom nonviolently, they were able to maintain identity without turf or sword, community without sovereignty. They thereby demonstrated pragmatically the viability of the ethic of Jeremiah and Jesus. In sum: *the Jews of the Diaspora were for over a millennium the closest thing to the ethic of Jesus* existing on any significant scale anywhere in Christendom." Yoder, Ibid., 60.

9. James C. Juhnke & Carol M. Hunter, *The Missing Peace: The Search for Nonviolent Alternatives in United States History* (Kitchener, Ont.: Pandora Press, 2001), 11.

10. Yoder, "Jesus the Jewish Pacifist," 50.

11. This is true too of various migrant groups "who are bound to other people in other places who are also heirs of the same story. Many migrant peoples over the centuries, especially refugee peoples, including in our day Armenians, Mennonites, Southeast Asians, and many others, have become unintentionally communities of a transnational character, depending on the grace of the nations which have given them refuge, bound to relatives in other lands." For Jews this cosmopolitan life has gone on for centuries through travel, intermarriage, or through the consultation of a prestigious rabbi being sent or invited from Babylon to Palestine, or from Spain to Egypt. Yoder, "Jesus the Jewish Pacifist," 57.

12. Ibid., 53.

13. In the Shalom Desktop publication of 1996, the chapter is titled "Paul the Judaizer."

14. Yoder makes reference to the ground breaking work of Krister Stendahl and a "whole generation of younger scholars" since Stendahl. On the Jewish side he makes significant use of the 1959 book by Hans Joachim Shoeps, *Paul: the Apostle's Theology in the Light of the History of Jewish Religion*.

15. Yoder puts it this way: "It was part of the messianic expectation that in the age to come all the nations would be drawn in, and would voluntarily want to know the will of God, which they would have to learn by asking Jews or by coming to Jerusalem. Paul simply puts two and two together. We recog-

nize in Jesus the in breaking of the messianic age. It is actually happening on a greater scale than before, that Gentiles who hear about Jesus come to the messianic synagogues. Conclusion: the will of God for our age is the active in-gathering of gentiles into a new kind of body." "Paul the Judaizer," (Elkhart, Ind.: Shalom Desktop, 1996), 71.

16. Ibid., 69. Yoder criticizes Rosemary Radford Reuther's argument in *Faith and Fratricide* for reading back into Paul later Christian supercessionism and antisemitism. Yoder argues that Reuther assumes the traditional Christian view that Paul "rejects the law." Yoder puts it this way: "Neither the ancient claim of institutional and legal supercession stretching from the apologetic fathers through medieval Catholicism nor the specific Lutheran way of seeing Christ as "the end of the Law" is faithful to what is really being said in Galatians and Romans. What Paul sees happening in Christ and in the Christian church, like what Jesus had said in Matthew, is the fulfillment and not the abolition of the meaning of Torah as covenant of grace. 'Fulfillment' is a permanently open border between what went before and what comes next" (72).

17. Ibid., 57.

18. Ibid., 59-60.

19. A. James Reimer, "Theological Orthodoxy and Jewish Christianity," in *The Wisdom of the Cross*, 447.

20. Ibid., 445.

21. "The view of Jesus being proposed here is more radically Nicene and Chalcedonian than other views. I do not here advocate an unheard-of modern understanding of Jesus. I ask rather that the implications of what the church has always said about Jesus as Word of the Father, as true God and true Man, be taken more seriously as relevant to our social problem, than ever before." John Howard Yoder, *The Politics of Jesus* 2nd. ed. (Grand Rapids: Eerdmans, 1994), 102.

22. Glen Stassen, D. M. Yeager, and John Howard Yoder. *Authentic Transformation: A New Vision of Christ and Culture*. (Nashville, Tenn.: Abingdon Press, 1996), 62.

23. Reimer, "Theological Orthodoxy and Jewish Christianity," 447.

24. See Yoder's article, "Meaning After Babble: With Jeffrey Stout beyond Relativism," *Journal of Religious Ethics*, 24:1 (Spring 1996): 125-138.

25. Ibid., 127. As we have already pointed out above, Yoder's concern is not Babel (This is God's gift.), but babble, "the intentional confusing of language by its human users," (127) and the belief in the inability in principle (what he calls "absolute relativism") of persons to communicate across cultural boundaries such that "accountable discourse is no longer possible." Examples (among others) of "programmatic hard relativism" are "the move beyond the fact of diversity to advocating epistemological nihilism," the formal denial of "the possibility of valid communication between/among communities with conflicting axioms," or "the claim to link the viability of a pluralist

society with relativism about truth." (128-129)

26. See Yoder's cautions about a highly centralized world government with no counter balances capable of limiting it. He prefers a modest role for the United Nations, and international cooperation that comes from widely dispersed contributions from sectors like agriculture, trade, and health, where the sanctions of coercive force are not just below the surface. See his *Christian Witness to the State* (Newton, Kan.: Faith and Life Press, 1964), 46.

27. Chris Huebner, Review of *Artists, Citizens, Philosophers: Seeking the Peace of the City* by Duane K. Friesen, in *The Mennonite Quarterly Review* 76:1 (January 2002) 137.

28. Yoder, *The Politics of Jesus*, 154.

29. John Howard Yoder *The Priestly Kingdom: Social Ethics as Gospel* (Notre Dame, Ind.: University of Notre Dame Press, 1984), 17, 36.

30. John Howard Yoder *The Christian Witness to the State* (Newton, Kan.: Faith and Life Press, 1964), 45.

31. There is not space in this paper to make the case that Gordon Kaufman's method for engagement with the larger society is similar to Yoder's, contrary to what many might think. Both support the practical engagement of the problems of society in the wider culture, consistent with a nonviolent ethic, on a case by case basis.

32. Gerald W. Schlabach, "Deuteronomic or Constantinian: What is the Most Basic Problem for Christian Social Ethics?" *The Wisdom of the Cross*, 450.

Chapter 8

ON EXILE: YODER, SAID, AND A THEOLOGY OF LAND AND RETURN

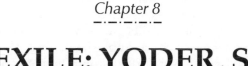

Alain Epp Weaver

We travel like other people, but we return to nowhere. As if traveling
Is the way of the clouds. We have buried our loved ones in the
Darkness of the clouds, between the roots of the trees.
And we said to our wives: go on giving birth to people like us
For hundreds of years so we can complete this journey
To the hour of a country, to a meter of the impossible.
We travel in the carriages of the psalms, sleep in the tents of the
Prophets and come out of the speech of the gypsies.
We measure space with a hoopoe's beak or sing to while away the
Distance and cleanse the light of the moon.
Your path is long so dream of seven women to bear this long path
On your shoulders. Shake for them palm trees so as to know their
Names and who'll be the mother of the boy of Galilee.
We have a country of words. Speak speak so we may know the end of
This travel.
—Mahmoud Darwish, "We Travel Like Other People" (1984)[1]

THE PALESTINIAN POET MAHMOUD DARWISH captures well the ambiguities of exile: travel without end; the pain of disconnection and the nostalgia of memory; the realization, encoded in the closing demand to

"Speak speak," that, for a people who have "a country of words," return from exile, the end of travel, will more likely than not be textual rather than physical. Darwish thus shows the reality of millions of Palestinians exiled from their land, living without fixed destination and sustained by the tenuous hope of return.

How should Palestinian exile, and exile more generally, be understood theologically? How should Christians understand the dreams of many exiles, dreams which often appear hopeless, of return to their homes? The late John Howard Yoder would probably have objected to starting with such general questions; they might have struck him as too "methodologistic," beginning theological reflection with abstract questions rather than with God's story in Scripture and the church.[2] Nevertheless, the drama of exile, especially as displayed in Jeremiah's call to the exiles to seek the peace of the city in which they find themselves (Jer. 29:7), played a key role in shaping Yoder's reading of Scripture, his ecclesiology and his missiology. As early as 1973 Yoder was probing the fruitfulness of the theme of exile for theology, writing in *Crosscurrents* of exile and exodus as two faces of liberation.[3] Exile, while painful, opens up a new chapter in the history of the people of God's radical reliance on God alone; God's people, for Yoder, are called to a nonviolent dependence on God which eschews the sovereignty of the sword in favor of embodying an alternative politics amid the Babylons of the world.

Yoder tentatively wondered about the relevance of this exilic, Jeremian vision for other exiled peoples. Was there "something about this Jewish vision of the dignity and ministry of the scattered people of God which might be echoed or replicated by other migrant peoples," Yoder asked. "Might there even be," he continued, "something helpful in this memory which would speak by a more distant analogy to the condition of peoples overwhelmed by imperial immigration, like the original Americans or Australians, or the Ainu or the Maori?"[4] Yoder recognized the potential affront of his question, I believe, and thus phrased it carefully. The provocation remains, however: Can those who have been violently uprooted from their lands embrace as good news the prophetic admonition to build houses and plant gardens in exile? What does Jeremiah's call mean for a return to one's land, for justice for the exiled refugee? Are justice and return endlessly deferred, postponed until the eschaton?

In this paper I seek to answer Yoder's question through an examination of the way in which the motif of exile functions in the thought and politics of the Palestinian-American critic Edward Said. After a summary of the role of exile in Yoder's reading of Scripture and his understanding of the church's mission, I turn to an examination of Edward Said's multifaceted appraisal of exile: while insisting on the harrowing character of exile, Said also expounds at length on the critical epistemological and moral possibilities opened up by exile. Finally, I sketch how an exilic consciousness of not being fully at home in one's home so long as injustice endures can contribute to a theology of living rightly and justly in the land, taking the particular case of justice in the land of Palestine/Israel as a springboard for my reflections; the view from exile, I suggest, poses a challenge to exclusionary politics which would deny a just place in the land for both Palestinian and Israeli.

JOHN HOWARD YODER ON
THE THEOLOGICAL POLITICS OF EXILE

Just as "Constantinianism" named for Yoder the perennial threat and temptation for the people of God, so did the Jeremian vision of the people of God living faithfully in exile form Yoder's positive vision for the church.[5] Grasping the importance of Jeremiah's call to the exiles for Yoder sheds light on his reading of Scripture, his understanding of church history, and his theology of Judaism.[6]

Let us begin with Scripture. Any Christian reading of the Old Testament must inevitably grapple with the plurality of voices and genres presented therein, interpreting its multiple strands and perspectives from God's definitive revelation in Jesus Christ.[7] The pacifist Christian, in particular, must struggle to understand the continuity of the two Testaments without resorting to a Marcionite dismissal of the God of the Old Testament and its wars of conquest as different from the God of love incarnated in Jesus Christ; rather, we must insist that the Triune God who reveals the nonviolent "grain of the universe" in Jesus' life, death and resurrection is the God of Israel.[8]

The theological vision from exile, Yoder argued, is one of "not being in charge." The exiles in Babylon do not rule the empire, or even a little corner of it, but instead live without sovereignty amid empire. Because "God is sovereign over history, there is no need . . . to seize (or subvert) sovereignty in order for God's will to be done." Living outside of the land, the community in Babylon relies solely on God for the sustaining of its life and becomes nonviolent in style and substance.[9] The continuity of this exilic vision with Yoder's ecclesiology should be clear: the church is the community called to go out into the world, into Diaspora (Matt. 25), a community which refuses to wield violent force, pointing instead to God's sovereignty and the conviction that Jesus has already triumphed over the powers of death, a triumph which will ultimately be revealed to all.[10]

If the continuity between Jeremiah's vision for the exiles and New Testament ecclesiology (as interpreted by Yoder) should be clear, the relationship between the call to exile and other parts of the Old Testament, such as the embrace of sovereign kingship in the land or the violent conquest of the land, might well appear to be one of tension, even conflict.[11] Yoder resolved this tension by focusing his attention on one thematic strand in the Old Testament, namely, that of Israel's radical dependence on God alone. Yoder did not deny and need not have denied that Scripture contains multiple strands, some of them in tension with one another. He did believe, however, that by identifying a strand within Scripture which repeatedly insists on God's absolute sovereignty and the people's accompanying dependence on God alone, one could highlight the continuity between YHWH the God of Israel and the Triune God incarnate in the nonviolent Messiah.[12]

Exile, Yoder suggested, did not simply equal punishment in Israel's history but represented a new opportunity for mission in the world and stood in continuity with God's previous gracious acts of dispersal, dispersal which highlighted the people of God's absolute dependence on God. Interpreting the Babel story in Genesis 11, Yoder wrote that "Diversity was the original divine intent; if God is good and diversity is good, then each of the many diverse identities which resulted from the multiplying of languages and the resultant scattering is also good."[13] The exile to Babylon then becomes on this reading another act of gracious dispersal: while the false prophets preach a premature return to the land, Jeremiah calls on the exiles to "seek the peace/salvation (*shalom*) of the city" (29:7).

Just as the exiles in Babylon live dependent on God and without reliance on their own sovereignty, so do the narratives of Exodus and the conquest of the land in the wars of YHWH exhibit a radical, completely dependent trust in God. "'Trust in JHWH [sic]/Adonai' is what opens the door to His saving intervention," claimed Yoder. "It is the opposite of making one's own political/military arrangements."[14] When addressing the question of Israelite monarchy with its violent exercise of sovereignty, Yoder turned to such texts as Judges 9, 1 Samuel 8 and Deuteronomy 17:14 and following, texts which exhibit "the antiroyal strand of the earlier history" of Israel which rejected any sovereign other than God. Exile, for Yoder, was not a brief hiatus between monarchy and the return to the land; rather, monarchy formed a problematic interruption in a history of dispersal as mission. "The move to Babylon," Yoder argued, "was not a two-generation parenthesis after which the Davidic or Solomonic project was supposed to take up again where it had left off. It was rather the beginning, under a firm, fresh prophetic mandate, of a new phase of the Mosaic project."[15] "Jeremiah's abandoning statehood for the future," Yoder continued, "is thus not so much forsaking an earlier hope as it is returning to the original trust in JHWH."[16]

Yoder thus identified a strand within the multiplicity of texts in the Old Testament which insists on complete dependence on God alone. Reading back from the Resurrection, we can not only observe that this strand stands in continuity with Jesus' nonviolent trust in God unto death but can identify certain aspects of that strand, such as Jeremiah's counsel to the exiles, as very close to the nonviolent coming of God in Jesus.[17] Jesus "rounds out" the mitigation of violence within the prophetic portions of the Old Testament, "and says that what it meant for Abraham to let God's future be in God's hands, and what it meant for Moses and Joshua to let the survival of the people be a miracle, means that now we don't have to kill anybody." This view is not "evolutionary" in that it does not assume some "survival of the fittest" in a contest of ideas, but Yoder concedes that its assumption of "organic growth under guidance" is in some ways similar to models which see evolutionary development within Scripture.[18]

"How can we sing the Lord's songs in a foreign land?" the Psalmist asks. "Painful as the question is," Yoder responded, "that is what the Jews learned to do, and do well."[19] Exile marked a new beginning in the history of God's people, one which would continue in the history of the early church and in the life of the Jewish people in Diaspora. While the church would lose sight of its calling to live as an embodied alternative to the violent politics of empire, becoming entangled in various forms of Constantinian compromise, Jewish communities in exile more successfully stayed true to the Jeremian call. "Occasionally privileged after the model of Joseph," Yoder noted, "more often emigrating, frequently suffering martyrdom nonviolently, [Jews] were able to maintain identity without turf or sword, community without sovereignty. They thereby demonstrated pragmatically the viability of the ethic of Jeremiah and Jesus.

In sum: the Jews of the Diaspora were for over a millennium the closest thing to the ethic of Jesus existing on any significant scale anywhere in Christendom."[20] Jewish communities in Diaspora thus lived as embodied critiques of Constantinian Christendom. Zionism, in contrast, as a late nineteenth-century form of European nationalism, represents a sharp departure from Jeremiah's exilic vision.[21]

An analysis of the ways in which Zionist discourse negates the Diaspora and an assessment of the possibilities of retrieving an exilic politics after Zionism will be my concern in the final part of this paper.

EDWARD SAID:
THE MORAL TASK OF THE EXILIC INTELLECTUAL

Yoder's appropriation of Jeremiah's call to the exiles has, I believe, undeniable power for an hermeneutics of Scripture, for an interpretation of church history, and for the articulation of a nonviolent ecclesiological politics. Can the call to seek the peace of the city of one's exile, however, also be heard as good news, even if only by "distant analogy," for the millions upon millions of people in the modern period violently uprooted by imperial and colonial practice? Is Jeremiah's call compatible with a struggle to return to one's land, with a struggle for justice? To answer these questions, I turn to a consideration of Palestinian dispossession and the writings of the most prolific, provocative, and insightful Palestinian intellectual, Edward Said, whose writings display the agonies and the promise of exile.

An initial caveat: Said, given his relentless critique of "religion," his stark opposition between "religious" (bad) and "secular" (good) criticism, and his desire to keep religion in proper bounds, might appear an odd thinker to bring into conversation with Yoder, someone who operated within an explicit theological horizon, who lived under the authority of God's Word and the church, and who resisted liberalism's attempts to confine the church's witness.[22] Apart from noting the similarities in the wide-ranging, "amateur" character of their intellects, what theologically useful observations can possibly come of bringing Yoder into conversation with such an aggressive, even dogmatic, secularist?[23]

Clearly, Said's treatment of religion is problematic at many levels. Nevertheless, I maintain that in Said's appropriation of exile we find a "distant analogy" (Yoder) to Jeremiah's vision for the people of God in exile; exploring these distant analogies, what Karl Barth called "secular parables of the kingdom," provides provocative material for reflection as Christians seek to articulate theologies of exile, land, and return.[24]

Palestinian existence is at root one of exile. Said observes that Palestinians form "a community, if at heart a community built on suffering and exile."[25] Palestinians are dispersed geographically, separated by borders, exiled from one another. In the Arab-Israeli war of 1948, in what Palestinians call *al-Nakba* ("the Catastrophe"), well over 700,000 Palestinians fled in fear from the fighting or were driven from their homes by Israeli military forces who destroyed over 400 villages. Many of these refugees and their descendants now live in U.N.-administered camps throughout the Middle East, denied the possibility of returning to their homes and properties. For the Palestinians left behind in what became the State of Israel, many were classified as "present absentees" under the Absentee Property Law of 1951 and denied return to their land.

Tens of thousands more Palestinians, many of them already refugees, became refugees once more in 1967, driven out of Mandate Palestine across the Jordan River by Israeli forces. Since 1967, for Palestinians in the occupied territories of the West Bank, East Jerusalem, and the Gaza Strip, dispossession has taken on a variety of forms. The Israeli civil administration confiscates land from Palestinians for the construction of colonies illegal under international law; Israeli bulldozers destroy Palestinian homes and rip up Palestinian orchards and vineyards; checkpoints and roadblocks separate Palestinian from Palestinian, making travel between, say, the West Bank and the Gaza Strip nearly impossible, while travel within the north and south of the West Bank becomes excruciatingly long, humiliating, and, at times, dangerous.[26]

Palestinians are thus continually ripped out of their contexts and find themselves travelers in a strange world. "The Palestinian is very much a person in transit," Said notes. "Suitcase or bundle of possessions in hand, each family vacates territory left behind for others, even as new boundaries are traversed, new opportunities created, new realities set up."[27] If, as Said indicates, exile creates "new opportunities" (to which we will return below), exile also is profoundly alienating. "Exile is a series of portraits without names, without contexts," Said observes. "Images that are largely unexplained, nameless, mute."[28]

Without continuity of place, Palestinians experience no continuity of identity. "Palestinian life is scattered, discontinuous, marked by the artificial and imposed arrangements of interrupted or confined space, by the dislocations and unsynchronized rhythms of disturbed time," Said explains, "where no straight line leads from home to birthplace to school to maturity, all events are accidents, all progress is a digression, all residence is exile."[29] De-centered, out of place, Palestinian life becomes one of travel without fixed destination: "Our truest reality is expressed in the way we cross over from one place to another," Said insists. "We are migrants and perhaps hybrids in, but not of, any situation in which we find ourselves. This is the deepest continuity of our lives as a nation in exile and constantly on the move."[30]

Rupture of continuity is the fate of the defeated, while the victors, the powerful, remain in place. "Continuity for *them*, the dominant population," Said notes, is opposed to "discontinuity for *us*, the dispossessed and dispersed."[31] Said's emphasis on the Palestinians' "privilege of obduracy," their steadfastness (*sumud*), the declaration that "Here we are, unmoved by your power, proceeding with our lives and with future generations," is a way of desperately trying to hold on amid the transit of exile, so that the de-centeredness of exile does not become dissolution.[32]

Said strenuously objects to any romanticizing of exile. "Exile is one of the saddest fates," he claims. "There has always been an association between the idea of exile and the terrors of being a leper, a social and moral untouchable."[33] For Palestinians, the experience of exile has not only been physically and emotionally painful, but has had negative effects on individual exiles and the exiled community as a whole. "Our collective history *fil-kharij* ('in the exterior') or in the *manfa* and *ghurba* ('exile' and 'estrangement') has been singularly unsuccessful," Said judges, "progressively graceless, unblessed, more and more eccentric, de-centered, and alienated."[34] Exile can turn people inward, generating a form of sectarian withdrawal which shuns those outside the community.[35] Exile is a "jealous state," Said observes, which can create "an exaggerated sense of group solidarity, and a passionate hostility to outsiders, even those who may in fact be in the same predicament as you."[36]

Ripped out of place, the exile often seeks solace in uncritical commitment to political parties and institutions, a tendency Said, a perpetual critic of the Palestine Liberation Organization, has carefully resisted. Those, meanwhile, who resist the temptation to subscribe blindly to political programs face the temptation of individualistic withdrawal away from all communities. Exile is marked, Said suggests, by "the sheer fact of isolation and displacement, which produces the kind of narcissistic masochism that resists all efforts at amelioration, acculturation, and community. At this extreme," Said warns, "the exile can make a fetish of exile, a practice that distances him or her from all connections and commitments."[37]

Warning against finding a moral within exile, Said demands that the reality of life in the refugee camp be given priority over the literature produced by such exiles as James Joyce and Vladimir Nabokov in any evaluation of exile. "Exiled poets and writers lend dignity to a condition legislated to deny dignity—to deny an identity to people," Said maintains. "To concentrate on exile as a contemporary political punishment," he counsels, "you must therefore map territories of experience beyond those mapped by the literature of exile itself. You must first set aside Joyce and Nabokov and think instead of the uncountable masses for whom U.N. agencies have been created."[38] Literature and religion, Said believes, run the risk of downplaying the horrors of exile in the interests of extracting new insights from exile itself. In contrast, Said insists that

> On the twentieth-century scale, exile is neither aesthetically nor humanistically comprehensible: at most the literature about exile objectifies an anguish and a predicament most people rarely experience first hand; but to think of the exile informing this literature as beneficially humanistic is to banalize its mutilations, the losses it inflicts on those who suffer them, the muteness with which it responds to any attempt to understand it as 'good for us.' Is it not true that the views of exile in literature and, moreover, in religion obscure what is truly horrendous: that exile is irremediably secular and unbearably historical?[39]

Here Said would appear to be challenging Yoder's theological appropriation of exile directly, accusing this religious view which uncovers a dignity of the vocation of the exilic community of banalizing the losses exile inflicts on those who undergo it.

Said's caution about an aesthetic or religious amelioration of exile's pains serves as a needed reminder not to lose sight of the fact that exile does not simply name a concept but names a condition in which millions of people live. That said, however, it is equally important to recognize that, just as Yoder articulates a missiological vocation for the people of God in exile, so Said argues that exile opens up an intellectual and moral space which provides a place for the intellectual from within which to resist attempts to co-opt him or her into becoming an apologist for power and which creates a discomfort with being settled in one's home so long as injustice forces homelessness on others. Exile, Said believes, is the proper *place* for the critic, the intellectual. "If you think about exile as a permanent state," Said says,

> both in the literal and in the intellectual sense, then it's a much
> more promising, if difficult, thing. Then you're really talking
> about movement, about homelessness in the sense in which
> [Georg] Lukacs talks about it in *The Theory of the Novel*—'tran-
> scendental homelessness'—which can acquire a particular intel-
> lectual mission that I associate with criticism.[40]

While exile, Said recognizes, "is an *actual* condition," it also functions
in Said's thought as "a *metaphorical* condition." Developing a distinction between insider and outsider intellectuals reminiscent of Yoder's
contrast between the Constantinian and free churches, Said differen-
tiates between

> those on the one hand who belong fully to the society as it is,
> who flourish in it without an overwhelming sense of dissonance
> or dissent, those who can be called yea-sayers; and on the other
> hand, the nay-sayers, the individuals at odds with their society
> and therefore outsiders and exiles so far as privileges, power,
> and honors are concerned.[41]

The responsibility of the intellectual, as articulated by Said in his
1993 Reith lectures, is to offer a critique from exile. "Exile for the intellectual in this metaphysical sense," Said explains, "is restlessness,
movement, constantly being unsettled, and unsettling others. You
cannot go back to some earlier and perhaps more stable condition of
being at home; and, alas, you can never fully arrive, be at one with
your new home or situation."[42]

Even those who have not experienced the pain of being physically uprooted from their homes can be marginal to the powers (of the
academy, government, the news media, and so forth) which reward
uncritical support for policies which oppress, exclude and dispossess. "Exile means that you are always going to be marginal," Said
claims. "Exile is a model for the intellectual who is tempted, and even
beset and overwhelmed, by the rewards of accommodation, yea-say-
ing, settling in."[43] Furthermore, the exilic intellectual should not suc-
cumb to a morose despair. "The intellectual in exile is," according to
Said, "necessarily ironic, skeptical, even playful—but not cynical."[44]

Even more than to Georg Lukacs' notion of "transcendental
homelessness," Said's positive appropriation of exile for his construal
of the intellectual vocation owes a debt to the reflections of the German Jewish theorist Theodor Adorno on dwelling. In his biographical

reflections, *Minima Moralia*, Adorno asserted that

> Dwelling, in the proper sense, is now impossible. The traditional residences we grew up in have grown intolerable: each trait of comfort in them is paid for with a betrayal of knowledge, each vestige of shelter with the musty pact of family interests. . . . The house is past . . . it is part of morality not to be at home in one's home.[45]

Adorno's insight, amplified by Said, is that particular economic and political configurations make the condition of having a home, of landedness one could also say, possible; it is "part of morality," then, to recognize how these economic and political systems also exclude others from the condition of landedness. In the case of Palestine/Israel, we will see, this insight can be deployed to suggest that no one, neither Palestinian nor Israeli, can truly be "at home" in the land so long as the structures which generate homelessness are perpetuated.

Adorno, having grasped the impossibility of dwelling securely given the knowledge of the conditions which make such dwelling possible, looked to the text, to literary production, for new dwelling. "In his text, the writer sets up house," Adorno suggested. "For a man who no longer has a homeland, writing becomes a place to live." Text provides only elusive comfort, however; Adorno noted that "In the end, the writer is not even allowed to live in his writing."[46]

Said develops Adorno's point, noting that the intellectual in his or her writing "achieves at most a provisional satisfaction, which is quickly ambushed by doubt, and a need to rewrite and redo that renders the text uninhabitable."[47] A comparison to Yoder proves useful at this point: while doubt and existential agony drive Said's exilic intellectual to rewrite her text again and again, the exilic community—the church—for Yoder is driven not by doubt but by the workings of the Holy Spirit to engage continually in the theological, missionary task of bringing the gospel into new thought worlds. Lacking any theological horizon, Said can only view the *poeisis* of the text as production and construction, whereas for the church the textual task of revising and renewing its proclamation of the gospel occurs within the framework of *pathos*, of a suffering receptivity to the Word of the Triune God.[48]

Said does, it turns out, "redeem" exile by stressing its moral possibilities; in particular, the exile, because she is not at home in her home, can resist accommodation to the powers, intellectual and political, which exclude and dispossess. Is this critically beneficial aspect

of exile, however, compatible with a struggle to end the physical condition of exile? Specifically, in the case of Palestinian refugees and
other Palestinians who have lost their lands, can one work for *al-
Awdah* (return) and not lose the moral perspective granted by exile?
This question relates to our earlier question of whether or not Yoder's
exilic politics could speak to a theology of landedness, of justice in the
land. To begin to tackle this question, let us examine how Said discusses the right of Palestinian refugees to return.

On the one hand, return is clearly not *only* a metaphorical concept
for Said. In a volume of essays examining Palestinian refugee rights
and ways to press for return and compensation, Said expresses dis-
may with what he views as the current Palestinian leadership's historical amnesia and willingness to forgo the demand for return; what
Palestinians must do, Said urges, is to "press the claims for return and
compensation in earnest with new leaders." Said cites as exemplary
the work of the Badil Refugee Resource Center and the Palestinian re-
searcher Salman Abu Sitta for their work on developing concrete
plans and campaigns for the actual return of refugees.[49]

On the other hand, Said also writes about return in a more
metaphorical fashion and warns against an easy symmetry between
exile and return which threatens to undermine the moral insights
exile provides. "All of us speak of *awdah*, 'return,'" Said notes,

> but do we mean that literally, or do we mean 'we must restore
> ourselves to ourselves'? The latter is the real point, I think, al-
> though I know of many Palestinians who want their houses and
> their way of life back, exactly. But is there any place that fits us,
> together with our accumulated memories and experiences?[50]

Exile, by separating people from place, threatens to separate people
from their history, de-centering and disorienting them to the point of
threatening their identity. What return would then mean is a "return
to oneself, that is to say, a return to history, so that we understand
what exactly happened, why it happened, and who we are. That we
are a people from that land, maybe not living there, but with important historical claims and roots."[51]

The greatness of Palestinian poet Mahmoud Darwish, Said argues, consists in his refusal in his poems to provide the reader with an
easy return, with simple closure: Darwish's work, Said contends,
"amounts to an epic effort to transform the lyrics of loss into the in-
definitely postponed drama of return. . . . The pathos of exile is in the
loss of contact with the solidity and the satisfaction of earth: home-

coming is out of the question."[52] A return which forsakes the moral insights of exile, a return which reaches back to retrieve a pristine past without concern for the human cost, must be avoided.

The Zionist project of a return to bring closure to Jewish exile stands for Said in marked contrast to the positive dimensions of Palestinian exile. Darwish, he believes, captures the key dimensions of the exilic experience, dimensions vital to the critical intellectual's task: "Fragments over wholes. Restless nomadic activity over the settlements of held territory. Criticism over resignation. . . . Attention, alertness, focus. To do as others do, but somehow to stand apart. To tell your story in pieces, *as it is*."[53] The openness of exile presents more powerful political and moral possibilities for the intellectual, Said emphasizes, than the closed symmetry of Zionist return.

The broken story of Palestinian exile, Said observes, occurs "alongside and intervening in a closed orbit of Jewish exile and a recuperated, much-celebrated patriotism of which Israel is the emblem. Better our wanderings," Said goes on to suggest, "than the horrid, clanging shutters of their return. The open secular element, and not the symmetry of redemption."[54]

AN EXILIC POLITICS OF LAND AND RETURN?

Said's positive appropriation of exile as a critical posture provides, I believe, a positive answer to Yoder's question about whether or not Jeremiah's vision for the exilic community might speak by "distant analogy" to other dispossessed peoples. Pressing questions remain, however. Can Yoder's exilic politics of the church as the nonviolent body of Christ in Diaspora speak to the call for justice and right living in the land, to the desire, the justice, of people returning to their homes? Gerald Schlabach, in a friendly challenge to Yoder's "Jeremian" reading of Scripture and church history, provides a helpful reminder of the "Deuteronomic" admonition to live rightly in the land (cf. Deut. 6-9). European-American Christians, particularly those in urban and suburban settings whose livelihoods are not dependent on the cultivation of the land, could be tempted to confuse Jeremiah's vision for life in exile with the rootless, virtual reality of much postmodernist thought. Such confusion would be self-deceptive, in that it would obscure the ways in which general North American prosperity has been built at the expense and on the land of its original inhabitants—and would further avoid the desire of many exiled peoples to return to live justly in the land. Schlabach sharply observes that "we do no favor to any dispossessed people if we think of land only in a figurative rather than an earthy sense."[55]

If, however, we do not avoid the challenges of return and justice, can we envision a politics of return, a politics of living rightly in the land, which does not simply replicate injustice and create new exiles in the wake of return?

To answer these questions, I will first examine how traditional Zionist discourse about a Jewish "return" from exile was not only dependent on a binary opposition between exile and return but that such discourse depended on the erasure of the indigenous Arab Palestinian presence. Posited was an "empty land" in which the drama of the return from exile might unfold.[56] In practice, as discussed above, this discourse translated into the expulsion of hundreds of thousands of Palestinians from their homes and continues to underwrite Palestinian dispossession today. For a future in Palestine/Israel which does not depend on the violent uprooting of others, we must paradoxically articulate *an exilic politics of land and return.* "Christians can live rightly in the 'land' that God gives," Schlabach suggests, "only if they sustain a tension with landedness itself."[57] Part of this tension, I suggest, is not being fully "at home" in the land so long as others are excluded from the benefits of landedness.

"The binarism of homeland/exile is central to Zionism," writes Laurence Silberstein in his perceptive study of "postzionist" debates within Israel.[58] The *homeland* of Eretz Yisrael and the *exile* of Jewish life elsewhere are not complementary in traditional Zionist discourse but stand, rather, in tension, even contradiction. Sander Gilman observes that Zionist discourse places the land at the center and diasporic communities on the periphery. This model, however, is not innocent of ideological baggage, however, but "is in truth a symbolic structure of the understanding of the impossibility of a Diasporic life within this model of center and periphery. Such a definition," Gilman continues, "demands the existence of a 'real' center and thus defines the Jews in terms of their relationships to that center."[59]

Silberstein delineates a series of binary oppositions issuing from the initial opposition of exile and homeland:

> homeland as a source of security, stability, refugee, nurturing, safety/exile as site of danger, insecurity, instability, threat, anxiety; heimlich/unheimlich; homeland is good/exile is bad; homeland is productive/exile is parasitic; homeland is conducive/exile is not conducive to redemption through labor; homeland is welcoming/exile is hostile; homeland is life-giv-

ing/exile is life-threatening; homeland is creative/exile is stulti-
fying; homeland is nurturing to Jewish national culture/exile is
destructive; homeland is unifying/exile is fragmenting.60

These oppositions present life in exile as an intolerable condition
whose only cure can be found in immigration to the "homeland." The
Hebrew word for immigration to Israel, *aliyah*, or ascent, encodes the
negative valuation which Zionism accords life in Diaspora; those
who grow disenchanted with life in Israel, meanwhile, are classified
as *yoridim*, or "those who descend."

Zionism, in most of its traditional forms, thus meant the "negation of the Diaspora" (*shelilat ha-galuth*). "The fulfillment of the Zionist dream," Silberstein explains, "depends upon acts of deterritorial-
ization and reterritorialization. . . . Jews and Jewish culture must be
deterritorialized from Diaspora spaces and reterritorialized in the
spaces of the homeland." Silberstein also perceptively notes that the
"reterritorialization" of Jewish immigrants into Mandate Palestine
eventually involved the "deterritorializing and reterritorializing of
large numbers of Palestinian Arabs, particularly during the 1948
War."61

Israeli political theorist Amnon Raz-Krakotzkin argues persua-
sively that the traditional Zionist negation of the Diaspora went
hand-in-hand with a negation of a prior Palestinian presence in the
land. "The definition of zionist settlement as an expression of '*shelilat
hagalut*'[negation of diaspora] and '*shivat haam*' [the return of the na-
tion] to its homeland," Raz-Krakotzkin contends, "prevented relating
to the collective yearnings of the local Arab population and its perspective. It [also] undoubtedly made it impossible to turn the fact of
this collective's existence into an essential foundation for establishing
a new Jewish identity."62

Raz-Krakotzkin argues that the Zionist valorization of a "return
to history" accepted the Christian and Enlightenment perception that
exilic existence had been an exclusion from history, an exclusion from
grace.63 The Zionist "return to history," sadly, has mirrored much of
the Christian West's violent and exclusivist practice. "The historical
conception of *shelilat hagalut*, the emptiness of Jewish time that sepa-
rates the loss of sovereignty over the land and its renewed settlement," Raz-Krakotzkin suggests, "is completed in a direct way
through the image of the land—the place for the realization and resolution of history—as an 'empty land.'"64 The distance between conceiving of the land as empty and actually emptying the land of its indigenous inhabitants proved unfortunately short.

To counter Zionist discourse and practice of dispossession, Raz-Krakotzkin proposes to recover exile, or *galut*, as a critical concept. Exile as a concept, for Raz-Krakotzkin, represents an "absence, the consciousness of being in an incomplete present, the consciousness of a blemished world." The absence, moreover, involves a lack of justice for Palestinians. To "return" from exile, then, must mean justice for the dispossessed. To yearn for redemption, Raz-Krakotzkin maintains, is to engage in political activity "that values the perspective of the oppressed, the only perspective from which a moral stance can develop."[65] A recovery of exile as a critical concept demands that Israeli Jews incorporate the consciousness of exiled Palestinians into their own aching for return. As Silberstein explains Raz-Krakotzkin's position, "By identifying with and assuming responsibility for, attending to, and responding to 'the consciousness of the conquered Palestinian,' the Jew recovers the 'principles embodied in the theological concept of galut.'"[66]

The critical use to which a secular political theorist like Raz-Krakotzkin puts exile finds a theological counterpart in the Jewish theologian Marc Ellis' recent insistence on exile as the proper *place* for prophetic Jewish communities. For Ellis, "the reality of exile is less the return to geography or tradition than it is a journey without return."[67] While certainly not downplaying the painful history of many Jewish communities in the Diaspora, Ellis also views as a threat to Jewish self-understanding the assimilation of Judaism in the United States and in Israel to the state and to power, a "Constantinian Judaism" which threatens to undermine the Jewish prophetic voice from exile. Ellis notes that "the assimilation to the state and power itself creates a wave of dissent," and that "there are Jews in Israel and the United States who oppose injustice and therefore refuse this assimilation." Amid such factors, Ellis envisions a community choosing exile from structures of power to stand in solidarity with those marginalized and excluded by power. Those in the exilic community then work together for a "return" which means justice for all, not simply landedness for some at the expense of others.[68]

A recovery of exile as a critical concept for political theory or for a theology of the people of God seeking shalom for all will be critical not only of exclusivist Zionist practice but also of any narrow nationalism, including Palestinian nationalism, which would threaten to exclude others from sharing in God's gift of landed security. In this critique Edward Said would again be an ally. While typically viewed as a champion of Palestinian nationalism, Said does not view Palestinian statehood as an end in itself, but rather as one potential way for bringing landed security to all in Palestine/Israel.

In recent years, in fact, Said has become increasingly critical of political arrangements in Palestine/Israel based on separation. "The idea of separation is an idea that I'm just sort of terminally opposed to," Said explains, "just as I'm opposed to most forms of nationalism, just as I'm opposed to secession, to isolation, to separatism of one sort or another."[69] Politics of separation too easily becomes a politics of apartheid, with one group enjoying benefits and privileges denied to the other.[70] As an alternative to the politics of separation, Said offers the model of the binational state in all of Mandate Palestine, a state in which Jews and Palestinians live as equal citizens. In a fascinating interview with Ari Shavit of the leading Israeli newspaper *Ha'aretz*, Said connects his appropriation of Adorno's critique of the home with his support for a binational state. "Adorno says that in the twentieth century the idea of home has been superseded," Said begins.

> I suppose part of my critique of Zionism is that it attaches too much importance to home. Saying, we need a home. And we'll do anything to get a home, even if it means making others homeless. Why do you think I'm so interested in the binational state? Because I want a rich fabric of some sort, which no one can fully comprehend, and no one can fully own. I never understood the idea of this is my place, and you are out. I do not appreciate going back to the origin, to the pure. Even if I were a Jew, I'd fight against it. And it won't last. Take it from me Ari. Take my word for it. I'm older than you. It won't even be remembered.

Shavit replies to Said, "You sound very Jewish," to which Said playfully and somewhat provocatively responds, "Of course. I'm the last Jewish intellectual. . . . The only true follower of Adorno. Let me put it this way: I'm a Jewish-Palestinian."[71]

Said, Ellis, and Raz-Krakotzkin all articulate in similar ways an exilic politics of land and return, a politics which embraces the challenge of living rightly in the land and nonviolently struggles for a return to the land of the dispossessed but which maintains an enduring tension with landedness. The late Palestinian-Israeli writer, Emile Habiby, summed up the necessary tensions of an exilic politics of land when he spoke of a "freedom of longing for the land within the land."[72] This "longing for the land within the land," suggests Raz-Krakotzkin, can be "a new starting point of all who dwell in the land, a basis for their partnership."[73]

John Howard Yoder, focused as he was on the church's calling to embody a nonviolent politics amid the Babylons of the worlds, was wary of attempts to theorize the shape of the ideal state, deeming such efforts as surreptitiously "Constantinian" attempts to identify the state rather than the church as the primary bearer of the gospel of reconciliation, renewal and redemption.[74] Yoder probably would therefore have been skeptical of the enthusiasm with which Said promotes the binational state.

That said, Yoder did not shy away from *ad hoc* engagements with state, encouraging Christians to target particular abuses rather than offering up grand political schemes. Yoder's understanding of the people of God as a political body living nonviolently amid empires while seeking their peace and welfare is, moreover, compatible with the exilic politics of land and return articulated by Ellis, Raz-Krakotzkin, and Said. This is the case even as it also operates within an eschatological horizon which animates Yoder's vision with more reasons for hope than can be provided by the secular proponents of an exilic politics like Said and Raz-Krakotzkin. Christians, together with others, must embrace the challenge of living rightly in the land: this can include calling for just distribution of land (see, for example, Yoder's treatment of the Jubilee), and working nonviolently for landed security for refugees.[75]

Part of living rightly in the land, however, will mean living lightly: Christians, as citizens of the heavenly city on pilgrimage in the Babylons of the world, will not use violence to establish justice in the land or to bring about a return to the land. Rather than pursue the sovereignty of the sword, they will pray unceasingly and work nonviolently, impelled by a "longing for the land within the land," for the day when all of God's children will dwell securely within the land which God so graciously gives.

NOTES

1. Mahmoud Darwish, "We Travel Like Other People," included in Larry Towell, *Then Palestine* (New York: Aperture, 1998), 32.

2. For Yoder on "methodologism," see his article, "Walk and Word: The Alternatives to Methodologism," in *Theology without Foundations: Religious Practice and the Future of Theological Truth*, ed. Stanley Hauerwas, Nancey Murphy, and Mark Nation (Nashville: Abingdon Press, 1994), 77-90.

3. .John Howard Yoder, "Exodus and Exile: Two Faces of Liberation," *Crosscurrents* (Fall 1973): 279-309.

4. John Howard Yoder, *For the Nations: Essays Public and Evangelical* (Grand Rapids: Eerdmans, 1997), 82.

5. For Yoder, "Constantinianism" did not simply name the church's alliance with and dissolution into the violent politics of empire, but also designated the perennial temptation for the church to abandon discipleship to its nonviolent Lord in favor of alignment with other, allegedly wider, social movements. For a nuanced treatment of Yoder on "Constantinianism," see Michael G. Cartwright, "Radical Reform, Radical Catholicity: John Howard Yoder's Vision of the Faithful Church," in John Howard Yoder, *The Royal Priesthood: Essays Ecclesiological and Ecumenical* (Grand Rapids: Eerdmans, 1994), esp. 5-14. See also Craig A. Carter, *The Politics of the Cross: The Theology and Social Ethics of John Howard Yoder* (Grand Rapids: Brazos Press, 2001), 155-178; and Alain Epp Weaver, "After Politics: John Howard Yoder, Body Politics, and the Witnessing Church," *The Review of Politics* 61:4 (Fall 1999): 649-652.

6. Yoder's unpublished writings on Judaism, mostly consisting of lectures delivered at Bethel College in Kansas, Earlham College in Indiana, and the Tantur Ecumenical Institute in Jerusalem, were collected by Yoder as *The Jewish-Christian Schism Revisited: A Bundle of Old Essays* (Elkhart, Ind.: Shalom Desktop Publication, 1996). These pioneering and provocative essays were published in the Radical Traditions series (*The Jewish-Chrisian Schism*, ed. Michael Cartwright and Peter Ochs (Grand Rapids: Eerdmans, 2003)). For a more thorough discussion of Yoder's appropriation of Jeremiah's call to the exiles for a reading of Scripture, an interpretation of church history, and a theology of Judaism, see Alain Epp Weaver, *Constantinianism, Zionism, Diaspora: Toward a Political Theology of Exile and Return* (Akron, Pa.: Mennonite Central Committee Occasional Paper #28, 2002), 13-22.

7. While I am sympathetic to those who wish to substitute the term *Hebrew Bible* for Old Testament, I do not believe that "Old" necessarily implies a supersessionist approach to Judaism: think of the wisdom of elders, for example, or the aging of a fine wine.

8. The phrase, "with the grain of the universe," is Yoder's. See his article, "Armaments and Eschatology," *Studies in Christian Ethics* 1 (1988): 43-61. Stanley Hauerwas recently appropriated it as the title of his Gifford lectures; see Hauerwas, *With the Grain of the Universe: The Church's Witness and Natural Theology* (Grand Rapids: Brazos Press, 2001). Both Yoder and Hauerwas assume in their writings that it is the same, Triune God to whom both Testaments witness and whose nonviolent, self-giving love embodies the true "grain of the universe." For seminal studies which emphasize the identity of the Triune God with YHWH, the God of Israel, see R. Kendall Soulen, *The God of Israel and Christian Theology* (Minneapolis: Fortress Press, 1996) and Scott Bader-Saye, *Church and Israel after Christendom: The Politics of Election* (Boulder, Colo.: Westview Press, 1996).

9. John Howard Yoder, "On Not Being in Charge," version of essay in *The Jewish-Christian Schism Revisited*, 138-139. This particular essay was also published in *War and Its Discontents: Pacifism and Quietism in the Abrahamic Traditions*, ed. J. Patout Burns (Washington, D.C.: Georgetown University Press, 1996), 74-90. Yoder also drew parallels between Jewish communities and Diaspora and the believers church vision of decentralized communities gathered around Scripture and animated by the Holy Spirit. Yoder, "On Not Being in Charge," 138.

10. Consider, for example, the following: "That Christian pacifism which has a theological basis in the character of God and the work of Jesus Christ is one in which the calculating link between our obedience and ultimate efficacy has been broken, since the triumph of God comes through resurrection and not through effective sovereignty or assured survival." Yoder, *The Politics of Jesus: Vicit Agnus Noster*, 2nd. rev. ed. (Grand Rapids: Eerdmans, 1994), 239.

11. For a current treatment of the theme of exile in Scripture, see the work of one of Yoder's students, Daniel Smith-Christopher, *A Biblical Theology of Exile: Overtures to Biblical Theology* (Minneapolis: Fortress Press, 2002).

12. Some might accuse Yoder of random selectivity in highlighting this particular strand in his attempt to provide a unified reading of the Old Testament which stands in continuity with the New. The selectivity was certainly not random, in that Yoder read Scripture, as should all Christians, through the lens of God incarnate in Jesus of Nazareth. To those who would reject the attempt to provide a coherent reading of Scripture, championing instead a "postmodernist" interplay of competing, conflicting voices within Scripture, it can only be answered that the postmodern valorization of a plurality of voices, none with more interpretive weight than the others, is itself a particular way of unifying the texts, one with its own implicit ethical and theological agenda, an agenda, one might add, which does not make the rejection of violence central to God's purposes in the world.

13. John Howard Yoder, "See How They Go with Their Face to the Sun," in *For the Nations: Essays Public and Evangelical* (Grand Rapids: Eerdmans, 1997), 64. For a more extended engagement with Genesis 11, see Yoder, "Meaning after Babble: With Jeffrey Stout beyond Relativism," *The Journal of Religious Ethics* 24 (Spring 1996): 125-39.

14. Yoder, "Jesus the Jewish Pacifist," in *The Jewish-Christian Schism Revisited*, 48. Yoder did not address, to my knowledge, the question most pressing to Palestinian Christians when reading the narratives of the Exodus and the entry into the Land, namely, the genocide of the native inhabitants. Yoder's appropriation of YHWH war is helpful and impressive; what one misses in Yoder is any appreciation for how these narratives leave the Canaanites and others outside of the sphere of moral concern. One can, of course, follow historical criticism and question the historicity of the exodus or the conquest, but one cannot escape the fact that the voice of the Canaanite is simply silent in

the texts. Instead, their cities and lands are taken over, a vision of landlessness which stands in haunting analogy to the destruction of over 400 Palestinian villages in 1948.

One can observe, of course, that other parts of Scripture clearly bring the nations, the Gentiles, within the orbit of God's redemptive action. What Yoder did not do (but, I would contend, should have done) was to argue that other parts of the Scriptural witness correct for the partially defective understanding of God present in the narratives of YHWH war.

For Yoder on exodus and exile, see "Exodus and Exile: Two Faces of Liberation," in *Crosscurrents*: 279-309. For a classic polemic noting the erasure of Canaanites and Palestinians from the sphere of moral concern, together with a critique of the attempt of a contemporary Jewish political theorist to appropriate Exodus as a model for radical politics, see Edward Said, "Michael Walzer's "Exodus and Revolution: A Canaanite Reading," in *Blaming the Victims: Spurious Scholarship and the Palestinian Question* (London: Verso, 1988), 161-78. Finally, for a challenging article noting how the exodus and conquest narratives have underwritten various forms of colonialist practice, see Michael Prior, "The Right to Expel: The Bible and Ethnic Cleansing," in *Palestinian Refugees: The Right of Return*, ed. Naseer Aruri (London: Pluto Press, 2001), 9-35.

15. Yoder, "See How They Go," 53.

16. Yoder, "Jesus the Jewish Pacifist," in *The Jewish-Christian Schism Revisited*, 48.

17. Yoder, "See How They Go," 74-75. A. James Reimer's critique, borrowing from John W. Miller, of Yoder's reading of the Old Testament that Babylon/exile never became the "exclusively normative symbol," either in the Old Testament or in the post-Temple Diaspora, does not mount an effective challenge to Yoder's approach. A. James Reimer, "Theological Orthodoxy and Jewish Christianity: A Personal Tribute to John Howard Yoder," in *The Wisdom of the Cross: Essays in Honor of John Howard Yoder*, ed. Stanley Hauerwas, Chris Huebner, Harry Huebner, Mark Nation (Grand Rapids.: Eerdmans, 1999), 446.

Yoder need not claim that the motif of a Jeremianic embrace of exile was necessarily dominant, but merely (1) that this strand continued both within the scriptural witness and within the history of post-biblical Judaism in the Diaspora and (2) that this strand is the one most in continuity with the gospel message. It should be clear, moreover, from even a cursory reading of Yoder's work, that John W. Miller's characterization of Yoder's theology as "Marcionite" is simply misguided and misleading. See Miller, "In the Footsteps of Marcion: Notes Toward an Understanding of John Yoder's Theology," *Conrad Grebel Review* 16 (Spring 1998): 82-92.

18. John Howard Yoder, *Christian Attitudes towards War, Peace, and Revolution: A Companion to Bainton* (Elkhart, Ind.: Distributed by Co-op Bookstore,

1983), 447.

19. Yoder, *For the Nations*, 56.

20. Yoder, "Jesus the Jewish Pacifist," 60. Sephardic Jews throughout the Arab world also lived in exilic communities, usually prospering and faring much better than Jews under Christendom.

21. Zionism, for Yoder, represents Judaism's full assimilation into the Christendom of the West: "The culmination of the Christianization of Judaism, then, is the development of Zionism. Zionism creates a secular democratic nation state after the model of the nation states of the West. It defines Jews, for the purpose of building the state, in such a way that it makes no difference if most of them are unbelieving or unobservant. In America the Jews are 'like a church' with a belief structure, life style commitments, and community meetings; in Israel Judaism is a nation and the belief dimension no longer matters. To be born in the state of Israel makes one less of a Jew, in the deep historical sense of the term, than to be born in a ghetto." Yoder, "Judaism as a Non-non-Christian Religion," in *The Jewish-Christian Schism Revisited*, 122.

I should stress here that the critique of Zionism I offer here is directed at Zionist theory and practice insofar as it assumed the necessity to exclude and dispossess Palestinians in order to establish Jewish sovereignty in *Eretz Yisrael*. This does not deny, of course, that Zionism was experienced as liberation by, for example, Jews who escaped Eurpoe during the 1930s and 1940s. Nor does it preclude the possibility of "Zionisms" which renew Jewish life in *Eretz Yisrael* in a way which does not exlude and dispossess the native Palestinian inhabitants.

22. The religious-secular opposition will surface several times in the following section. Rather than attempting to parse the different, and, to my mind, ultimately incoherent ways in which Said deploys this opposition, I will only note that I find the opposition to lack critical persuasiveness. For a helpful critique of Said on "religious" and "secular" criticism, see William D. Hart, *Edward Said and the Religious Effects of Culture* (Cambridge, England: Cambridge University Press, 2000).

On the question of Yoder's relationship to liberalism, Oliver O'Donovan has claimed that Yoder fell prey to the latter's consumerist voluntarism. O'Donovan, *The Desire of the Nations: Rediscovering the Roots of Political Theology* (Cambridge: Cambridge University Press, 1996), 223-224. For critiques of O'Donovan's characterization of Yoder on this point, see Alain Epp Weaver, "After Politics," 658-659; and P. Travis Kroeker, "Why O'Donovan's Christendom is Not Constantinian and Yoder's Voluntareity is Not Hobbesian: A Debate in Theological Politics Redefined," *The Annual of the Society of Christian Ethics* 20 (2000): 41-64.

23. Said's defense of "amateurism," as an intellectual stance which revels "in making connections across lines and barriers, in refusing to be tied down

to a specialty, in caring for ideas and values despite the restrictions of a profession." *Representations of the Intellectual* (London: Vintage, 1994), 57, brings to mind Yoder's wide-ranging intellect and his fruitful bringing together of scholarship in Biblical studies, church history, ethics, theology and beyond.

24. For Barth's treatment of "secular parables of the kingdom," see *Church Dogmatics* IV/3:1, par. 69, sec. 2. Both Barth and Yoder—contrary to some simplistic characterizations—could embrace truth *extra muros ecclesiae*. See Alain Epp Weaver, "Parables of the Kingdom and Religious Plurality: With Barth and Yoder towards a Nonresistant Public Theology," *The Mennonite Quarterly Review* 72 (July 1998): 411-40.

25. Edward Said, *After the Last Sky: Palestinian Lives* (London: Vintage, 1986), 5.

26. For treatments of the war of 1948 and the Palestinian *Nakba*, see *The War for Palestine: Rewriting the History of 1948*, ed. Eugene L. Rogan and Avi Shlaim (Cambridge: Cambridge University Press, 2001); Ilan Pappe, *The Making of the Arab-Israeli Conflict, 1947-1951* (London: I.B. Tauris, 1992); Benny Morris, *The Birth of the Palestinian Refugee Problem, 1947-1949* (Cambridge: Cambridge University Press, 1987); Avi Shlaim, *Collusion Across the Jordan: King Abdullah, the Zionist Movement, and the Partition of Palestine* (Oxford, England: Clarendon Press, 1988); Nur Musalha, *Expulsion of the Palestinians: The Concept of "Transfer" in Zionist Political Thought, 1882-1948* (Washington, D.C.: Institute for Palestine Studies, 1992); *All That Remains: The Palestinian Villages Occupied and Depopulated by Israel in 1948*, ed. Walid Khalidi (Washington, D.C.: Institute for Palestine Studies, 1992); Meron Benvenisti, *Sacred Landscape: The Buried History of the Holy Land since 1948* (Berkeley: University of California Press, 2000). For a recent study which debunks many myths concerning the Arab-Israeli conflict, see Avi Shlaim, *The Iron Wall: Israel and the Arab World* (New York: W. W. Norton, 2000). Finally, for a strong collection of essays analyzing the current Palestinian uprising, or *intifada*, against Israeli occupation, see *The New Intifada: Resisting Israel's Apartheid*, ed. Roane Carey (London: Verso, 2001).

27. Said, *After the Last Sky*, 130.

28. Ibid., 12.

29. Ibid., 20-21.

30. Ibid., 164.

31. Ibid., 20-21.

32. Ibid., 68.

33. Said, *Representations of the Intellectual*, 35.

34. Said, *After the Last Sky*, 51.

35. The endless claims that Yoder's theology is "sectarian" in precisely this sense are sorely misguided. For one explanation of why Yoder's theology is not sectarian, see my "After Politics," 653-656.

36. Edward Said, *Reflections on Exile and Other Essays* (Cambridge: Harvard

University Press, 2000), 178.

37. Ibid., 183.

38. Ibid., 175.

39. Ibid., 174. "Secular" in this context appears to mean for Said that exile cannot be placed into a larger, transcendental, theological context of meaning; it is an agonizingly concrete situation with no hope for amelioration (other than what the exile him- or herself can produce).

40. Edward Said, *Power, Politics, and Culture: Interviews with Edward Said*, ed. Gauri Viswanathan (New York: Pantheon Books 2001), 56.

41. Said, *Representations*, 39. For Said the critic is tempted not only to be a yea-sayer for the community at large, but within one's own community; Said, it should be noted, has been a vociferous critic of the PLO and its often misguided handling of the Palestinian struggle. Yoder, too, was no "yea-sayer," or apologist, for the Mennonite community, but rather reserved his most polemical barbs for critiques of the Mennonite churches. See for example "Anabaptist Vision and Mennonite Reality," in *Consultation on Anabaptist-Mennonite Theology: Papers Read at the 1969 Aspen Conference*, ed. A. J. Klassen (Fresno, Calif.: Council of Mennonite Seminaries, 1970), 1-46.

42. Said, *Representations*, 39.

43. Ibid., 46.

44. Ibid., 45.

45. Theodor Adorno, *Minima Moralia: Reflections from Damaged Life* (London: New Left Books, 1951), 38-39. Quoted in Said, *Reflections on Exile*, 564-565.

46. Adorno, *Minima Moralia*, 87. Quoted in Said, *Reflections on Exile*, 568.

47. Said, *Reflections on Exile*, 568.

48. For a highly useful and persuasive discussion of *pathos* in theology and the role of *poeisis* within that *pathos*, see Reinhard Hütter, *Suffering Divine Things: Theology as Church Practice* (Grand Rapids: Eerdmans, 2000).

49. Edward Said, "Introduction: The Right of Return At Last," in *Palestinian Refugees: The Right of Return*, ed. Naseer Aruri (London: Pluto Press, 2001), 6.

50. Said, *After the Last Sky*, 33.

51. Said, *Power, Politics, and Culture*, 429.

52. Said, *Reflections on Exile*, 179.

53. Said, *After the Last Sky*, 150.

54. Ibid. Note once more Said's rather wooden use of the religious-secular opposition. What Said cannot imagine is a religious criticism which prizes the "open" character of exile precisely because it confesses God's redeeming defeat of the powers of sin.

55. Gerald Schlabach, "Deuteronomic or Constantinian: What Is the Most Basic Problem for Christian Social Ethics?" in *The Wisdom of the Cross*, 463.

56. I do not mean, through this analysis of the ways in which Zionist dis-

course and practice have worked historically to dispossess Palestinians, to deny the possibility that other forms of Zionism, Zionisms not dependent upon the dispossession of others, might be possible. The "cultural Zionism," for example, of an Ahad Haam or a Judah Magnes, would be cases in point. In his interview with Ari Shavit, Said rejects any talk of "de-Zionization" or a simple dismissal of "Zionism" as a valid term. Jews should be able to be Zionists, Said believes, and "assert their Jewish identity and their connection to the land, so long as it doesn't keep the others out so manifestly." Said, *Power, Politics, and Culture*, 451

57. Schlabach, "Deuteronomic or Constantinian," 470.

58. Laurence Silberstein, *The Postzionism Debates: Knowledge and Power in Israeli Culture* (Routledge: New York and London, 1999), 20.

59. Sander Gilman, "Introduction," in *Jewries at the Frontier: Accommodation, Identity, Conflict*, ed. Sander Gilman and Milton Shain (Urbana and Chicago: University of Illinois Press, 1999), 5.

60. Silberstein, 22-23.

61. Ibid., 20.

62. Quoted and translated in Silberstein, *The Postzionism Debate*, 179. For the original Hebrew, see Amnon Raz-Krakotzkin, "Exile in the Midst of Sovereignty: A Critique of 'Shelilat HaGalut' in Israeli Culture," *Theory and Criticism (Theoria ve-Bikoret)* 4 (Fall 1993): 44.

63. Raz Krakotzkin, "Redemption and Colonialism: Exile, History and the Nationalization of Jewish Memory," available at http://www.nyu.edu/gsas/program/neareast/raz-krakotzkin.html. This conclusion bears remarkable similarities to Yoder's critique of Zionism, noted above, as a Jewish assimilation to Christendom.

64. Quoted and translated in Silberstein, 178-179; Raz-Krakotzkin, "Exile in the Midst of Sovereignty," 44.

65. Quoted and translated in Silberstein, 181; Raz-Krakotzkin, "Exile in the Midst of Sovereignty," 39.

66. Silberstein, 181, citing Raz-Krakotzkin, "Exile in the Midst of Sovereignty," 49.

67. Marc H. Ellis, *Revolutionary Forgiveness: Essays on Judaism, Christianity, and the Future of Religious Life* (Waco, Tex.: Baylor University Press, 2000), 121.

68. Ellis, *Revolutionary Forgiveness*, 271. See also Marc Ellis, *Practicing Exile: The Religious Odyssey of an American Jew* (Minneapolis: Fortress Press, 2001).

69. Said, *Power, Politics, and Culture*, 425.

70. Commentators of various political persuasions increasingly describe the reality in the occupied Palestinian territories as one of apartheid. See for example, several of the essays in *The New Intifada: Resisting Israel's Apartheid*, ed. Roane Carey (London: Verso, 2001).

71. Edward Said, *Power, Politics, and Culture*, 457-58. Some Israeli writers share aspects of Said's binational vision. Raz-Krakotzin, for one, believes that

galut as a critical concept makes possible "a Jewish identity based on the recognition of the potential embodied in the bi-nationality of the land." Quoted and translated in Silberstein, 181; Raz-Krakotzkin, "Exile in the Midst of Sovereignty," 49.

72. Quoted and translated in Silberstein, 182; Emile Habiby, *Ehtayeh*, translated from Arabic into Hebrew by Anton Shammas (Tel Aviv: Am Oved, 1988), 9.

73. Quoted and translated in Silberstein, 182; Raz-Krakotzkin, "Exile in the Midst of Sovereignty," 52.

74. See, for example, John Howard Yoder, *The Christian Witness to the State* (Newton, Ks.: Faith and Life Press, 1964), 77. I discuss Yoder's ad hoc approach to engagements with the state in my article, "After Politics," 669-671.

75. For Yoder's treatment of the Jubilee, see *The Politics of Jesus*, 60-75. Christians, as followers of a nonviolent Lord, cannot, of course, support refugee return which would mean the violent displacement of others in turn. For a discussion of the debate on Palestinian refugee return, see Alain Epp Weaver, "Right of Return: Can Palestinians Go Back Home?" *The Christian Century* (May 2, 2001): 8-9.

Chapter 9

Share The House: Yoder and Hauerwas Among the Nations[1]

Paul Doerksen

AN INVESTIGATION OF THE THEOLOGICAL LEGACY of John Howard Yoder invariably includes a discussion of Stanley Hauerwas' work. Hauerwas has consistently been forthright concerning the extent of Yoder's impact and has even described his own work as "a rather modest statement of a position that has been articulated by people like John Howard Yoder for years."[2] Hauerwas has been quite personal in his comments, and his admiration of Yoder is obvious. Perhaps Hauerwas could be described as wanting to do things as Yoder wanted them to be done.[3]

While Hauerwas is open about Yoder's impact, Yoder's engagement with Hauerwas' work is very rarely undertaken directly,[4] and then not always usefully, as when Yoder scolds Hauerwas for use of the term _primer_ in the subtitle of _The Peaceable Kingdom_ because the book does not function as an initial coat of paint.[5] While Yoder does not often engage Hauerwas' work directly, Hauerwas is often the motivation behind Yoder's examples, and perhaps even behind the choice of some book titles.[6]

Hauerwas' self-described status as a "Mennonite camp follower"[7] should be understood as having been initiated by and carried forward in large part by Yoder's work. This has led to the scenario in which Hauerwas' more widely read work often serves as an initiation/introduction to Yoder, a situation viewed with some ambivalence by commentators such as Michael Cartwright and Craig Carter.[8] I do not share this ambivalence, in large part because I share with Yoder, Hauerwas and others the view that one cannot find a "scratch point" from which to begin reading anyone. If one reads Hauerwas as a way to Yoder, at the very least Yoder is being read with some sympathy. Reading Yoder by way of Hauerwas is probably better than reading Yoder through the brothers Niebuhr, for example.

While the fact of significant affinity between the work of Yoder and Hauerwas is easy enough to identify, the description of the nature of any continuities or discontinuities must be approached with care. One might locate the difference between the two men in their respective approaches to novels. Hauerwas, in a piece centered on Ralph McInerny's mystery novels, notes wryly, "I suspect Yoder was not a reader of mysteries,"[9] while Yoder describes Hauerwas as being "underawed by the study of real (unsaved) history. He would rather read novels."[10] But obviously the differences run deeper than literary taste and habit.

Part of the difficulty in capturing the distinctions between Yoder and Hauerwas has to do with the striking similarity of approach to the theological/ethical task. I will therefore show that their conceptions of church and world reveal remarkable convergence, while real differences exist regarding their respective understanding of voluntarism, and the relationship of worship and ethics.

The relationship of church and world as understood by Yoder and Hauerwas proceeds with a refusal to find a "scratch point." Hauerwas' nonfoundationalism can be summarized by his statement that "in a world without foundations all we have is the church."[11] Yoder is similarly committed to the rejection of a foundationalism or methodologism. In the introduction to *For the Nations*, Yoder explicitly states, "One reason I do not start from scratch to do a book on just one subject is that there is no scratch from which to start."[12] Rather, Yoder's refusal to be committed to some kind of scratch point, or foundation, or method, is based on his "commitment to a community which is in turn committed to canonical accountability."[13] Or to put it another way, "What must replace the prolegomenal search for 'scratch' is the confession of rootedness in historical community. Then one directs one's critical acuity toward making clear the distance between that community's charter or covenant and its present faithfulness."[14] Clearly this notion also has implications for the interpretation of Scripture, seen by both men as necessarily performed within the interpretive community of the church.[15]

Hauerwas and Yoder are also in considerable agreement regarding the danger of Constantinianism to the church. Yoder's definition of Constantinianism is worth quoting at some length, since it is so crucial to the ecclesiology of both Hauerwas and Yoder. As Yoder views Constantiniasm,

> the term refers to the conception of Christianity which took shape in the century between the Edict of Milan and the *City of God*. The central nature of this change, which Constantine himself did not invent or force upon the church, is not a matter of doctrine or polity; it is the identification of church and world in the mutual approval and support exchanged by Constantine and the bishops. The church is no longer the obedient suffering line of the true prophets; she has a vested interest in the present order of things and uses the cultic means at their disposal to legitimize that order. She does not preach ethics, judgment, repentance, separation from the world; she dispenses sacraments and holds society together. Christian ethics no longer means the study of what God wants of man; since all of society is Christian (by definition, i.e., by baptism), Christian ethics must be workable for all of society.[16]

Hauerwas makes Yoder's notion of Constantinianism the basis of what he refers to as a "Christian critique of America." Drawing on Yoder's construal of Constantinianism as depicted in *The Priestly Kingdom*,[17] Hauerwas launches an extended critique he insists must be made by understanding a shift in the logic of moral argument that occurred when Christians ceased to be a minority and accepted Caesar as a member of the church. The shift results in Christians believing that everyone is a member of the church and occasions the need to develop a doctrine of the "invisible church." Hauerwas implores Christians to give up this Constantinian habit of thought to return to Christian ways of thinking.

It is important to note that Hauerwas follows Yoder so closely in this section that not only is he criticizing Christian America; he is simultaneously conducting an apologetical defense of Yoder's thought. The extensive notes on this section are a running commentary on Yoder.[18] Ian Barns' description of Yoder as trying "to overcome the depoliticization of the church resulting from its Constantinian subversion and to recover the self-understanding of the church as a political community"[19] is also an apt description of Hauerwas' ecclesiology.

The striking similarity of approach is often overshadowed by attempts to capture the distinction between Yoder and Hauerwas in the titles of their respective books, *For The Nations* and *Against The Nations*. This way of seeing things has actually come about at least in part from Hauerwas' and Yoder's own commentary on the matter. For example, Hauerwas refers specifically to the differences between himself and Yoder in an essay intended for an Australian audience:

> Yoder does not feel the need to be polemical, at least not as polemical as my work tends to be, because he does not need to emphasize the differences, coming as he does from a position of difference.... Michael Cartwright recently noted that one way to describe the difference between Yoder and myself is that Yoder thinks of the church as being "for the nations" whereas I tend to think of the church as being "against the nations." Such a characterization is certainly fair insofar as I have come from mainstream Protestant Christianity in America and find it necessary to confront what I perceive to be the accommodation of that tradition to the religiosity of America. Yoder feels no such compunction and he is certainly right to remind us that the church exists to serve the nations.[20]

For his part, Yoder sees Hauerwas as maximizing "the provocative edge of the dissenting posture with titles like *Against the Nations* or *Resident Aliens*."[21] Therefore the for/against distinction is not without merit, especially since Hauerwas tends to use what has been termed as contrarian language, making use of sweeping denunciations, especially of movements.[22]

However, in my view, Yoder and Hauerwas view the relationship of the church to the nations in very similar ways, although Hauerwas' language makes it more difficult than necessary to see this.[23] In fact, use of such language makes Hauerwas too easy a mark for those searching for the stench of sectarianism. The difference between Hauerwas and Yoder cannot be characterized by saying that one is for and one against the nations. The similarities between their ecclesiologies are far greater than any dissimilarities.

Further, it is somewhat unclear just how much weight ought to be given to the choice of the term *against* in the title of Hauerwas' book. In the preface to the separately published lecture "Should War be

Eliminated?"[24] the listing of some of Hauerwas' publications to that date includes a manuscript in preparation described as "a book on war and other related topics called *Living Among the Nations: Reflections on War, Democracy, and Survival.*" When the book was published, it came out as *Against the Nations: War and Survival in a Liberal Society.* It is unclear what impression Hauerwas' work might give if for example "among" replaced "against" language. His book *Sanctify Them in the Truth* includes a section entitled 'Speaking Truthfully In, For, and Against the World.' However, within this section is the previously published essay, "No Enemy, No Christianity: Preaching Between 'Worlds,'" as well as an essay provocatively titled "The Nonviolent Terrorist: In Defense of Christian Fanaticism."[25] This kind of against language has added to the perception that Hauerwas is indeed a sectarian. It is hard to pin down to what extent such language is rooted in personal style versus theology.[26] My close reading of Hauerwas has shown that he appears to take extremely strong positions but often mitigates these positions with less absolutist nuances.

More recently, Hauerwas has affirmed his perception that Yoder was more willing to work within the world as he found it.[27] In *A Better Hope*, Hauerwas contends that it is a mistake to allow life to be determined by enemies, and this book is his attempt to make "for" the more determinative factor. (I was somewhat relieved to see that in the next breath of the same introductory essay, Hauerwas is "still mad as hell at Christians").[28]

While not as provocative as Hauerwas, Yoder also has described the posture of the church as one of being against the nations, as clearly seen in *Body Politics*.[29] The church is determinative for Christians; it precedes the world and thus values which contradict Jesus must be subordinated or rejected.[30] In *Christian Existence Today*, Hauerwas argues that it should not be assumed that there are only two stark options regarding involvement—complete involvement or complete withdrawal. He sees the issue as "how the church can provide the interpretive categories to help Christians better understand the positive and negative aspects of their societies and guide their subsequent selective participation."[31] Thus both men see the church as shaping how the nations should be engaged.

Even if my contention that Hauerwas and Yoder conceptualize the relationship of church and world in closely related ways holds, at least two areas of significant difference exist. First is Hauerwas' criticism of the Mennonite and specifically Yoderian emphasis on the voluntary nature of the church. In *The Priestly Kingdom*, Yoder describes his Mennonitism as "my own ethnic and denominational orientation, by birth and by choice."[32] Fair enough, says Hauerwas, but if your church is voluntary, then why is everyone named Epp or Bender?[33]

Yoder's emphasis on the voluntary nature of the church is perhaps most clearly delineated in his essay "The Hermeneutics of Peoplehood."[34] Here Yoder contends that Western intellectual history since the post-Reformation era "has been a pendulum swinging between the collective and the individual."[35] Yoder argues for a third option that does more than simply mix elements of the other two. "Communities which are genuinely voluntary can affirm individual dignity (at the point of the uncoerced adherence of the member) without enshrining individualism. They can likewise realize community without authorizing lordship or establishment."[36] This is an assertion for freedom, but instead of freedom of choice, it is freedom of confession that is at stake, a particular understanding that allows for the creation of a "voluntary community which has about it neither the coercive givenness of establishment nor the atomistic isolation of individualism."[37] This line of understanding of the voluntary nature of the church can be found throughout Yoder's work in various discussions of baptism, binding and loosing, and so on.[38]

Hauerwas is clearly uncomfortable with and critical of such an understanding, although it should be said that his own ecclesial position is not nearly as clear as his discomfort. In Hauerwas' highly personal reflections in "Confessions of a Mennonite Camp Follower," he confesses to what he refers to as his own ecclesially unintelligible experience, one in which he "whores after" what he takes to be faithful to the gospel. In the same article, he argues that Christianity has become voluntary, but that voluntariness constituted by modernity makes it impossible to maintain the disciplines necessary to be nonviolent.[39]

To Hauerwas, the notion of a voluntary church is problematic because of the liberal understanding and practice of atomistic choice. This is further illustrated in an essay in which Hauerwas finds himself expressing admiration for what goes on in the small Irish village of Sneem, where on the day of the feast of Ascension, all the little girls and boys dress in white robes and join in first communion. Hauerwas claims that if this kind of practice is a vestige of Constantinianism, he likes it. Indeed, he seemingly cannot stop himself from comparing Sneem to Second Baptist of Houston, a church growth movement megachurch of 17, 000. The reason Hauerwas gives for his preference of Sneem is "the 'obligatory' nature of what goes on in Sneem."[40]

However, this raises the question of whether a place with practices like Sneem can be sustained without a state. Here Yoder enters Hauerwas' thoughts, via a memo, challenging Hauerwas' narration of these matters and particularly the understanding of Sneem as Constantinian rather than "a celebration of primitive pagan (i.e. village) religiosity, covered with a Catholic veneer by St. Patrick."[41] Hauerwas concludes that he is simply "looking for traditioned practices or disciplines where imposed will and total freedom are not assumed to be the only alternatives."[42]

Despite Yoder's attempts to position himself somewhere else than at one of those two poles, Hauerwas remains unconvinced. John Milbank, in a public discussion with Hauerwas at Wheaton College, suggests it is difficult to get into clear focus a kind of overrating of process and method in Hauerwas that may be modern. Hauerwas' response is to highlight his own criticism of Yoder because "John's language of the voluntary is overdetermined in modernity exactly because it puts too much stress on process separate from the material convictions you want the process to serve."[43]

Hauerwas finds support for his criticism of Yoder in the work of Oxford theologian Oliver O'Donovan, who accuses Yoder of emphasizing voluntariety at the expense of belief. O'Donovan admits that a church defined by faith must of course be free, for "coerced faith" is a contradiction in terms. However, asks O'Donovan, does this legitimate a voluntary society—one that could be left without incurring grave or irremediable loss? "Is Yoder, in the name of nonconformity, not championing a great conformism, lining the church up with sports clubs, friendly societies, colleges, symphony subscription-guilds, political parties and so on, just to prove that the church offers late-modern order no serious threat?"[44] Hauerwas, although somewhat critical of O'Donovan's larger project, allows that O'Donovan is onto something in this criticism of Yoder's "'voluntarism,' which can too easily, particularly in modernity, underwrite rationalistic accounts of faith."[45]

Hauerwas is also onto something here, although just what it is is not quite clear. While it is true that Yoder did not say much about how Christian communities shape Christians to be Christian in their moral behavior,[46] Yoder is clearly not advocating consumer choice when he speaks of the voluntary church.[47] Surely not every choice or each incident of voluntary behavior can be classified as crass, liberal freedom of choice. While Travis Kroeker has observed an "ironic lack of attention to the complex character and (trans)formation of the human *vol-*

untas in Yoder's voluntariety,"[48] he argues convincingly that O'Donovan's' portrayal of Yoder as advocating some sort of neo-liberalism is badly misleading (and cranky). Yoder's voluntarism is different from the political voluntarism of social contract theory, since freedom in Christ after all, is very different from freedom of choice.[49] These fruitful lines of analysis regarding both O'Donovan and Yoder seem right to me, and the critique of O'Donovan's portrayal of Yoder might well be directed at Hauerwas' complaints against Yoder as well.

Nonetheless, it is important to listen to Hauerwas and O'Donovan (and others) on this matter. What does the notion of a voluntary church, along with attendant practices such as adult baptism, look like or require in a society in which all churches are "free" and when baptism is unrelated to issues of status or citizenry within the state? Even if Yoder (and others) can show that voluntary is not equal to free choice, freedom to believe, or some such liberal notion, do Christians within free churches make the necessary distinctions? The danger exists here that disciplined practices will collapse into serial "voluntary" memberships or even temporary covenants with whatever church persons happen to want to attend in a given year, as though association and membership can somehow be equated.

Yet voluntarism is intrinsic to free church theology, ecclesiology, and ethics, as James Reimer points out in an essay presented at the sixteenth Believers Church Conference in Hamilton, Ontario. Reimer, writing from within the tradition, incisively observes that the dilemma Anabaptists face is that voluntarism strengthens ethics at one end through responsibility and free will, and at the other end the definition of personhood as free will calls into question the humanity of fetuses and thus threatens their existence. In such dilemmas lie the kinds of questions that deserve further exploration of just how the voluntarism of Mennonites occupies a place between establishment and arbitrary individualism. Reimer suggests that such an understanding must take into account an understanding of human agency that is derivative from, dependent upon, and accountable to divine agency.[50]

Writing in the same collection of essays, James McClendon seeks to redefine freedom as not a good or a goal or in isolation from the gospel, but rather part of that good news. Given this understanding, what is meant by voluntary must be determined case by case, a suggestion then described in particular situations, as McClendon taught so well.[51] All this to say that the work Reimer, McClendon, and others have done signals work that remains to be done if the voluntary church Anabaptists espouse is not to become that which Hauerwas is afraid we already are.

A second area of considerable agreement but also some divergence between Hauerwas and Yoder is the connection of worship or liturgy with ethics. Yoder addresses the connection in a positive light, describing Jesus as using the image of a scribe to fulfill a "function of social knowing," an image that appears to treat the "function of 'worship' as constituting a group ever anew around its common memory."[52] Yoder cautions against making too much of the point, since he does not see a specific activity labeled as worship in the New Testament. Nevertheless, in the same essay, Yoder returns to the topic and asserts that it is indeed fitting to affirm the unity of worship and morality, defining worship as "the communal cultivation of an alternative construction of society and history."[53]

In a later essay (subsequently expanded into a book), Yoder returns to address the interrelationship of worship and ethics, carefully distinguishing his approach from those that see worship as character formation or motivational—that is to say, those approaches which seek to build some kind of a bridge between worship and ethics.[54] Yoder then describes five communal practices which have in common the notion "that each of them concerns *both* the internal activities of the gathered Christian congregation *and* the way in which the church interacts with the world."[55] The five practices are (1) fraternal admonition, (2) the universality of charisma, (3) the Spirit's freedom in the meeting, (4) breaking bread, and (5) induction into the new humanity.[56]

Yoder admits several of these practices do not ordinarily fall under accepted understandings of worship or liturgy. Yet he would like them designated as worship, since "each is a practice, which can be described formally and which is carried out when believers gather for reasons evidently derived from their faith."[57] Therefore, for Yoder, worship is essential within our understanding of social ethics, since the practices of the church are the way in which culture is transformed. However, the connections Yoder makes between worship and ethics lack a significant emphasis on the experience of individual believers, focusing instead on communal life.

Hauerwas' work includes a well-developed emphasis on the connection of liturgy and ethics.[58] Observance of the liturgical church year is seen by Hauerwas as crucial to the understanding of Scripture, since this "prevents any one part of Scripture from being given undue emphasis in relation to the narrative line of Scripture."[59] Jeffrey Siker has observed that Hauerwas' appeals to Scripture as well as his published sermons often come in liturgical contexts and draw on the lectionary reading.[60]

Hauerwas' emphasis on the connection between liturgy and ethics is clearly stated in his treatment of the importance of the sacraments of baptism and the celebration of the Eucharist for the church. He argues that "the sacraments are means crucial to shaping and preparing us to tell and hear"[61] the story of Jesus. Through the sacraments the church learns who we are, but they do not function as motives or causes for social work. Rather "these liturgies are our effective social work. For if the church is rather than has a social ethic, these actions are our most important social work."[62]

The strength of Hauerwas' connection between liturgy and ethics is perhaps best exemplified by the structure of an ethics course he teaches. In a chapter entitled "The Liturgical Shape of the Christian Life: Teaching Christian Ethics as Worship,"[63] Hauerwas reports on the rationale, structure, and content of the course. He hopes to embody the presumption that nothing is more important to Christian people than praising God, and to defeat the "and" of "theology and worship."[64]

In a recent article, Hauerwas extends this elimination of "and." Here Hauerwas posits the notions that "when all is said and done, liturgy and ethics are just ways to do theology, and theology so understood might again be understood as worship."[65] This is not to say that any of these subjects of study cannot be considered separately, but such distinctions ought to be seen as part of the church's ministry reflected in diversity of gifts.[66] Hauerwas succinctly states, "I have staked my work and life on the presumption that if, in some small way, I can help the church recover liturgical integrity, questions about the relation between worship, evangelism, and ethics will no longer be asked."[67]

Hauerwas also uses eucharistic logic to argue that the church is

> the necessary correlative of an apocalyptic narration of existence. It is the eucharistic community that is the epistemological prerequisite for understanding "how things are." Only as we stand in the reality of the Eucharist can we see that 'the causal point of view' is not the final truth of our lives. Instead, we can see that our world is not determined by the powers, that we do not have to submit to the necessities that we are told are unavoidable.[68]

So while certain affinities are evident in the way Yoder and Hauerwas connect ethics and worship, Hauerwas is consistently critical of the instrumentalist account and practice of worship he sees in Mennonites, practice he describes as generally rationalistic and aesthetically thin.[69] Therefore, while Hauerwas is being accused by his fellow Methodists of emphasizing liturgy to the point of being indistinguishable from Catholicism,[70] Yoder's work continues to be criticized for ignoring any dimension of worship not specifically ethical in nature.

Here Hauerwas is not alone in his criticism. Travis Kroeker has observed that Yoder's deep-seated concern to distance himself from any form of "pietism" has created a body of work in which everything has to do with the cosmos, and virtually nothing to do with the human self. Thus, "Yoder's inattention to the rich sacramental meaning of the marks of the church is lamentably characteristic of the 'free church' tradition."[71] Yoder's tendency to reduce worship to social ethics is lamented by other Mennonite theologians. James Reimer has complained that "Yoder offers a powerful political reading of the New Testament which unfortunately devalues the existential-sacramental power of Jesus' message—that part having to do with divine grace, the personal forgiveness of sin, the inner renewal of the spirit, and the individual's stance before God," a complaint echoed by Mark Thiessen Nation.[72]

In my view, Michael Cartwright's assessment of the instrumentalist account of worship in Christian formation that floats throughout Yoder's work is important in understanding a real difference between Hauerwas and Yoder. Cartwright, a sensitive and insightful interpreter of Yoder, describes him as having an account of sacramentality that is oddly one-dimensional, as though the only human faculty shaped by God's grace is the intellect. Further, Cartwright pegs the critical difference between Yoder's neo-Anabaptist account of the sacraments and those within the sacramental traditions as follows:

> For Yoder, regardless of the practices that are embodied before the eyes of the watching world, the Word of God can only be experienced as an "Inner Word" to which the gathered community of faith testifies, whereas for Protestants like John Wesley and John Calvin as well as for those who stand within the Roman Catholic tradition, the Word of God is believed to come to us in audible forms such as preaching and is made visible in sacraments like the Eucharist.[73]

Later in the same article, Cartwright states, with reference to discussion of hermeneutics, that the ongoing argument between himself and Yoder "had everything to do with the traditions from within which we stood, and beyond which we continued to engage each other's writings."[74] Cartwright's conclusion seems exactly right to me, and I wish to extend this description of the matter to differences between Hauerwas and Yoder, which have everything to do with disparate traditions within which they have engaged each other's work. Hauerwas writes as a deeply committed Methodist;[75] Yoder writes as a Mennonite by birth and by choice. When they turn to speak to their own respective traditions, they are often critical. When they engage the world, they sound very similar. When they disagree, they do so as Methodist and Mennonite.[76]

NOTES

1. The title is a take on Michael Cartwright, "Sharing The House of God: Learning to Read Scripture With Anabaptists," *Mennonite Quarterly Review* 74:4 (October 2000): 593-621.

2. Stanley Hauerwas, *In Good Company: The Church as Polis*, (Notre Dame, Ind.: University of Notre Dame Press, 1995), 51. Hauerwas is here referring to what he and Will Willimon were attempting in *Resident Aliens*.

3. See for example Stanley Hauerwas's comments at Yoder's memorial service, held at Goshen College Mennonite Church on January 3, 1998, in *Conrad Grebel Review* 16:2 (Spring 1998): 98-100, as well as Hauerwas, "When the Politics of Jesus Makes a Difference," *Christian Century* 10 (October 1993): 982-987; and Hauerwas, *Dispatches From the Front: Theological Engagements With The Secular*, (Durham: Duke University Press, 1994), 21-25.

4. Jorge Garcia, "A Public Prophet?" *First Things* 75 (February 1999): 49.

5. John Howard Yoder, *For The Nations: Essays Public and Evangelical* (Grand Rapids: Eerdmans, 1997), 9 n.24. Stanley Hauerwas, *The Peaceable Kingdom: A Primer in Christian Ethics*, (Notre Dame, Ind.: University of Notre Dame Press, 1983).

6. I take this way of putting the matter from Chris Huebner, "Globalization, Theory, and Dialogical Vulnerability: John Howard Yoder and the Possibility of a Pacifist Epistemology," *Mennonite Quarterly Review* 76:1 (January 2002): 55 n.17.

7. Stanley Hauerwas, "Confessions of a Mennonite Camp Follower," *Mennonite Quarterly Review* 74:4 (October 2000): 511-522.

8. Michael Cartwright, "Radical Reform, Radical Catholicity: John Howard Yoder's Vision of the Faithful Church," in *The Royal Priesthood: Essays Ecclesiological and Ecumenical*, ed. Michael Cartwright (Grand Rapids: W. B.

Eerdmans, 1994). Cartwright notes that while Hauerwas has made Yoder more known to people, that representation has contributed indirectly to a misidentification of Yoder's position with Hauerwas's work (15, n.25). Craig Carter cites Cartwright to make the same point in Carter, *The Politics of the Cross: The Theology and Social Ethics of John Howard Yoder* (Grand Rapids: Brazos Press, 2001), 68, 227. In a foreword to Carter's book, Hauerwas declares his hope that anyone reading him (Hauerwas) might be led to read Yoder (10, 11).

9. Stanley Hauerwas, *A Better Hope: Resources for a Church Confronting Capitalism, Democracy, and Postmodernity*, (Grand Rapids: Brazos Press, 2000), 280, n.17.

10. Carter, *The Politics of the Cross*, 69. Carter is quoting "Absolute Relativism is an Oxymoron," an unpublished Yoder paper.

11. Stanley Hauerwas, Nancey Murphy, and Mark Nation, eds., *Theology Without Foundations: Religious Practice and the Future of Theological Truth* (Nashville: Abingdon Press, 1994), 144.

12. Yoder, *For The Nations*, 10. Here Yoder also refers to Hauerwas's so-called "primer" in Christian ethics, *The Peaceable Kingdom*, as an example of something that is not really a primer in any sense of the word, but "as selective and idiosyncratic as Hauerwas's earlier writings, even though it differed from them in having been written in one piece. Were I to try to write a book like that, I do not know what it would be about" (9). Hauerwas relates a conversation in which an unnamed theologian informed him that it was high time to write the "big book" in Christian ethics. Hauerwas's response is remarkably similar to Yoder's statement in that he replies that "after Wittgenstein, I simply had no idea what it would mean to write the 'big book' in Christian ethics." Hauerwas, *Sanctify Them in the Truth: Holiness Exemplified* (Nashville: Abingdon Press, 1998), 8.

13. Yoder, "Walk and Word: The Alternatives to Methodologism," in *Theology Without Foundations*, 87.

14. Quoted in Hauerwas, "When the Politics of Jesus Makes a Difference," 983.

15. The topic of the church as interpretive community goes beyond the scope of this essay. However, it should be noted that there has developed an interesting line of discussion that ties both Yoder and Hauerwas to the work of Stanley Fish. See Mark Thiessen Nation, "Theology as Witness: Reflections on Yoder, Fish, and Interpretive Communities," *Faith and Freedom* 5:1, 2 (June 1996): 42-47; Hauerwas, "Stanley Fish, the Pope, and the Bible," in *Unleashing the Scripture*, 19-28; and Alan Jacobs, "A Tale of Two Stanleys," *First Things* 44 (June/July 1994): 18-21; Scott Saye, "The Wild and Crooked Tree: Barth, Fish, and Interpretive Communities," *Modern Theology* 13 (1996): 435-458; Hauerwas and Stephen Long, " Interpreting the Bible as a Political Act," *Religion and Intellectual Life*, 6:3, 4 (1989): 134-142.

16. John Howard Yoder, *The Original Revolution: Essays on Christian Pacifism* (Scottdale, Pa.: Herald Press, 1971, 1977), 65, 66.

17. John Howard Yoder, *The Priestly Kingdom: Social Ethics as Gospel,* (Notre Dame, Ind.: University of Notre Dame Press, 1984). See especially his essay, "The Constantinian Sources of Western Social Ethics," 135-147.

18. Stanley Hauerwas, *Christian Existence Today: Essays on the Church, World, and Living In Between,* (Durham, N.C.: Labyrinth Press, 1988), 180-185. For the notes I referred to see 189-190. For a more extended development of the relationship of Hauerwas and Yoder in this regard see Samuel Wells, "How the Church Performs the Jesus Story: Improvising on the Theological Ethics of Stanley Hauerwas," (Unpublished Ph.D. Thesis, University of Durham, England, 1995), 99-134.

19. Ian Barns, "Toward an Australian 'Post-Constantinian' Public Theology," *Faith and Freedom* 5:1, 2 (June 1996): 29-38.

20. Stanley Hauerwas, "Reading Yoder Down Under," *Faith and Freedom* 5: 1, 2 (June, 1996): 41.

21. Yoder, *For the Nations*, 3. Duane Friesen claims that "Yoder is much more ready to see connections between what the church stands for and movements in culture at large." "Toward a Theology of Culture," *Conrad Grebel Review* 16: 2 (Spring 1998): 63. Unfortunately, Friesen does not provide support for his assertion, but follows up his assertion by noting a disagreement between Yoder and Hauerwas by only giving Yoder's side of the issue, and not including Hauerwas' explicit reply to Yoder. The disagreement has to do with civil, or social arrangements in society. See Yoder, "Meaning After Babble: With Jeffrey Stout Beyond Relativism," *Journal of Religious Ethics* 24:1 (Spring 1996): 135; Hauerwas, *Wilderness Wanderings*, 21.

22. See Cartwright, "Radical Reform," 15, n.25, and Richard Fox, "Thorn in the Side," *Christian Century* 118 (November 21-28): 18. Douglas Harink has shown that Hauerwas and Yoder understand and use the term *nations* differently, but that people are ready to listen to Yoder precisely because of Hauerwas. Douglas Harink, "For and Against the Nations: Yoder and Hauerwas, What's the Difference?" *Toronto Journal of Theology* 17:1 (2001): 183.

23. Chris Huebner, "Globalization, Theory, and Dialogical Vulnerability," 55, n.17.

24. Stanley Hauerwas, *Should War Be Eliminated? Philosophical and Theological Investigations,* (Milwaukee, Wis.: Marquette University Press, 1984). The essay appeared later in *Against the Nations*.

25. Hauerwas, *Sanctify Them in the Truth*.

26. For example, Hauerwas makes the cryptic, probably jocular remark, "Why say carefully what you can say offensively?" in "Tribute to John Howard Yoder," 99.

27. See Hauerwas, "The Christian Difference: Or, Surviving Postmodernism," *A Better Hope*, 227, n.39.

28. Ibid., 10.

29. "A church that is not 'against the world' in fundamental ways has nothing worth saying to and for the world." Quoted by Carter, *Politics of the Cross*, 205.

30. Yoder's way of putting the matter is that "The church precedes the world epistemologically. We know more fully from Jesus Christ and in the context of the confessed faith than we know in other ways. The meaning and validity and limits of concepts like "nature" or "science" are best seen not when looked at alone but in light of the confession of Jesus Christ. The church precedes the world as well axiologically, in that the lordship of Christ is the center which must guide critical value choices, so that we may be called to subordinate or even to reject those values which contradict Jesus." Yoder, *The Priestly Kingdom*, 11.

31. "If the Church does become isolated, it will not be from withdrawal or deliberately provoking the world's violence. It may however mean that the only available path of resistance is to leave one place for another. Christians are at home in no nation: their only home is the Church itself." Samuel Wells, "How the Church Performs the Jesus Story," 109. Wells refers here to a Hauerwas statement from "Will the Real Sectarian Please Stand Up?" in which Hauerwas, referring to the Anabaptists, states that their "forced withdrawal became a self-fulfilling prophecy as Anabaptists misdescribed their own theological and social commitments by making a virtue of necessity" (91). It seems that Hauerwas is here warning Anabaptists about the dangers of being 'against the nations' as it affects our sociological position.

32. Yoder,*The Priestly Kingdom*, 15.

33. In *In Good Company*, 65. This question compelled a friend to note that perhaps Hauerwas needs to bone up on statistics that show the number of African Mennonites, for example.

34. Yoder, *The Priestly Kingdom*, 15-45.

35. Ibid., 25.

36. Ibid. Hauerwas also claims to like the notion of being a member rather than belonging, since one can belong to something without being a member. *Sanctify Them in the Truth*, 160.

37. Yoder, "Hermeneutics of Peoplehood," 25.

38. See for example, "A 'Free Church' Perspective on Baptism, Eucharist and Ministry," in *The Royal Priesthood*, 277-288.

39. Hauerwas, "Confessions," 515, 521. It seems Hauerwas has experienced some personal discomfort with his own practice of "choosing" to attend Aldersgate after reproducing precisely the kind of church shopping he wishes to defeat. *Sanctify Them in the Truth*, 163.

40. Hauerwas, *In Good Company*, 227, n.2.

41. Ibid., 228.

42. Ibid.

43. Stanley Hauerwas, John Milbank, "Christian Peace" (Wheaton College: unpublished transcript of public debate, March 17, 2000), 13.

44. Oliver O'Donovan, *The Desire of Nations: Rediscovering the Roots of Political Theology* (Cambridge, England: Cambridge University Press, 1996), 224.

45. Stanley Hauerwas and Jim Fodor, "Remaining in Babylon: Oliver O'-Donovan's Defense of Christendom," in *Wilderness Wanderings : Probing Twentieth-Century Theology and Philosophy,* (Boulder, Col.: Westview Press, 1997), 224, n.15.

46. Mark Thiessen Nation, "The Ecumenical Patience and Vocation of John Howard Yoder: A Study in Theological Ethics" (Pasadena, Calif: Fuller Theological Seminary, unpublished Ph.D. dissertation), 239.

47. Alain Epp Weaver, "After Politics: John Howard Yoder, Body Politics, and the Witnessing Church," *Review of Politics* 61:4 (Fall 1999): 637-674. Weaver tries to make the point that the new that is created in people has already begun, and thus we meet the kingdom, and do not in any sense create it by voluntarily joining it. Epp Weaver's argument attempts to show that Yoder does not have a low view of the church, but a high view of grace.

48. P. Travis Kroeker, "Why O'Donovan's Christendom is not Constantinianism and Yoder's Voluntariety is not Hobbesian: A Debate in Theological Ethics Re-Defined," *The Annual of the Society of Christian Ethics* 20 (2000): 58.

49. Ibid., 55.

50. A. James Reimer, "The Adequacy of a Voluntaristic Theology for a Voluntaristic Age," in *The Believers Church: A Voluntary Church*, ed. William Brackney, (Kitchener, Ont.: Pandora Press, 1998), 137-148.

51. James McClendon, "The Voluntary Church in the Twenty-First Century," in *The Believers Church: A Voluntary Church*, 179-198.

52. Yoder, "The Hermeneutics of Peoplehood," in *The Priestly Kingdom*, 30, 31, The scribal function is to serve the community and communal memory, a practical moral reasoner who "remembers expertly, charismatically the store of memorable, identity-confirming acts of faithfulness praised and of failure repented" (31).

53. Ibid., 43.

54. Yoder, "Sacrament as Social Process: Christ the Transformer of Culture," in *The Royal Priesthood*, 360, 361.

55. Ibid., 361. Emphasis Yoder's.

56. Ibid., 361-373. Each of these practices form the topic of individual chapters in Yoder's expanded book-length discussion. They are renamed and reordered in the book. See Yoder, *Body Politics: Five Practices of the Christian Community Before the Watching World,* (Nashville, Tenn.: Discipleship Resources, 1992).

57. Ibid., 71.

58. The words *worship* and *liturgy* are often used without substantive distinctions intended. Yoder uses both terms in a virtually interchangeable way.

Hauerwas, however, seems to prefer liturgy, a choice which seems to me to be not merely semantic, as will become clear in this section.

59. Stanley Hauerwas, *A Community of Character: Toward a Constructive Christian Social Ethic*, (Notre Dame, Ind.: University of Notre Dame Press, 1981), 240, n.9.

60. Jeffrey Siker, *Scripture and Ethics: Twentieth Century Portraits*, (New York: Oxford University Press, 1997), 9. This insight into Hauerwas's way of reading Scripture is confirmed by Richard Hays, *The Moral Vision of The New Testament: A Contemporary Introduction to New Testament Ethics* (San Francisco: Harper Collins, 1996), 256.

61. Hauerwas, *The Peaceable Kingdom*, 107, 108.

62. Ibid., 108. William Placher, in describing Hauerwas's emphasis on worship, suggests that Hauerwas does not say much about the church as a sacramental community, adding in a note that perhaps Hauerwas should publish more on this. Placher, *Narratives of a Vulnerable God: Christ, Theology, and Scripture*, (Louisville, Ky.: Westminster John Knox Press, 1994), 143, 156 n.22. I find this comment mystifying, since Hauerwas often refers especially to the celebration of the Eucharist as central to the worship of the church.

63. Hauerwas, *In Good Company*, 153-168. He includes his course outline as an appendix, 164. The basic structure is as follows: Gathering and Greeting; Confession and Sin; Scripture and Proclamation; Baptism; Offering, Sacrifice, and Eucharist; Sending Forth. The sending forth of the eucharistic service is for Hauerwas evidence that the church can never be a sect, since the question of whether to serve the world is not asked, only the question of how to serve the world. He goes on to claim that "after teaching such a course for twenty-five years, I hope to have half of the Methodist clergy of North Carolina feeling guilty for not serving the Eucharist every Sunday." "Storytelling: A Response to 'Mennonites on Hauerwas,'" *Conrad Grebel Review* 13:2 (1995): 169.

64. Hauerwas, *In Good Company*, 154, 155.

65. Stanley Hauerwas, "Worship, Evangelism, Ethics: On Eliminating the 'And,'" in *Liturgy and the Moral Self: Humanity at Full Stretch Before God*, ed. E. Byron Anderson, Bruce Morrill (Collegeville, Minn.: Liturgical Press, 1998), 99, 100. This essay is now also published in *A Better Hope*, 155-161.

66. Ibid., 106.

67. Hauerwas, *Sanctify Them in the Truth*, 11. This book is interesting in that Hauerwas is very explicit about his Wesleyan church commitments, evidenced especially in his series of essays under the rubric of "The Truth About Sanctification: Holiness Exemplified."

68. Hauerwas, *Dispatches*, 112-113. The parallel to Yoder's thought here is striking indeed. See Yoder, *The Priestly Kingdom*, 11.

69. Hauerwas, "Confessions," 521. In an earlier treatment of these matters, Hauerwas criticizes Harold Bender for omitting worship as part of the Anabaptist vision, and goes on to declare that he finds in Anabaptist worship a

lingering Zwinglian rationalism incompatible with other practices. *In Good Company*, 76.

70. Hauerwas *A Better Hope*, 155. Hauerwas's only defense is to claim that it is precisely because of Methodism's refusal to separate theology and piety that he focuses so much on liturgy. Ibid., 156.

71. Kroeker, "Why O'Donovan," 64 n.84.

72. A. James Reimer, "Mennonites, Christ, and Culture: The Yoder Legacy." *Conrad Grebel Review* 16:2 (Spring 1998):8. Mark Thiessen Nation, "The Ecumenical Patience and Vocation of John Howard Yoder," 236. Nation is following the work of David Layman. See also Craig Carter, *The Politics of the Cross*, 237.

73. Cartwright, "Sharing The House of God," 608. The larger account is found 606-608. I recognize that Reimer and Cartwright are offering different criticisms. Their similarity lies in the complaint that Yoder's work paid attention only to social ethics. I acknowledge a helpful discussion with Harry Huebner on this point.

74. Ibid., 613, 614.

75. Hauerwas, *In Good Company*, 61.

76. I am grateful for the input of several friends in the writing of this paper, especially Dr. Denny Smith, the most theologically astute dentist I know.

Chapter 10

The Public Ethics of John Howard Yoder and Stanley Hauerwas: Difference or Disagreement?

Craig R. Hovey

INTRODUCTION

Stanley Hauerwas has claimed that "everything John Howard Yoder believes, I think is true."[1] Indeed, this is also a common assumption regarding the two theologians, since Hauerwas is better known and also makes plain his indebtedness to Yoder in nearly every essay and book. However, Craig Carter recently wrote that "The biggest problem in Yoder interpretation arises with regard to Stanley Hauerwas."[2] This is because many readers come to Yoder by way of Hauerwas and, as a consequence, impose an interpretive grid whereby the differences between the two are overlooked.

Some have tried to address this concern by pointing out various differences between the two theologians. Next they either suggest (as Kent Reames has done[3]) that those who find Hauerwas problematic need not also find Yoder problematic (or at least, not for the same reasons), or they suggest (as Douglas Harink has done[4]) that the differences do not finally amount to any substantive disagreement and we would do well not to feel the need to choose between them. Therefore, though the space between Yoder and Hauerwas is certainly small relative to some others, it is worth examining some of what makes up this particular space. This kind of examination is rendered particularly difficult, though, by Hauerwas' own admission that "if there is in fact a difference—which may even amount to a disagreement—between Yoder and me, no one should be tempted to side with me."[5]

Nevertheless, one may not need to take sides to present important differences, or even disagreements. Comparing these two theologians is not a simple matter of placing them side by side. Hauerwas draws so frequently and deeply from Yoder that we cannot merely point out where they overlap; rather we must specify the places where Hauerwas has adopted Yoder's thinking and those places where he has not. Because instances when Yoder engages Hauerwas are comparatively rare (and, even then, commonly in footnotes), I intend to look at ways Hauerwas diverges from Yoder and not the other way around. By putting the matter this way, I do not wish to deny that Hauerwas may have influenced Yoder; indeed, he may have, even significantly. However, the influence has happened so strongly in the other direction that it warrants particular attention.

Much is often made of the suggestion that Yoder is essentially "for the nations" and Hauerwas is essentially "against the nations," following their respective book titles. However, this invites a simplistic, reductionistic kind of characterization that we can do without. It may certainly be the case that Hauerwas is more of a contrarian than Yoder, but such an observation does not say much that is particularly new or interesting. In what follows, I hope to engage this topic on another level. I point out three closely related areas under the topic of the church's public witness where Hauerwas has intentionally not gone along with Yoder. These are the issues of Constantinianism in modernity, pluralism,translatability, and the world's response to the church's witness.

Showing where Hauerwas' thinking departs from Yoder's may make some feel that this requires too much focus on Hauerwas and not enough on Yoder. This may indeed be true. Nevertheless, I hope this will prove to be a productive strategy for treating two thinkers who are far more interested in taking on those who differ significantly from themselves. Their writings are often directed at different audiences, serve different purposes, and treat different topics. By attending to the ways Hauerwas has not adopted every aspect of Yoder's program, I hope to advance understanding of the contributions of both to the ongoing consideration and practice of the church's faithful witness in the world.

CONSTANTINIANISM IN MODERNITY

Yoder and Hauerwas are certainly both opposed to Constantinianism, that is, the presumption that the church must take responsibility for making history come out right by aligning itself with state power. It was on this assumption that the church resorted to violence in the name of securing a future for itself and lost its critical edge and its distinctiveness.

For Hauerwas, however, the more persistent enemy of the church is liberalism. Liberalism is the modern belief that reason is grounded in rationality *qua* rationality and is therefore the reason of any clearly thinking person. In a word, it is universal. To be sure, Yoder was opposed to the Enlightenment concept of rationality too but not to the extent that Hauerwas is. Yet the difference is not simply a matter of degree, as though Yoder hates the Enlightenment but Hauerwas *really* hates the Enlightenment. Instead, Hauerwas identifies the Enlightenment with Constantinianism in a way that Yoder rarely if ever did.

Indeed, Yoder showed how the Constantinian temptation has taken different forms. Just because the church is no longer in the position to claim imperial dominance does not mean that it has not found new ways of being Constantinian; it has just done so through variations on the same theme. The social position of the church in liberal democracies has tended to be what Yoder calls "neo-neo-Constantinianism"—that is, the stage of the original Constantinian project "where the church blesses her society (and particularly her own national society) without a formal identification therewith, or without religious rootage in the common people."[6] Nations (at least, outwardly) are no longer empires which attempt to be universal in their scope and no longer rely on formal links with the church nor ostensibly consider themselves to be Christian. Thus the church cannot hold a Constantinian stance in the original sense. Nevertheless, the aims of a neo-neo-Constantinian strategy represent but a secularization of a Constantinian dream.[7]

The concern that fuels Hauerwas' polemic against liberalism, however, is not primarily rooted in the church's response to a modern ethos (although it includes this); but it involves a thoroughgoing critique of the liberal project itself. Here he draws significantly on the work of philosopher Alasdair MacIntyre. Jeffrey Stout writes, "It is not clear how Hauerwas proposes to combine [the] anti-Constantinian narrative with the anti-modern narrative he takes over from MacIntyre."[8] Nevertheless, it is clear that Hauerwas does combine them. From MacIntyre, Hauerwas adopts the view that, in the Enlightenment, theories of rationality suffered a great blow when they presumed to achieve universal significance by dispensing with the narrative framework which gave rationality coherence. As a consequence, moral reasoning no longer depended on systems of thought and practice. Therefore, in the modern period, not only did the church maintain a Constantinian stance, as Yoder contends, but also the world lost contact with the very conditions necessary for it to be virtuous.

For Hauerwas, the false universalism of liberalism is but a form of Constantinianism. He writes, "Christian adherence to foundationalist epistemologies—that is, the kind of position we find exemplified in thinkers such as Kant—was commensurate with social strategies of Christendom" and "I am not asking the church to withdraw, but rather to give up the presumptions of Constantinian power, particularly when those take the form of liberal universalism."[9] This means that a church that rejects the strategies of Christendom cannot help but find itself incommensurate with liberalism. This is because both Christendom and liberalism rely on false universals.

It is important to note that Yoder is not committed to incommensurability between the church and the world as Hauerwas is. This is because he does not connect the project of Christendom with the project of the Enlightenment as Hauerwas does, even though he is often vigorously critical of both. Hauerwas represents, therefore, a combination of Yoder and MacIntyre, in his notion of incommensurability. Indeed, he notes, "It is probably a sign of the unusual times in which we live that I can be at once influenced by Alasdair MacIntyre and John Howard Yoder without feeling a deep sense of contradiction."[10] These unusual times, no doubt, involve the temptation toward absolutizing Christian claims to power over history on the grounds that the dominant forms of rationality not only make such absolutizing possible but, in some sense, inevitable.

Stout observes this when he writes, "One cannot stand in a church conceived in Yoder's terms, while describing the world surrounding it in the way MacIntyre describes liberal society, without implicitly adopting a stance that is rigidly dualistic. . . . "[11] However, saying that the church and the world are incommensurate with one another is not necessarily the same as dualism if by dualism we mean some kind of ontological separation. Ontologically, the church and the world are both under the lordship of Christ and have been given the same possibilities. Hauerwas follows Yoder in maintaining that if there is a duality, it is not over the domain of Christ's lordship but over agency: "between the basic personal postures of men, some of whom confess and others of whom do not confess that Jesus Christ is Lord."[12] There may be a descriptive dualism but not an ontological one or, better, not a necessary dualism but a contingent one.[13]

In the same way, incommensurability is not a way of talking about the church's relationship to the world at all times and places. For example, Constantine did not become Constantinian because he shared liberal presuppositions regarding universal reason, but because he got wrong "the course of history, its direction, and meaningfulness."[14] In the modern period, the Constantinian temptation was legitimated in a new way; its legitimation sanctioned the support of nation states since the church no longer held political power as the church. When it held power, it was only due to its close affiliation to the nation state. In this situation, as long as the church confronts the epistemological assumptions of liberalism, which make inevitable a demand that the church adopt either a Constantinian social strategy or admit irrelevance, it cannot help but exist incommensurably with such a world.

PLURALISM

Of course, this state of affairs has potentially been reshaped by pluralist and relativist critiques. Recently, Hauerwas suggested that a possible form of the church's witness might involve being "tactical allies of the pluralism/relativist questioning of the secular orthodoxies that promise certainty through coercion."[15] Hauerwas warns, however, against exalting relativism on its own terms, even as relativism may make a useful partner in the struggle against the Enlightenment. In suggesting this strategy, Hauerwas deliberately follows Yoder's use of the term "tactical allies" from Yoder's essay, "But We Do See Jesus."[16]

It is telling that Hauerwas does not take up Yoder's suggestion that we might ally ourselves even with the Enlightenment. This is the one thing that Christians have been more than willing to do and so, it could be argued, the church is in no position to make an alliance with such a seductive enemy. Certainly too much could be made of this point, especially since it argues from silence (i.e. from what Hauerwas does *not* say) and both theologians have written far too much to warrant an argument from silence. Yet it is instructive in a paradigmatic way of a subtle but real difference between these two theologians.

For one, Yoder does not want to reject some of the fruits of modern liberalism to the extent that Hauerwas wants. He is sympathetic to a "soft pluralism." He writes, "From the gospel perspective, modern pluralism is not a setback but a providential occasion for clarification."[17] He goes on to suggest that pluralism can make life more livable for minority voices and so is preferable to the alternatives. Of course, it is a form of Constantinianism when we begin to ask what the best form of government is[18] but the state is under divine lordship to "maintain the order needed for the church to live as a witness to a new form of social relations."[19]

But Hauerwas does not think that what we have should be called pluralism since it has produced enormously conformist consumers in a capitalist economy.[20] This conformity is, in some sense, achieved in the name of pluralism, that is, under the illusion of free choice. Following Nicholas Boyle, Hauerwas is suspicious of suggestions that the global expression of so-called pluralism may, in fact, provide a better ethos for the church. Indeed, it may be just as tempting, "For the new order is a kind of universality whose ambition is to rule minds and bodies just as nations did so effectively in the past."[21]

Even worse, the language of pluralism admits to a variety of so-called postmodern discourse which is still essentially modern. Hauerwas says that he is not convinced that "postmodernism, either as an intellectual position or as a cultural style, is post-anything."[22] Instead, it is the "bastard offspring"[23] of modernism to the extent that it continues to presuppose an ahistorical viewpoint based around the false presumption of personal liberty. The language of pluralism relies on a notion of relativism that is still a modern description.

Even though Yoder wants to maintain pluralism, he reminds Stout that the assumption that "relativism is something recent and threatening, rests upon nostalgia for a prior epoch of Establishment. There never was an homogeneous moral language; it only seemed that there was because the other voices were not heard."[24] The charge of relativism, like the charge of sectarianism, is only a version of the modernist ethos that makes notions like relativism and sectarianism inevitable. It is the language that postmodernists revert to in a way that betrays their modernist commitments. Instead, if objectivism is false, it is not false because relativism is true, but because neither objectivism nor relativism has merit as a distinct category. But for Yoder, the hearing of the unheard voices that is so crucial for dismantling the false universalism of modernity is accomplished by a modern pluralism that Hauerwas essentially rejects on the grounds that such minority voices are not given a voice so much as they have been made to think that they have relatively little to say. With Yoder, Hauerwas rejects the language of relativism as essentially modern, but with MacIntyre he suspects that the language of pluralism is too.

I have been trying to show that Yoder and Hauerwas conceive of Constantinianism's modern expression somewhat differently. It should not be surprising that, comparatively, Hauerwas rarely even uses the term *Constantinian*, instead preferring to name liberalism on its own. This owes to Hauerwas' particular combination of MacIntyre's identification of liberalism with the Christendom fantasy. Put simply (and at the risk of oversimplification), when it comes to Constantinianism and liberalism, the difference between Yoder and Hauerwas is MacIntyre. Next, I will attempt to show how this difference bears on how these two theologians represent the church's witness in the public sphere.

TRANSLATABILITY

Middle axioms

Much of Yoder's work was devoted to articulating how the church could be involved in more secular peace movements and work for justice and so forth in the public arena. Yoder's first and most influential suggestion in this regard came in his book *The Christian Witness to the State* (1964, reprinted 1977).[25] There, Yoder employs the concept of "middle axioms," a popular concept in ecumenical circles at the time. By it, he meant that the church should employ ways of addressing specific actions of the state, not in the native language of the church but in the language of the state. Christians, therefore, witness to the state by selectively calling the state to live up to the state's own highest ideals and stated principles.

Making these kinds of appeals to the state would then involve the *ad hoc* deployment of Christian norms formulated in "pagan terms" such as, Yoder suggests, liberty, equality, fraternity, education, democracy, and human rights.[26] The pagan terms do not have an existence of their own but have a temporary usefulness to the Christian who knows that "the ultimate ground for their validity is the love of

Christ."[27] "No metaphysical value is ascribed to the middle axioms outside of Christ"[28]

A significant difference arises here between Yoder and Hauerwas because Hauerwas has "a number of theological and philosophical misgivings about the very idea of translation."[29] Of course, Hauerwas had in mind bigger offenders than Yoder (most notably James Gustafson) when he expressed his misgivings. Nevertheless, one suspects that, for him, middle axioms come too close to the kind of Enlightenment project that produced the accommodationist church in America. But perhaps more importantly, the idea of translation as a means to communicate is philosophically problematic.

Following Ludwig Wittgenstein, Hauerwas asserts that language is intelligible only within determinate settings—or linguistic communities—which arise from shared skills and practices.[30] Intelligibility is not intrinsic to language or even to a particular message but depends on the recipient being able to understand what is said as communication based on using these skills and practices. In other words, much of what we typically refer to as translation is really the speaking of a second message. To speak in a different context and have it count as communication requires training in the second form of life and learning to speak that language. This is not translation since the bearer of meaningful utterance is not semantic but communal in nature. Put differently, the world cannot know what Christians might mean by human rights without entering into worship.

Since the language of liberalism, in Hauerwas' words, "has been and is the speech that dominates our lives,"[31] the church is challenged to inhabit an alternative speech community that takes seriously the inability to separate language from the world. Pagan terms cannot help but communicate pagan meaning even when Christians use them. Even when intended as a translation of *agape*, the language of liberty does not challenge the presumption that the freedom of the individual is primary, a notion incompatible with God's love. For Hauerwas, Christian speech not only resists translation on account of the material content of Christian convictions—although this is true— but it resists translation primarily because the very idea of translation is spurious.

The difference with Yoder is significant but subtle. Yoder is not the best representative of the position that Hauerwas argues against. After all, middle axioms, for Yoder, are not perfect translations and some translations are not defensible. He laments, for example, the "ease with which the word 'freedom' replaces the name 'Jesus'" among oppressed peoples who sing of liberation. The problem is not that a translation has happened but, instead, we need to ask "whether the word 'freedom,' with all the freight of meaning which it has come to have in the contemporary movement, is big enough and true enough to say everything that the name of Jesus must mean."[32]

Nevertheless, in the concept of middle axioms, Yoder relied on the ability of Christians to translate their convictions into the language used by the state. The state is thus called to approximate Christian norms more closely even though the translated message need not have recourse to the language of those norms in their biblical and traditional formulations.

Michael Cartwright correctly observes that, over time, Yoder dropped the language of middle axioms although he never specifically repudiated it as a notion.[33] What is clear, however, is that Yoder began increasingly to focus the language of witness on the church side of the church-world distinction. It is an open question whether middle axioms dropped out of his vocabulary and the role of translatability in political witness was diminished due to misgivings over translatability or for some other reason. Yoder's essay on "The Christian Case for Democracy," for example, clearly relies on a kind of translation across three "semantic frames": how the faith community speaks internally, how it speaks to the nations, and how the nations speak on their own terms.[34] Here, it could be argued that Yoder essentially retained the notion of middle axioms but dropped the terminology.

The five practices of witness

In several essays and eventually in book form (*Body Politics*[35]), Yoder set forth what appears to be his own improvement to the previous notion of "middle axioms," namely a set of "five practices of the Christian community before the watching world."[36] The advantage of the practices of *Body Politics* over middle axioms lies in the fact that the practices are meant to be *constitutive* of the church's very existence; they are a part of what the church *is* rather than what the church *does*. Of course, by definition, a practice is something that is done, but in the case of the particular practices Yoder suggests, he does not intend for us to imagine the church even existing apart from these kinds of practices. Put simply, the church does not do what it does because the world is watching but because it is called to faithfulness. The substance of Yoder's approach here derives from the acknowledgement that worship and ethics are not, in the end, separable.

Yet "each of these practices can function as a paradigm for ways in which other social groups might operate" since "they are accessible to the public. People who do not share the faith or join the community can learn from them."[37] This way of putting witness is much closer to Hauerwas' than was the language of middle axioms.

Even though he is careful to indicate that these five practices are meant to be crucial to the life of the church, Yoder has in mind that they also cannot help but witness to the world. He notes that, in addition to being a form of the church's faithfulness to God, a practice "at the same time offers a paradigm for the life of the larger society."[38] For example, in the Eucharist, we find the normative Christian affirmation that disciples break bread together. This involves feeding the hungry and all eating in turn regardless of rank or class. For Yoder, a churchly practice has an identifiable, social dimension which witnesses to the world and "is a paradigm, not only for soup kitchens and hospitality houses, but also for social security and negative income tax."[39]

However, by focusing on practices, Yoder does not give up entirely on the project of translation. He insists that the practices *are* translatable because they are not "religious" activities but "are by nature 'lay' or 'public' phenomena."[40] Perhaps with Hauerwas in mind, Yoder addresses the concern over the use of mediating language:

> Some have warned me that it is dangerous to borrow such worldly words as "egalitarian" or "freedom" since those concepts are not only hard to define but are the property of the liberal establishment, which is an oppressive elite. These friends are right in thus warning me. If I were to think that those contemporary terms have a univocal normative meaning, and if I were proposing that they simply be "baptized," I should have sold out. But those warning friends are wrong if they suggest that some other, less liberal words (for example "virtue," "narrative," "community") would be safer from abuse. The right corrective is not to seek fail-safe words never yet corrupted but rather to renew daily the action of preempting the extant vocabulary, rendering every creature subject to God's rule in Christ. What is needed is to surface the criteria whereby we can tell whether, in the appropriation of each new language, the meaning of Jesus is authentically reenacted or abandoned.[41]

Here Yoder comes close to addressing Hauerwas' philosophical misgivings about translatability. He is making one of two possible moves. On the one hand, Yoder may be primarily defending the integrity of practices and language. "Preempting the extant vocabulary" might take the form of inhabiting "liberal" words with new practices and the "criteria" he has in mind for determining whether a language is true to Jesus are themselves practices. On the other hand, Yoder may be primarily defending the practice of translation where practices make the translation authentic. So when the church speaks about freedom, for example, and knows that it means something different from the liberal meaning, its truthful living supports its redeemed use.

In either case, Yoder is clearly onto a project quite different from middle axioms and, in significant respects, closer to Hauerwas. However Yoder intends to support the witnessing power of churchly practices, he does not intend to suggest that the state be called to live up to its own, highest stated ideals. Instead, the church, as part of its internal worship life, is of service to the world. It suggests possibilities that, apart from the presence of an alternative community of belief, the world could not know. These possibilities are not only normative for the church but for the whole world since Jesus is Lord over all.

THE WORLD'S RESPONSE
TO THE CHURCH'S WITNESS

For both Yoder and Hauerwas, the witness of the church is primarily a matter of being a visible, real, alternative community of belief in a world of unbelief.[42] This community lives as though the kingdom has come in Jesus Christ and so is equipped to live in a new way. As such, the church is a model to the world of what has been made possible since Jesus is Lord over the whole world.

The two theologians, however, differ over the kind of response to witness that the church can normally expect from the world. In this, they differ quite apart from the issue of translation. Yoder is much more optimistic about the world's response. The new possibilities made real in the life of the church for the wider society are made explicit in practices which do not necessarily require translation, as we have seen.

According to Hauerwas, however, the world may well convert as a result of the Church's witness but such witness is more likely to yield contempt than awe. The watching world is more likely to reject the church's witness than learn from it. This is because the truthfulness of the church's witness runs so contrary to the world that the world will not immediately recognize it as true. Even in the event that the church's witness is met with conversion, it is the result of a crisis. The world may learn from the church's refusal to live according to violence, for example, but not without radical discontinuity with the world's whole public program which seems to require violence. Here Hauerwas adopts MacIntyre's notion of an epistemological crisis.

According to MacIntyre, incommensurable traditions are domains that cannot simultaneously have purchase on the human agent or community and the movement from one to the other requires an epistemological crisis.[43] Hauerwas notes that witness is disruptive: "That Christians are first and foremost called to be witnesses by necessity creates epistemological crises for those who do not worship the God of Jesus Christ."[44] The church witnesses to the truth about the way that the world has been made new on account of the cross and resurrection. The problem is that the world does not know that the world as it appears is not the way things really are. The church's witness challenges the belief that the world is in possession of ultimate reality by living according to the new age.

This throws the one who does not believe into an epistemological crisis which calls into question the narrative that gives rise to the unquestioned assumption about the reality of the world. Hauerwas notes that a "new narrative is required for the resolution of an epistemological crisis. Such a narrative must enable the agent to understand both how they could have intelligibly held their former beliefs and how they may have been misled by them."[45] Conversion, then, is fitting one's life into the narrative that resolves the crisis.

Of course, putting the matter this way is simplistic, insofar as it suggests that an epistemological crisis is followed by a dramatic and immediate resolution. Hauerwas follows MacIntyre in arguing that traditions may, for a long period of time, coexist without resolving conflict, which is to say, without the recognition that a crisis exists.[46] Hauerwas draws attention to war as the necessary result when "traditions are unable to recognize the crises they create for each other."[47]

Similarly, learning to see one's life in the ongoing narrative of Jesus and of the church is a lifelong process of learning the reality of what was accomplished in baptism. This is also more generally true of the church's witness to the world. Without the presence of the church as an alternative community that lives in a way newly made possible in Christ, the world, in Hauerwas' words, "cannot know that it is the world."[48] It cannot know that all along, it has been assuming that the world is the full extent of all possibilities unless an alternative possibility exists to challenge that assumption.

Even though much of the language of the "alternative community" is Yoder's, Yoder does not see witness as involving much of a crisis. This is because, for him, the practical rationality of the church is commensurate with that of the world. The world is in need only of a truthful message proclaimed and witnessed with integrity. With Hauerwas, Yoder maintains that the church's witness is a witness regarding the way the world really is. The difference is that, according to Hauerwas, the world cannot readily recognize the world as it is apart from adopting the very practices of worship and so forth that allow for the acknowledgement that the material content of the church's witness might, in fact, be true.

It should be clear that the epistemological crisis is a corollary of Hauerwas' views on translatability and incommensurability. It is the means by which one tradition adopts another or, better, converts from one to the other. There is no significant translation of the Christian message but, instead, the display of the effective causes for an epistemological crisis should the world turn and believe. Put differently, the practices of Christian worship and service are, for Yoder, the carrier of the message and, at times, the message itself; whereas, for Hauerwas, such practices are also the means by which the practitioner comes to see the truthfulness and reality of the message.

CONCLUSION

Noting that Yoder is "For the Nations" and Hauerwas is "Against the Nations" is not to say much on its own. Both theologians deserve much more attention than that unfortunate characterization. Certainly there are differences; there may in fact be disagreements. The differences I have noted between Yoder and Hauerwas may be subtle but they are real. They bear on the nature of the church, the world, and the church's witness to the world.

But what are we to make of these differences? It is not at all clear to me whether a Mennonite needs Wittgenstein (or MacIntyre) as much as does a Methodist graduate of Yale. Hauerwas's Yale mistook particularity for universality in a way that the Mennonite world was never privileged to do. Put more contentiously, maybe Mennonites do not need a prophet against liberalism as badly as the rest of us do.[49] I suspect this is a reason that only a John Howard Yoder could write against methodologism as effortlessly as he did; he knew what most of us do not, namely, a "concrete social genuineness of the community's reasoning together in the Spirit."[50]

If we insist on making a distinction between being for or against the nations, we do so at the expense of more thoughtful attention to the way of God in the world. Perhaps Yoder, himself, said it best:

> For the people of God to be over against the world at those points where "the world" is defined by its rebellion against God and for us to be in, with and for the world, as anticipation of the shape of redemption, are not alternative strategies. We are not free to choose between them, depending on whether our tastes are more "catholic" or more "baptist," or depending on whether we think the times are friendly just now or not. Each dimension of our stance is the prerequisite for the validity of the other. A church that is not "against the world" in fundamental ways has nothing worth saying to and for the world. Conversion and separation are not the way to become otherworldly; they are the only way to be present, relevantly and redemptively, in the midst of things.[51]

NOTES

1. Debate with Paige Patterson at Southeastern Baptist Theological Seminary, September 18, 2002.

2. Craig A. Carter, *The Politics of the Cross* (Grand Rapids: Brazos, 2001), 227.

3. Kent Reames, "Why Yoder is not Hauerwas and Why it Matters," presented at the Society of Christian Ethics Annual Meeting, 1999.

4. Douglas Harink, "For or Against the Nations: Yoder and Hauerwas, What's the Difference?" *Toronto Journal of Theology* 17:1 (2001).

5. Stanley Hauerwas, foreword to Craig Carter, *The Politics of the Cross* (Grand Rapids: Brazos, 2001), 10.

6. John Howard Yoder, *The Original Revolution* (Scottdale, Pa.: Herald Press, 1971), 152.

7. Ibid., 151.

8. Jeffrey Stout, "Virtue and the Way of the World: Reflections on Hauerwas," 6. (Paper presented in Berlin, Societas Ethica Annual Conference, August, 2001, used with the author's permission). Page numbers refer to author's copy of manuscript.

9. Stanley Hauerwas, *After Christendom* (Nashville: Abingdon, 1991), 15, 18.

10. Ibid., 9.

11. Stout, "Virtue and the Way of the World," 3.

12. Yoder, *Original Revolution*, 116. See also Stanley Hauerwas, "Messianic Pacifism," *Worldview* 16:6 (June 1973): 32.

13. Yoder characterized some Mennonite theology, such as Hershberger's, as holding an ontological dualism in which Christians live by nonviolence and the state lives by violence. *Nevertheless: The Varieties and Shortcomings of Religious Pacifism*, rev. and expanded ed. (Scottdale, Pa.: Herald Press, 1992), 113.

14. Yoder, *Original Revolution*, 148.

15. Stanley Hauerwas, *With the Grain of the Universe: The Church's Witness and Natural Theology* (Grand Rapids: Brazos, 2001), 224-225

16. John Howard Yoder, *The Priestly Kingdom* (Notre Dame, Ind.: University of Notre Dame Press, 1984), 61.

17. John Howard Yoder, "Meaning after Babble," *Journal of Religious Ethics* 24: 1 (spring 1996): 135.

18. Yoder, *Priestly Kingdom*, 154.

19. Alain Epp Weaver, "After Politics: John Howard Yoder, Body Politics, and the Witnessing Church," *The Review of Politics* 16:4 (Fall 1999): 663.

20. See *After Christendom*, 97-98.

21. Stanley Hauerwas, *A Better Hope: Resources for a Church Confronting Capitalism, Democracy, and Postmodernity* (Grand Rapids: Brazos, 2000), 45.

22. Ibid., 37.

23. Ibid., 38.

24. Yoder, "Meaning after Babble," 134-135.

25. John Howard Yoder, *The Christian Witness to the State*, (Eugene, Ore.: Wipf & Stock Publishers, 1997 reprint of 1964/1977 Newton, Kan. Faith and Life Press ed.).

26. Ibid., 73.

27. Ibid.

28. Epp Weaver "After Politics," 670.

29. Stanley Hauerwas, *Wilderness Wanderings: Probing Twentieth-Century Theology and Philosophy* (Boulder, Col.: Westview, 1997), 3.

30. See Brad Kallenberg, *Ethics as Grammar* (Notre Dame, Ind.: University of Notre Dame Press, 2001), 119-133.

31. Stanley Hauerwas, "Failure of Communication or A Case of Uncomprehending Feminism," *Scottish Journal of Theology* 50:2 (1997): 231.

32. John Howard Yoder, *For the Nations: Essays Public and Evangelical* (Grand Rapids: Eerdmans, 1997), 121.

33. Michael Cartwright, "Radical Reform, Radical Catholicity: John Howard Yoder's Vision of the Faithful Church," *The Royal Priesthood: Essays Ecclesiological and Ecumenical*, ed. Michael Cartwright (Grand Rapids: Eerdmans, 1994), 17.

34. Yoder, *The Priestly Kingdom*, 160-161. See also164: "It is sufficient to be aware of the relativity of our linguistic rulings to be able to translate from one frame to the other."

35. John Howard Yoder, *Body Politics: Five Practices of the Christian Commu-*

nity Before the Watching World (Scottdale, Pa.: Herald Press, 1992, 2001).

36. This is the subtitle to *Body Politics*.

37. Yoder, *Royal Priesthood*, 369.

38. Yoder, *Body Politics*, x.

39. Yoder, *Royal Priesthood*, 370.

40. Ibid.

41. Ibid.

42. Yoder, *Original Revolution*, 116. This is the thesis of Stanley Hauerwas and William H. Willimon, *Resident Aliens: Life in the Christian Colony* (Nashville, Tenn.: Abingdon, 1989).

43. See Alasdair MacIntyre, "Epistemological Crises, Dramatic Narrative, and the Philosophy of Science," *Why Narrative?* ed. Stanley Hauerwas and L. Gregory Jones (Eugene, Ore.: Wipf and Stock, 1997), 138-157.

44. Stanley Hauerwas, *Sanctify Them in the Truth: Holiness Exemplified* (Nashville, Tenn.: Abingdon, 1998), 187.

45. Ibid., 186.

46. Ibid., 187.

47. Ibid.

48. Hauerwas and Willimon, *Resident Aliens*, 94.

49. I interpret James McClendon as claiming that Hauerwas is a prophet against liberalism in his review of *Christian Existence Today. Theology Today* 46:4 (Jan. 1990): 427.

50. John Howard Yoder, "Walk and Word: The Alternatives to Methodologism" in *Theology Without Foundations: Religious Practice and the Future of Theological Truth*, ed. Stanley Hauerwas, Nancey Murphy, and Mark Nation (Nashville, Tenn.: Abingdon, 1994), 87.

51. Yoder, *Body Politics*, 78.

Chapter 11

The Christian Witness in the Earthly City: John H. Yoder as Augustinian Interlocutor

Gerald W. Schlabach

SEEK THE PEACE OF THE CITY—its welfare, its prosperity, its shalom. After all the violence and humiliation at the hands of the nations, after all the temptations to counter-hubris and patriotic self-exaltation, after all the promise and hiddenness of a covenant-making God, after all the epiphanies and betrayals of loyalty to this God, after all the disorientation of land loss and forced exile—this was Jeremiah's last word to Israel's exiles in Babylon.[1] The social stance to which it called them was supple and manifold, requiring them both to stubbornly preserve their identity and accept the suffering of serving the common good they shared even with their conquering enemy. They must be "in but not of"—long before that phrase became a cliché barely able to move us anymore with its rich social creativity.

And so too both Augustine of Hippo and John Howard Yoder. Intriguingly, each in his own way ended long reflections about the role of the church in the world at this same point, exhorting Christians to follow the model of Jeremiah's exiles in Babylon. This, I will argue, is no mere coincidence. For Augustine's last word on how the "heav-

221

enly city" of Christians still on pilgrimage should live amid the "earthly city" has served Christian traditions in the West not so much as a final answer to the question of how they should order politics within the passing societies of every age, but as a definitive stating of the question. We can thus construe Yoder's pacifist, ecclesial social ethic as a late answer—perhaps the best answer—to the very question Augustine did so much to sharpen but ultimately left hanging: Just how *are* we to seek the peace of the city without eroding our loyalty to that better one in whose hope we move and live?

John Howard Yoder was, in other words, far more deeply embedded in Augustinian problematics and debates than we usually recognize. Even to recognize this possibility, however, the reader may need also to recognize at least some of the assumptions by which I will proceed. First, what is true of most "authorities" in the Christian tradition is prototypically true of Augustine: By being pilgrims they left traces along multiple paths by which we may now construe their legacies. Second, the fidelity of one especially creative thinker to another greatly influential one may only be traceable through deep and imaginative reading, not merely the counting of citations. Third, sometimes those with whom we argue are the ones who influence us most.

CONVERGING UPON JEREMIAH

St. Augustine of Hippo has exercised such an abiding influence on political thought in the West for a curious reason: Intrinsic to his vision of human society is the insight that we can never quite set our affairs in order and never quite get our politics right. The world's best possible peace is a shadowy one; its most stable order is a tenuous one; its fullest possible justice is always only somewhat more just than current arrangements. In fact, the very effort to forge a definitive political order lies at the root of many of humanity's gravest injustices, disorders and conflicts. For when the earthly city imagines itself to be too like the heavenly city—eternal and approaching the glory that is proper only to God—it intensifies the very conditions of human fallenness and thus invites its own falling.

Inevitably if not explicitly, therefore, politics according to Augustine must always be temporal, tentative, and revisable.[2] This leaves every generation with a remainder to rework. And that makes Augustinian political thought itself into an ongoing debate that no age, system or ideology can definitively capture.[3] Paradoxically, it thrives upon the recognition of human limitations—but that must include the limits of any particular "political Augustinianism."[4]

If the politics Augustine charted for the earthly city is *necessarily* and *rightly* incomplete, however, the same cannot be said of Augustine's ecclesiology. Given the rigor of Augustine's critique of the Roman Empire in *City of God*, and the depth of political insight that his critique occasioned, one might have expected from him an ecclesiology at least as thorough as his political theory. If an adequate account of the life of the church must include not just a theological metaphysic but a practicable sociology, however, Augustine's ecclesiology is elusive and suggestive at best.[5]

In a strictly theological sense, no doubt, Augustine's ecclesiology is immensely rich. For Augustine, the church is nothing short of shared participation in God's own trinitarian life of mutual love.[6] Such communion is possible insofar as the earthy, bloody incarnation of God in Christ, together with the outpouring of love into our hearts by the Holy Spirit, heals both our divided wills and our disordered relationships. If the church remains a hospital for convalescents, and the mystery of healing renders an invisible quality to the final identities of the church's members, that is because the church lives in an eschatological tension between already-in-communion and not-yet-fully transformed. In short, Augustine's ecclesiology is seamlessly integrated with his trinitarian theology with his doctrine of love with his eschatology.

In fact, Augustine's vision of the church was not devoid of practical, sociological, or political specification either. Virtually all of Augustine's writings were "occasional" in some way, insofar as they responded to specific controversies, accusations, or pastoral challenges. Whatever else *City of God* became through its twenty-two lengthy "books," therefore, it began as a response to an accusation.[7] Roman aristocrats were saying that the reason their city had been sacked in 410 was that Christianity had weakened its citizens' virtue and diverted their devotion away from the gods. So when Augustine countered that Rome (the most immediate instantiation of "the earthly city") had slipped because it had risen too high, had deteriorated because it had overextended itself, was humbled because it had grown through imperial pride,[8] his critique came with lessons for that other society which was making its way through the earthly city.

The pilgrim heavenly city which is the church must thrive by humbling itself and glorifying God not self, nor the collective self of nation; its love cannot be for domination, but for God, neighbor and even enemy. And though no one may mistake Augustine for a pacifist, he certainly recognized that the church had in fact extended itself through the faithfulness of the martyrs and the witness of a people who, like the Hebrews, "was gathered and united in a kind of community designed to perform [the] sacred function of revelation" through "signs and symbols appropriate to the times."[9] This witnessing presence in the world hints at the affirmation of the Second Vatican Council that the church itself is the sacrament of the world's salvation. It also hints at the truthful power of what John Howard Yoder called the creative minority whose presence is the "original revolution" in the world.

But by now we are *only* talking about hints. What Augustine's ecclesiology lacks is a politics or sociology to chart out how Christians are to live simultaneously in the earthly and heavenly cities, without confusing their loyalties or conflating their duties. To be sure, just as no politics for the earthly city can be definitive—given the eschatological tension of the age—likewise any polity for the heavenly city that is intermixed within the earthly must have a certain open-ended quality. After all, Christians must not only anticipate variations according to culture, history and circumstances, but must remember precisely that they *are* on pilgrimage, never fully settled but intermixed within the earthly city, and thus still being perfected.

What we may rightly wish of Augustine, however, is that he had at least been clearer about whether and when his political commentary on the earthly city applied normatively to Christians. A passage often assumed to settle the case may illustrate. How are we to interpret book 19 of the *City of God* in general, and the identity of "our wise man" the reluctant judge of *City of God* 19.6 in particular? The chapter begins with recognition that even in human cities that are relatively at peace, some must pass judgments upon others. For those judgments to be just, Roman jurisprudence could not imagine the interrogation of suspects without recourse to torture. But anyone informed by the best wisdom of human philosophy (the subject of previous chapters) would recognize how imperfect was the juridical process. Torturing suspects to extract the truth might prompt the innocent to lie—and all the more quickly if they too heeded the philosophers, who counseled courage to welcome death and escape the miseries of this life!

Doing one's duty to preserve justice in the earthly city thus necessitated an array of tragic choices: release the innocent only after undeserved torture, execute the innocent upon false confession, or execute an actual criminal without certainty of the grounds. Because "our wise man" saw "this darkness that attends the life of human society" without flinching, he would accept its claims, do his duty, and sit on the bench without shirking. "Here we have what I call the wretchedness of man's situation," wrote Augustine. And if the wise man was not to be called wicked, that was only because he hated the very "necessity of his own actions," was learning a further wisdom from devotion to God, and cried out for deliverance from his necessities.

To most interpreters, the lesson we should take from Augustine has seemed obvious. In the following chapter, *City of God* 19.7, "our wise man" turned "wise judge" serves as template for explaining why even the best and wisest philosopher officials will not only punish wrongdoers but wage wars, though they will wage even just wars reluctantly. But although that much is straightforward in the text, the standard interpretation goes farther than the text itself warrants. For when it makes "our wise man" into the exemplar for any politician informed by Augustinian sensibilities—and thus for any politically involved Christian—it assumes that Augustine's purpose was to provide a normative argument rather than a description of the human predicament apart from God.

Most of *City of God* 19 is about indictment, not guidance. It is one of Augustine's many and characteristic endeavors to drive his readers to despair precisely in order that they like he will look elsewhere for hope, recognize their need for God and cry out for deliverance.[10] The first chapters of *City of God* 19 constitute the climax to a long series of similarly structured indictments that build upon each other and thus constitute the master argument of the tome: The Roman aristocrats who accuse Christianity of weakening Roman virtue are the ones who have weakened the empire by failing to match the virtues of the old Romans.[11] But the virtues of the old and founding Romans in fact had rested on vices—love of glory, praise, domination, and self—so that whatever glories they had in fact achieved in this world, "they have received their reward" and could look forward to nothing eternal (Matt. 6:2, 5, 16).[12]

Ancient philosophers offered somewhat better counsel about where to lodge one's hope and how to pursue the human good; of all the various philosophical sects Platonism came closest to an answer by recognizing that we must look beyond this life for life's happiness.[13] But even they fell short by seeking their good through pride in their own efforts, rather than faith in God.[14] And if the one thing the philosophers all agreed upon was that the human good must be social, the best that human society had to offer was a "shadowy peace" still full of ills, enmity, and tragic choices.[15] Such is the panorama of misery Augustine has just finished presenting in *City of God* 19.5.

"Our wise man" of 19.6, then, was the one who had learned all these lessons—the best that Roman civic culture and antique philosophical eclecticism had to offer. He was Stoic in composure, Platonic in aspiration, and perhaps somewhere upon the threshold of Christian devotion to God, but no more than that was certain. What he should do next in his official capacity simply was not the driving point of Augustine's argument.

Augustine knew and counselled many such men, of course. He had been one, and though he had once renounced public life he later found himself re-immersed in it as a bishop. The *City of God* itself he directed to Marcellinus, a genuinely pious Christian and a Roman official in North Africa. When Count Boniface was considering the monastery—wishing deliverance from his necessities, perhaps—Augustine urged him to stay in the military, only to see his moral stature deteriorate in the following years.[16]

Such pastoral counsel often responded as much to Augustine's pragmatism as his principle, however.[17] Disjunctures between his systematic reflection and his occasional letters are as much a sign that he himself was unsettled about what "our wise man" and judge should do next, once devoted to God, as they are an authoritative template for Christian political engagement. To Boniface he wrote famously, for example, that his only objective in war should be peace, not vengeance. Yet Augustine's more systematic reflections in *City of God* 19.12 demonstrate that all creatures, even monsters, seek peace as their ultimate end anyway. So only that "only" in Augustine's counsel to Boniface is normative, and it risks of devolving into platitude. Further, even that "only" is problematic, for of all Church Fathers, Augustine knew better than any that no one can really know one's own intentions, leaving no way to verify when one is acting justly in war.[18]

The normative guidance that Augustine did offer to worldly wise Christians in *City of God* 19, was that they look to God for hope, look to the heavenly city for citizenship, and look at the earthly city as no better than a "captivity."[19] They should not cease to be "a society of resident aliens" drawn from many languages and cultures—not abandon therefore the status that Christians had embraced before Constantine.[20] The inadequate, shadowy peace of the earthly city surely had value insofar as it gave the church time and space to grow in the worship of God, but Christians should merely *use* this earthly peace not rest in it or identify with it as their own.[21]

To "seek the peace of the city" was in fact an obligation for members of the pilgriming heavenly city, but they should do so precisely as did the captive exiles to whom Jeremiah once wrote.[22] If Jeremiah's exiles were the template for Christian political engagement (and if the young Jewish men in the Babylon of the book of Daniel have a historical basis) then yes, one way to seek the peace of the city might be to work as civil servants. But unlike the Roman officials with whom Augustine corresponded, Diaspora Jews had had little trouble remembering themselves to be captives. They dare not forgot that they *were* in Babylon, that resistance to imperial idolatry could never cease to be an option, and that they belonged first to God and God's people.

For all practical purposes, Jeremiah's final exhortation was Augustine's last word on politics and Christian engagement in *City of God*. It does not solve but rather leaves hanging the fruitful question of *how* exactly Christians are to seek the peace of the earthly city. To take the practices of Augustine's wise but more-Stoic-than-Christian judge as our final answer to the question of how to seek the peace of the city is to misread his larger argument. Such a move ignores his rhetorical practices and above all begs the question Augustine left hanging. The "wise man" of *City of God* 19 then serves as a blank for later interpreters to fill in with whatever they have already decided to be the best wisdom of their age; Augustine's "necessities" become whatever they think they must do when they "do what they have to do" on other grounds. And if Augustine himself could only barely imagine a Christian politics that helped answer the wise man's cry for deliverance—if he himself assumed that the best his Christian friends in high places could do was act like "our wise man" and carry out their "necessities" with purer intentions and authentic grief in their hearts—that only means that he too was begging the question that Jeremiah put to *him*, even as he posed it definitively for later Christian traditions.

Now, what if a later interpreter accepted the contours of Augustine's critique of the earthly city but did more than he to explore the implications of Jeremiah's guidance for life in exile and Diaspora? What if he did at least as much to help Christian "resident aliens" remain clear about where their ultimate loyalties lie? And what if he thus identified a more complete and creative politics for the pilgriming heavenly city that is obliged to seek the peace of the earthly city? It would hardly seem remarkable for someone to describe that interpreter as deeply engaged in the Augustinian project.

Except of course that I refer to John Howard Yoder.

DIVERGING FROM NIEBUHR

Reinhold Niebuhr's name appears only rarely in the last book John H. Yoder prepared for publication, *For the Nations*.[23] Yet as Yoder turned to Jeremiah and Diaspora for models of constructive social engagement, he was answering—one more time, in one more way, in earshot of still other conversations—the Niebuhrian charge that often seems to have shaped his career.[24] That charge: Christians who embrace the nonviolent ethic of Jesus may get Jesus right, but they at the same time render themselves politically irrelevant and socially irresponsible.

Diaspora Judaism belied this charge. What Jeremiah had made clear when he wrote to the first exiles, urging them to seek the peace of the city, was that living in exile without political sovereignty was an opportunity for mission and constructive contribution to the good of other cultures. Though countercultural in one sense it was pro-cultural and "for the nations" in another. Jeremiah's injunction could be translated far more forcefully, according to Yoder: "'seek the salvation of the culture to which God has sent you.'"[25] Diaspora Jews down through the centuries may have done this in ways that were sometimes "grudging and clumsy" or sometimes "wholehearted and creative."[26] But doing so had depended on neither their own ability to gain access to reins of power nor their host culture's ability to comprehend on its own terms the *shalom* to which God's people were contributing.[27]

Diaspora Jews had contributed more not less to Near Eastern and European societies, precisely because they repeatedly became fluent in other peoples' cultural "languages" without losing the thought world of their own particular "language" or identity.[28] While their social posture might be sectarian in some technical sociological sense, it was that very posture that gave them resources to be more rather than less socially engaged, responsible, and efficacious—in other words, to be anything *but* sectarian in the pejorative ethical sense.[29]

So even though Yoder did not set out intentionally to critique one strand of Augustinian political thought by drawing upon another, closer attention to Jeremiah's exiles showed that "our wise man's" necessities might not be quite so necessary after all. Reinhold Niebuhr was nothing if not a twentieth century American version of that "wise man," at least according to the standard interpretation of *City of God* 19 that Niebuhr himself has helped to make seem obvious. He was worldly wise according to the best wisdom of his age, he claimed remorse for actions that fell short of God's true peace, yet he was "tough-minded" enough to recognize his necessities and do what apparently had to be done. As such, having become a "wise judge" presiding over the court of public opinion in mid-century Protestant America and among its Washington elite, Niebuhr like the Stoic of *City of God* 19.6 provided a template for "wise" warriors to follow.[30]

For Yoder to move inadvertently closer to Augustine when he critiqued the putatively Augustinian Niebuhr on eminently Augustinian grounds was nothing new, however. Niebuhr sometimes portrayed his own work as a recovery of Augustine's orthodox doctrine of sin and human limitation in the face of misguided liberal optimism about human perfectability.[31] Yet by his own admission Niebuhr turned his attention only belatedly to a doctrine of grace that would correspond to his doctrine of sin,[32] while he incorporated a doctrine of eschatology only fitfully,[33] and wrote on ecclesiology hardly at all.[34] Yoder had pointed out how impoverished was Niebuhr's orthodoxy already in the early 1950s.

"Despite the appearance of the label 'neo-orthodox,'" wrote Yoder in his 1954 essay on *Reinhold Niebuhr and Christian Pacifism*, he "is far from what a historian of theology could call orthodox."[35] While countering Niebuhr's characterization and rejection of Christian pacifism in various ways in the pamphlet, Yoder insisted that the "most significant" objection to Niebuhrianism went "still deeper." Although Niebuhr's recovery of an orthodox doctrine of sin constituted a proper and largely biblical diagnosis of the human predicament, according to Yoder, it "consistently slighted" all "those Christian doctrines which relate to [God's] redemption" and point to the Bible's answer to our deepest human need.

Yoder reminded Niebuhrians, therefore, of the resurrection and the "new ethical possibilities" that it opens up through grace and regeneration. Anticipating themes in his later work, he pointed out the absence of the church in Niebuhr's thought and corrected this omission by pointing toward ways in which that "divine-human society, the church, the body of Christ," as a "supernational society," can break with the patterns of group egoism that Niebuhr thought demonstrated the inevitability of war.

Of course that break is not complete in the human society of the church, but in 1954 Yoder was also preparing to counter positions such as Niebuhr's by stressing the need for an adequate eschatology.[36] Meanwhile, as Yoder observed in *Reinhold Niebuhr and Christian Pacifism*, "the common denominator of the above-mentioned doctrines of resurrection, the church, and regeneration is that all are works of the Holy Spirit, and the Holy Spirit is likewise neglected in Niebuhr's ethics."[37]

Though Yoder did not say so, his theology was at least moving toward Augustine. A theology that took the reality of sin seriously yet continued to chart the course of a multinational society of pilgrims being transformed truly if only partly in this life through the love of God "poured into our hearts through the Holy Spirit that has been given to us"[38]—well, this was a theology that became more not less Augustinian even as it challenged Niebuhr. Ecclesiology, eschatology, pneumatology, and grace were precisely the Augustinian doctrines Niebuhr had slighted.

Yoder's long debate with Niebuhr, on terms surprisingly Augustinian both early and late in his career does not make Yoder himself an "Augustinian," of course. Yoder could be alternately charitable and caustic about the role Augustine had played in launching the just war tradition and consolidating the Constantinian synthesis of church and state,[39] but he surely would not have called himself an Augustinian. Characteristic of his lifelong approach to ethical debate and ecumenical conversation alike was that very willingness he associated with Diaspora Judaism to learn other people's languages and engage them on their own terms, without confusing linguistic systems or endorsing his interlocutors' ethics and worldviews. A willingness to debate all comers, one after another, was Yoder's alternative to what he considered dubious efforts to build a universal theological system that might anticipate every challenge, foundation, and common principle in advance.[40]

Yet one wonders. If nothing else, the length and breadth of Yoder's debate with Niebuhrianism makes it something more than one conversation among Yoder's many. For Yoder to chart his way through such a formative debate using so many Augustinian markers would seem to result from or result in *some* kind of Augustinian formation.[41] Given the subtle but pervasive way that Augustine has shaped political and theological problematics in subsequent Western thought, exact lines of influence may be too amorphous to trace in a way that will satisfy skeptics.[42] In whatever way Augustinian assumptions got into Yoder's thought, however, they continued to surface even when Yoder moved from critique of Niebuhrian politics to constructive proposals for political engagement according to his own peace church tradition.

The primary audience for Yoder's *The Christian Witness to the State* was "nonresistant Christians" who doubted that they could or should address policy deliberations by the state at all.[43] Niebuhr had reinforced this doubt, of course, and so *The Christian Witness* constitutes one more chapter in Yoder's engagement with Niebuhrianism—but it is much more than that. Where Yoder worked from assumptions that coincide with Augustine's we may safely suppose that they respond to his own desire to articulate a biblical theology, rather than to respond to the more constraining rhetorical task of meeting Niebuhr's agenda.[44]

A reader familiar with characteristic ways of thought in both Augustine and Yoder will note that Yoder's Christian witness to the state corresponds with Augustine's attitudes toward the earthly city in numerous ways:

(1) Both Augustine and Yoder shared a *markedly eschatological frame of reference*, and a corresponding recognition that the present challenge for God's people is to live "between the times." Augustine's famous contrast between the earthly city and the heavenly city is not a static ontology, for the heavenly city on earth knows itself to be on pilgrimage home to the fullness of communion with God and all creatures who love God. These pilgrim people live in tension, as resident aliens, not only because they are away from home but because the current world is a contested zone, in which the angelic citizenry of each city (the faithful and the rebellious angels) vie to direct our loves and our loyalties toward opposing ends.[45] Yoder in turn set the stage for Christian witness to the state by describing how "the present historical period is characterized by the coexistence of two ages or aeons," in which Christ is already reigning, although the powers governing the world still refuse to acknowledge that he is Lord precisely through the triumph of the cross. Still, this coexistence is not perpetual, for ultimately "the church and the reign of Christ will one day be englobed in the same kingdom."[46]

(2) For Augustine and Yoder, however, eschatology was not just a question of time, but a question of space, wherein *the two societies are presently intermixed—yet distinguished according to their ends, loyalties, and loves*. Augustine spoke of co-mixture, Yoder of coexistence. Both described the church as societies spread around the world, across borders and cultures, united by the character of their love. What distinguished the two societies for Augustine is that the citizens of the earthly city glorify themselves, lust for domination, and love themselves to the point of contempt for God—while the citizens of the heavenly city glorify God, seek to serve one another in love, and love God to the point of contempt for self. Likewise for Yoder, the distinc-

tion between church and world was not the kind of *dualism* that would imagine that the church could separate itself entirely from the world, but rather a *duality* based on faith and unbelief, allegiances in opposite directions, and social relationships patterned according to the contrasting logics of self-interest and Christ-like love.[47]

(3) For both Augustine and Yoder, *the purpose of history and the good of the social order are never knowable on their own terms.* Augustine argued at some length that when the ancient Romans built up their empire, they were not doing what they thought they were doing. They might think they were establishing themselves through their own glorious strength and virtue, or by the power of their gods. But in fact even their virtue had vice at its base, and their gods were demons seeking the glory that belonged to God. It was the one God who was ruling for purposes that were ultimately inscrutable but surely included such ends as establishing that partial earthly peace of which believers were to make use but not trust, and providing lessons concerning virtue and vice from which believers could learn.[48]

Yoder was of course more blunt: "The Christian church knows why the state exists—knows, in fact, better than the state itself." The state merely provides the "'scaffolding' service" within which the church can evangelize. Christ's triumph is what "has already guaranteed that the ultimate meaning of history will not be found in the course of earthly empires or the development of proud cultures, but in the calling together of the 'chosen race, royal priesthood, holy nation,' which is the church of Christ."[49]

(4) To be sure, nations tend to think otherwise, so in turn, Augustine and Yoder identified pride as the great problem for the state and *made thorough-going critiques of imperial presumption.* The problem with the earthly city that Augustine knew best was not just that the Romans had been ignorant of God's purposes. In addition, they had willfully overstretched themselves in their pride, were falling all the harder, and in the process had inflicted great suffering on other peoples. The grandeur of empire was a fragile illusion at best; look closely and imperialism turned out to be brigandage on a grand scale. The power of the gods who projected Roman values was a "poverty-stricken kind of power," scrambling for lost dominions, claiming honors proper only to God.[50]

Pressing the issue, Yoder insisted that such pretension is a problem for all states, not just empires, and not just self-deifying ones that explicitly asked for worship. Certainly in every attempt to create an ideal society, rulers act on pride—"the one sin that most surely leads to a fall, even already within history." But the "universal temptation" of all states was not to neglect the policing duties God had assigned them according to Romans 13; rather, it was to overdo the function. Thus idolatry does not have to be explicit, nor apostasy cultic, to express "essential rebellion against God," since violent domination and nationalism are always "intrinsically self-glorifying."[51]

(5) Still, even though the capacity of the state to effect true peace with justice is always limited—and to think otherwise is to invite the very pride that tends toward greater injustice—Augustine and Yoder both expect that *Christians can always call the social order and the state to do somewhat better*. Augustine's qualified appreciation for the virtues of the old Romans, despite their grounding in vices like self-glorification, implies as much. So too does his appreciation for the peace of the earthly city, even though it is but a shadow of God's ultimate peace and in fact falls short of the harmony of purpose that is possible already in this life for those who share in the love of God.

Hence the Jeremiah-like injunction to seek the peace of the earthly city.[52] Yoder's task of explaining how a pacifist church can witness to "the social order at large" even though he could not expect it "to function without the use of force," required him to specify still more clearly why (and how) pacifist Christians can expect policies that are less violent and more just. Christians can expect the contribution of the state to be "modest," "constantly shifting but nevertheless definable." In asking civil authorities to do their "second best" even if they cannot imagine acting according to the fullness of the gospel, pacifist Christians ask something of them that "does not cease to be gospel by virtue of the fact that we relate it to [their] present available options." Policy proposals cannot be total. But they will expose "one injustice at a time, pointing each time to a less evil way which the statesman can understand and follow;" it is thus realistic to hope for "improvement in the tolerability of the social compromise and thus in a certain sense progress."[53]

(6) Finally, Augustine and Yoder stated *similar motivations for seeking the peace of the earthly city*: the aid it afforded to the mission of the church which is the true purpose of history, and love of neighbor. "While this Heavenly City . . . is on pilgrimage in this world," wrote Augustine, "she calls out citizens from all nations and so collects a society of aliens, speaking all languages"—thus making "use of the earthly peace." What is more, the pilgrim people places earthly peace into relationship with heavenly peace. How? By faith they already possess and live that peace which "is the perfectly ordered and com-

pletely harmonious fellowship in the enjoyment of God, and of each other in God;" in view of the fullness of that peace they perform "every good action . . . in relation to God and in relation to a neighbor, since the life of a city is inevitably a social life."[54] Yoder described the state as performing a scaffolding function" that helps the church to evangelize. He also emphasized, however, that on many particulars a primary reason for Christians to witness to the state is "the very personal and very concrete concern" Christians have for the welfare of the neighbor, the stranger, and even the enemy.[55]

Of course, Augustine and Yoder certainly differed too. Where they did, the thought of each can sometimes push the other in ways both subtle and blunt. Take the issues that prompted Yoder's turn to the conceptual device of "middle axioms."[56] Yoder was sure Christian pacifists could not appeal as traditional social ethics had done to principles "somehow built into the nature of man or of the social order." Convinced that God's will for human social life is only accessible in "definite and knowable" ways through Christ, they instead must translate truths known through Christ into terms that are concrete, practical and accessible to those operating from other ethical convictions. Such translations "mediate between the general principles of Christological ethics and the concrete problems of political application. They claim no metaphysical status but serve usefully as rules of thumb to make meaningful the impact of Christian social thought."[57]

"Usefully," had Augustine employed this device of middle axioms as self-consciously as Yoder, he might have had a far easier time addressing Roman officials without becoming one himself according to the Constantinian synthesis that was solidifying throughout his career. Since Augustine would recognize in *any* truthful principle a reflection of God's created order, middle axioms must have *some* kind of "metaphysical status" for him. But this would hardly make them less "useful" to an Augustinian social ethic. For resident aliens who maintain primary loyalty to their heavenly, eschatological home, middle axioms are a practical way to negotiate the "already" and "not yet" of pilgrimage through the earthly city while contributing to its peace. What Augustine's vision most lacks is the practical explication that would give "our wise man" somewhere to turn for guidance besides the dubious wisdom of the age.

If Yoder's thought can nudge Augustinian thought toward greater faithfulness not only to Jeremiah's injunction but to Augustine's own vision, however, Augustinianism can serve to probe Yoder's as well. For what is unclear about middle axioms, in Yoder's hands, is whether they can ever become anything *more* than "useful"—whether, in other words, they ever dare make truth claims or instead must devolve into the truces, compromises, and contracts of a liberal pragmatism. (Such pragmatism has its own violent and manipulative proclivities, and is thus at least as dangerous an ally for pacifists as Augustinianism allegedly is.) Despite renouncing natural law principles built into human nature and social life, Yoder did want to affirm that "there exists a level of human values, not specifically Christian but somehow subject to Christian formative influences, where the real movement of history takes place."[58]

What are those "human values?" What is that "level"? What constitutes the "human"? Logically, Yoder still needed *some* theology of creation.[59] Thankfully, Stanley Hauerwas has begun charting a way forward by arguing in his Gifford lectures for a natural theology that is not autonomous from but rather enclosed within the yet-prior claims of Christology.[60] Certainly, such a formulation need not coincide at every point with Augustine's. But finally, any development of Yoder's insight that the cross does "run with the grain of the universe" must offer a theology of creation as robust as Augustine's own, thus allowing for stronger truth claims than his use of "middle axioms" seemed to allow.

TESTING THE COUNTER-INTUITIVE

Of course Augustine and Yoder differed more bluntly still in their respective acceptance and rejection of Christian participation in war. If that difference is incommensurable, my purpose is not to domesticate Augustine for pacifists but to make it all the harder for non-pacifist Christians to marginalize Yoder's witness. Stated cautiously, my claim is that Yoder's pacifist ecclesial social ethic is a surprisingly Augustinian answer to this eminently Augustinian question: How *shall* the heavenly city on pilgrimage within the earthly city seek the peace of that earthly city? Stated more strongly, my claim is that an Augustinian can be pacifist and a pacifist Augustinian.[61] Stated most strongly, my claim might be that they *must*—but I am not so foolish as to expect a single paper to establish such a claim in either direction, much less simultaneously. The moderate claim that one can be both a pacifist and an Augustinian is counter-intuitive and challenging enough. To make it imaginable is therefore response enough. It is imaginable because John Howard Yoder himself was a serious contender for, within, and not strictly over-against the Augustinian legacy.

Yet this claim will prove stronger still if the counter-intuitive intuits more than expected. Hauerwas, in the final chapter of *Peaceable Kingdom*,[62] has already tested the counter-intuition by showing why pacifists need something of an Augustinian spirituality to sustain their struggle and witness. And he has done so by drawing on that Augustinian sensibility which Reinhold Niebuhr did properly share.

A "spirituality of peaceableness" must sustain joy, thankfulness, and hope even while training us to face the tragedy of our world— nay, our own love of self-delusion—with unblinking honesty. This was Hauerwas's conclusion as he surveyed the classic 1932 debate in the pages of *The Christian Century* between H. Richard and Reinhold Niebuhr over Japan's invasion of Manchuria.[63] At the time Richard Niebuhr remained a pacifist, unlike Reinhold, and throughout his career he would remain the more ecclesial theologian of the two brothers. Facing the sense many had at the time that nothing could be done to arrest the historical forces moving toward war in Asia, he argued that some ways of *apparently* doing nothing were theologically significant and fruitful. For they slowly planted seeds of change, while trusting God's ultimate work in history, and creating the cells for a "Christian international" throughout the nations.

Such a vision was by implication a Jeremiah-like Diaspora, one akin to Yoder's later politics; the fact that Reinhold did not address his brother on this front might actually be a sign of his *lack* of political imagination. Instead he charged Richard with an incoherent faith because he trusted God to use the brutal forces of history to eventually bring about a just and loving social order but would not allow Christians to use those same forces to achieve an imperfect measure of relative justice. Hope was appropriate, but must look beyond history for the fulfillment of history; Richard's mistake was to gloss over the perennial tragedy of human history.[64]

The lesson to learn from the brothers Niebuhr, according to Hauerwas, was not that we must choose between them, but that we cannot sustain "the kind of position represented by H. Richard Niebuhr . . . without a spirituality very much like that hinted at by Reinhold." Though we rarely think of Reinhold Niebuhr as providing a spirituality, Hauerwas noted, he was training us in the very spiritual disciplines we need to sustain a struggle for justice—one not surprised by setbacks nor deceived by relative gains.

God's peace is dangerous. It exposes the lies upon which human beings "to a greater or lesser extent" have built all "social orders and institutions." The "normalcy and safety" we long for come in ways we prefer to repress, "at the expense of others." If in our interpersonal relationships "we 'use' even our love and those whom we love" to secure our needs, and if our larger circles of friendship become "a conspiracy of intimacy to protect each of our illusions" and allow us a measure of "peace," then all the more do we fear and defend ourselves against the stranger who would challenge our illusions. Unless, that is, we are hospitable to the God who is our ultimate stranger and challenger of our self-images. Unless, that is, we welcome the hope we only truly find on the far side of our human tragedy. Namely, neither can we save ourselves nor can we transform our world through violence, precisely because God has already won our peace through the cross and resurrection of Jesus. "Joy is thus finally a result of our being dispossessed of the illusion of security and power that is the breeding ground of our violence."[65]

But all of this is deeply Augustinian.[66] If Hauerwas is right, then the claim that we do not have to choose between H. Richard and Reinhold Niebuhr is interesting, but far more is at stake. What H. Richard Niebuhr got right about the hope we must live out through cells of that Christian international we call the church, Yoder would later explain at greater length and in finer detail. What Reinhold Niebuhr got right about facing our illusions unblinkingly, Augustine was training us to do all along.

Surely what matters most is that we choose the way of Jeremiah and Jesus, the gift God gave us long before Augustine and Yoder. Between these two witnesses, however, we need not choose.

NOTES

1. Jeremiah 29:7.

2. The broad interpretative claims so far in this paragraph are substantiated in the references to Augustine on pp. 231-234, along with corresponding notes.

3. For a fuller argument that the Augustinian tradition has been a resilient and living tradition precisely because of its inherent capacity for self-correction, see Gerald W. Schlabach, "The Correction of the Augustinians: A Case Study in the Critical Appropriation of a Suspect Tradition," in *The Early Church and the Free Church: Bridging the Historical and Theological Divide*, ed. Daniel H. Williams (Grand Rapids: Eerdmans, 2002), 47-74.

4. Robert Markus, in his influential *Saeculum: History and Society in the Theology of St. Augustine*, 2nd. ed., reprint, 1970 (Cambridge, England: University Press, 1988), may have overstated his case when he portrayed Augustine as

laying the basis for political liberalism by desacralizing every temporal order. My intention is not to weigh in on the growing, revisionist debate concerning Markus's thesis, reflected for example in Mark Vessey, Karla Pollmann, and Allan D. Fitzgerald, eds. *History, Apocalypse, and the Secular Imagination: New Essays on Augustine's City of God* (Bowling Green, Oh.: Philosophy Documentation Center, Bowling Green State University, 1999). Still, I simply cannot imagine how Augustinian political thought can ever do without some sense of the limitations of human politics, whether or not those limitations are now construed to require political liberalism. I thus assume that the summary statements in this paragraph will reflect an uncontroverted consensus however the debate between Markus and his revisionists proceeds.

5. H. Richard Niebuhr suggested something similar when he noted in *Christ and Culture* that Augustine's *City of God* lacked an ecclesiology to match its philosophy of history. See *Christ and Culture*, Harper Torchbooks/Cloister Library (New York: Harper & Row, 1956), 215-16.

6. Cf. Augustine, *The Trinity* 6.5.7, and Oliver O'Donovan's comments in *The Problem of Self-Love in St. Augustine* (New Haven, Conn.: Yale University Press, 1980), 128.

7. Augustine, *City of God* 1.1. The translation I am quoting in this is Augustine, *The City of God*, trans. Henry Bettenson, with introduction by David Knowles (Harmondsworth, Middlesex, England: Penguin, 1972).

8. These are themes and arguments that run throughout *City of God*, but that Augustine anticipated already in the preface to book one when he noted "how great is the effort needed to convince the proud of the power and excellence of humility," in contrast to the pride, arrogance and lust of domination that God was surely resisting according to the promise of James 4:6.

9. Augustine, *City of God* 7.32 (quoted); 18.50.

10. On this characteristic rhetorical practice, see John Cavadini, "The Structure and Intention of Augustine's *De Trinitate*," *Augustinian Studies* 23 (1992): 103-23; John C. Cavadini, "Time and Ascent in *Confessions* XI," in *Augustine: Presbyter Factus Sum*, papers originally presented at a conference at Marquette University, Milwaukee, Wis., November 1990, ed. Joseph T. Lienhard, Earl C. Muller, and Roland J. Teske, Collectanea Augustiniana (New York: Peter Lang Publishing, 1993), 171-85.

11. Augustine, *City of God* 1.1, 1.33, 2.2.

12. Ibid., 5.12-20.

13. Ibid., 10.1, 19.1-4.

14. Ibid., 10.29.

15. Ibid., 19.5.

16. Augustine, *Letters* 189 and 220.

17. Cf. Robert Dodaro, "Eloquent Lies, Just Wars and the Politics of Persuasion: Reading Augustine's *City of God* in a 'Postmodern' World," *Augustinian Studies* 25 (1994): 77-138.

18. For a masterful argument as to why Augustine's just war theory falls apart precisely at this point, see Robert L. Holmes, "St. Augustine and the Just War Theory," in *The Augustinian Tradition*, ed. Gareth B. Matthews, Philosophical Traditions, no. 8 (University of California Press, 1998), 332.

19. Augustine, *City of God* 19.17.

20. Ibid. Cf. the *Epistle of Mathetes to Diognetus* 5-6; *Shepherd of Hermas* s. 1; Clement of Alexandria, *Stromata* 6.5-6; Tertullian, *The Apology* 38; Origen, *Against Celsus* 8.75; *The Life and Passion of Cyprian* 11; Gregory of Nazianzen, *Oration* 43.49.

21. Augustine, *City of God* 19.10, 19.17.

22. Ibid., 19.26.

23. John Howard Yoder, *For the Nations: Essays Public and Evangelical* (Grand Rapids: Eerdmans, 1997).

24. Long-time students of Yoder will hardly need evidence that the debate with Niebuhr, Niebuhrianism, and the assumptions that other non-pacifist Christians had held but that Niebuhr definitively articulated, run like a thread throughout his career. Mennonite students of Yoder will also recognize that the response to Niebuhr's charge had already begun in the decade or two before Yoder began writing. The following references, therefore, are only a sample of the most forthright statements recognizing the task of taking on Niebuhr, chosen because they thread back a half a century: Guy Franklin Hershberger, *War, Peace, and Nonresistance*, 3rd. ed., reprint 1944, Christian Peace Shelf Selection (Scottdale, Pa.: Herald Press, 1969), 236-54; John H. Yoder, *Reinhold Niebuhr and Christian Pacifism*, reprint 1955, A Concern Reprint (Scottdale, Pa.: Concern, n.d.); John Howard Yoder, *The Christian Witness to the State*, Institute of Mennonite Studies Series, no. 3 (Newton, Kan.: Faith and Life Press, 1964), 5-8, noting n.4 p. 7; John H. Yoder, *The Politics of Jesus* (Grand Rapids: Eerdmans, 1972), 11-25 (noting especially nn. 4, 7), 110-13; John Howard Yoder, *The Priestly Kingdom: Social Ethics as Gospel* (Notre Dame, Ind.: University of Notre Dame Press, 1984), 90-91, 100-01.

25. Yoder, *For the Nations*, 76 n.60.

26. Yoder, *For the Nations*, 1.

27. Yoder, *For the Nations*, 33-34, 67-68.

28. Yoder, *For the Nations*, 71. Cf. John Howard Yoder, "On Not Being Ashamed of the Gospel: Particularity, Pluralism, and Validation," *Faith and Philosophy* 9:3 (July 1992): 290-291.

29. Yoder, *For the Nations*, 3-5. Yoder prepared and entitled *For the Nations* in part to clarify that his own position was less contrarian than his former colleague Stanley Hauerwas's often appeared to be. Hauerwas, after all, had published *Against the Nations*. (Cf. the hint of this purpose in n.6 on p. 4 of *For the Nations*.) Long-time readers of Yoder, of course, know he had regularly drawn up lists of ways a prophetic minority, creative minority, Abrahamic community, Jeremianic Diaspora community, or any other preferred term for

a putatively sectarian group provides societies-at-large with the resources for constructive social change. See for example *Christian Witness to the State*, 18-22; John Howard Yoder "Christ, the Hope of the World," *The Original Revolution: Essays on Christian Pacifism*, Christian Peace Shelf (Scottdale, Pa.: Herald Press, 1971), 203-07; Yoder, "The Biblical Mandate for Evangelical Social Action," *For the Nations*, 184-89; John Howard Yoder *Body Politics: Five Practices of the Christian Community Before the Watching World* (Nashville, Tenn.: Discipleship Resources, 1992).

30. For a fresh account of the role that Niebuhr played in the emerging managerial elite of mid-century America, see Eugene McCarraher, *Christian Critics: Religion and the Impasse in Modern American Social Thought* (Ithaca, N.Y.: Cornell University Press, 2000), 64-70, 91-97.

31. Reinhold Niebuhr, "Reply to Interpretation and Criticism," in *Reinhold Niebuhr: His Religious, Social, and Political Thought*, ed. Charles W. Kegley and Robert W. Bretall, The Library of Living Theology, vol. 11 (New York: The Macmillan Company, 1956), 436; Reinhold Niebuhr, "Intellectual Autobiography," in *Reinhold Niebuhr: His Religious, Social, and Political Thought*, 9; Reinhold Niebuhr, *Human Nature*, vol. 1 of *The Nature and Destiny of Man*, reprint 1941, The Scribner Lyceum Editions Library (New York: Scribner's, 1964), 49; Reinhold Niebuhr, *The Irony of American History*, The Scribner Lyceum Editions Library (New York: Scribner's, 1952), 17.

32. Against charges that he had been preoccupied with original sin, Niebuhr wrote: "I must plead guilty to this charge in the sense that it was a long time before I paid as much attention to the Christian conception of the cure as to the diagnosis, to 'grace' as well as to sin." "Intellectual Autobiography," 10.

33. Note Niebuhr's doubts about the wisdom of having drawn on eschatological themes when he wrote the preface to a reprint of *Human Nature*, ix.

34. In *Human Destiny*, Niebuhr's longest sustained discussion of ecclesiology offered no constructive proposal but only a critique of Roman Catholicism, along with what he considered its essentially Augustinian doctrine of grace. See *Human Destiny*, vol. 2 of *The Nature and Destiny of Man*, reprint 1943, The Scribner Lyceum Editions Library (New York: Scribner's, 1964), 138-39, 144-152.

35. Yoder, *Reinhold Niebuhr and Christian Pacifism*, 4.

36. See Yoder's essay "Peace Without Eschatology?" published in various versions: "If Christ is Truly Lord," in *The Original Revolution*, 64; "Peace Without Eschatology?" in John Howard Yoder, *The Royal Priesthood: Essays Ecclesiological and Ecumenical*, ed. Michael G. Cartwright (Grand Rapids: Eerdmans, 1994), 152-53.

37. Unless otherwise indicated, all quotations from this paragraph are from Yoder, *Reinhold Niebuhr and Christian Pacifism*, 17-19. For an explicit statement of Yoder's acceptance of "Niebuhr's real service to theology, and to

pacifism, in making real the omnipresence of sin," see p. 19.

38. The quotation from Romans 5:5 is one Augustine often cited in explicating his conception of Christian love.

39. Compare *The Priestly Kingdom*, 75, where Yoder said that "Ambrose and Augustine did the best they could," with *The Royal Priesthood*, 89, where Augustine appears midway in a dynamic leading from Constantine to the Inquisition.

40. On this matter I can offer personal confirmation. Some months after I had finished a review essay of *The Royal Priesthood*, but before its publication, I sent Yoder a copy. Although he quibbled with various points, on one matter he supplied the kind of unambiguous affirmation that most of his students will recognize as rare, when he simply wrote "well summarized" in response to the following paragraph:

> What may not have been so clear without the accumulation of reminders that Cartwright's anthology affords is that a truly ecumenical conversation in the free church style is Yoder's alternative to theological system-building. Yoder's theological method itself is an open-ended conversation with all comers, in respect for the dignity even of opponents, and vulnerability to their insights. If one does not attempt to construct a system that will solve all problems in advance, one may nonetheless act on the very-particular yet also-universal faith that because Jesus Christ is Lord, conversation is in principle possible with persons of any particular 'tribe' or tradition or ideology or position. Because *this* Lord is the lamb that was slain, one should not coerce those persons to believe using one's overarching system any more than one coerces with superior weaponry. And if unbelief is possible, so is intractable disagreement. But in principle, if the gospel is knowable and believable within any culture, so is translation and agreement across traditions. There is no way to know without the discipline of actually conversing—again and again.

See Gerald W. Schlabach, "Anthology in Lieu of System: John H. Yoder's Ecumenical Conversations as Systematic Theology," review essay on *The Royal Priesthood: Essays Ecclesiological and Ecumenical* by John Howard Yoder and Michael G. Cartwright, ed., *Mennonite Quarterly Review* 71:2 (April 1997): 305-309.

41. To be sure, Yoder once remarked that the "imperatives of dialogue with majority mentalities [had] skewed" the emphasis in his own position. Does that mean if Yoder's arguments sometimes take an Augustinian shape or form, this is in fact a Niebuhrian de-formation? Some will want to say so, yet the paragraph I am citing makes clear that if anything Yoder's positions would have come across as *more* orthodox and pious if unconstrained by the parameters of debate with Niebuhrians. Yoder's remark occurs in a one-paragraph concluding section with the title, "Back to True North"; thus I have

long wondered whether with this Yoder was not leaving us a commentary on his own entire career. See Yoder, *The Priestly Kingdom*, 101.

42. If one did wish to trace a more exact genealogy of ideas, however, the place to begin would probably be in the influence of historian Herbert Butterfield. References to Butterfield occur occasionally in Yoder's work. In June of 1954 he submitted a book review of Butterfield's *Christianity, Diplomacy and War.* (New York: Abingdon-Cokesbury Press, 1953) to Guy F. Hershberger for the *Mennonite Quarterly Review* (never published). In the cover letter he told Hershberger that "This book has made a great impression on me, chiefly in the direction of demonstrating the lines along which the study of history can and should contribute to the church's prophetic witness to the state, precisely because the anabaptist (N.T.) [*sic*] doctrine of the State is not only a doctrine but also a historical reality" (Guy F. Hershberger papers, Archives of the Mennonite Church, Goshen, Ind., box 10, file 23).

What Yoder found confirmed in Butterfield's historiography was precisely what I am arguing appears also in Augustine—a circumscribed conception of the state in which the police function is legitimate, but when wars "go beyond this limit [police action] and claim ideological value or religious or philosophical sanction," they become more harmful, hypocritical, and "rend the fabric of society more than they protect it." As to the influence of Augustine on Butterfield see the suggestive remark on p. 3 of H. Butterfield, *Christianity and History* (New York: Charles Scribner's Sons, 1949), and a more extended discussion in Herbert Butterfield, *Writings on Christianity and History*, ed. C. T. McIntire (New York: Oxford University Press, 1978), 124-32.

43. Yoder, *Christian Witness to the State*, 6.

44. Cf. note 41.

45. Augustine, *City of God* 10.7, 11.1, 15.2, 18.1, with Augustine's entire march through history closing in upon the final judgement (book 20), eternal punishment (book 21), and "the eternal bliss of the City of God" (book 22, as introduced in 22.1).

46. Yoder, *Christian Witness to the State*, 8-11, 13, 17; quotations from pp. 8, 17.

47. Augustine, *City of God* 1.35; 10.32, 14.1, 14.4, 14. Yoder, *Christian Witness to the State*, 17, 28-31, 42, 72-73. Among the Augustine passages, note that in 1.35 Augustine's discussion of co- or inter-mixture does not imply an "invisible church" in which pacifism is scarcely imaginable because Christians look so much like non-Christians, but rather leads to pacifist possibilities, because among the enemies of the heavenly city are hidden its future citizens, who must therefore be treated patiently, until they convert.

48. Augustine, *City of God* 5-11-21, but especially 5.16 and 21, and cf. 19.17.

49. Yoder, *Christian Witness to the State*, 10-11, 13, 16, 17, 36, 40; quotations are from pp. 16, 11 and 13.

50. Augustine, *City of God* 4.3-6, 11.1, 12.1, 14.3-4, 13, 14.28, 15.7; quotation is from 11.1.

51. Yoder, *Christian Witness to the State*, 37-38.

52. Augustine, *City of God* 5.12-15, 19.10-14, 19.17, 19.21, 19.26-27.

53. Yoder, *Christian Witness to the State*, 6, 7, 13, 25, 32-33, 38-39, 42, 71-73; quotations are from pp. 6, 25 and 39. Key to Yoder's approach was the notion of "middle axioms," which he mentions on p. 32 and treats at greater length on pp. 71-73. I will give greater attention to middle axioms below.

54. Augustine, *City of God* 19.7.

55. Yoder, *Christian Witness to the State*, 10-11, 14, 41-42.

56. I state the matter carefully in order to avoid what would otherwise be the laughable anachronism of expecting Augustine to have had access the same conceptual toolbox Yoder had in the mid-twentieth century. Yet it is not historically irresponsible to imagine Augustine himself thinking up a concept *like* "middle axioms." His pre-Christian career, after all, was that of a professor of rhetoric, which requires appealing to the presuppositions of diverse audiences and interlocutors in order to score one's own points. Augustine continued practicing exactly this in both his many theological controversies and his regular correspondence with government officials.

57. Yoder, *Christian Witness to the State*, 32-33.

58. Ibid., 40.

59. Although, for reasons of both principle and humility Yoder never claimed to be a philosopher, the power of his intellectual rigor rarely left him making logical blunders. Two sentences on p. 29 of *Christian Witness to the State* are deeply puzzling, therefore. Yoder was arguing (correctly) that the question of whether Christian principles are relevant to the social order is misleadingly simple. As part of this argument he wrote, "Whether or not, or in what sense, non-Christians or the non-Christian society *should* love, forgive, and otherwise behave like Christians is a speculative question. The spiritual resources for making such redeemed behavior a real possibility are lacking." Paired, these two statements constitute a non-sequitur, apparently based on the confusion of "ought" (or here, "should") with the "is" of spiritual resourcelessness. What is puzzling becomes troubling when we linger over the first sentence. If Yoder must not only be humble about specifying exactly what God's will is for a non-Christian social order (which is surely appropriate) but must refuse even to say whether God's will for non-Christians is that they love and forgive—because such a question is "speculative"—then he surely needed a more robust theology of creation. Failing to provide one only helps reinstate the case for some kind of natural law theory.

60. Stanley Hauerwas, *With the Grain of the Universe: The Church's Witness and Natural Theology*, Gifford Lectures delivered at the University of St. Andrews, Scotland, in 2001 (Grand Rapids: Brazos Press, 2001). While drawing most explicitly on Karl Barth, Hauerwas's *With the Grain of the Universe* honors Yoder by pursuing Yoder's own hints that it is only unbelief which prevents us from seeing that the cross does "run with the grain" of all God's cre-

ation after all. For the source of that title phrase, see John Howard Yoder, "Armaments and Eschatology," *Studies in Christian Ethics* 1:1 (1988): 58; Yoder, *The Politics of Jesus*, 246.

61. Though the purpose of this paper was not to reply to James Turner Johnson's ill-considered claim in the pages of the *Journal of Religious Ethics* that a pacifist can hardly begin to understand much less interpret Augustine, it obviously does constitute one reply. See "Can A Pacifist Have A Conversation with Augustine? A Response to Alain Epp Weaver," *Journal of Religious Ethics* 29:1 (Spring 2001): 87-93.

62. Stanley Hauerwas, "Tragedy and Joy: The Spirituality of Peaceableness," chap. 8 in *The Peaceable Kingdom: A Primer in Christian Ethics* (Notre Dame, Ind.: University of Notre Dame Press, 1983), 135-151.

63. H. Richard Niebuhr, "The Grace of Doing Nothing," *Christian Century* 49 (23 March 1932): 378-80; Reinhold Niebuhr, "Must we Do Nothing?" *Christian Century* 49 (30 March 1932): 415-17.

64. Hauerwas, "Tragedy and Joy," 135-40.

65. Ibid., 141-48.

66. The current paper has demonstrated Augustine's unblinking social critique as practiced in *The City of God* and his practices of thorough-going self-examination are famous from his own *Confessions*. For an exposition of Augustine's analysis of friendship and the illusions by which we subtly but wrongly use our friends, see Gerald W. Schlabach, "Friendship as Adultery: Social Reality and Sexual Metaphor in Augustine's Doctrine of Original Sin," *Augustinian Studies* 23 (1992): 125-47.

Chapter 12

"I came not to abolish the law but to fulfill it": A Positive Theology of Law and Civil Institutions[1]

A. James Reimer

Do not think that I have come to abolish the law or the prophets; I have come not to abolish but to fulfill. For truly I tell you, until heaven and earth pass away, not one letter, not one stroke of a letter, will pass from the law until all is accomplished. Therefore, whoever breaks one of the least of these commandments, and teaches others to do the same, will be called least in the kingdom of heaven; but whoever does them and teaches them will be great in the kingdom of heaven. For I tell you, unless your righteousness exceeds that of the scribes and Pharisees, you will never enter the kingdom of heaven. —Matthew 5:17-20

THIS TEXT IS THE PROLEGOMENON TO THE SIX precepts of Jesus that have been foundational to the Anabaptist-Mennonite understanding of the Christian imperative to live a life of discipleship, peace, and nonviolent love (inadequately expressed with the term *pacifism*). What might it mean to take seriously Jesus' words in Matthew—"I have come not to abolish but to fulfill the law"—in relation to the specific problematic I am concerned with in this project? I am thinking here of the importance of law and civil institutions for a religious community characterized by three dynamics: (1) The community has historically put great stock in following quite literally (not necessarily literalistically) the words of Jesus as commands to be obeyed in all areas of life (discipleship). (2) The community is one for which especially Matthew, and within Matthew the Sermon on the Mount, and within the Sermon on the Mount, the call of Jesus to "love the enemy," "turn the other cheek," and "not resist evil," has functioned as a kind of "canon within a canon." (3) However, this same community has not understood "law," as used here by Jesus, to apply to religious and moral *as well* as civil law the way the ancient Hebrews (and Jesus?) must surely have understood it.

I come to this topic as a historical and systematic theologian and also as an ethicist, one who loves the Bible and thinks it critical for all theological work and Christian life, but not as one trained in exegesis. For this I rely on scholars in the field of biblical studies. For my purposes in this work I concentrate less on the minutiae of textual analysis than on general thematic and conceptual motifs that may have been present in or behind Jesus' assertion. My biblical reflections on law are part of a larger project on which I am now working.

THE LARGER PROJECT

A number of years ago I was challenged by Oliver O'Donovan, moral philosopher and canon of Christ Church, Oxford, who claimed that he could not find any coherent and systematic treatment of pacifist social theory by Anabaptist or Mennonite writers. I denied this at the time but have since then pondered his comments at length and come to suspect that he may be at least partly right. It's not that we don't have biblical, historical and ethical apologetics for our peace position but we lack a systematic political theory in which the positive role of civil institutions outside of the church is elaborated from the perspective of the Historic Peace Church tradition. We have worked out systematically our own view of Christian social ethics from within the womb of the church but not thought a great deal about the positive function of the whole range of human institutions outside church and para-church agencies. It is this task to which I turn my attention in a longer project of which this essay is but a small part.

This longer project is tentatively entitled "When Law and Civil Institutions are Just: Honesty in Pacifist Thinking." In 1984 John H. Yoder published a book entitled *When War is Unjust: Being Honest in Just-War Thinking*. In it he rightly presses those in the just war tradition (most mainline Christians) to apply the criteria of just war thinking consistently. Were they to do so, he argues, they would virtually in all cases join with pacifists in condemning war. In my longer project, worked at while on a six-month sabbatical at the Center of Theological Inquiry, Princeton, New Jersey, I turn Yoder's argument on its head, and apply it to those of us who call ourselves pacifists. I urge Mennonites and others in the Historic Peace Church tradition to overcome their frequently dishonest disjunction between abstract theories of pacifism, on the one hand, and their actual human life within civil society, on the other.

I am not recommending the deriving of an "ought" from an "is," although I revisit the relation of these two, nor of giving up our calling as Mennonites to witness to this central part of the gospel (nonviolent love). I am, however, encouraging us to be honest: not to use high-sounding theological and moral rhetoric (1) ideologically to distort or disguise the situation in which we actually find ourselves in our family, professional, business, political, civil, and church lives; and (2) selectively to read the Bible and history and undervalue the positive mandate for institutional life found in the biblical narrative as well as in our own Anabaptist-Mennonite heritage.

In short, we need a more honest theology of law and civil institutions and their function in helping to shape and preserve human and nonhuman life in a fallen world, as mandated in the Christian doctrines of creation, redemption and reconciliation. Whether these institutions are to be understood primarily as themselves fallen and therefore as post-lapsarian (the Augustinian position) or part of the intent of creation itself and consequently pre-lapsarian (the Aristotelian-Thomistic position) remains to be argued—I in fact defend a particular combination of these two.

In any case, they are not to be dispensed with in favor of some kind of "evangelical anarchy"—a prevalent assumption among some that if only we were truly obedient to the Lordship of Christ we would not need institutions. Institutions, I hold, are indeed in some sense "ordained" by God and need to be given critical support as necessary for life.

Furthermore, the institutions that need our support and participation are not to be relegated to those that have some direct or indirect structural connection with the church and its ministries, although the latter are themselves instances of institutional life which deserve our support. When social ethics are positioned exclusively within or derived from a discussion of the doctrine of the church, as found in most Mennonite confessions of faith and in virtually all Mennonite theologizing, there is a problem: The true theological significance of "God-ordained" institutions throughout human history, by which God preserves the world from total chaos and disintegration, is not adequately understood or acknowledged.

This problem becomes even more pronounced when, as is the case in the believers church tradition, the church is understood not in a universal, comprehensive sense, but as a small group of believers visibly gathered from out of the larger culture and society. In this scenario, how God governs the world "outside the perfection" of Christ remains largely unaddressed, the focus being primarily, if not exclusively, on what it means to be faithful "inside the perfection of Christ," with little analysis on what positive role human institutions of family, tribe, ethnicity, nationality, law and government play in the divine economy of the world at large and the cosmos as a whole.

The church is of course, for Christians, the primary community of allegiance—the community within which our ultimate values and commitments are shaped. However, the church is not the only venue of our faithful activity. Good and godly things happen outside the church and church-related ministries. In fact, there are occasions when individuals are called on in concrete times and concrete places to give provisional priority to working outside the standard institutions of the church as a form of Christian faithfulness—Dietrich Bonhoeffer, despite the ambiguity of his choices, could be cited as an example here, as could Martin Luther King Jr.

HISTORY AND THE SOCIAL SCIENCES: REVISITING THE ISSUE OF "IS" AND "OUGHT"

Yoder never tired of telling us you can't get an ought from an is. This was one of his main responses to Niebuhr's political realism. To skeptics who challenged him by saying nonviolence doesn't work he most often answered that whether it "works" or not in the usual understanding of that word (i.e., effectiveness) is not a criterion for truth. Sometimes he responded by saying "You haven't really tried it." In short, a description of how we live—the human condition—is not a factor in determining how we are called to live by the gospel.

The human condition and the social and political situation in which we find ourselves are not the sources out of which our ethical norms emerge. Our standard comes from the Word of God in Christ. Yoder is thoroughly Barthian and Neo-orthodox in this, although he draws some different conclusions. It is on the basis of this underlying conviction that Yoder could claim, in his 1964 *The Christian Witness to the State,* unlike Niebuhr, that sin is not a variable when Christian ethics is done in the context of the believers church.

The line Yoder draws between the "is" and the "ought," between the "Mennonite reality" and the "Anabaptist ideal," is too clean. The human condition and the way Mennonites have lived and survived historically, how they live now and are likely to continue to live in the future, have a bearing on how we understand the moral and ethical demands placed on us. Theologically, this can be argued on the basis of a Trinitarian understanding of God and reality: God *has* created the world good, God *has* redeemed the world in Christ, and God *is* reconciling the world to himself through the Holy Spirit. This is not the place to examine each of these claims in greater depth except to say that each of them has an "objective/is" quality. If, for example, Christians believe that God *is* doing something reconciliatory in the world through the Holy Spirit both inside and outside the church, then there is insight to be gained from looking empirically at what *is* happening in cosmic and human history—past, present, future.

The social historians and social scientists have much to offer us in this regard. They show us how we as people have lived out our lives beyond the first generation of visionaries as families, farmers, skilled laborers, business people, professionals (teachers, lawyers, dentists, doctors, nurses, politicians), artists, bureaucrats, technocrats, pastors, and so on. Institutions are indispensable in each of these. The "is" disciplines (historians, sociologists *et al*) are particularly indispensable in keeping the "ought" disciplines (theology, philosophy, ethics *et al*) honest through their insight into the sociology of knowledge. The "ought" without the "is" (and there never is a pure ought) is prone to ideological distortion of reality just as easily as the "is" without the "ought."

The prophets of the "ought" are themselves unavoidably socially located interpreters of the "ought." Yoder himself cannot be understood apart from (1) his Swiss Mennonite background, (2) his American citizenship and the way this fact determined the questions he asked, and the answers he gave, (3) his academic training in America under Bender and in Europe under Barth, (4) his emerging Anabaptist and free church self-consciousness in the context of post-World War II Europe reconstruction and the Concern group discussions, (5) his impressive ecumenical connections and conversations in which he sharpened his debating skills and his own ethical convictions, and (6) modern and postmodern intellectual developments in the West.

It is illuminating to follow the careers of the other members of that Europe-centered Concern group (other than Yoder), a number of whom departed significantly from their earlier positions and Yoder's views: A. Orley Swartzentruber became an Episcopalian priest; Calvin Redekop has devoted his life to sociology and playing a significant role in MEDA (Mennonite Economic Development Agency) trying to foster an ethically responsible form of capitalist entrepreneurialism; John W. Miller is an Old Testament scholar who departs significantly from Yoder's reading of the Jewish story, as we will see below.

To gain a better understanding of how Mennonites might understand civil institutions and their involvement in such institutions theologically I have chosen, in my larger project, to look at social ethics through the prism of a theology of "law" (*nomos*) as a way of structuring love. I begin with (1) methodological considerations and Trinitarian foundations; then (2) look at the biblical understanding of law and ethics (the topic of this essay). Further (3), I survey the historical development of Western legal traditions, including the Constantinian legacy; medieval refinements of notions of divine, eternal, natural and civil law; the Reformation and early modern legal developments, with particular focus on the Anabaptists and the natural law tradition; and finally law, freedom of conscience, and pluralism within modern and postmodern nation states.

SYNAGOGUE AS FREE CHURCH PROTOTYPE

In the following biblical essay I ask what it might mean to take Jesus' words in Matthew seriously: "I came not to abolish the law but to fulfill it." I come to this question not as someone trained in biblical scholarship but as an historical and systematic theologian with strong ethical interests. Jesus' assertion has a *formal* and a *material* aspect. The formal issues have to do with whether there is continuity or discontinuity between the Hebrew Scriptures and the Christian Scriptures, or between Judaism and the early Christian community on law. The material question relates to what the substance of that continuity or discontinuity is—that is, what Jesus understood the law he was not abolishing but fulfilling to be.

Ever since World War II and the waking of Western Christianity to its complicity in the horrific, genocidal action against European Jews by virtue of the anti-Semitism implicit if not explicit in Christian thought reaching back right to the beginning, even into its sacred texts, biblical scholars have deliberately re-examined assumptions that long remained for the most part unquestioned. One assumption was the rather unnuanced distinction between law and gospel; the other was the supercession of the Christian Scriptures and teachings over the Hebrew Scriptures and its teachings. A virtual consensus appears to have developed among biblical scholars arguing for the continuity between the Jewish canon (Law, Prophets, and Writings) and the additional Christian writings (Gospels, Acts, Paul's Epistles, General Epistles, Pastoral Epistles, and Revelation). Where differences do occur it concerns whether there is any novelty in the Christian Scriptures at all and what the nature of the new is.

The way one deals with this question of continuity and discontinuity has serious ramifications for understanding of law and gospel in general, but especially for Mennonites and our rather singular ethical concerns. Yoder's Christocentric theology and ethics is a case in point. Yoder's whole theological and ethical project stands or falls on the absolute centrality of Jesus' life and teachings of nonviolent love—confirmed by his death and resurrection, and the realistic possibility of followers of Jesus to live out this messianic ethic in this world.

In his last years Yoder was preoccupied with tracing this messianic ethic back into the Hebrew narrative. He was concerned with Diaspora, messianic, synagogue, rabbinic Judaism as a free-church prototype, which was an alternative to temple-priestly Judaism and all forms of centralized political, religious, or legal authority. It was a prototype which continued in the early Jewish-Christian communities but was largely lost with the Constantinianization of the church (itself a renewal of the temple-monarchical prototype). However, it was kept alive in the various medieval sectaries and picked up most explicitly again by the Radical Reformation in the sixteenth century and is reborn now in postmodern non-foundationalism.[2]

Yoder's particular way of retrieving Jewish-Christianity as a prototype for his free church ecclesiology—going back to exilic-Diaspora synagogue Judaism, itself anticipated in the dispersion of languages and cultures at Babel—stands in some tension with his strong, almost Marcion-like Christocentricism as a basis for his uncompromising nonviolent ethic. Yoder's reading of the Hebrew tradition and, consequently, also of the Christian tradition suffers from two inadequacies: First, he provides a too-selective and one-dimensional reading of the Jewish story. Although the mission of the Jewish Diaspora is to be a blessing to all the nations as "resident aliens" in foreign cultures, whether and how God was also present during the monarchy and in Jewish temple culture, and how God is universally present in all cultures and nations of the world outside of Judaism is not addressed. Second, given his apparent interest in demonstrating the continuity of free church ecclesiology, messianism and ethics with the Jewish prophetic tradition, any spelling out of how the Torah can in fact give Christians material ethical guidance seems to be lacking, with the exception of a few favourite themes, such as Jubilee.

If we are to take seriously Jesus' self-perception as someone who came not to abolish but to fulfill Torah, then we will need to look at the Hebrew Scriptures the way the Jews themselves understood it at the time. Furthermore, in our shaping of a Christian ethic, we will need to draw on the full range of Jewish ethical literature. Any discontinuities with that literature will need to be argued intentionally and self-consciously to avoid the triumphalist and supercessionist mistakes of the past. In the development of my own position I begin with a look at the recent work of John W. Miller and Waldemar Janzen.

SECOND-TEMPLE JUDAISM AS
PROTOTYPE FOR A WORLD ORDER

Within contemporary Mennonite theology, it is the Old Testament scholars who have perhaps the most to contribute to the present debate and yet are the least listened to. John W. Miller, Yoder's contemporary and one of the seven original members of the Concern group in Europe, like Yoder studied with Barth in Basel, where he received his Th.D., has spent much of his professional academic life immersed in the Hebrew Scriptures and in recent years has been especially preoccupied with canon criticism and canon-formation studies. He and Yoder share some underlying concerns but also part company at critical points. Miller agrees with Yoder that the mission of the Christian church is not to rule the world but to witness to it. For Miller, this mission was already pioneered by second-temple Judaism, which was a fulfillment of the prophetic message, especially the new covenant of Jeremiah and second and third Isaiah (Isa. 40-60), a fulfillment without restoration of the Davidic monarchy. Through faithfulness in worship both at the temple in Jerusalem and in the Diaspora, and not by means of a powerful, dominating kingdom as in the visions of Daniel (which inspired the Jewish uprisings in the first two centuries after Christ), the Jews would become a blessing and light to all the nations of the world. So far there is remarkable agreement between Yoder and Miller, except for the greater importance Miller places on Jewish temple worship.[3]

Where Miller parts company with Yoder is in his much greater stress on the positive role of the foreign nations in God's providential design for the world. The Ezra-Nehemiah reforms and the rebuilding of the temple take place under the beneficent jurisdiction of Persian rulers (Cyrus) and conclude the theology of the Tanakh. In this theology God is portrayed as the ruler of the nations, and the nations play a highly significant role for human betterment:

> The temple was to be a house of prayer for all nations (Isa. 56:1-8), in time the gathering place for a union of the nations that would be the prelude to disarmament and world wide peace [Miller sees this same vision animating the United Nations today]. Biblical Judaism has the nations totally in focus in its vision of things to come and in its understanding of why it existed. . . . Genesis 1-11 was drafted at this point as a prelude to the retelling of Israel's story as we now have it in Genesis to Kings. This prelude locates Israel's story within the setting of a new world order created after the flood (to overcome the anarchy that existed before the restraint against lawless and random spilling of human blood (murder). This is the narrator's recognition of an existent order that obtains in every nation on earth. This order is traced to an action of God in the post-diluvian epoch.[4]

Miller thinks Yoder tried to marginalize this Noachide epoch and its global vision, even though it was highly significant for Jewish theology. Consequently Yoder also marginalized the role of the state in New Testament teaching. In Yoder's "relentless one-sided interpretation of the cross of Christ as the politics of God," he did not come to terms with the legitimate, God-ordained role of magistrates and state authorities in dealing with wrongdoers.

It is this more global and universal vision that I believe needs to be kept in mind when interpreting Jesus' self-perception as a fulfiller of the law and the prophets and developing a positive theology of law and civil institutions for today. There is, however, both in Yoder and in Miller as I read them, an historical optimism about the possibilities of a messianic ethic that skewers the nature of law and civil institutions. In the case of Miller this involves his hope for a United Nations-led new world order; for Yoder the optimism revolves around the vision of a small messianic community actualizing the politics of Jesus. Both enact a reading of the Christian Scriptures in which the Hellenistic influence appears diminished.

This is most evident in their understanding of Paul. I maintain that the Hellenistic (Greek) strain can be found within the Hebraic literature itself, particularly the Wisdom literature, but also in how some Jews interpreted Torah. Philo the Alexandrian Jew is an interesting example of this more mystical and philosophical reading of Torah and might be considered a Pauline type.[5] The theme of law (*nomos*) and institutional life as a post-lapsarian setting of limits and boundaries (their negative role) is in the Bible but greatly strengthened under the influence of Platonic thought in Paul and Augustine. This theme is not adequately represented in Miller's view of civil institutions. His more positive understanding of law and civil institutions is a prelapsarian means of furthering the good in human society and is more Aristotelian and Thomistic than Augustinian. This view is dominant in early Hebraic literature, flowers in late Medieval renaissance, and becomes especially strong during the Enlightenment. In my own work I hope to give each of these (the Platonic-Augustinian and the Aristotelian-Thomistic) views of the state their rightful place.

Miller is especially insistent on seeing Christ and the Christian story as "a clarifying fulfillment within a fulfillment [second-temple Judaism as the first fulfillment]—a powerful activation of an already strong Israelite calling—a continuation of Israel's story not its replacement. . . . ."[6] He credits the early church, and in particular Irenaeus, for insuring the inclusion of the Hebrew Scriptures within the Christian canon in its fight against Marcion. He puts great weight on the ordering of the Christian writings which were added to the Jewish Scriptures. In all but one of the earliest codices the Gospels and Acts came first, then the General Epistles (which highlight the Jerusalem Christian church), only then Paul's letters to the seven churches, and finally additional letters and the book of Revelation. He calls the addition of the Christian Scriptures to the biblical canon the third canon-forming epoch of Israel, the first being the Deuteronomic and the second the Ezra-Nehemiahic.

The Christian story now becomes part of the world story which begins with Genesis and ends with Revelation: "Creation and history are not two different things. History is an outgrowth of creation and the goal of creation. The narrative as such repudiates Marcion's bifurcation between creation, history and redemption."[7]

With the Constantinianization of the church, thinks Miller, the order of the Christian Scriptures was reshaped once more. From the fourth and fifth centuries onward, Paul's epistles were placed before the General Epistles to reflect the primacy of Paul and Gentile Christianity over the Jerusalem church and the letters of James, Peter, John, and Jude. In other words, this reordering reflected the break with the Jewish community.[8] Furthermore, the Hebrew Scriptures themselves are re-arranged by Gentile Christians in a supercessionist fashion: Whereas earlier the scrolls of the prophets were in the middle, between the first canon-formation period (Deuteronomistic) and the second (Ezra-Nehemiah), now the prophets are placed at the end to highlight the notion that the Christian Scriptures are what the prophets are anticipating. This now contributes to the bifurcation of Old and New Testaments.

Miller's is an important voice for Mennonites to hear. He calls on us to read the whole Bible in its narrative unity and comprehensiveness, not to limit ourselves to a highly selective supercessionist— even Christomonistic—reading of the biblical text driven by a nonresistant, pacifist ethic. Miller is himself an ardent free-church pacifist but finds himself in the older pre-Yoder generation of thinkers who continued to believe in a strong state, ordained by God to punish the evil and protect the good in the world, but a state quite separate from the church, which is called to follow Christ nonviolently.[9] It is our vocation to witness to Christ's nonviolent love in the world. The term Miller prefers for this witness is "vocational pacifism."

Three criticisms (further to the ones made above) that might be leveled against Miller are these: First, he places too much emphasis on the early ordering of the Hebrew scrolls; their arrangement, I have been told, was much more fluid before their fixing in the Christian canon than Miller wants them to be for the sake of his argument. Second, he gives Paul too much of a secondary status in the Christian writings, and the legitimacy he does give to Paul is colored by his distinctive reading of the Hebrew Scriptures. Third, he does not allow enough possibility for the breaking in of the new. To call the addition of the Christian writings simply the third canon-forming epoch of the Jewish story is overstating the case and underestimating the early tension between believing Jews and Gentiles and non-Christian Jews already present in Paul.

RE-ENFRANCHISING THE OLD TESTAMENT
LAW FOR A CHRISTIAN VIEW OF CIVIL LIFE

Waldemar Janzen, who received his doctorate in Near Eastern Languages and Literatures from Harvard, is an ordained Mennonite minister and a Professor Emeritus at Canadian Mennonite University, Winnipeg, Manitoba. He is also someone who has devoted a considerable portion of his academic life to the Hebrew Scriptures. He too laments the Marcion-like tendency of the Anabaptist-Mennonite tradition (including Yoder) to think of the New Testament as having superceded the Old Testament if not outrightly replaced it. He is critical of Mennonites who have disdain for those mainline traditions which still depend on the Old Testament for their views of law, politics, and war.[10] The Anabaptist reduction of the canon to the New Testament is a serious hermeneutical deficiency.

The consequence is that Mennonites can dispense with explicit theological reflection on the world outside the church, and large areas of life that have had importance for Mennonites throughout their history (e.g., family and land).[11] Unlike the Old Testament, the New Testament does not give us much ethical guidance on family and land. Other areas of life given virtually no attention theologically due to a supercessionist approach include these: creation (land, place, nature, body, medicine); political society (government, law and justice, human rights and liberation); economic society (business, work, play); and family (children before baptism, children outside the church).[12] The result is that we seek guidance on these issues outside of theology.

Agreeing with my own call for reading the Bible as a whole in the context of the believing community, Janzen pleads for a re-enfranchising of the Old Testament for theological and ethical reflection, such that the whole canon becomes a source of authority for the Christian community without threatening the Anabaptist concern for obedience to the radical call of Jesus. He disagrees, however, with my claim that what unifies the canonical literature is the "creation-fall-redemption-consummation" schema, and my call to read the canonical literature through confessional (kerygmatic, rule of faith, Apostolic creedal) eyes. What the canon has to say to us ought not to be controlled in this way, he says.[13]

Instead, Janzen proposes a polyphonic rather than a homophonic, a synchronic rather than a diachronic reading of the whole canonical text to gain guidance for ethical questions.[14] No part of the canon would have priority over another (gospel over law, Sermon on the Mount, story of Jesus) but rather the biblical exegete would move freely through the whole canon to find texts relevant for the issue under consideration:

> Texts will support, challenge, modify or supplement each other. At points they will appear to be contradictory. Such diversity will be evident just as much *within* each Testament as *between* the Testaments. Thus an Old Testament apparently advocating war will find itself in just as much tension with other Old Testament texts advocating peace as with New Testament texts.[15]

In the pursuit of insight, there would be an ever wider circle of texts in dialogue with each other in the context of communal discernment. Though long and painful, such an approach can lead to closure on a topic, as the universal consensus against slave-holding exemplifies.[16]

There is much to be said for Janzen's canonical approach, which is especially useful in my own project, although I am less confident than Janzen that communal discernment can reach consensus in canonical interpretation of a given issue without *confessional* mediation of some kind, and possibly an institutional teaching authority ("magisterium"). His own assertion that the canonical texts "all speak within the framework of assuming one sovereign God, creator of the world and shaper of its history and destiny," is itself a creedal assertion.[17] Furthermore, considering his strong Christological conclusion: "We need, rather, to reread the exodus in the light of Jesus Christ. . . . We would recognize the need of both [Israelites and Egyptians] to be saved by the means demonstrated in the suffering servant love of Jesus." Here Janzen confirms his own strong confessional hermeneutical perspective.[18]

Nevertheless, the helpful way Hebrew Scriptures can be used to give ethical guidance is shown especially clearly by Janzen in his article, "The Biblical Basis of Stewardship of Land."[19] The restoration of humanity's right relation to the land—that is, fulfillment of the original Genesis commission to be good administrators and stewards of God's good land—says Janzen, is an ever-present theme of God's salvation of humanity. Israel's many detailed laws and institutions were meant to emphasize her duty, as "long-term guests" (another way of saying "strangers and sojourners" or "landed immigrants"), to be good caretakers of God's property.[20] The various laws of Moses were an answer to the question, "What does it mean to be good stewards of their God-given land?" and were summarized as: "You shall love the Lord your God with all your heart, and with all your soul, and with all your might" (Deut.6:5), made more explicit by Jesus' addition: "You shall love your neighbor as yourself" (Mark 12:31, citing Lev. 19:18).[21]

The many Israelite laws, including (1) return of first fruits to God, (2) the prohibition against eating blood, (3) the various food laws, (4) fair distribution of land, and (5) Sabbath laws are simply detailed application and elaboration of these central theological principles.[22] The spiritual, the ascetic, poverty, suffering are not glorified for their own sake: "God wants for everyone the good life, the life that can be enjoyed and that leads to rejoicing and praise (Lev. 23:39-43; Deut. 10:7; 16:9-12; 26:11)."[23]

Jesus and the New Testament, while devoting proportionately less space to the land, nevertheless continue in the same vein. If anything, the New Testament widens and globalizes the scope of material well-being to all people and places: "All places and lands are now potential promised land, holy land, where God can manifest himself."[24] In no way can Jesus be understood to reject the fundamental principles of the Old Testament *vis-a-vis* the human stewardship of land and its resources, but stewardship is expanded to include the redemption of all of nature.

"While the Old Testament pictures the fulfillment of human redemption in an earthly rule of God (or his law, or the Messiah), extending from Jerusalem over all nations, the New Testament translates these events into God's eternity."[25] This eternal, universal redemption of nature, however, begins here in the earthly sphere through good stewardship of the land, through healing the sick, feeding the hungry, and visiting the imprisoned.

Janzen represents a critical minority voice within contemporary Mennonite theology calling for a much more positive understanding of law and public civil and institutional life than is the case in what might be termed the Yoder school of thought. This can be explained at least partly by the fact that Janzen is an Old Testament scholar who draws on the Old as well as New Testaments for his social ethics; that he belongs to another Anabaptist-Mennonite historical stream—the Dutch, North German, Russian, General Conference tradition which has from the start had a more fluid understanding of the relation between church and larger culture, society and state; and that he is a Canadian with a stronger sense of the common good and the benevolent role of the state in public, including religious, life—a more benign view of the "principalities and the powers."

There continues to be in Janzen a strong sense of the Christian calling to follow Jesus in living nonviolently, but this vocation is seen to be compatible with a selective participation in public life on many levels, including the artistic, cultural, economic, and political. There is, in this approach to public life, a close parallel between Mennonites and Jews in their attempt to hold together a minority ethnic/cultural and a religious identity within the context of larger dominant cultures. There are some illuminating studies of the relation of the Mennonite and Jewish communities in southern Russia in the nineteenth century in this regard. The very essence of the Christian faith (parallel to the Jewish faith) is the holding together of corporal life in all its aspects and belief, and a resistance to an atomization and individualization of that life and faith.

This has its strengths but also its dangers as we shall see below. Such a vision bears some resemblance to the Christian communities Stanley Hauerwas envisions: narrative communities devoted to the formation of Christian character and virtues among Christians who exist as "resident aliens" within larger culture but act as salt and leaven in that larger world. However, the extent to which such communities draw nourishment from, participate positively in, and contribute to the civil life of that larger world—the fluidity of the boundaries—is not emphasized by Hauerwas nor by Yoder, whom Hauerwas has adopted as his theological and ethical mentor.

Precisely this "in between" space is the locus of my own present project. Or more accurately put, I seek to find how it is that individual communities, such as the Jewish or in my case Mennonite-Christian, can as communities influence the shape of the common good and in turn are themselves nourished and preserved by the common realm.

JESUS, PAUL, AND TORAH

Recent biblical scholarship has made considerable strides in understanding law in the Old and New Testaments in a number of ways: (1) There appears to be a virtual consensus that the traditional Lutheran reading of Paul in terms of the strict law-gospel distinction does not do justice to the way gospel (divine benevolence or grace) is at the heart of law in the Hebraic tradition and law is intrinsic to the gospel in the Christian Scriptures. If a distinction is to be made between law and gospel—and there is some justification in not simply collapsing the two; Luther's insights on this continue to have validity—that distinction is present from the beginning. (2) There is no homogeneous understanding of Torah among the Jews; the law meant/means many different things.

Here I have found Dale C. Allison Jr.'s book, *The New Moses: A Matthean Typology*, particularly helpful. His detailed look at how Moses represented many different types not only in Christian figures (like Jesus, Peter, Paul, Constantine, to name only a few) but also in Hebrew figures (like Joshua, Gideon, David, Elijah, Jeremiah, the Suffering Servant, the Messiah and so on) confirmed for me this diversity.[26] I am fully persuaded by Allison against W. D. Davies that the parallels between the Matthean Jesus and Moses are numerous and intentional.[27] However, in the light of his study alone, it is not self-evident which particular view of the law Jesus was not abolishing but fulfilling. One is left with such a diversity of typologies, all with considerable validity, that one remains theologically dissatisfied.

I turn, therefore, in my concluding pages to two recent studies which I believe move the discussion forward beyond someone like Allison: Richard B. Hays' *The Moral Vision of the New Testament* and Robert C. Tannehill's *The Narrative Unity of Luke-Acts: A Literary Interpretation: Volume Two: The Acts of the Apostles*. I restrict myself here to one small fragment in each of these works: Hays' treatment of the Matthean Jesus and Tannehill's understanding of Paul's defense speeches before civil authorities in Acts.

THE MATTHEAN JESUS

The Jesus of Matthew is a Moses-like, authoritative teacher, with the didactic Sermon on the Mount programmatically placed at the beginning of the gospel. The continuity of Jesus with the Torah is a theme throughout, but "rather than reading the Law's requirements as rules that fix the normative standards of righteousness, Matthew's Jesus sees them as pointers to a more radical righteousness of the heart, intensifying the demand of God far beyond the letter of the Law."[28] One of the ways Jesus fulfills the law is by disclosing the "inner intent" of the law. Another way is that in his life he completes numerous Old Testament prophecies. In this way Matthew demonstrates the identification of Jesus with the Torah both in his person and in his teaching, thereby harmonizing Law and Gospel. But Hays is careful not to reduce the teachings of Jesus to an inner, subjective, individual "spiritualized" righteousness: Jesus calls people to a new community of disciples who put Jesus' teachings into practice—an alternative to society at large.

When compared to the detailed prescriptions of community life in the Mishnah or at Qumran, Matthew's program appears incomplete: "Despite his emphasis on the church's commission to teach obedience to Jesus' commandments, Matthew sees such teaching as instrumental to a deeper goal: the transformation of character and of the heart."[29] Although Matthew's moral vision has much in common with the wisdom tradition of the Hebrews, he is more concerned with character formation within a community than with the cultivation of individual virtues and wisdom. Matthew in effect transforms the Hebraic understanding of law. He does so by making the double love command—"'You shall love the Lord your God with all your heart, and with all your soul, and with all your mind'. . . . 'You shall love your neighbor as yourself'" (Matt. 22:37-39)—the "hermeneutical filter" that governs the community's whole understanding of the law.

This is consistent with the Hebraic view (see Hosea 6:6, "For I desire steadfast love and not sacrifice, the knowledge of God rather than burnt offerings"), but with Jesus detailed specifications of law are consistently subordinated to the law's inner intent—love and mercy. Yet also in Jesus there remains a tension between mercy and rigor, forgiveness and communal discipline, as reflected in "the order [or law] of Christ" found in Matt. 18:15-20. Sin is not ignored or tolerated, and the community has power to "loose and bind" (Matt.16:19).[30]

The teaching and disciplining authority of the church is understood by Matthew as *ekklesia*. This involves a small group of believers, as in Matthew 18:20: "For where two or three are gathered in my name, I am there among you." Matthew's vision—also suggestive of the rabbinic tradition of two or three gathered around the Torah—is grounded not on an authoritative institution or text but on the personal presence of the risen Christ.[31]

The historical situatedness of Matthew is important. It was probably written in Antioch, after the destruction of the temple (70 CE), in the last twenty years of the first century, shortly after the split between church and synagogue, leaving bad feelings between the two groups. Each community (rabbinic Judaism and Jewish-Christians) claimed the authentic interpretation of the Torah. The Matthean community tended to spiritualize the Torah by emphasizing a hermeneutic of love, thereby reaching out to the Gentiles. More important was their claim that Jesus was the fulfillment of the Torah. Matthew was a master synthesizer and church diplomat who wove diverse elements into a master narrative in which Jesus proclaims a message both rigorous and flexible.[32]

I find Hays' treatment compelling in its depiction of early Christianity as firmly rooted in the Hebraic story *and* transforming that story into something new without being supercessionist. In the process, however, something is lost. It has to do with the historical specificity of the requirements of the law even for Christians. Hays wants to retain the tension of the external "rigor" of the Christian life and the internal intention of the law—"love of God" and "love of neighbor (mercy)." However, the specifics of moral life and responsibility in the world are weakened.

Let me illustrate. For the majority of Anabaptists, and Mennonites historically, the hard sayings of Jesus in the Sermon on the Mount had very specific, concrete, ethical and political ramifications: the rejection of all participation in warfare. Yoder calls this "biblical realism."[33] There is always the temptation to spiritualize the precepts of Jesus, to idealize them, or to see them as an interim ethic, but if Jesus' teachings as found in Matthew are taken to be realistically demanded of the disciplining community, how does that translate into historical, economic, and political life? Or, to go the route of Waldemar Janzen above, how are the many relevant "laws" of the Old Testament having to do with our stewardship of creation (e.g.,"cultural mandates"), political society, economic life, family relationship related to the Matthean vision of Jesus as the new Torah?

I don not see Hays addressing these tough issues. I grant that my tradition has focused too narrowly on the specific imperatives of Jesus in Matthew 5; this is precisely why I am urging us to read the whole canon, and why I am exploring the problem of the rightful place of law and civil institutions for Christians as well as non-Christians. I do believe there may very well be a place for well-articulated specifications of what is and what is not required of the Christian in daily life, a form of "canon law." The question then becomes how that is related to public, civil law.

LUKE-ACTS: PAUL AND THE CIVIL AUTHORITIES

I have for some time thought that especially those of us in the "pacifist" traditions might fruitfully examine more carefully Paul's relation to the Jewish and Roman authorities in the Acts of the apostles. It would give us a helpful counterpoint to the usual New Testament texts cited in relation to church-state and Christian use of force issues. Such an alternate paradigm might help us see with fresh eyes the conversion of Cornelius the centurion without reference to his leaving his profession (Acts 10); Jesus's cleansing of the temple with a whip (John 2:15); Jesus statements "I came not to send peace, but a sword" (Matt. 10:34) and "He that hath no sword, let him sell his garment and buy one," (Luke 22:35-38); Jesus's saying "Render to Caesar the things that are Caesar's and to God the things that are God's" (Mark 12:17); subjection to divinely instituted authority which bears the sword for the preservation of the good and the restraining of evil, and the legitimate payment of taxes (Rom. 13: 1-7); and of course the so-called "hard sayings" of Jesus (Matt. 5) and a similar Pauline text on "marks of the true Christian" (Rom. 12: 9-21), to name a few.

What we find in Acts is Paul taking advantage of the "police function" of the state for his own protection, and the use of secular courts as a Roman citizen. The Roman authorities, despite their opportunism, are generally portrayed by the author of Luke-Acts as friendlier and more concerned with justice than are the non-believing Jews, who repeatedly charge Paul with betraying the laws of Moses. On numerous occasions Roman militia rescue and protect Paul against mob violence (Acts 21:32, Acts 23:10, Acts 23:23-24). They are described as friendly guardians of Paul on the long trip to Rome (Acts 27-28). Paul at no time refuses this protection and friendship. In fact, he shows every sign of respect to the political authorities. On at least three occasions Paul demands his rights as a Roman citizen, and in the end demands to be heard by the highest court of the land: the Roman Emperor himself (Acts 25:10). Whether he ever did appear before the Emperor is left open at the end of the book. Robert C. Tannehill does a fine job of giving the reader a detailed and colourful account of Paul's imprisonment, appearances before the various authorities, including his three defense speeches, and the dramatic last trip to Rome.

One gets the sense that Paul's real quarrel is with his coreligionists, not with the Roman authorities. His arrest and first defence speech before the Roman tribunal and a Jewish audience (Acts 21:17–22-29) have to do with the basic charge that Paul is anti-Jewish, defiling the temple by bringing Greeks into it and not requiring them to follow the Jewish law. The narrator and Paul claim their loyalty to Israel but are committed to a mission which "relativizes Israel's place in the scheme of things. They are not willing to allow Jewish rejection to stand in the way of the world mission."[34] In his defense Paul argues that he is a zealous Jew, he is educated and loyal to Jewish law, and his universal mission to the Gentiles emerges out of the heart of the Jewish tradition itself (in fact he received his call to the universal mission in a vision in the temple).[35] Earlier in Luke 2:30-32, it was in the temple that Simeon had declared that in Jesus God's salvation has come as a light to all peoples, and in Acts 3:25 Peter recalls in Solomon's portico the divine promise to Abraham that in his "descendants all the families of the earth shall be blessed."

In subsequent defence scenes, Paul appears before the Jewish Sanhedrin, two Roman Governors and the Jewish King Agrippa. Before the Sanhedrin (Acts 22:30–23:11) he begins to shift the line of debate to the question of the Jewish hope and the resurrection, initially defending the concept of the general resurrection rather than the specific resurrection of Jesus, claiming that he is being a faithful Pharisee.[36] Next Paul appears before two Roman governors, Felix and Festus, who are portrayed ambiguously by the author. While open to hearing the truth about Paul's innocence, they are ultimately swayed by self-interest and the need for Jewish support. The Tribune Lysias decisively intervenes three times to save Paul (Acts 21:31-36, 23:10, 23:12-35), on the last occasion saving Paul's life from an ambush. God uses natural forces and human decisions without their knowledge to fulfill his divine purpose.[37]

With his transfer to Judean Governor Felix, his Jewish opponents change their charge; now Paul is a threat to Roman society. After complimenting Felix, Paul shifts attention to his Jewish accusers, defending again his fidelity to the law and the prophets but effectively using his defense speech to witness both to the Jews and to the Roman officials. Felix is attracted to Paul but in the end his self-interest wins out. Finally, both the religious and the Roman leaders are more interested in the status quo than the truth.[38] The second governor before whom Paul appears, Festus of Caesarea (Acts 25:1-12), is also depicted as a biased judge who is on the verge of giving in to Jewish demands that Paul be sent for trial to Jerusalem. Paul continues to defend himself against charges that he has committed offenses against Jews, the temple, and Caesar and successfully avoids going to Jerusalem. He insists on going before the Emperor not for his own sake (not as "the legal maneuver of a desperate prisoner") but for an opportunity to go to Rome to witness to the Roman Jews and to Caesar.[39]

Paul's defence speeches reach a climax with his appearance before King Agrippa, who with his sister Bernice is visiting Festus (Acts 25:13–26:32). Festus, reviewing the case for the sake of Agrippa, deceptively tries to paint himself favorably as someone primarily interested in justice, although he has been motivated by favoritism toward the Jewish opponents for political reasons. Then Festus asks Agrippa to hear Paul and to give an opinion. Agrippa is Jewish, familiar with Jewish affairs, "believes the prophets," and knows about the Christian "way," so Paul can speak to him as an insider.

Paul's great speech is basically autobiographical, a review of his ministry, reaching back to John the Baptist, Jesus, the apostles, and moving into the present with proclamation and an appeal to the king himself. Paul outlines again his own Jewishness (strict upbringing, zeal as a persecutor, using the terms "my nation," "our religions," "our fathers," "our twelve tribes"[40]), his encounter with the Lord, and repeats his message of hope and resurrection, call for repentance, release of sins, and salvation for both Jews and Gentiles. He conveys the irony of being accused of having the hope that the twelve tribes themselves seek—the hope of the resurrection. He now becomes much more Christological, linking the general resurrection to the resurrection of the Messiah, a hope for both the Jews and the Gentiles. Agrippa's response is either one of surprise or cynicism: "This man could have been set free if he had not appealed to Caesar."[41]

Tannehill's best chapter, and for my purposes the most important, is the second to last one, dealing with Paul's sea journey to Rome (Acts 27:1–28:16). Tannehill, together with the narrator, understand the journey of the ship through the stormy sea as a grand metaphor for the Christian church in relation to the larger world. Woven into the account is the early promise of the survival of the whole mixed company, each of whom contributes to their final rescue but especially Paul, through his interventions at critical points, and the cooperation of the military leader Julius. The chief protagonists of the story are the centurion Julius and his soldiers, the sailors, and of course Paul himself. A close friendship and trust develops right from the start between Julius and Paul, a relationship that in the end results in the rescue of all on the ship, virtually all of them pagans who worship other gods.

The meal on the ship has eucharistic overtones and "Even though the boundary of the church is not completely eliminated, the meal on the ship is an act that benefits all, Christian and non-Christian, and an act in which community is created across religious lines."[42] Because the universal "salvation" theme is so central in the whole Luke-Acts narrative, beginning with Luke 3:6 ("all flesh will see the salvation of God") the identification of the rescue of all on the ship with the salvation of all humanity is an especially significant conclusion to Acts.

The most remarkable facets of the story, however, are these: First, Paul makes no reference to faith in Christ as a precondition for rescue/salvation. Second, the non-believing centurion and sailors play an important role in the unfolding drama of God's saving design for the passengers, who symbolize all of humanity. There is no indication that Paul preached Christ to the passengers or the peoples of Malta—God's saving work in this case does not seem to depend on the rejection or acceptance of the message.[43] While the case for "universal salvation"—every single person will be saved whether believer or not—cannot be inferred from this, nevertheless some kind of universality is implied. Furthermore, human agency is critical in reaching the goal. It is remarkable that in the context of a Christian minority within Roman society, the "possibility of salvation in the social and political sphere depends on Christians and non-Christians being willing to follow the lead of Paul, Julius, and the sailors when they are acting for the good of all."[44]

Even the so-called "barbarian" islanders of Malta and their chief Publius, not part of Greco-Roman culture and depicted as having superstitious religious views (Paul is thought of as a "divine man" when not harmed by the bite of the viper), show warm hospitality to the entourage. "The narrative," as Tannehill observes, "undermines any tendency for Christians to regard the world in general as hostile and evil."[45] Paul stays on the island for three months, and like Jesus, performs many miracles of healing, but we are told nothing about any preaching that he may have done to the Maltans. They are allowed to remain pagan, demonstrating once again the cooperation between pagan society and Christians in contributing instrumentally in fulfilling a more general divine purpose.

Despite this positive portrayal of pagans and Gentiles, Paul remains a prisoner, and his unsuccessful mission to the Roman Jewish community ends the narrative of Luke-Acts with an unresolved tension. In the end, there is no evidence that the "salvation of all flesh" promised in Luke 3:6 is anywhere near being fulfilled. There are many parallels to Jesus' last days, and like Jesus, Paul's mission ends in rejection by his people and suffering. There is a tragic-ironic tone to the end of Acts: the Gentiles are ready to hear but the Jews are deaf and blind. Paul remains courageous and faithful to the end, but only a few Jewish listeners seem interested. The ending is left open: We are not told whether or not Paul finally did appear before the Emperor nor are we told about his martyrdom. The question of the acceptance or rejection of the Messianic hope by the Jewish people remains unresolved.[46]

For pacifists, and particularly for Mennonites, reading this interpretation of Paul's appearance before Jewish and Roman authorities, his defending of his rights as a Roman citizen in the "secular" courts of the land, his insistence to be heard by the Emperor, his interaction with the captain and crew of the ship, and his most remarkable reception and ministry among the "pagan" Maltans raises some provocative questions:

(1) Could not one characterize the activities of the Roman "militias" as found in the book of Acts as a form of "police" action, to be distinguished from "war-making" activities?

(2) What role does such "policing" have in society—both locally and regionally as well as nationally and internationally?

(3) Can Christians intentionally benefit from or even participate in such policing?

(4) What role do secular courts of law play in the Christian scheme of things? Can Christians, like Paul, demand their rights as citizens of a country in the context of secular courts?

(5) Are there public laws (in the arena of the common good) that play a significant, even normative role for the Christian community? For most Christians in history since the time of Constantine up to the present the response to these questions has been self-evident. It is "yes" to all of the above. For some minority groups, like the Mennonites, this conclusion has been not at all obvious. In my current project I explore the complex issues raised by these questions and give a qualified and conditional, affirmative answer.

PARTICULARITY AS MEANS TO UNIVERSALITY: EXCLUSIVE COMMUNITIES, PUBLIC ORTHODOXIES, AND THE COMMON GOOD

In light of the rejection by a majority of the Jews of the Christian messianic message that leads to the separation of church and synagogue, one can see why a supercessionist reading of Paul and his ministry is such a strong temptation for Gentile Christians. We have in Acts, as interpreted particularly by Tannehill, a highly one-sided reading of the story, narrated by someone from within the Jewish-Christian community. One wonders how someone like Philo, a virtual contemporary—I would call him a kind of non-Christian-Jewish Paul—would have interpreted the same events.

Jon D. Levenson is an example of a Jewish theologian who articulates for Jews the issues and tensions that apply also to a minority Christian group such as the Anabaptist-Mennonite: How is it that a small community of believers, with exclusive truth claims, can coexist peacefully with other such communities with other exclusive truth claims, within some notion of a common good which inevitably itself is grounded in a "public orthodoxy" of some kind? I agree with D'-Costa and Levenson that there is no such thing as a "pluralist position"—either on the level of inter-religious dialogue or on the level of public policy—when that is conceived as an ideologically neutral vantage point from which to tolerate all viewpoints equally within its horizon. Within the field of interreligious discourse, pluralism and inclusivism are subtypes of exclusivism; each based on some notions or criteria of what is true and what is false, what is acceptable and what is not. In the realm of public social policy, every so-called "pluralistic" society, in which there coexist groups with exclusive worldviews, will be governed by some form of "public orthodoxy."[47]

The unanswered questions are these: What will be the nature of that public orthodoxy? How is it determined? Is it simply an enforced public orthodoxy by the dominant group? Or is it conceived as some type of liberal social contract, along the lines envisioned by John Rawls? And if the latter, are the rules arrived at purely prudential and ad hoc or is there some more universal rational or metaphysical basis for them? Levenson claims Rawls' contractualism itself reflects Western, liberal Protestant values. Can some form of natural law, or in theological language, "general revelation"—a bare minimum of social ethical principles that apply to all diverse groups in late modern societies—be retained while at the same time respecting the exclusive truth claims of each particular social grouping? The present conflict between Israelis and Palestinians in the Middle East, exclusive groups claiming rights to the same ancestral territories, makes this issue much more than an interesting academic parlor game.

I want to argue that there are such universal principles but that they are always mediated through particular communities, frequently religious. While there is no neutral vantage point through which universal moral and ethical principles can be mediated—the universal is always mediated through the particular—nevertheless, there are universals which can be translated into public law and civil institutions. In the subsequent pages I very tentatively suggest how this might be conceptualized from the perspective of the Jewish-Christian narrative. To begin with, I return to Jon D. Levenson and an article on "The Exodus and Biblical Theology: A Rejoinder to John J. Collins."[48]

Levenson argues here against those Marxist or liberation theologians who use the exodus story as an unqualified prototype of a universal message of liberation of the poor and enslaved ("preferential option for the poor"). He does not deny the universalistic elements in the story but rejects the notion that it or the law given to the Jews is a manifesto for a modern charter of freedom: Such law ignores "'the cold fact that the biblical criteria for inclusion among those who benefit from the exodus are not poverty, oppression, suffering, or anything of the kind' but only 'descent from a common ancestor, Jacob/Israel son of Isaac son of Abraham.'"[49] It ignores the "familial-national" aspects in favour of the "social-ethical." In fact, slavery is not condemned universally at all.

This does not preclude social activists like Martin Luther King Jr. from drawing on the exodus story for their own social justice agenda—every community, even the Jewish, draws and builds on the past, selects certain themes giving them priority over others. But such dependence on the story can be legitimate only when it *"brings the past, the story of Israel, to bear upon the present"* by means of appropriation not projection.[50] The difference between the Egyptian social order of the Pharaohs and the book of Exodus is not that the latter is more egalitarian than the former—as though there were a neutral standard by which to judge each—but that it was a contest between two masters: the Pharaoh and JHWH. "The social obligations that the Hebrew Bible associates with the exodus are never subordinated therein to any autonomous ethic of egalitarianism, and the identification of justice with equality is not native to Israelite culture. That is why the legal corpora and prophetic preachings alike can combine the most thoroughly egalitarian and the most grossly inegalitarian elements without a problem."[51]

Where does this leave us? Levenson has correctly identified the illegitimacy of simply projecting onto the exodus story and the Torah retrospectively our modern Western, egalitarian, social-political agenda. Still he leaves room for the universal element—there is a universalistic, social-ethical dimension to Exodus and Torah, but it is always rooted in a particular covenantal relationship: "Israel's special degree of responsibility is grounded in JHWH's prior benefactions."[52]

I say that any personal, communal, or public ethic derived from the Jewish-Christian tradition will understand that ethic not simply in contractual terms but as presupposing such divine benefaction, agency and command. Let me suggest from the vantage point of a Christian theologian—himself rooted in a particular communal and "covenantal" tradition—that the narrative of the Jewish story, as it gradually unfolds in the Hebraic literature, and within which the

Jewish-Christian and Gentile-Christian narrative emerges, is the narrative of the birth and growing clarity with which the people of God come to understand that divine agency and command.

In the process, the particularity of the familial-national comes to be relativized and subordinated to another particularity, the believing community. That community, made up of a diverse familial-national grouping, seeks to fulfill a universal mission. It is how this new community understands its make-up and conceptualizes its universal vocation that causes the tensions and ruptures between the earliest Jewish-Christians, Gentile-Christians, and non-Christian Jews.

CONCLUSION

What was the law that Jesus was fullfilling?[53] I can here only suggest, with Michael Welker and others, that the law Jesus and early Christian writers had in mind included cultic, religious (moral), *and* civil law. There has been considerable debate over exactly how Jewish law can be classified into types.[54] Nevertheless, the general division into cultic, religious, and civil seems to prevail. Welker has suggested the helpful categories of legal, cultic and mercy codes which parallel the above. (1) The legal categories involve laws (e.g., Deut. 20-23) that have to do with restorative justice and setting limits through abstraction from individual cases. (2) Cultic laws are related to specific times and places of worship and to the prohibition against idolatry. (3) The mercy codes focus on the routinization of rights for the weaker and marginalized in society, not only as recipients but also as active participants in social, economic and judicial processes.[55]

Although there were many similarities between Hebraic law codes and other Ancient Near Eastern legal formulations, there were at least two fundamental differences: First, Jewish laws were seen as God's commands. Second, Jewish laws had two further unique characteristics. They had to do with a direct encounter with that God (verticality) and, intrinsically linked to that encounter, they entailed a responsibility for fellow humanity and the created order (horizontality).[56]

In the best sense, Jews did not understand law self-righteously or legalistically but as based on divine encounter and grace, most specifically as experienced in the covenant and deliverance from bondage in Egypt. It can be argued, and Welker and others do so, that Jewish law codes are prototypes for later constitutional law and therefore are foundational for the development of Western civil law and the entrenchment of individual and corporate rights and natural justice. The implications of this for the way Christians, including Mennonites, see themselves and their responsibiltiies for and within larger culture is what I explore in my ongoing extended project.

NOTES

1. This is a modification and fusion of two papers: one presented at the conference "Assessing the Theological Legacy of John Howard Yoder," (Notre Dame, Ind.: University of Notre Dame, March 7-9, 2002), the other at the Center of Theological Inquiry (Princeton, N.J., April 10, 2002).

2. See especially "See How They Go with Their Face to the Sun," in John Howard Yoder, *For The Nations: Essays Public and Evangelical* (Grand Rapids: Eerdmans, 1997), 51-78. I have outlined Yoder's position, as found in the above article as well as some of his later unpublished essays, in my "Theological Orthodoxy and Jewish Christianity: A Personal Tribute to John Howard Yoder," in *The Wisdom of the Cross: Essays in Honor of John Howard Yoder*, ed. Stanley Hauerwas, Chris K. Huebner, Harry J. Huebner, Mark Thiessen Nation (Grand Rapids: Eerdmans, 1999), 430-448.

3. For my information on Miller and Yoder in the paragraphs above and below, I gratefully acknowledge personal correspondence with John W. Miller (email March 4, 2002) and his sharing with me his unofficially produced manuscript: *Reading Israel's Story: Hope for the World: A Canon History Approach to the Narrative and Message of the Bible.*

4. Personal email Miller to Reimer, March 4, 2002.

5. See Peder Boren, "Philo of Alexandria," *The Anchor Bible Dictionary*, vol. 5, 333-342; also Peter Frick, *Divine Providence in Philo of Alexandria* (Tübingen: Mohr Siebeck, 1999).

6. Email Miller to Reimer, March 4, 2002.

7. Miller, *Reading Israel's Story*, 70.

8. Ibid., 79.

9. Although, as we have pointed out above, Miller has a more optimistic view of the positive role of the state in the creation of international order than those earlier Mennonites would have had.

10. Cf. Waldemar Janzen, "A Canonical Rethinking of the Anabaptist-Mennonite New Testament Orientation," *The Church as Theological Community: Essays in Honour of David Schroeder*, ed. Harry Huebner (Winnipeg, Man.: CMBC Publications, 1990), 90-112, 92. In personal correspondence, Janzen clarifies that "My position is not that Mennonites should follow mainline denominations in deriving their views of law, politics, and war from the Old Testament (which even mainline denominations do not do exclusively), but that Mennonites should draw Old Testament texts into the discussion of such areas within a canonical inter-textual dialogue." Email Waldemar Janzen to

A. James Reimer, May 1, 2002.

11. Janzen, "A Canonical Rethinking," 97-100.

12. Ibid., 99. It should be noted that Janzen does not want to limit the derivation of Old Testament ethics to law. It derives from various genres. Email Janzen to Reimer, May 1, 2002.

13. Janzen, "A Canonical Rethinking," 104-105.

14. Janzen elaborates: "Yoder and others approach this matter diachronically, i.e. treat the Testaments in historical sequence. I, on the other hand, am calling for a 'synchronic' (though not flat) use of the whole canon, both Testaments, as a basis for Christian ethics." Email Janzen to Reimer, May 1, 2002.

15. Janzen, "A Canonical Rethinking," 109.

16. Commenting on this section, in personal correspondence, Janzen says: "That whole paragraph . . . , though correct in what it says about my position, omits the strong eschatological emphasis that runs through my whole canonical approach. In other words, I see ethical living in both Testaments as an eschatologically oriented living out of 'signs' of the Day of Jahweh/Kingdom of God. Whether it is justice, peace, feeding the hungry, or whatever else, believers in both Testaments are 'pre-living' the shalom of God that marks God's will for both creation and eschaton. In that sense, the New Testament is 'nearer' to God's goal; but not because it is less primitive, more perfect, etc." Email Janzen to Reimer, May 1, 2002.

17. Ibid., 108.

18. Ibid., 112.

19. Waldemar Janzen, "The Biblical Basis of Stewardship of Land," in *Still in the Image: Essays in Biblical Theology and Anthropology* (Newton, Kan.: Faith and Life Press, 1982), 158-169.

20. Ibid., 160.

21. Ibid., 161.

22. Ibid., 162-163.

23. Ibid., 164.

24. Ibid., 166.

25. Ibid., 168-169.

26. "Both Moses and Jesus were many things, and they occupied several common offices. Moses was the paradigmatic prophet-king, the Messiah's model, a worker of miracles, the giver of Torah, the mediator for Israel, and a suffering servant. And Jesus was similarly a suffering servant, the mediator for Israel, the giver of Torah, a worker of miracles, the Mosaic Messiah, and the eschatological prophet-king." Dale C. Allison Jr., *A Matthean Typology* (Minneapolis: Fortress Press, 1993), 275.

27. Ibid., 298-306.

28. Richard B. Hays, *The Moral Vision of the New Testament: A Contemporary Introduction to New Testament Ethics* (San Francisco: HarperSanFrancisco, 1996), 95.

29. Ibid., 98.

30. Ibid., 101-102.

31. Ibid., 105.

32. Ibid., 108-109.

33. John Howard Yoder, *The Politics of Jesus* (Grand Rapids: Eerdmans, 1972).

34. Robert C. Tannehill, *The Narrative Unity of Luke—Acts: Volume Two: The Acts of the Apostles* (Minneapolis: Fortress, 1994), 272.

35. Ibid., 268-284.

36. Ibid., 285-292.

37. Ibid., 293-296.

38. Ibid., 297-304.

39. Ibid., 305-308.

40. Ibid., 318.

41. Ibid., 309-329.

42. Ibid., 335.

43. Ibid., 337.

44. Ibid., 338-339.

45. Ibid., 340.

46. Ibid., 344-357.

47. Cf. Gavin D'Costa, "The Impossibility of a Pluralist View of Religion," *Religious Studies* 32 (1996): 223-232; John Hick, "The Possibility of Religious Pluralism: A Reply to Gavin D'Costa," *Religious Studies* 33 (1997):161-166; a conversation between members of the Center of Theological Inquiry and Jon Levenson (Princeton, N.J., March 22, 2002).

48. Jon D. Levenson, "The Exodus and Biblical Theology: A Rejoinder to John J. Collins," in *Jews, Christians, and the Theology of the Hebrew Scriptures*, ed. Alice Ogden Bellis and Joel S. Kaminsky (Atlanta: Society of Biblical Literature, 2000), 263-275.

49. Ibid., 264.

50. Ibid., 265.

51. Ibid., 274.

52. Ibid., 273.

53. Janzen in personal correspondence has suggested that "it might be good to check all [biblical] occurrences of 'law' and ask whether it means what modern readers understand as 'law,' or what Jews understand as 'law' in the sense of 'statutes, commandments, and ordinances,' or what the Old Testament understands as Torah, 'teaching.'" Email Janzen to Reimer, May 1, 2002.

54. Cf. E. P. Sanders, *The Anchor Bible Dictionary*, Vol. 4, 252 ff.

55. Michael Welker, "Security of Expectations," *Journal of Religion* 66:3 (July 1986):237-260.

56. See Sanders,*Anchor Bible Dictionary*, Vol 4. 264.

Chapter 13

The Anabaptist and the Apostle: John Howard Yoder as a Pauline Theologian

Douglas Harink

JOHN HOWARD YODER'S *THE POLITICS OF JESUS* is widely acknowledged as having made a significant contribution to the political reading of the canonical gospels. Moreover, quite apart from its own contribution and influence, the basic thesis of *The Politics of Jesus* has been vindicated in much recent scholarly research on Jesus. Today there are few accounts of Jesus that do not consider an understanding of the socio-political context and character of his mission as central to the task of delineating Jesus' theological import for the church and discipleship.

It is quite otherwise with Paul. Paul is still often thought of in mainstream Protestant theology, conservative and liberal alike, as the apostle who turned Jesus' local, Jewish, and perhaps political mission into a universal, 'spiritual' message about how sinful individual human beings (in general) are 'saved'"from God's righteous judgment and 'justified' before God through "faith in Jesus Christ." Perhaps there may be a sociopolitical stance or orientation implied by or derivable from that message, but it is just that, implied or derived;

274

and it is often either a conservative or liberal orientation (it doesn't matter which) easily compatible with the ideals and aims of the modern liberal-democratic nation-state and the market economy. On this understanding there is no sociopolitical truth, consistent with the politics of Jesus, *intrinsic* to Paul's theology.

What is often forgotten about Yoder's *Politics of Jesus* is that a large portion of it (at least a third) was devoted to challenging just those interpretations of Paul which render him irrelevant or perhaps even hostile to the politics of the Jesus of the Gospels. In fact, I believe Yoder in his life-work finally wrote more about Paul than about Jesus. The result is that Yoder presents us a theology that is thoroughly Pauline in shape and character, even if in some profound respects very different from what is usually construed as "Pauline" in mainstream Protestant theology. Further, Yoder's post-Protestant reading of Paul, as was his reading of Jesus, is now also being vindicated by a good deal of recent Paul scholarship.

In what follows I draw attention to two significant themes in Pauline theology which are of crucial importance in understanding Yoder: first, the apocalyptic origin and orientation of Paul's theology; and second, justification by "the faithfulness of Jesus Christ." I will suggest in relation to a third theme in Paul, God's election of Israel, that Yoder's important work on the theology of the Jews and Judaism falls somewhat short of the full Pauline vision.

THE APOCALYPSE OF
JESUS CHRIST AND THE POWERS

The claim that Paul is a thoroughly apocalyptic theologian goes back as far as Albert Schweitzer and finds more recent notable proponents in Ernst Käsemann, J. Christiaan Beker and J. Louis Martyn. Martyn in particular has put forward a vigorous and compelling apocalyptic interpretation of Paul in his recent commentary on the epistle to the Galatians.[1]

One of Martyn's central theses, following the work of Martinus de Boer, is that Paul works with a "cosmic apocalyptic eschatology" rather than a "forensic apocalyptic theology." Briefly stated, a forensic apocalyptic theology emphasizes human responsibility for creating the sinful human condition through a willful rejection of God. God's righteous judgment therefore stands against humanity in its culpable sinfulness. Nevertheless, God intervenes in the human situation by providing forgiveness of sins and setting before humans two ways, the way of life and the way of death. Humans must choose the way of life to be saved and assured of eternal life.

According to many interpretations of Paul, Paul found in Jesus Christ just such forgiveness of sins and the offer of salvation through faith in him, and called on his hearers to make a decision for Jesus Christ. Martyn, however, rejects such "forensic" interpretations. He suggests, rather, that they are precisely what Paul is arguing *against* in his letter to the Galatians.[2]

By contrast, cosmic apocalyptic eschatology emphasizes that the *cosmos* is in bondage to rebellious, "anti-God" powers from which both the cosmos and humans await deliverance. God's sending of his Son, Jesus Christ, and in particular the Son's crucifixion, is the event in which God invades the enslaved cosmos and delivers it from these powers, thereby creating a new cosmos in which human beings are enabled again to become obedient to God through the effective new-creation power of the Holy Spirit. The *ecclesia* is created in the "space" of the new creation opened up by God's liberating cosmic action and, by living the way of the cross, the ecclesia itself becomes the visible sign of God's new creation through the cross of Christ.[3]

Limited space prevents my setting out here Martyn's many compelling arguments for interpreting Paul in terms of cosmic apocalyptic eschatology. What is significant is that Martyn construes the *"apokalypsis* of Jesus Christ," which is at the very core of Paul's theology, as most thoroughly the *action of God in and toward the cosmos*, creating the very ontic and moral conditions under which human obedience becomes concretely possible and actual. That is the significance of Paul's theology of the cosmos and of the powers which enslave it, and of God's defeat of these enslaving powers through the crucifixion and resurrection of Jesus.

Anyone familiar with Yoder's *Politics of Jesus* or any number of his other writings recognizes this language immediately. The chapter on "Christ and the Powers" in *Politics*, drawing on the work of others, moves the theme of "the principalities and powers" from the "mythological" periphery to the very center of Paul's theology. The principalities and powers in Paul's writings name supra-human structures, institutions, ideologies and "isms"—whether economic, social, political, or religious in nature—which on the one hand make human life possible but on the other hand also enslave humans. It is these powers Christ conquers and subdues through his obedient death on the cross. The redemption of human life in all its dimensions begins with and depends upon God's defeat of the powers through Christ and his action of re-ordering them to serve his purposes. That re-ordering begins in the new social reality of the ecclesia.

Yoder thus, without using the phrase, makes "cosmic apocalyptic eschatology" a determinative feature of his theology. He explores it explicitly in a number of writings, but it is, I believe, foundational to everything he does. Yoder's theological interest is not first in the condition of the human "heart" but in the shape of the cosmic and moral order as it is revealed in the death and resurrection of Jesus. Ontic and moral order are intrinsic to one another. That is the very meaning of apocalyptic for both Paul and Yoder.[4] Such a Pauline apocalyptic vision enables Yoder to affirm simultaneously that God is sovereign over the cosmos and that that sovereignty is none other than the rule of the Crucified Jesus. The church is the people which is called to participate in God's cosmic reign by itself living a cruciform life. "People who bear crosses are working with the grain of the universe."[5]

As I have noted, Yoder argued in *The Politics of Jesus* that the language of the principalities and powers in Paul should be interpreted as referring to the multi-layered and multi-faceted social, economic, political, and religious systems in which human beings always find themselves. Christ's conquest, subjugation, and reconciliation of the powers then is itself immediately the bringing about of a new sociopolitical situation. In other words, Paul's apocalyptic gospel is not implicitly or derivatively 'relevant' to social and political order, but itself directly and explicitly creates a new order, manifest concretely as the church.

Such a political reading of Paul was, at the time of the first publication of *The Politics of Jesus*, fairly unheard of. In the past decade or more, however, the political character of Paul's theology has been rediscovered and explicated in remarkable ways. Recent works by Richard Horsley, Karl Donfried, Neil Elliott, Dieter Georgi, N. T. Wright and others draw attention to the ways in which Paul's language, concepts, and practices promote an alternative social and political vision to that of the Roman empire.[6] The confession that "Jesus is Lord," made in the contexts of the Roman imperial order established in the cities of Greece and Asia Minor, consigns the early Gentile Jesus-communities to sociopolitical liminality and vulnerability, a situation addressed in various ways in the letters to the Thessalonians, Philippians, and Galatians.

That confession creates a new people whose citizenship, (*politeuma*) social practice, and internal and external affairs are shaped by the pattern of life of Christ crucified—crucified on a cross which is the very symbol of Roman domination and suppression of political opposition. The messianic community of Jews and Gentiles engaged in common worship, table-fellowship, and mutual service thus constitutes a specific alternative, and often contrastive, form of sociopolitical life under the reign of Christ within the very empire created by the "rulers of this age" who crucified "the Lord of glory."

As such, this community exists in the world both as God's judgment upon the world and as its only hope. Jesus Christ and his Body is God's apocalyptic invasion of the nations for the salvation of the nations. That is the central theme of Paul's theology, which Yoder has also made central to his own.

THE FAITHFULNESS OF JESUS CHRIST AND DISCIPLESHIP

It may come as a surprise to many Protestant readers of Paul that he nowhere provides us with a phenomenology of "faith" or "trust" as a dimension of human experience, nor does he give us any warrant for developing such a phenomenology as a task of *theological* importance. Indeed, I propose that Paul does not seem very interested in faith at all. But how could that be true? Is not justification *by faith*— that is, by believing or putting one's utmost trust in Jesus Christ for forgiveness and salvation—the very center of Paul's theology? That is certainly the consensus of the Protestant tradition since Luther.

But there is now a growing, though not unanimous, consensus in Paul scholarship that one of the phrases crucial to understanding the meaning of justification in Paul has been mistranslated, at least from the time of Luther onward.[7] Since Luther, virtually all translations have rendered the phrase *pistis Jesou Christou* as an objective genitive, "faith *in* Jesus Christ." The phrase tells the story of how humans are justified not by the good deeds they do, but by placing their faith wholly in the work and 'merit' of Jesus Christ, through whose atoning death God deals with sin. Faith is understood as the purely passive, inward *receiving* of justification, God's verdict of righteousness upon sinners through Jesus' death, apart from any work or co-operation on the part of the sinner.

Recent Paul scholarship has been rethinking the phrase *pistis Jesou Christou*, largely as a result of the ground-breaking 1981 doctoral dissertation by Richard B. Hays, *The Faith of Jesus Christ: An Investigation of the Narrative Substructure of Galatians 3:1–4:11* (published in

1983).[8] Many Paul scholars have accepted Hays's rendering of *pistis Jesou Christou* as a subjective genitive, "the faith *of* Jesus Christ."[9] Hays's argument for this rendering is only partly based in linguistic considerations, which even he admits are not conclusive in themselves. Far more important is his persuasive argument that the phrase *pistis Jesou Christou* tells a story not about the general human disposition, attitude or consciousness whereby God's salvation in Jesus Christ is appropriated; rather, the phrase encapsulates a story or narrative about Jesus Christ and his obedience or faithfulness. Only so, says Hays, can one make good sense out of the arguments which Paul puts forward in texts such as Galatians 3 and 4 and Romans 3.

The focus of attention thus shifts from an anthropological narrative (what must we do to be justified?—have faith) to a christological narrative (what has Jesus Christ done for our justification—he was faithful to the point of death, even death on a cross). In Romans 5:12-21 Paul can speak at length about how humans are justified without even mentioning our "faith," but he speaks emphatically about the "one act of righteousness" and the "obedience" of Jesus Christ by which humans are justified and made righteous.

For Paul, the language of justification or rectification is consistently language about God's faithful action of apocalyptic vindication (resurrection) with respect to Jesus' action of obedience and faithfulness (crucifixion). Jesus is certainly on the one hand "sent" or "put forward" by God; that is, the coming of Jesus is itself God's own faithful action toward the cosmos. But it is also the case that Jesus Christ himself acts faithfully, toward God and within God's faithful action, for the deliverance of the cosmos.

Furthermore, in a central passage like Philippians 2:5-11, Jesus Christ's faithfulness in humbling himself is put forward as a normative pattern of life for the Christian community. Just so justification "by faith" is for Paul a theological and christological doctrine which has little to do with our faith. It is God's faithful action, through Jesus' faithful action, making possible and calling forth corresponding and participating faithful action from Christians and the Christian community. In other words, Paul is almost wholly indifferent to what evangelicals, liberals, and existentialists alike have pursued under the rubric of "the doctrine of faith."

Yoder nowhere, as far as I know, makes an argument for the translation of *pistis Jesou Christou* one way or the other. He seems to be unaware of the discussion, which I find somewhat strange, given that Yoder did pay close attention to some of the more important major shifts in Pauline interpretation during his time. In one footnote in the chapter on justification in *The Politics of Jesus* he does write that "in general the New Testament word *pistis* would better not be translated 'faith,' with the concentration that word has for modern readers upon either a belief *content* or the *act* of believing; 'faithfulness' would generally be a more accurate rendering of its meaning."[10] But Yoder cites no scholarly literature at this point, nor does he provide linguistic or exegetical reasons for his suggestion. He does not suggest that we must first of all speak of Jesus Christ's faithfulness before our own. Even in the second edition (1994) he makes no reference to the work of Richard Hays, which had been available for a decade.[11] This is even odder, because I believe Yoder's theology everywhere presupposes and depends upon the reality of "the faithfulness of Jesus Christ," and would be considerably strengthened by attending to and embracing that translation of *pistis Jesou Christou*.

As a critical example, consider the hinge chapter in *Politics*, "The Disciple of Christ and the Way of Jesus." There Yoder addresses the question whether the sociopolitical meaning of the way and cross of Jesus Christ ever made it beyond first-century Palestine into the life of the early Christian communities. More specifically, did that meaning make it into the Gentile churches via Paul's proclamation of the gospel? Yoder shows by way of a lengthy series of quotations from the epistles that in fact it did make its way to the Gentiles, particularly by way of the language of the imitation of Christ, participation in Christ, and suffering with Christ.

Despite the fact that such language has often in Christendom been interpreted in silly, pietistic, mystical, or morbid ways, it does not function that way in the New Testament. Yoder concludes that "if we may posit—as after the preceding pages we must—that the apostles had and taught at least a core memory of their Lord's earthly ministry in its blunt historicity [i.e., as intrinsically political/social in its context], then this centering of the apostolic ethic upon the disciple's cross evidences *a substantial, binding, and sometimes costly social stance*."[12]

In other words, in the Pauline call to imitate Christ, participate in Christ, and suffer with Christ, Jesus Christ himself exemplifies a specifiable way of faithful social-political existence which must be taken up by his disciples. "To follow after Christ is not simply to learn from him, but also to share his destiny." It means to be faithful in the way Jesus himself was faithful. "The 'cross' of Jesus was a political punishment; and when Christians are made to suffer by government it is usually because of the practical import of their faith, and the doubt they cast upon the rulers' claim to be 'Benefactor.'"[13]

My point is simply this: Yoder's Christology is a Christology of "the faithfulness of Jesus Christ" in its significance both as atonement and as normative pattern for the life of the Christian community. Just so also for Paul: the Gentiles are saved by God's right-making action (justification) through the right-making obedience of "the one man" Jesus, and in turn participate in that salvation by taking up a corresponding right-making obedience in the power of the right-making Holy Spirit.

Justification and Christian social ethics are each intrinsic to the other. The story of the "faithfulness of Jesus Christ" in Pauline theology is the crucial link to the Jesus of the canonical gospels, a link Yoder's work is always intent on making.[14]

GOD'S ELECTION OF ISRAEL AND EXEMPLARY JUDAISM

In his later years Yoder devoted increasing attention to the question of the theological significance of the Jews and Judaism for Christian theology. Central to Yoder's theological engagement with Judaism is his thesis that the history of Diaspora Judaism, from the time of the Babylonian exile to the present day, might be read from a Christian perspective as a history of God's call of his people into a world mission not possible when Israel was settled in Judea.

Yoder's thesis is set forth most clearly in an essay "See How They Go With Their Face to the Sun,"[15] a reflection on the significance of the Jewish Diaspora for understanding the role of the people of God among the nations. According to Yoder, the impact of the Babylonian conquest on Israel was historically inestimable and theologically fruitful. The Jews, under God's judgment enacted through the Babylonians, are led into exile. While this event is certainly in one sense a disaster for the nation of Israel, in another sense the exile under Jeremiah's prophetic instruction becomes a calling and a task. Without king, temple, and land the Jews are called into an alternative way of living as a specific people among the nations.

> Thus says the Lord of hosts, the God of Israel, to all the exiles whom I have sent into exile from Jerusalem to Babylon: Build houses and live in them; plant gardens and eat what they produce. Take wives for your sons, and give your daughters in mar-

riage, that they may bear sons and daughters; multiply there and do not decrease. But seek the welfare of the city where I have sent you into exile, and pray to the Lord on its behalf, for in its welfare you will find your welfare. (Jer. 29:4-7)

Yoder argues that this "Jeremianic dispersion existence," this Diaspora mode of being Jewish among the nations, became a *normative* pattern for Judaism—its divinely appointed mission. "To be scattered is not an hiatus, after which normalcy will resume. From Jeremiah's time on, rather, . . . dispersion shall be the calling of the Jewish faith community."[16] The theology of return, resettlement, and re-conquest, played out by Ezra and Nehemiah, the Maccabees, the Zealots and Sadducees, and the messianic revolts up to Bar Kochba in 135, did not become normative. Rather, the stories of Joseph, Daniel, and Esther, being at once faithful to YHWH and publicly useful in the context of their pagan environments, became the normative, canonical stories for a people no longer at home in its own land and no longer in charge of its political destiny.

Paul himself must be seen as fitting within this history of Diaspora Judaism. He never gave up his Jewishness, certainly not in this respect. What Paul establishes as churches through the preaching of the gospel to the Gentiles are not intended by Paul to be anything other than a thoroughly Jewish phenomenon, religiously, ethically, intellectually, and most importantly, socio-politically and theologically. Paul intended no "schism" with Diaspora Judaism as a form of life, no departure from already existing ways of being Jewish. Rather, "What Paul added [to an already existing pattern of Diaspora Jewishness] . . . was the pastoral and political power of a strong mind and will, with which he founded and led *messianic synagogues in this already available style.*"[17]

> This meant structuring a confessing community on non-geographical grounds, an identity that could be voluntarily sustained by a minority of people scattered in lands under other sovereignties. There were two groups of Jews who did this successfully. . . . There were the messianists, later called Christians, and there were the rabbis.
>
> Both of these movements were Jewish. Neither was more Jewish than the other, although the "Christian" side of the tension had been crystallized earlier. They had almost the same moral traditions, almost the same social structures. They differed from one another only about one very Jewish but also very

theological question, namely on whether the presence of the Messianic Age should be conceived of as future or also already as present. [18]

In other words, Paul was simply taking the Jeremianic dispersion mode of being God's people among the nations and applying it to the new messianic, predominantly Gentile communities which were being formed through his preaching about Jesus the Messiah. He established these communities in a thoroughly Jewish way of life marked by an identity focussed on the worship of the one God of Israel and his Messiah Jesus, the study of the Jewish Scriptures, local communal gathering, peaceable relations with the wider world, and a system of networks with messianic communities in other cities.

I find this a compelling, important, and theologically fruitful vision of what Paul was doing. I believe a careful examination of his missionary and ecclesial strategies as reflected in his letters will bear out Yoder's understanding of them. For a variety of reasons Yoder proposes his understanding as a valuable and helpful orientation to Jewish-Christian dialogue. And he may be right. But surprisingly, Yoder nowhere addresses the *theological* consideration Paul gives to the reality of non-messianic Judaism in Romans 9-11. Yoder finally gives far more attention to the question of *Jewish* faithfulness than to that of *God's* faithfulness.

Paul, by contrast, is finally not concerned to address the question of the Jews in God's purpose in terms of a moral history of the Jews and Judaism, that is, to tell a lengthy story either of the *sin* of the Jews (as N. T. Wright emphasizes in his recent studies of Paul on the Jews) or of the *virtue* of the Jews who remain faithful in Diaspora (as Yoder emphasizes). Rather, Paul concerns himself with what *God* is doing with Israel, given the fact that the larger part of Israel is not believing Paul's gospel and accepting his mission. Paul's answer in Romans 8-11 is that God will not, cannot, contradict his election of carnal Israel, but rather sustains that election in and through the apocalypse of Jesus Christ. Nothing in all creation can separate the elect people from God's love in Christ Jesus (Rom 8:31-39). Just for that reason the Gentiles who are grafted into Israel can be assured of their own participation in God's salvation. Jews, even non-messianic Jews, continue to be sharers in and recipients of the strange differential movement of God's mercy-showing.[19]

Paul does not in Romans or his other letters engage in a *moral history* of Judaism. He focuses rather on the *election* of Israel. Yoder on the other hand shows almost no interest in the doctrine of Israel's non-superseded election, even as he at the same time also seems to assume it. Yoder is finally interested in a form of "Jewishness." He emphasizes the Jewishness of the Diaspora form of life as the peculiar gift of the Jews to the world. The biblical and Pauline doctrine of God's election of a specific, non-substitutable, fleshly historical people tends to disappear behind a set of "Jewish" ideas or practices.

Because Yoder does not make the election of Israel the point of departure in his theology of the Jews, his attention is drawn toward the moral and even voluntary character of Judaism. He chooses to concentrate on Jewishness as a way of life, to be freely reaffirmed by Jews and taken up by Gentiles, as the place to focus the discussion of the relation between Jews and Christians.

There is a great deal to be learned from that focus about how to be God's people in the world. However, from a Pauline perspective it is not the primary or most promising theme for beginning a theological discussion of the relation between messianic Jews and Gentiles on the one hand and non-messianic Jews on the other.[20] The question which begs to be asked at this point, but which I cannot pursue further, is whether there can be an adequate ecclesiology which does not give priority to election over ethics, the faithfulness of God over the faithfulness of Jews and Gentiles. Paul would say no! So too, I think, would Yoder. But he does not develop a response to that question in his essays on Judaism.

CONCLUSION

What I have presented here is, by reason of length, only a sketch, and that too only of a few themes in Yoder's theology which are on the one hand deeply Pauline in character, and on the other hand crucial for understanding Yoder's theology.[21] I submit that Yoder is a Pauline theologian in the most vigorous sense, as worthy of the designation "Pauline" as the likes of Augustine, Luther, Calvin, and Barth. What makes Yoder's Paulinism so compelling is that it accords with some of the best and most important insights of recent Paul scholarship, and that it is such a vital vision for the renewal of the church and its mission in our time.

NOTES

1. J. Louis Martyn, *Galatians, The Anchor Bible*, vol. 33A (New York: Doubleday, 1997); *idem, Theological Issues in the Letters of Paul* (Nashville: Abingdon, 1997). The most accessible brief introduction to Martyn's interpretation of Paul is "The Apocalyptic Gospel in Galatians," *Interpretation* 54 (2000): 246-266. Martyn is indebted to the work of Martinus C. de Boer for his understanding of Pauline apocalyptic; de Boer has recently also published a very accessible and helpful essay on this theme: "Paul, Theologian of God□s Apocalypse," *Interpretation* 56 (2002): 21-33.

2. For Martyn's description of forensic apocalyptic eschatology see "God's Way of Making Right What is Wrong," in *Theological Issues in the Letters of Paul*, 141-148; and "The Apocalyptic Gospel in Galatians," 246-252.

3. For Martyn's description of cosmic apocalyptic eschatology see "God's Way of Making Right What is Wrong," 148-156; and "The Apocalyptic Gospel in Galatians," 252-259.

4. In his essay, "Armaments and Eschatology," *Studies in Christian Ethics* 1 (1988): 43-61, Yoder, drawing on recent studies of Jewish apocalyptic in New Testament times, lists a number of features of the "apocalyptic world-view" (49). Notable in this list is the blending of cosmic and moral features of the enslaved and corrupt condition of creation, and of the interruptive, invasive character of God's action to make things right, to rectify or "justify" things.

5. Yoder, "Armaments and Eschatology," 58. This quote supplied Stanley Hauerwas with the title of his 2001 Gifford Lectures, *With the Grain of the Universe: The Church□s Witness and Natural Theology* (Grand Rapids: Brazos Press, 2001).

6. Representative essays by these and other authors may be found in two volumes ed. Richard Horsley: *Paul and Empire: Religion and Power in Roman Imperial Society* (Harrisburg, Pa.: Trinity Press International, 1997); *Paul and Politics: Ekklesia, Israel, Imperium, Interpretation: Essays in Honor of Krister Stendahl* (Harrisburg: Trinity Press International, 2000).

7. See George Howard, "Faith of Christ," in *Anchor Bible Dictionary*, vol. 2, ed. David Noel Freedman (New York: Doubleday, 1992), 759. Howard shows that before Luther the Pauline phrase *"pistis Jesou Christou"* was consistently translated as a subjective rather than objective genitive; that is, as "the faith *of* Jesus Christ" rather than "faith *in* Jesus Christ." The subjective genitive may be found in the Vulgate and even in older editions of the Authorized version. Howard's article concludes with an excellent bibliography on the question.

8. Richard B. Hays, *The Faith of Jesus Christ: An Investigation of the Narrative Substructure of Galatians 3:1–4:11* (Chico, CA: Scholars Press, 1983). A second edition has now been published (Grand Rapids: Eerdmans, 2002) which includes some valuable new work by Hays: a new introduction (xxi-lii), and an essay, "Πίστις and Pauline Christology: What Is at Stake? (Appendix 2, 272-297). In addition, there is an essay by James D. G. Dunn, "Once More, ΠΙΣΤΙΣ

ΧΡΙΣΤΟΥ" (Appendix 1, 249-271), in which Dunn gives a vigourous defense of the traditional reading, "faith *in* Jesus Christ." These two essays were first published in *Pauline Theology, Volume IV: Looking Back, Pressing On*, ed. E. Elizabeth Johnson and David M. Hay (Atlanta, Ga.: Scholars Press, 1997), 35-60 and 61-81, respectively.

9. See the bibliography and Hays's own more recent statement of his thesis in "Πίστις and Pauline Christology: What is at Stake?"

10. Yoder, *The Politics of Jesus*, 221 n.9.

11. Yoder's only interaction with Hays's work is a response to Hays's book, *The Moral Vision of the New Testament: A Contemporary Introduction to New Testament Ethics* (New York: HarperCollins, 1996): see Yoder "Epilogue: On Being Read by Richard Hays," *To Hear the Word* (Eugene, OR: Wipf and Stock, 2001), 155-163. In that essay Yoder does not engage Hays's work on Christology; he only offers a rather cranky response to Part Three of Hays's book, in which Yoder's work (among others) is appreciatively discussed.

12. *The Politics of Jesus*, 127 (emphasis added).

13. Ibid., 124-125.

14. Therefore Yoder's Pauline social ethics should be read in conjunction with the kind of work done by Richard Hays in *The Moral Vision of the New Testament*, 16-59, and Michael J. Gorman, *Cruciformity: Paul's Narrative Spirituality of the Cross* (Grand Rapids: Eerdmans, 2001), both of whom demonstrate the way the language of the faithfulness of Jesus Christ links Pauline theology with the traditions about Jesus which form the heart of the gospel narratives.

15. The essay appears in Yoder's *For the Nations: Essays Public and Evangelical* (Grand Rapids: Eerdmans, 1997), 51-78. Many of Yoder's essays on Jews and Judaism were in quasi-"unpublished" manuscript form at the time of his death. These were available to me as a manuscript packet directly from Yoder as a desktop publication, under the title The Jewish-Christian Schism Revisited: A Bundle of Old Essays (Notre Dame, Ind.: Shalom Desktop Publications, 1996). My references to these essays are from this source. See now *The Jewish Christian Schism Revisited* (ed. Michael Cartwright and Peter Ochs; Grand Rapids: Eerdmans, 2003). Other published essays in which Yoder addresses the theme of Jewish Diaspora include "On Not Being in Charge," in *War and Its Discontents: Pacifism and Quietism in the Abrahamic Traditions*, ed. J. Patout Burns (Washington, D.C.: Georgetown University Press, 1996), 74-90; "War as a Moral Problem in the Early Church: The Historian's Hermeneutical Assumptions," *The Pacifist Impulse in Historical Perspective*, ed. Harvey L. Dyck (Toronto: University of Toronto Press, 1996), 90-110.

16. *For the Nations*, 52. Yoder at this point is summing up the message of the play *Jeremiah* by Jewish poet, Stephan Zweig. That message becomes the thesis of Yoder's essay. A similar proposal about Diaspora as the calling of the Jewish community has been made recently by Daniel Boyarin in *A Radical Jew: Paul and the Politics of Identity* (Berkeley and Los Angeles: University of

California Press, 1994), 242-260.

17. *The Jewish-Christian Schism Revisited* (Shalom Desktop Publications, 1996), 8 (emphasis added).

18. Ibid., 25.

19. For understanding the theme, shape and argument of Romans 9-11, I am especially reliant, in various ways, on: Scott Bader-Saye, *Church and Israel after Christendom: The Politics of Election* (Boulder, Col.: Westview Press, 1999), 100-102; Neil Elliott, "Figure and Ground in the Interpretation of Romans 9-11," in *The Theological Interpretation of Scripture: Classic and Contemporary Readings*, ed. Stephen E. Fowl (Oxford and Cambridge, Mass.: Blackwell Publishers, 1997), 371-389; Lloyd Gaston, *Paul and the Torah* (Vancouver, B.C.: University of British Columbia Press, 1987), 116-150; Richard B. Hays, *Echoes of Scripture in the Letters of Paul* (New Haven and London: Yale University Press, 1989), 63-83; E. Elizabeth Johnson, "Romans 9-11: The Faithfulness and Impartiality of God," in *Pauline Theology, Volume III: Romans*, ed. David M. Hay and E. Elizabeth Johnson, 211-239; *idem*, "Divine Initiative and Human Response," in *Theological Interpretation of Scripture*, ed. Stephen Fowl, 356-370; R. Kendall Soulen, *The God of Israel and Christian Theology* (Minneapolis: Fortress Press, 1996), 109-177; Stanley K. Stowers, *A Rereading of Romans: Justice, Jews, and Gentiles* (New Haven: Yale University Press, 1994). Many supersessionist readings of Romans 9-11 may be found in the classic commentaries on this text, from Origen and Augustine to Käsemann, Cranfield and, most recently and vigorously, N. T. Wright.

20. This judgment is not intended to undervalue in any way the importance of Yoder's attention to "Jewishness" for understanding the nature and mission of the church, only to set it in its proper theological order. For further detailed exploration of some of the themes that Yoder opens up, and a confirmation of the fruitfulness of those themes, see the important recent work by Markus Bockmuehl, *Jewish Law in Gentile Churches: Halakhah and the Beginning of Christian Public Ethics* (Edinburgh, Scotland: T & T Clark, 2000).

21. I address each of the themes raised in this essay, in both Paul and Yoder (and others), in much greater length and detail in my book, *Paul among the Postliberals: Pauline Theology beyond Christendom and Modernity* (Grand Rapids: Brazos Press, 2003).

Chapter 14

Smelting for Gold: Jesus and Jubilee in John H. Yoder's *Politics of Jesus*

Willard M. Swartley

JOHN H. YODER'S WRITING ON JUBILEE[1] is indebted to André Trocmé's *Jesus and the Nonviolent Revolution*.[2] Trocmé proposes that Jesus began his ministry in a sabbatical year and proclaimed the Jubilee.[3] Luke introduces Jesus with the Spirit-anointed mandate that concludes with "proclaiming the favorable year of the Lord" (Luke 4:18-19). Yoder sets forth his interpretation of Jesus as a third perspective to two dominant trends: a spiritualization that internalizes Jesus' teachings or the revolutionary portrait popularized by S. G. F. Brandon.[4] In chapter 2 of *Politics of Jesus* Yoder explicates lead-motifs of Luke's gospel to show that Jesus' teaching was socio-economic and political in nature, is thus relevant to social ethics, and calls for a new ordering of politics and economics. Luke 4:18-19 is the "Platform" for Jesus' ministry. Jesus claims that the *today-fulfilled* text of Isaiah testifies to a prophetic event. That fulfillment

> is a social event . . . a visible social-political, economic restructuring of relations among the people of God, achieved by his intervention in the person of Jesus as the one Anointed and endued with the Spirit. (38//32)

Several quotes help us grasp the power of Yoder's contribution on the portrait of Jesus:[5]

> Jesus was not just a moralist whose teaching had some political implications; he was not primarily a teacher of spirituality whose public ministry unfortunately was seen in a political light; he was not just a sacrificial lamb preparing for his immolation, or a God-man whose divine status calls us to disregard his humanity. Jesus was in his divinely mandated prophethood, priesthood, and kingship, the bearer of a new possibility of human, social, and therefore, political relationship. His baptism is the inauguration and his cross is the culmination of that new regime in which his disciples are called to share. Men may choose to consider that kingdom as not real, or not relevant, or not possible, or not inviting; but no longer may we come to this choice in the name of systematic theology or honest hermeneutics (62-63//52-53).

> We understand Jesus only if we can empathize with this three-fold rejection; the self-evident, axiomatic, sweeping rejection of both quietism and establishment responsibility, and the difficult constantly reopened, genuinely attractive option of the crusade (98//97).

To critically analyze Yoder's contribution in this area, I raise the following questions:
- In Yoder's portrait of Jesus, are there particular emphases that upon close examination of the text are not fully justified? I.e., does Yoder push the text beyond its intention?
- Is there additional evidence, especially in Luke, that further supports Yoder's portrait of Jesus?
- Are there additional ways of thinking about the Jubilee theme in Luke's Gospel that if explored would further strengthen but also alter Yoder's portrait of Jesus?

ARE PARTICULAR EMPHASES IN YODER NOT JUSTIFIED BY THE TEXT?

In response to the first question, which asks whether Yoder has pushed any texts beyond their clear intention, the following items merit notice:

(1) In his review of *Politics* Stephen Charles Mott disagrees with Yoder's exegesis of the temptations as economic and sociopolitical in

character.[6] While it is true that the text does not explicitly support Yoder's interpretation, understanding the temptations within the emphases of the whole Gospel may lend credence to Yoder's interpretation. The reductionism of Jesus' temptations to this one central theme by Yoder triggered Jeffrey Gibson's doctoral dissertation's analysis of eight temptations of Jesus in Mark and Q sources. His close study contends that in every one of these testings (*peirasmoi*), Jesus' faithfulness to his baptismal designation as Son, Servant, Beloved One is tested, precisely whether he will continue to be God's *peacemaker* (*eirēnopoios*) refusing vengeance against enemies or whether he will seek to secure the future through violence. Gibson's study largely substantiates Yoder's thesis,[7] though not all will agree with his exegetical decisions. Susan Garrett's study of *The Temptations of Jesus in Mark*[8] emphasizes also the personal (Jesus vs. Satan) dimensions of Jesus' testings and wider themes as well.

(2) A more crucial potential exegetical weakness is Yoder's use of Luke 4:16-30. Luke 4:18-19 is Jesus' reading and/or Luke's quotation (Yoder does not say *which*[9]) from Isaiah 61:1-2. Several problems arise in Yoder's treatment of this important authorizing text for Jubilee. First, the fact that 4:18-19 does not fully cite Isaiah 61:1-2 but omits a line from it and adds a line from Isaiah 58:6 means that this is likely Lukan construction, since no scroll text of Isaiah 61:1-2 read exactly that way. It is not impossible that Jesus made the change in the reading, but it is unlikely. Hence Luke adapted what Jesus actually read, for a reason, to which we return later.

Second, Ben Ollenburger points out in his study of Jubilee that the Jubilee legislation in Leviticus 25 (the Holiness Code) does not include remission of debts, while Deuteronomy 15 (the Deuteronomic Code) speaks of remission of debts but does not mention Jubilee.[10] However, as Ollenburger observes, the LXX translation of *release* (*derôr*) of land in Lev. 25:11-13 and "Jubilee" (*yôbēl*) in Lev. 25 and 27 uses the same Greek word (*aphesis*) as it does also for *debt-remission* (*šemit*) in Deut. 15:2, 3, 9. Further, Isa. 61:1 in LXX uses *aphesis*, and thus the way is paved for Luke, writing in Greek and depending on the LXX, to assimilate these two types of *release* into one.[11] But the differences in these Hebrew texts caution us against reading all aspects of *release* into Jubilee and into Jesus' words in Luke also. Yoder makes much of debt-release in his exposition of Luke, but this point particularly is not explicit in the Hebrew text of *Jubilee* legislation.

Third, Yoder notes that the story that follows this quotation speaks not about Jubilee, but about the opening of the New Age to the

Gentiles. Yoder says: "This second thrust does not seem to be derived from the Jubilee proclamation, it grows rather out of Jesus' response to the disbelief bred in his hearers by their familiarity with his family" (*Politics*, 39//32). *If* this is true, then it must be asked: Does Luke really intend to develop the Jubilee emphasis? We must ask whether or not and how these themes of Jubilee and turning to 'outsiders' are related (see below).[12]

(3) Another point qualifying Yoder's thesis is that Luke does not use the word *debts* in the Lord's Prayer, but Matthew does. Parallel printing of Matthew and Luke shows the difference (Throckmorton and Aland):

Matthew 6:12	Luke 11:4
And forgive *(aphes)* us	and forgive *(aphes)* us
our debts *(opheilēmata)*	our sins *(hamartias)*
As we also have forgiven	for we ourselves forgive
(aphēkamen)	*(aphiomen)*
our debtors *(opheiletais)*	everyone who is indebted
	(opheilonti) to us.

In the second line Matthew uses "debts"; Luke uses "sins."[13] One could argue that the technical term for the Jubilee cancelation of debts (*aphes* from *aphiēmi*; noun, *aphesis*) occurs in Luke[14] for human relationships and that it is appropriate to substitute "sins" for "debts" in the divine-human relationship. Nonetheless, the point counts against Yoder's emphasis since it raises the question whether Luke, the Gospel Yoder selected as the primary gospel text for chapter 2 of *Politics* to anticipate his Jubilee thesis, does not in fact have a larger notion in mind in Jesus' announcement of the "favorable year of the Lord."

In texts Yoder does not mention, Luke uses the debt-cancellation term, *aphiēmi*, to often refer to the forgiveness of sins without any reference to sociopolitical dimensions (5:20-24, 4 times; 7:47-49, 4 times; 17:4; total of nine times). One can argue, however, that these examples illustrate Jubilee forgiveness (since sins are debts!) and that these forgiven persons indeed become members of the messianic community. But Yoder does not develop this emphasis. Further, the Lukan parable Yoder uses to illustrate the debt-cancellation transaction (parable of the dishonest steward, Luke 16:1-8) does not use *aphiēmi*. Matthew's alternate parable (merciless servant, 18:23-35) uses the term three times (vv. 27, 32, 35), but the parable clearly stands in support of Jesus' emphasis on forgiveness, broadly understood (see vv. 21-22).

Additionally, Yoder's treatment of the cleansing of the temple draws more on Mark and Matthew than on Luke, for Luke's account is very brief, owing to his larger positive portrait of the temple. Also, Yoder's treatment of the role of the Twelve as carrying socio-political significance is clearer in Matthew and Mark than in Luke.

Perhaps these weaknesses should be tempered by noting that Yoder's real interest is Jesus, not Luke *per se*. Yoder's thesis clearly states that his portrait of Jesus is supported by all the Gospels, but Luke is his selected sample to simplify his endeavor.[15] That this is Yoder's viewpoint is made clear indeed at numerous points in the book. This approach would justify Yoder's occasional reference to the other Gospels to bolster his exegesis of Luke. So why criticize Yoder on this account?

Considerations here, however, are twofold: (1) reviewers of Yoder's *Politics* commonly say that whereas Yoder presents a Jubilean portrait of Jesus, his "treatment justifies only a more modest claim such as 'the social ethic of Luke.' To emphasize continually—as he does—the social ethic of *Jesus* is a position that few New Testament critics will espouse"[16] and (2) Yoder's treatment does not in fact show that any of the other Gospels would consistently substantiate the Jubilee thesis. To critically defend Yoder's portrait of Jesus, one must either demonstrate more clearly one Gospel's Jubilee portrait or test the claim that all the Gospels witness to this portrait.

Since Yoder used Matthew and Mark at times to make his case, it appears that the Jubilee theme passes the test of historical authenticity on the criteria of multiple attestation (i.e., in triple tradition of Matt., Mark, and Luke) and multiple genre. So perhaps Yoder's claim is more correct than Johnsson's and other reviewers' critiques. But is it? We noted earlier that Luke 4:18-19 is not an exact reading of Isa. 61:1-2, but it includes a line from Isa. 58 that enables the word *release* to be used twice. The point shows in its chiastic form:

a To preach good news (*euangelisasthai*) to the poor,

  b To proclaim (*kēruxai*) release (*aphesin*) to the captives,

    c And recovering of sight to the blind,

  b' To send forth the oppressed in release (*en aphesei*)

a' To proclaim (*kēruxai*) the acceptable year of the Lord.

The italicized key English words (WMS trans.) highlight the recurring use of release in b and b'. By dropping one line of Isaiah 61:1, "to bind up the brokenhearted," and inserting one line (b') from Isaiah 58:6, "to let the oppressed go free (release),"[17] Luke stresses the theme of release.[18] This telling point confirms that Luke is a good sample to make Yoder's point, but it is also a vexation for his thesis, in that the social ethic of Luke reflects *Luke's* emphasis. But even in this case the economic concern is not dominant over others, for Luke also collapses the next two lines from Isaiah 61:2 into one and brings in a line as the center of his chiasm, a point that evokes messianic fulfillment of Isaiah 35, "to give sight to the blind" (note Acts 26:18). This does not deny that the Jubilean emphasis arose with Jesus, but to establish that takes work beyond Yoder's treatment.[19]

DOES ADDITIONAL
EVIDENCE SUPPORT YODER'S JESUS?

The second question regarding Yoder's portrait of Jesus asks whether there is additional evidence in Luke to support Yoder's portrait of Jesus. The text in Luke 23:2, which Yoder does not mention, presents Jesus accused of political subversion, as well as forbidding the payment of tax to Caesar. Does this support Brandon or Yoder? In the context of the larger gospel portrait of Jesus, I believe it supports Yoder's thesis, for the same reason as does Luke 23:30, a text referring to the dry wood and the green wood. This means that while the people understood Jesus to be a violent revolutionary ("the dry wood"), Jesus was in fact comparatively not that at all, but was rather the green wood. On this verse Oscar Cullmann presents a portrait of Jesus much akin to Yoder's.[20]

A larger consideration is whether Luke's extensive use of the term *peace* (*eirēnē*) does or does not support Yoder's portrait of a nonviolent socio-political Jesus. The results of my investigation of the fourteen uses of *eirēnē* in Luke indicate that Yoder's view is bolstered by Luke's peace emphasis. Conzelmann's view, however, that Luke is a political apologetic to advance Rome's Pax Romana is not supported since none of his key texts are interconnected with the *eirēnē* texts. Nor is the part of Cassidy's view that Luke's Jesus is a political threat to the Empire, maintaining a defiant stance against Jewish leaders.[21] These texts also are not connected with the *eirēnē* texts. The part of Cassidy's thesis that emphasizes Jesus' alternative social and political model is interconnected with the *eirēnē* texts; these thus join Yoder's selection of texts.

As I have shown earlier in my essay, God's new peoplehood of peace has its own kingdom mission and agenda. It neither courts nor condemns Rome or the contemporary nations of this world. Nor does it give its main energies to aid or block the imperialistic pacification programs, of which the Pax Romana was a grand model. Rather, the new humanity of Christ's body welcomes people to become "children of peace," freed from the tyranny of the powers in whatever personal, national, socioeconomic, political, or ideological guise they manifest themselves.[22] This new humanity, in contrast to the dominant cultural power structures, expends its primary energies building communities of faith, hope, love, and peace. Further, Luke presents Jesus as a Savior who cries out in lament: if only you would know those things that make for peace (Luke 19:42).

DO ADDITIONAL WAYS OF THINKING ABOUT JUBILEE SUPPORT LUKE'S JESUS?

Taking up the third question, we ask if there are more ways of thinking about the Jubilee theme that, if explored, would further support Luke's Jubilee portrait of Jesus. Such possible emphases are—

Luke's recurring statements of blessings to the poor and stern warnings toward the rich. Almost all of chapters 12 and 16, the end of 18, and the beginning of 19 treat this theme. This emphasis has been widely recognized by New Testament scholars. What a congenial theme to the Jubilean platform!

Luke's frequent emphasis on the important role of women in the gospel drama: Elizabeth, Mary, Anna, the women from Galilee included among Jesus' disciples, Martha and Mary, and the women at the tomb. Although the role of women is not an intrinsic part of the Old Testament Jubilee theme, the emphasis upon women in Luke's Gospel may be viewed as an expression of Jubilee justice and concern for equality.

Luke's strong emphasis on Jesus' acceptance of sinners, outcasts, and outsiders. Note especially Luke 7:36-50[23] and all of chapter 15. Jubilee means that the forgiven prostitute and prodigal have a future in Jesus' messianic kingdom and community, a concrete fulfillment of the synagogue address. Precisely at this point the connection between the two parts of Luke 4:16-30 is apparent, since the Gentiles in 4:24-30 are, from a Jewish point of view, outcasts and outsiders. This point contrasts sharply to the use made of Isa. 61 in the Qumran community, where vengeance on the outsiders—the part not quoted from Isa. (61:2b) by Jesus in Luke—is the main emphasis in 11QMelch.[24]

Luke's clear intent is to highlight the ministry of Jesus as "gospelizing," a literal translation of *euangelisasthai* in line *a* of the Nazareth synagogue reading. This *euangel* verb occurs twenty-five times in Luke-Acts to stress the spread of the gospel under the leading of the Holy Spirit. This evangelistic shower of blessing demonstrates too that Jesus' messianic kingdom breaks racial and national boundaries. In Acts it includes Samaritans, Gentiles, of whom one was Ethiopian. The main story line tells of the gospel's spread through Asia Minor, Macedonia, and finally to Rome. Luke-Acts is aptly titled, "From the temple to Rome."[25]

Luke strongly emphasizes the gospel's *release* of people from Satan's power, and that occurs explicitly throughout both volumes. The feature has generated extended study of Luke's portrayal of the gospel's deliverance from Satan's powers and specifically magical powers (Acts 8, 12, 16, 19). I have treated this theme in Luke elsewhere and Susan Garrett has studied it more broadly in Luke-Acts.[26]

Specific citations make the point. When John the Baptist in prison sends messengers to Jesus to ask if he is the one to come, or shall we look for another, Luke precedes Jesus' answer with, "Jesus had just cured many people of diseases, plagues, and evil spirits, and had given sight to many who were blind" (7:21). Hence, Jesus' healing and exorcisms attest to his messianic mission.

Likewise, Luke's summary of Jesus' mission in Peter's sermon celebrating the gospel's inclusion of Gentile Cornelius is that God's message of "preaching (*euangelizomenos!*) peace by Jesus Christ" consisted of Jesus going "about doing good and healing all who were oppressed by the devil, for God was with him" (Acts 10:36-38).

In Paul's final defense speech to King Agrippa, Paul sums up his mission, as portrayed by Luke, with these words, as God's commission to him, "'I will rescue you from your people and from the Gentiles—to whom I am sending you to open their eyes so that they may turn from the power of Satan to God, so that they may receive forgiveness of sins and a place among those who are sanctified by faith in me" (Acts 26:18-19).

These texts are crucially placed in Luke's two-volume work and are interpretive of the Nazareth synagogue sermon in Luke 4:18-19 on the Sabbath.[27] Their emphases are not immediately socio-political or socio-economic (though might become such as in Acts 19). Lack of attention to this in Yoder renders Yoder's exposition of the Jubilee proclamation reductionist, by Lukan standards.

These five points, taken together,[28] constitute a fuller portrait of the Jubilee mission of the servant Messiah. The significance of these exegetical observations means that Yoder's presentation of Jesus' jubilean mission needs to be qualified and broadened. Yoder's portrait of Jesus needs to be qualified by recognizing that for Luke Jubilee is broader in appropriation than Yoder shows it. Also, that while Matthew and Mark may be cited to bolster this stream of emphasis, neither Gospel develops a Jubilee motif *per se*. Yoder thus misses the opportunity to join Luke in stressing those themes that portray the contextualization of Jubilee into a wider theological, ethical, and spiritual—even personal—dimension. Not all of what Luke regards as fulfillment of Jubilee is sociopolitical or economic. "Release" from the devil's oppression (Acts 10:38) is personal and spiritual to the core.

Thus, Yoder's goal to show that Jesus is relevant to social ethics resulted in a Jesus-portrait that "screened" out important spiritual emphases of the Jubilee theme that Luke indeed intended to present.

YODER'S CONTRIBUTION ON JUBILEE AND ITS HERMENEUTICAL *PERFORMANCE*

To assess the hermeneutical *performance* of Yoder's Jubilee contribution, some explanation of what is intended by this term is fitting here. Stephen Barton, in a recent book,[29] calls New Testament interpretation to a new model, the metaphor or paradigm of *performance*. Building on the contributions of Nicholas Lash, Rowan Williams, and Frances Young (who in turn are indebted to Alasdair MacIntyre), Barton proposes that the most appropriate hermeneutic model is that in which *performance* of the text in the life of the church becomes authentic biblical interpretation. The metaphor is drawn from the worlds of music and theatre, in which performance is essentially different from analysis of the musical score or expertise in music history. So also *performance* of Scripture is diachronic in nature, expression through time, rather than synchronic, the analytic methods of most biblical interpreters in the New Testament guild.

Further, *performance* is communally expressed, in worship, Eucharist, and daily life. This emphasis is akin to what Wayne Meeks called "The Hermeneutic of Social Embodiment"[30] and Richard Hays has called "Scripture-Shaped Community,"[31] but it adds the rich dimension of comparing authentic interpretation, i.e., embodying the gospel in life, with musical/art *performance*, the mode by which we grasp and witness truly to Scripture's meaning.[32]

In assessing the *performance* of the Jubilee teaching of the Gospels *a la* Yoder's exposition of it, his work has performed well in that many of his students and readers have shaped their theological thinking by this emphasis spelled out by Yoder.[33] At Associated Mennonite Biblical Seminary, Luke is the favorite gospel of the majority of students, and students regularly cite as their rationale the Jubilee motif and its relevancy to socioeconomic and political critique.[34] The permeation of Yoder's emphases within the Mennonite churches staffed by AMBS grads is astounding. I would venture that Luke 4:18-19 has been used more often in pulpits and conference programs within Mennonite circles than any other Scripture. I believe this has generated self-consciousness for the denomination that extends to the work of the Mennonite Central Committee and other peace and justice ministries.

Further, some of the Lukan-contextualized Jubilee themes above have been included in this motif, though often not with careful exegetical basis. But, the fifth theme, release from Satan's power, has not been included in any performative sense, except by a few persons. These few often query whether the Mennonite church has not got it wrong, thinking that political and economic structures are evil, rather than seeing these as potentially infected by evil powers, *a.k.a.* Satan, devil, and demons.

Beyond the Mennonite church, the impact of Yoder's teaching has been enormous. Numerous dissertations and writings have appeared in the last generation that respond to and extend or question Yoder's contribution; Yoder's 1994 *Politics* edition reports on and evaluates these.[35] Likewise, organizations of various sorts have used *Jubilee* as an authorizing rationale, including the worldwide organization Jubilee 2000 urging the United States to forgive debts in developing countries crippled by huge debts to U.S.

Yoder strikes gold in the performance of Scripture in his theological-ethical contribution on the topic of Jubilee. My aim has been to show that the church, Mennonite and larger ecumenical, has incorporated into its thought and witness a faithful rendition of Yoder's exegesis of this biblical pillar for social ethics. However, one might ask if the *fullness* of Luke's Jubilee emphases is manifest in the life of the community, the key test of performance.[36] If there is deficiency in this regard, I suggest it arises from failure to link Luke's Jubilee manifesto of contextualized liberation to evangelism (this despite Yoder's good work on theology of mission) and deliverance from Satan's power, including exorcism and healing, however those emphases are appropriated theologically and practically. Thus while Yoder brilliantly recovered the New Testament for social ethics, the associative dimensions of Jubilee themes in personal and communal practices have been short-changed, both in Yoder's work and in the ecclesial communities that Yoder's contribution so much influenced.

NOTES

1. John H. Yoder, *The Politics of Jesus: Vicit Agnus Noster* (Grand Rapids: Eerdmans, 1st. ed., 1972; 2nd. ed., 1994), chs. 2-3. I will cite both editions for specific pagination, using / / between the cited pagination, with the 1st. ed. first. Another basic biblical exposition with similar import is his chapter on the Sermon on the Mount in *The Original Revolution* (Scottdale, Pa.: Herald Press, 1972), ch. 2, "The Political Axioms of the Sermon on the Mount, 34-54.

2. André Trocmé, *Jesus and the Nonviolent Revolution* Trans. Michael H. Shank and Marlin E. Miller (Scottdale, Pa.: Herald Press, 1973).

3. Trocmé, 39-40. Neither Trocmé nor Yoder clarifies how literally the Jubilee prescriptions were intended to be enacted by Jesus or Luke. In his 1994 *Politics* ed., Yoder, in answer to a query as to whether 1976 should be a Jubilee year since 1976 is a fifty-year multiple of A.D. 26, Yoder says that neither he nor Trocmé ever intended to imply that Jesus was reinstituting an every-fifty year Jubilee, but that Jesus' in his proclamation of God's kingdom coming lifted the *periodic* practice. Rather, Jesus' Jubilee is a "permanently defining trait of the new order" (Yoder, 71).

Similar to Trocmé, Margaret Barker argues that Jesus' ministry began within the first seven years of a Jubilee cycle, which ended in the fulfillment of Jesus' judgment-warnings, in the Jewish war of 66-70 CE. Taking her cue from Josiah's reform re-instituting Jubilee, she extends her calculation, correlating it with a series of ten Jubilees fulfilling the seventy weeks of years in Daniel. "The Time Is Fulfilled: Jesus and Jubilee," *SJT* 53:1 (2000):27.

4. S. G. F. Brandon, *Jesus and the Zealots: A Study of the Political Factor in Primitive Christianity* (New York: Charles Scribner's Sons, 1967).

5. I used these quotations also in a 1976 paper, "Yoder's *Politics of Jesus*: An Analysis of its Biblical Rootage."

6. Stephen Charles Mott, "'The Politics of Jesus' and our Responsibilities." *The Reformed Journal* (Feb. 1976), 7-10.

7. Jeffrey B. Gibson, *The Temptations of Jesus in Early Christianity* JSNTSS 112 (Sheffield, England: Sheffield Academic Press, 1995), esp. 110 and the Summaries to every chapter. Even "the testing" connected with the divorce controversy involves the same issue, for to speak against divorce jeopardized Jesus' security under Herod's political control, since Herod notoriously violated the prohibition (285-87). See pp. 10-12 for Gibson's quoting Yoder and querying whether testing of the early Christians in this sense occasioned the writing of Hebrews, even though it states that Jesus was tempted in all ways as we are (2:18; 5:2). Gibson reports on P. G. Bretcher's study of *The Temptations in Matthew* (St. Louis: Concordia Seminary, 1966, Th.D. dissertation), which while concurring on the basic point that the temptations revolve around faithfulness to God's call, does not specify the content of that call in the way Gibson does, but explains it along the general lines of the "wisdom of obedience" (116-117 n.92).

8. Susan R. Garrett, *The Temptations of Jesus in Mark's Gospel* (Grand Rapids and Cambridge, England: Eerdmans, 1998). Garrett sets Jesus' temptations in the broader biblical context of the nature of temptation, and thus sees other dimensions of struggle in the "testings" that Jesus encounters.

9. Yoder does enter the debate on whether Jesus chose the text or whether it was the set lectionary reading. He tilts to the side that it was not the lection text, but Jesus selected it. *Politics of Jesus*, 34-35 n.10//28-29 n.10.

10. Ben C. Ollenburger "Jubilee: 'The land is mine; you are aliens and tenants with me,'" in *Reclaiming the Old Testament: Essays in Honor of Waldemar Janzen*, ed. Gordon Zerbe (Winnipeg, Man.: CMBC Publications, 2001), 214-215, 222. A summary chart on 220 shows the differences between the three Pentateuchal Codes. The Jubilee text of Lev. 25 also does not mention slave-release in the seventh year, but only in the fiftieth. Its emphasis falls on land release, with differing provisions for country and city.

11. Ollenburger, 228-29. See also James A. Sanders, "From Isaiah 61 to Luke 4," in *Christianity, Judaism, and Other Greco-Roman Cults* Vol. 12, part 1, ed. Jacob Neusner (Leiden: E. J. Brill, 1975), 97. Sanders comments extensively on the Qumran text, 11QMelch, which he says "is a midrash on the idea of release in the Jubilee texts of Lev 25, Deut 15, and Isa 61" (97). But since Qumran Covenanters used Hebrew texts the term *Jubilee* is not in two of these texts. It would be more correct to say that 11QMelch is a midrash on the theme of "release/remission." Even more precisely, the Isa. 61:1-2 text is a midrash, holds Merrill P. Miller, on Lev. 25:12; Isa. 52:7; and Ps. 82:1-2—one text each from the Torah, the Prophets, and the Writings. In 11QMelch Melchizedek becomes the anointed herald—thus a pesher on Isa. 52:7—who combines the motifs of God's favor and vengeance. "The Function of Isa. 61:1-2 in 11Q Melchizedek," *JBL* 88 (1969): 467-469.

By the first two centuries BCE, however, the tradition, exemplified in the LXX, may have telescoped Lev. 25; Deut. 15; and Isa. 61:1-2 (and possibly others) into a unity of thought. Margaret Barker asserts this point, saying in the second temple period during the Maccabees the people took a solemn oath to obey the law in threefold dimension: not to intermarry with outsiders, not to trade on the Sabbath, and to forego all crops and exaction of debts in the seventh year (Neh. 10:30ff.). See "The Time is Fulfilled," 23.

12. Sanders emphasizes the contrast between Qumran's and Jesus-in-Luke's uses of Isa. 61. In the Qumran midrash, the favorable year is limited only to the Qumran faithful. In Luke, the favorable/acceptable (*dekton*) year is immediately exposited by the two narratives that follow, both showing favor to the outsiders. This is the point that infuriates the people, who initially spoke well of him at his gracious words (101)!

13. In his review of *Politics*, Edward Glynn says that Yoder's treatment of the Lord's Prayer does not in fact support his thesis since Luke does not use *opheilēmata* and Yoder resorts to Matthew to bolster his Lucan interpretation,

in *America* 129 (1973), 131. Glynn, however, disregards Luke's other three uses of *aphiēmi*.

14. Yoder rightly observes that the LXX uses *aphesis* in Lev. 25 for forgiving debts (66, n.4 //62 n.5).

15. *Politics*, 23-24, see esp. n.14 on p. 24//11-12 and n.17 on p. 12. Yoder deals with this issue in his 1994 "Epilogue" to ch. 2; see p. 54 n.60. In noting that his point might have been made just as sharply by reference to Matthew and the Sermon on the Mount (for this see his *The Original Revolution*, 34ff.), Yoder says, "Since all the Gospels say enough of the same things to make my point, I have no stake in preferring one school of Gospel criticism to another" (54).

16. William G. Johnsson, *Andrews Theological Seminary Studies* 13 (1975): 96-97.

17. A textual variant does retain the Isa. 61 line, but the ms. support is weaker than that for its omission. Further, those mss. including it reflect the scribal tendency to correct what appears as an error.

18. So Sanders' point also, 97.

19. Mark H. Rich, in a paper at the 2001 Annual Society of Biblical Literature Meeting (Denver), "Was the Jesus Movement Jubilee-Based?: An Examination of the Evidence," argues that a quite wide selection of texts contain jubilean emphases, such as Jesus' answer to John's objection to baptizing him, "'Let it be so now, for it is proper for us in this way to fulfill all righteousness'" (Matt. 3:15). The Greek for "Let it be so now" is *aphes arti*, which could be translated, "Release it now." In other words, let the Jubilee release begin now in my baptism! Rich argued similarly for the word "left" in Mark 10:28-29, proposing that these disciples reminded Jesus that they consciously "released themselves" from home and families to join a "Jubilee" movement. If Rich's arguments are valid, then Jubilee is a pervasive theme in the Synoptics. But that does not tell us how Jubilee is to be understood specifically in each of the Gospels. Yoder's primary appeal is to Luke, but his thesis is a claim about Jesus. My contention is that Luke identifies Jesus' ministry of "gospelizing," forgiving sins, healing and exorcism as the Jubilee emphases of Luke 4:18-19, along with the other themes mentioned above.

20. Cullmann's interpretation is as follows:

> On the way to the place of execution Jesus says to the weeping women (in Luke 23:28-30), "Daughters of Jerusalem, do not weep for me, but weep for yourselves and for your children. . . . For if they do this to the green wood, what shall be done to the dry?" All exegetes agree that Jesus refers to himself as the green wood. But who are the subject of "they do"? And why does Jesus refer to himself as the green wood? I believe there can be no doubt in this situation, where Jesus is being led to the place of execution by the Romans, that only the Romans can be the subject of the sentence. Then the saying of Jesus can have only the

following meaning: If the Romans execute me as a Zealot, who am no Zealot and who have always warned against Zealotism, what will they do then to the true Zealots: For the Romans Jesus was in reality green wood, for he had indeed renounced Zealotism. Then this saying of Jesus expresses exactly what I have endeavored to show here: 1) Throughout his entire ministry Jesus had to come to terms with Zealotism; 2) He renounced Zealotism, although he also assumed a critical attitude toward the Roman State; 3) He was condemned to death as a Zealot by the Romans. *The State in the New Testament* (New York: Charles Scribner's Sons, 1956), 48.

21. Richard Cassidy, *Jesus, Politics, and Society* (New York: Orbis Books, 1978), 50-85. I have summarized his views in my article, "Politics and Peace (*Eirēnē*) in Luke's Gospel," in *Political Issues in Luke-Acts*, ed. Richard J. Cassidy and Philip J. Scharper (Maryknoll, N.Y.: Orbis Books, 1983), 26-38.

22. See my essay, "Politics and Peace (Eirene) in Luke's Gospel," 33-35. On this topic see now also Anna Janzen, *Der Friede im lukanischen Doppelwerk vor dem Hintergrund der Pax Romana* (Frankfurt am Main: Peter Lang, 2002). Janzen argues that Luke reflects some of the good elements in the Pax Romana, such as the "benefactor" convention of the rich assisting the poor, but it is not a political apologetic.

23. James A. Sanders develops this point at length, that Luke makes of the woman's anointing something quite different than occurs in the other three Gospels. This is so because Luke wants it to be a Jubilee manifesto. In the inner core of the story the Greek word *echarisato* from *charizomai*, meaning "freely remit or graciously grant" occurs twice. The latter part of the story stresses the importance of forgiveness (verb forms of *aphesis*) and the pronouncement of forgiveness ("Your sins are forgiven," v. 48). In "Sins, Debts, and Jubilee Release," in *Luke and Sacred Scripture: The Function of Sacred Scripture in Luke-Acts*, ed. Craig A. Evans and James A. Sanders (Minneapolis: Fortress Press, 1993), 84-92.

24. Sanders puts it provocatively: "Is it not possible that Jesus might have used the *Essene second axiom as a foil* against which he gave his prophetic understanding of the judgements and grace of God in the End Time—and thereby so deeply offended some of his compatriots (was not *dektos* [accepted] in his own *patris*)." In "From Isaiah 61 to Luke 4," 101.

25. See Swartley, *Israel's Scripture Tradition and the Synoptic Gospels: Story Shaping Story* (Peabody, Mass.: Hendrickson, 1994), 78-80.

26. Susan R. Garrett, *The Demise of the Devil: Magic and the Demonic in Luke-Acts* (Minneapolis: Augsburg/Fortress, 1989); *idem.*, "Exodus from Bondage: Luke 9:31 and Acts 12:1-24," *CBQ* 52 (1990): 656-80; Swartley, *Israel's Scripture Tradition*, 85-88.

27. Often overlooked is the Sabbath setting for this text. Jubilee is inherently related to Sabbath liberation, as Richard H. Lowery, in *Sabbath and Ju-*

bilee (St. Louis: Chalice Press, 2000), helpfully shows, including present-day appropriation of these deep structure biblical themes.

28. A sixth point might be Luke's Jubilee emphases in the "Song of Zechariah" in Luke 1:68-79. Robin J. Dewitt Knauth presented a paper at the 2002 Society for Biblical Literature Annual Meeting (*SBL Abstracts* S23-53, 2002), 183, arguing this point. The paper argues that following Cyrus's edict to permit captive Israel to return to the land, major reinterpretation of the Jubilee legislation occurs, emphasizing hope for restoration and eschatological hope, so clearly enunciated as "in-fulfillment" in Zechariah's Song.

29. Stephen C. Barton, *Life Together: Family, Sexuality, and Community in the New Testament and Today* (Edinburgh and New York: T. & T. Clark, 2001), 223-250.

30. Wayne A. Meeks, "A Hermeneutic of Social Embodiment," *HTR* 79: 1-3 (1986): 176-86.

31. Richard B. Hays, "Scripture-Shaped Community: The Problem of Method in New Testament Ethics," *Interpretation* 41 (1990): 42-55.

32. Compare the oft-quoted Hans Denck, "No one can know Christ truly except by following him in life."

33. The impact of Yoder's thought has been aided by Donald B. Kraybill's popularization of *Politics* in *The Upside-Down Kingdom* (Scottdale, Pa. and Waterloo, Ont.: 1978, 2nd. ed. 1990, 3rd. ed. 2003). This has been used widely in undergraduate courses at Mennonite colleges.

34. This became clear to me in teaching Theology and Ethics of the Gospels these past years. I ask students which Gospel is their favorite and why. My comments are based on information from these interactions.

35. See pp. 72-75. These include Sloan, Ringe, Blosser, and Elias. Yoder also notes that Marshall, Tiede, and Danker have affirmed the jubilee dimension in Luke. So also my *Israel's Scripture Traditions*, 74-87.

36. Barton, *Life Together*, 230, 247.

Chapter 15

Yoder's Mischievous Contribution to Mennonite Views on Anselmian Atonement

Rachel Reesor-Taylor

INTRODUCTION

The doctrine of atonement and more specifically, Anselm's Satisfaction theory were not an area of research for Yoder. They might therefore not appear to be the place to assess his legacy. However, his discussion of the subject has clearly been influential simply by virtue of his stature, and is significantly evident in two Mennonite books published on atonement in the past twenty years. John Driver's *Understanding the atonement for the Mission of the Church*[1] shows an almost exclusive reliance upon Yoder's discussion for his own evaluation of Anselm's Satisfaction theory. J. Denny Weaver's recent work, *The Nonviolent Atonement*[2] also reflects Yoder's treatment of Anselm, even though Weaver includes his own research to draw conclusions that go beyond those of Yoder.

It seems appropriate, therefore, to consider these discussions as one indication of Yoder's legacy. [3] And what do we discover about his legacy in these works? Driver and Weaver took up Yoder's critique of Anselm, which did not contribute much beyond what was commonly recited in Liberal Protestant circles, influenced by Adolf von Harnack[4] and Gustaf Aulen[5]. This is understandable since the critique, which was at points devastating, is what formed the weight of Yoder's discussion. Nevertheless, Yoder did note certain significant strengths that should keep the careful reader from presuming to dispense too quickly with Anselm's Satisfaction theory entirely. Both Driver and Weaver reflect and build on Yoder's critique, arriving at different conclusions, but neither one clearly heeds the statements Yoder made about the strengths of Anselm's *Cur Deus Homo* (CDH). Weaver is much closer to a thoroughgoing rejection of Anselm's Satisfaction theory than Yoder was apparently ready to advocate, and Driver simply leaves Anselm's contribution criticized on the sidelines.

There is thus a discernable difference between Yoder and his two interpreters, neither of whom explicitly suggests any departure from Yoder's estimation of Anselm. Is this due to their carelessness or also to something in the nature of Yoder's work? His writing was contextual rather than systematic. It was complex, to be sure; was it also ambiguous? Or was it perhaps mischievous? Yoder's legacy on the question of atonement does indeed reflect a certain mischievousness, for he articulated his critique in a way that might entice readers to a more thoroughgoing rejection of Anselm's Satisfaction theory than he himself was prepared to advocate—and for good reason.

YODER ON ANSELM:
SERIOUS PROBLEMS BUT THE BEST WE HAVE

Yoder's critique of Anselm's atonement theory is multivalent and more complex than one might at first conclude. He approached the question from the point of view of biblical studies, theology, and ethical commitments. It is more complex than one might be tempted to believe, because he *did* grant Anselm a lot, despite the serious weaknesses he outlined. At the outset of his lecture notes on the *Cur Deus Homo*, Yoder mentioned the arguments in favour of Anselm's theory:

> It answers the question; it makes Christ's blameless death an absolute juridical necessity, the only way to reconcile God's Holiness and His love. . . . it takes sin seriously, . . . and it is also capable of integrating the various imageries in which the Bible speaks of the Work of Christ, especially those of sacrifice (and blood) and of redemption.[6]

It is easy to skip over these introductory comments, but there they are as a sort of reminder to maintain some humility in the face of a tradition that he later noted called forth "praise, gratitude, (and) commitment" (304). The warning almost gets lost, however, because the bulk of the discussion is a presentation of all that is wrong with Anselm, capped with a thumbnail sketch of the necessary elements of a better theory, enticing all those who dare to do better than anyone has so far—even Anselm. Consider, then, the details of his critique of Anselm's theory, for no sooner had he signalled the strengths than he proceeded to explain the "damaging criticisms to which this view is subject" (299).

Yoder's critiques from a biblical point of view

Yoder cited what would then have been relatively recent biblical scholarship to evaluate Anselm's argument in CDH and to find it biblically unsatisfactory. What was so unsatisfactory? First, according to Yoder, Anselm depicted "God's offended holiness as the definition of perdition," and in so doing "abandon(ed) the NT affirmation that God is the Agent, not the object, of reconciliation (2 Cor 5:18-20). . . . [T]he Gospel reveals God taking the initiative for our redemption, and (*humanity*) as needing to be reconciled." (Yoder referred to James Stewart, *A Man in Christ: The Vital Elements of St. Paul's Religion,* [London: Hodder and Stoughton, 1935], 209ff., 221ff.; and V. Taylor, *The Atonement in New Testament Teaching,* [London: Epworth, 1958] 171ff., 299).

Second, Yoder noted that exegetes see in Scripture that Christ died *for us,* on our behalf or as our representative, but *not* as our *substitute.* Yet he understood Anselm to portray Christ as our substitute.

A third problem from the point of view of biblical scholarship is that in the biblical account, the guilt of (past) sin is not the real problem of atonement. The New Testament points to two other foci that ". . . define the lost condition: separation from God and incapacity to do the *good.* "Thus salvation is not primarily the remission of guilt or the cancellation of punishment, it is reconciliation (reestablishment of communion) and obedience, i.e. discipleship" (300).

A further exegetical problem has to do with the meaning of the Hebrew sacrificial system which is not well understood. What is clear to Yoder is that the power of Anselm's theory rests on the "easy juxtaposition of civil punishment with bloody sacrifice" (301, n. 6), which is to misunderstand sacrifice in the Hebrew Bible. Sacrifice was not about punishment and death, but about gift and offering and identification with God (301). Finally, Yoder considered that Anselm omitted the biblical idea of "union with Christ" (306).

Yoder's statement integrating the various exegetical problems with Anselm's CDH goes like this:

> Every strand of NT literature makes clear that God's purpose with humanity is to establish obedience in His communion, not only to expiate juridical guilt. . . . Forgiveness in the sense of removal of an obstacle to communion with God is evidently part of His purpose; but we do not find Him preoccupied with our guilt, in the sense of our deserving punishment. Guilt in this sense seems rather to be an anthropopathism carried over by Anselm from human concepts of just retribution. (301)

Critiques from a systematic theology point of view

In addition to the exegetical issues, Yoder identified weaknesses from the point of view of systematic theology. First, he maintained that CDH "forces us to a tritheistic doctrine of God. . . . The idea of Father and Son as having separate wills and identities to the point of having transactions with one another has no grounds in the orthodox doctrine of the Trinity, and still less in the New Testament" (302).

Second, "there is the danger of an *opus operatum* view of Christ's work" (302), which tends to have universal validity, whether individuals want it or not. Yoder observed that Anselm's theory does not need the faith of the believer.

Third, "it grew out of the penitential practice" (302) where human work has saving merit, so "Christ's death remains a human initiative directed Godward" (302).

Finally, Yoder held that Anselm succeeded in "working pardon into the legal system of just rewards . . . " so, as he put it, the "legal structure is intact" (302). Yoder found this contrary to God's grace which is in fact "a flexing of the law, not its rigid, destructive application" (302).

Critiques from a discipleship point of view

In addition to the biblical and systematic considerations, Yoder brought questions from the point of view of the Anabaptist emphasis on discipleship. He suggested that it is significant that proponents of Anselm's view have had trouble relating sanctification to justification since his view was formed in a state-church context, where, in Yoder's words, "sacraments mattered more than ethics. . . " (302). In Yoder's estimation, "the concept of discipleship is most clearly taught in precisely those New Testament texts which speak of the Christian's sufferings (or "cross") as somehow parallel to Christ's" (303). Yoder cited Matthew 10:38; Mark 8:34f, 10:38ff.; Luke 14:27; John 15:20; 2 Corinthians 1:5; Philippians 1:29, 2:5-8, 3:10; Colossians 1:24f; Hebrews 12:1-4; 1 Peter 2:21ff.; Revelation 12:11. However, in the satisfaction theory, these passages make no sense, claimed Yoder, for the believer's sufferings"do not placate an offended Holiness" nor are they"a transaction with the Father" (303). The only way to make sense of the parallel of the Christian's cross with that of Christ in the New Testament is if the cross of Christ has an ethical sense.

Yoder saw a connection between an Anselmian atonement theory, a downplaying of the parallel between the cross of Christ and the cross of the Christian, and a downplaying of discipleship. Yoder determined that the early Anabaptists who did emphasize discipleship managed to hold an Anselmian view *only* by *adding their own qualification*. Michael Sattler and Jacob Kautz (and Hans Denck) used the language of satisfaction but with an addition/critique:"The benefit of the death of Christ applies only to the person whose acceptance of it includes discipleship, the inward appropriation of the broken will and the outward following in his steps" (303).

The Satisfaction theory alone, without this added stipulation of obedience, makes no required link between the cross of Christ and the Christian's obedience or even acceptance of the cross. Yoder noted another aspect of a missing link regarding obedience. The description of how atonement is brought about has no necessary relationship to the life of Jesus as a man—his particular life and obedience (303). So, obedience is not linked to salvation for people, and salvation is not linked to the obedient life of Jesus.

Having outlined the exegetical, theological, and discipleship problems with Anselm's theory of atonement, Yoder added final observations that might certainly be construed as flaws in the theory. From the point of view of the history of dogma, naive people who imagine that Anselm's theory is straight from the Bible should note that it is actually the youngest of the theories (only from the twelfth century). Also, in comparison to the other theories, it is the one "tied most precisely to a particular model of thought, namely the court room" (304). In Yoder's estimation CDH would be a more adequate explanation of why Jesus had to die if it needed the resurrection and if it were in history, rather than in the mind of God or in some heavenly courtroom (307).

It is interesting that Yoder dismissed the objections that New Testament scholar Vincent Taylor laid on humanitarian grounds, namely, that punishing an innocent one is immoral, and that "imputed righteousness is nonsense." In Yoder's estimation, these objections only reflect Taylor's prejudices for, in fact, God is free to do these things (304). Unlike Taylor, then, Yoder was not intending to base any objections on any ground so shifting as a "humanitarian" one, but only on the firm foundations of "Scripture."

To sum up, then: In Yoder's view, the weaknesses with Anselm's Satisfaction theory concern an inappropriate preoccupation with guilt instead of future obedience; a depiction of God as unwilling to forgive without the payment offered by the Son as our substitute, suggesting a fractured Trinity with transactions between members of the Godhead; and finally God as the *object* rather than the *agent* of the reconciliation, so that salvation is a result of human efforts and payments, even if real human beings are not required to be obedient. These were the objections he passed along, gathered together from New Testament scholars, systematic theologians, church historians and his own Anabaptist emphasis on discipleship.

But let us not forget the comments with which he began. He ventured that "on first view" Anselm's Satisfaction view had "a number of considerations in its favor." Namely, it "appeared to answer the question . . . it takes sins seriously"—unlike the other available models. One might expect him to go on to show that none of these first impressions are accurate and that what appears to be the case is only appearance. In fact, by the end, he concluded that we need to recognize that

> the satisfaction theories are *the most serious answers found in the history of Christian theology*, in the sense that they answer the question of piety. They make sense in prayer. They call forth praise, gratitude, commitment. Therefore, they are deeply rooted in the life of the common believer. We need to recognize and respect the theory because of that moral strength (304, emphasis added).
>
> That was the first of the 'two clear findings.' At the same time, the second clear finding was that 'it is not a biblically satisfactory theory' (304).

Where does that leave his readers or students? With the task of taking the Bible and answering the question of atonement better than any of the six models Yoder outlined from the history of the Christian church! But do recall: *the Satisfaction theory is the most serious so far*. Surely that is saying a lot! Note also that although Yoder suggests the guilt of past sin is not the *primary* concern, it is not eliminated as *a* concern. Given these warnings, ambiguous or shrouded as they might be, I suggest that the wise student will not soon scrap the Satisfaction theory. Yet that is what many of us who came to the point of reading Yoder's *Preface* were just aching to do! And he gave us the reasons to do it—along with the subtle warnings about taking that route.

DRIVER ON ANSELM: SERIOUS PROBLEMS BUT MIGHT BE ONE OF THE MIX

Driver's interpretation of Anselm relied heavily on Yoder's treatment of CDH in *Preface to Theology*.[7] Since Driver's project was not to examine Anselm, but to catalogue the images of atonement in the Bible, he did not need to examine Anselmian scholarship and Yoder's interpretation sufficed. Driver attempted to do justice to the host of images found in the Bible, not settling on just one theory. As such, he did not explicitly dismiss Anselm's Satisfaction theory of atonement. Nevertheless, his critique of the "Satisfaction view" emerges as a refrain throughout the book and he did not grant the place to Anselm that Yoder did, although his reliance on Yoder for his understanding of Anselm is evident from the fact that his work follows Yoder's critique of Anselm in *Preface* so closely.

WEAVER ON ANSELM: INSURMOUNTABLE FLAWS AND THEREFORE TO BE REJECTED

While J. Denny Weaver's earlier works on atonement included a treatment of Anselm reminiscent of Yoder's, his more recent discussions have focused the critique more sharply.[8] The problem is not simply that an ethic derived from Jesus is not intrinsically required by Anselm's Satisfaction theory. In fact, it is worse than that, for there *is* a value or an ethic assumed in CDH, but it is not a Christian one, according to Weaver's discussion. In Weaver's attempt to articulate a contemporary atonement theology, he concluded that Anselm's satisfaction theory of atonement is "based on divinely sanctioned, retributive violence."[9] It depends upon the assumption that "doing justice means to punish" (225). Anselm's doctrine of atonement must therefore be rejected by Christians who are "uncomfortable with the idea of God who sanctions violence, a God who sends the Son so that his death can satisfy a divine requirement. . . ." (225).

PERTINENT ELEMENTS IN YODER'S BROADER WORK SUGGESTING HESITATION

There is ample evidence that testifies to Yoder's eagerness for an Anabaptist, peace church or free church articulation of atonement. Back in the 1980s he noted and encouraged the efforts of Driver, C. Norman Kraus, and Perry Yoder in this endeavor. So, it is clear why many Mennonites would reject Anselm after reading Yoder. He did point out damaging criticisms and concluded that we might want a theory that is more biblically satisfactory. Nevertheless, there were those initial statements about it being the strongest statement so far. Perhaps it was not intended, but this does give me pause. It makes sense in piety; it calls forth praise, gratitude, and commitment. These are certainly an important start and one would have to have great self-confidence to presume to do better than the best so far. At least it would be prudent to hold on to the "best so far" and improve on it, until a better substitute is in place.

Other comments by Yoder that shed light on the question suggest that a more careful reading of Anselm might be necessary before rejecting his theory out of hand. Furthermore, these might be used to evaluate Weaver's rejection of Anselm based on slightly different conclusions regarding justice and punishment. In two related discussions, one of punishment and the other of the death penalty, Yoder made arguments with implications for Anselm's satisfaction theory. On the matter of punishment, he warned his friends not to make their case against the death penalty on the grounds that all punishment is inherently evil. He made a more complex case regarding punishment, outlining how it is "anthropologically normal" and how it is better to acknowledge the presence of punishment in all societies and its role rather than to "bemoan it or declare it immoral."[10]

Now, turning to the New Testament, Yoder noted that, of course, punishment is not the *last* word. However, it must nevertheless be allowed to stand as the *first* word.[11] This suggests that a desire for some sort of consequence, even punishment or payment for past sin might not be wrong-headed, but a human requirement that God acknowledges and answers in the cross. This would further indicate that not all talk of punishment is to be termed "violence."

Yoder also noted, in building the biblical case against the death penalty, that Jesus' death on the cross is understood sacrificially in Hebrews, making further sacrifices unnecessary:

> It is the clear testimony of the NT, especially of the epistle to the Hebrews, that the ceremonial requirements of the Old Covenant find their end—both in the sense of fulfillment and in the sense of termination—in the high-priestly sacrifice of Christ. 'Once for all' is the good news. Not only is the sacrifice of bulls and goats, turtledoves and wheatcakes at an end; the fact that Christ died for our sins, once for all, the righteous one for the godless (Heb. 9:26-28; 1 Peter 3:18), puts an end to the entire expiatory system, whether it be enforced by priests in Jerusalem or by executioners anywhere else.[12]

Atonement was not the topic of the discussion in which this statement was uttered, but the implications are clear. It is not *in*appropriate to speak of the cross in terms of sacrifice—nor even in terms of expiation! In fact, Yoder did note, in *Preface*, that "a major challenge to our own understanding, is the portrayal of Jesus' death as a sacrifice in some continuity with the blood animal sacrifices of the mosaic legislation."[13] Although this is not an explicit reference to Anselm, there are implications, since Anselm's satisfaction theory involved sacrifice. Further, when Yoder spelled out at length how Jesus is to be followed as our example in the *Politics of Jesus*, he did not reject the more commonly acknowledged claim of Jesus as sacrifice. Rather, his stated intention was to highlight what had hitherto been ignored, namely "Jesus as teacher and example, not only *as sacrifice.*"[14] (emphasis added).

REJECTION DESPITE THE STRENGTHS?

Or did Yoder intend an essential rejection of Anselm's satisfaction theory, since he invited us to do better? If so, why the apparently strong statements about the strengths of Anselm's model? Was he just covering his tracks, to make sure he was not dismissed out of hand by more orthodox Christians? I choose to take these statements as genuine comments not to be dismissed, but that might in fact be critical. Just as I would take the "only" in his statement about Jesus being not *only* sacrifice but also example as especially noteworthy.

After reading Yoder's chapter, the cautious and serious attempt to articulate a doctrine of the atonement would necessitate a revisitation of the theory that had called forth gratitude, praise, and commitment—from a "truly great mind of the Middle Ages." (293) Might Yoder's own reading of the *Cur Deus Homo* need critique? Indeed, the conscientious Christian scholar of atonement might want to do more to understand Anselm than Yoder who was not a scholar of Anselm, or indeed of medieval theology. Imagine surveying two thousand years of Christian experience and saying to your students that none of the great ones have got it right. So scrap their attempts, take the Bible, and work out a doctrine at least as good as Anselm's. Isn't that just a little mischievous? Wouldn't a wise approach be to hold onto the one that was heralded as the best, even if it needs to be revised, reinterpreted? And wouldn't a caring teacher emphasize that route to the students?

Instead, I see in Yoder, a thrill with being as alternative and free as possible, unfettered by any external authority other than the Bible. But I also see someone whose views, amazingly enough, rarely rejected what was affirmed in orthodoxy. I see someone who was not so naive as to think that the Bible can be interpreted by an individual, in isolation from the church—locally, globally, and over the ages.

WHY YODER'S HESITATION WAS WELL-FOUNDED

It is doubtless because I have discovered Anselm's CDH to be a careful and profound reflection on why Jesus had to die, and compatible with the biblical witness, that I am inclined to highlight the evidence of Yoder's refusal to dismiss it entirely. The positive reading of CDH emerges when it is understood in the context of Anselm's medieval catholic, *viz* sacramental, theology and worldview. That is clearly the only setting in which it can properly be understood. However, it has been ripped out of that web and transplanted into a Protestant theology, where its character appears quite differently. It is perhaps for this reason that some Mennonites believe Satisfaction incompatible with a peace theology which advocates restorative justice rather than retributive justice, and understands nonviolence as inherent in true discipleship. Interpreted within the context of Anselm's theology, it is evident that CDH is indeed compatible with a theology committed to social justice and nonviolence.[15]

Rather than summarizing again all of Yoder's objections, it will be best simply to mention some and to describe an alternative interpretation of CDH that makes Yoder's characterization seem misplaced. The various objections were, not surprisingly, related. First, concerning the relevance of the guilt of past sin, although salvation is not primarily a matter of salvation from the guilt of past sin, that is certainly a part of it. Yoder objected to the *degree* of attention paid to the guilt of past sin, and not to the mention of it *per se*, as a matter for concern. So, on the question of whether something might need to be done about past sin, or whether such sin can simply be ignored, Yoder might side with Anselm as well as with Howard Zehr of the restorative justice movement, since both see payment or reparation as inherent in justice.[16]

A consideration of what Anselm meant by "rectitude," and the justice and honor of God, using recent interpretations of *CDH* from Catholic and Anglican instead of strictly Protestant theologians, suggests an image of God where the restoration of humanity and the whole creation is wanted. The God of CDH emerges as the defender of the weak rather than as von Harnack's "Mighty Private Man"[17] who lingers behind Yoder's description of Anselm's God. The love of God is revealed in the justice of God that is not simply legal, but moral, theological, and restorative, like the biblical idea of *shalom*.

This is a justice not at odds with mercy even though satisfaction must be made for evil—the distortion of relationships and the creation. God is loving, self-giving, merciful, willing even to die, to assure the restoration of creation. The love of God, the justice of God, or the mercy of God refuses simply to overlook evil, which would betray the victims. But the love of God is also not content only to punish the sin. The love of God opts for satisfaction, to restore the broken creation, and relationships—that is both just and merciful.[18]

The matter of sacrifice is also significant, and an area Yoder noted would need more attention by Protestants, for whom it is quite foreign, although it is biblical. Yoder believed it was clear that the power of Anselm's theory rests on the "easy juxtaposition of civil punishment with bloody sacrifice." [19] He argued that the Satisfaction theory misunderstood the meaning of sacrifice by concentrating on the death. In fact, it was not Anselm who misunderstood sacrifice, assuming that sacrifice had to do with death. It so happens that the offering/sacrifice that served as the satisfaction involved the offering of Jesus' whole life, as Yoder noted that a real sacrifice would (301), and that the offering of his life in obedience resulted in his death—the ultimate of offering one's whole life. So not so much Anselm but later interpreters of Anselm misunderstood sacrifice and read substitutionary punishment into CDH. Anselm did not speak of civil punishment but only of sacrifice. He explicitly said that Jesus' death was *not* the enacting or exacting of a punishment, but the offering of a sacrifice that made satisfaction *instead of* undergoing punishment: Jesus's death was an offering or gift—a sacrifice.[20] It is easy to confuse sacrifice with punishment because they can both involve death. However, there is a world of difference between an offering of self—even unto death, and a death penalty. Anselm knew the difference.

Anselm also knew about other critical distinctions. One might even say that was his specialty! A number of Yoder's objections are related to the unity and separation of Jesus, human beings, and God. He charged that Anselm's theory omitted the idea of "union with Christ," [21] built upon the notion of substitution which Yoder claimed was not biblical, and fractured the Trinity with transactions between the members of the Godhead. These isolating views of Anselm's argument are actually quite surprising, given Anselm's more organic worldview and his metaphysic which envisioned real union and a participatory relationship between people, and specifically between the humanity of Jesus and human beings, or between Jesus as the second person of the Trinity and the First Person of the Trinity.

Furthermore, the "transactions" between the members of the Trinity do not appear to be fracturing when one holds seriously to the doctrine of the incarnation, which is precisely the subject of Anselm's meditation in this work! To say that in CDH God was unwilling to forgive without the payment offered by the Son as our substitute and therefore not the agent of reconciliation—and that this suggests a fractured Trinity with transactions between members of the Godhead—ignores Anselm's underlying assumption of the incarnation.

For Anselm, the whole story was a matter of God taking action, through the incarnation, to do on behalf of humanity, with human participation, what humanity or human beings could not do, but needed to do. Yoder at once complained that in CDH salvation is the result of "human effort and payments" or "a human initiative directed Godward" (302) in Jesus, and also critiqued the theory because it did not require human obedience or action (302). Apparently Yoder wanted a clear demarcation of roles here: God initiates and human beings respond. This would however not require anything so complex as the incarnation or the Trinity.

But the incarnation was necessary (and the cross) because human beings were not able even to respond, hence the need for substitution and participation. Precisely because Anselm recognized the real union or participation between human beings and the humanity of Jesus, the work of Jesus is not separate from the work of all human beings and human beings are not exempt from obedience in Anselm's view. In Anselm's worldview God was really present and active in Jesus. So the offering by Jesus to God is not a fracturing of the Trinity, but an expression of the love and the three-ness in the unity—especially because it was also God in Christ doing the offering on behalf of humanity.

CONCLUSION:

Yoder was not ready to reject Anselm altogether. No doubt he knew that he had not taken the time to study and understand this statement that had called forth praise, commitment, gratitude—even though there were obvious problems with popular versions and interpretations of it. He did not rule out entirely the legitimacy of punishment, which is a key element in Weaver's critique of the underlying, deep structure of Anselm's argument. He also knew that it was entirely biblical to speak of Jesus' cross as a sacrifice—even though he knew that many modern people, especially Protestants, do not understand sacrifice. Perhaps Yoder intuited that Anselm, being a medieval man , with a sacramental theology and piety, might have understood more about sacrifice. Perhaps he sensed that Anselm's commitment to justice and human participation in salvation might turn out to have something to offer a Christian faith that emphasizes discipleship and peace.

I believe Yoder's reluctance to scrap Anselm's Satisfaction theory is clear. It is apparently not clear enough. And if it is not clear (enough), then we are justified in being perturbed with him. He took a mischievous route. He was brilliant in his ability to sort out the finest points and perspectives, often catching people for asking the wrong question, making a faulty assumption, or failing to see another option. It was certainly within his ability to spell things out clearly, so that his readers would not fall into the ditches that he so artfully dodged. Yet he chose not to do so.

As a sort of postscript or suggestion for further consideration, I would add that there are indications that this mischievousness might not be just an isolated incident. Alain Epp Weaver has argued that many inheritors of Yoder's work show less nuance *vis-à-vis* the creeds than he did.[22] Furthermore, an addendum in the second edition of *The Politics of Jesus* indicates that Yoder had to refer many readers back to certain lines in his chapter 7 on Justification because these certain few lines had been ignored, leading to a misrepresentation or an incomplete grasp of Yoder's own position.[23] Again we are led to wonder whether Yoder might have been more deliberate in helping his readers to avoid traps he himself carefully side-stepped—that is, whether he might have been less mischievous.

NOTES

1. John Driver, *Understanding the Atonement for the Mission of the Church* (Scottdale, Pa.: Herald Press, 1986).

2. J. Denny Weaver, *The Nonviolent Atonement* (Grand Rapids: Eerdmans, 2001).

3. C. Norman Kraus also discussed Atonement in his work on Christology, but with less treatment of Anselm directly, since his setting was more a pre-Christian rather than a post-Christian one. He did emphasize that Jesus' work was not about paying an "equivalent penalty in order to satisfy God's anger or justice."*Jesus Christ Our Lord: Christology from a Disciple's Perspective* (Scottdale, Pa.:Herald Press, 1987), 225-226.

4. Adolph von Harnack, *History of Dogma*, vol. 6, trans. Neil Buchanan, (New York: Dover Publications, 1961).

5. Gustaf Aulen, *Christus Victor. An Historical Study of the Three Main Types of the Idea of the Atonement* (London: SPCK, 1931; reprint, London: SPCK, 1920).

6. Yoder, *Preface to Theology: Christology and Theological Method* (Grand Rapids: Brazos Press, 2002), 299.

7. Driver, 55-64.

8. There are a number of articles and a book, *Keeping Salvation Ethical: Mennonite and Amish Atonement Theology in the Late Nineteenth Century* (Scottdale, Pa.: Herald Press, 1997).

9. Weaver, *The Nonviolent Atonement*, 225.

10. "The Case for Punishment" unpublished, 1995. Available as "You Have It Coming: Good Punishment. The Legitimate Social Function of Punitive Behavior" (Notre Dame, Ind.: Shalom Desktop Publishing, 1995.) Also retrieve at John Howard Yoder's website at http://www.nd.edu/~theo/jhy/writings/home/ind-punish.htm.

11. Ibid., ch. 13. Yoder referred to Larry Miller, "Christianisme et Societe dans la Premiere Lettre de Pierre" (Strasbourg, France: Universite des Sciences Humaines de Strasbourg, Faculte de Theologie Protestante, 1995, Ph.D. dissertation).

12. John Howard Yoder, "Noah's Covenant & the Purpose of Punishment" in *Readings in Christian Ethics*, vol. 2, ed. David K. Clark and Robert V. Rakestraw (Grand Rapids: Baker Books, 1996), 471-481. Excerpted from *The Death Penalty: A Debate*, ed. John Howard Yoder and H. Wayne House (Dallas:

Word, 1991), 479.

13. Yoder, *Preface*, 287.

14. John Howard Yoder, *The Politics of Jesus* (Grand Rapids: Eerdmans, 1999), 226-227.

15. See the works on Anselm written by Robert Crouse, Eugene Fairweather, Joseph Komonchak, Hunter Brown, R. W. Southern, Katherin Rogers, and A. E. McGrath.

16. Howard Zehr argued that "reparation ought to be at the center of justice" in "Justice, Stumbling toward a Restorative Vision," in *Justice: The Restorative Vision*, (Akron, Pa.: Mennonite Central Committee, 1989), 9.

17. von Harnack, *History of Dogma*, vol. 6, 77-78.

18. This is from the conclusion of my unpublished paper, "St. Anselm's *Cur Deus Homo*: A Nuanced Doctrine of the Love of God," read at Christian Systematic Theology Group (Denver, Col. Annual Meeting of The American Academy of Religion, November 2001). The whole question is discussed in detail in my dissertation in progress, "Anselm and an Anabaptist Peace Theology: the Compatibility of Nonviolence and Sacrificial Atonement" at McGill University, under the supervision of Douglas Farrow.

19. Yoder, *Preface*, 301

20. "... *either* satisfaction *or* punishment must follow upon every sin."(emphasis added). Anselm, *Why God Became a Man (Cur Deus Homo)*, translated and edited by Jaspar Hopkins and Herbert Richardson (Lewistown, NY: Edwin Mellen Press, 1980), 73.

21. Yoder, *Preface*, 306.

22. Alain Epp Weaver, "Missionary Christology: John Howard Yoder and the Creeds" *Mennonite Quarterly Review* 76:3 (July 2000):439.

23. Yoder, *Politics*, 227.

Chapter 16

Did Yoder Reduce Theology To Ethics?

Thomas Finger

FOR SEVERAL GENERATIONS MOST BELIEVERS church traditions have produced scholars in biblical studies, and often in history—at least of their denominations. Many such believers churches now include academically trained ethicists and/or missiologists, depending on their priorities.

However, explicit theologizing in the believers church tradition, often called *systematic* or *constructive*, is only about a generation old. Before this, biblical scholars, historians, ethicists and missiologists in these churches were often called "theologians" and still are today. Indeed, since they sometimes ranged beyond their disciplines and made explicit theological statements, this label was somewhat accurate. Among the best-known was surely John Howard Yoder.

Why have believers churches taken up formal theology so belatedly? Partly due to long-standing suspicion of the discipline, which has been the most academic of religious studies. Until recently, many believers churches have been distant from the academy. Perhaps more importantly, believers churches emphasize lived, practical faith, and fear that sophisticated speculation might dilute the vibrancy of devotion, discipleship, and mission. Just why, their members often ask, need we reflect on anything more than biblical texts, and on our own behavior, outreach, and history?

Theologians commonly respond that today's world differs significantly from those worlds where the Scriptures and the various believers churches originated. Consequently, it is not always clear what biblical and traditional terms actually mean today. For example, Christian medical professionals want to care for whole persons. Their religious resources, however, often refer to what persons truly are by terms such as *soul*. Yet many functions once attributed to souls are apparently being explained biologically. What, then, does *soul* mean today? How do medical people find whatever it indicates? How do they treat it?

Such questions stretch far beyond medicine. For instance, as life is increasingly shaped by materialistic explanations and values, interest is rising in *spirituality*. Numerous claims about spiritual reality are circulating, some unknown in biblical or even recent church history. How can believers churches help people, including their own members, distinguish genuine claims from bogus?

Systematic or constructive theology can help, I believe, because it does not simply describe what Scripture or a church tradition has said on such themes, even if it regards one or both as authoritative. Instead, it considers all reality in light of one overarching concept. This is "God," the one "ultimate point of reference in terms of which our human life and its problems and possibilities must be understood."[1] That is, theology examines both traditional Christian and contemporary scientific, religious and other understandings of reality; and how they differ, correspond or intersect. It seeks to express what terms like *soul* actually mean in light of these understandings.[2]

Theology need not *substantiate* its affirmations by criteria from these other domains. Yet it will give some account of what criteria and sources it uses. Neither, of course, can any theology treat all of these areas fully. Yet if it regards all things in light of their ultimate Origin and Purpose, theology will at least move in these directions.[3]

Despite this broad orientation, theology, as I understand it, is not chiefly an academic endeavor. It is undertaken by the church, to enhance its life and ministries. The issues I just mentioned—medicine and spirituality—touch the daily lives of many Christians. They are pastoral and mission issues.

To be sure, biblical scholars, church historians, ethicists, and missiologists also explore current understandings of reality, and seek to connect with them. Yoder for instance did not simply focus on the biblical Jesus. Instead, as James Reimer puts it, Yoder viewed "every event, text and theory" through "sharply focused ethical glasses," and excelled in rendering Jesus' ethical significance vivid and concrete for our day.[4]

Constructive or systematic theology, then, differs from ethics and other theological studies not simply because it considers contemporary conceptualities, but because it explores them and their relations to biblical and traditional languages more comprehensively. Theology, accordingly, can provide a vantage-point for raising questions about the broader significance of Yoder's work. It can ask, with Reimer, whether Yoder's ethical glasses tended to "filter out" other dimensions of meaning; indeed, whether Yoder actually adopted an *historicist* worldview which eliminated a transcendent or spiritual realm, and reduced theology to social ethics.[5] A theologian might conclude, with Craig Carter, that Yoder avoided this reduction. Nonetheless, Carter's helpful and comprehensive treatment proposes that this issue may be foremost in evaluating Yoder's broader legacy.[6]

Yoder's influence has spread far beyond ethics, not least because he pioneered believers church *systematic theology*.[7] I myself have learned much from him, and, along with my colleagues in the field, will continue to. At present, I think we can profit from carefully examining whatever Yoder said that is relevant to the reductionism issue, especially because society today is much more interested in and open to "spiritual" reality than when Yoder started writing.

This issue already agitates believers church theology. It often crystallizes around Christology—where the divine and human most intimately intersect. Some theologians, like Reimer, believe that Yoder minimized, largely ignored, or even denied the transcendent, ontological dimensions of classical Christology. Some such theologians, with Reimer, deplore this. Others welcome it, usually because classical Christology, for them, clashes with emphasizing Jesus' ethics. Still others, like Carter, find Yoder affirming the transcendent: "protecting, declaring, and unpacking the claims of classical Christology is what Yoder is about."[8]

Accordingly, my main questions will be these: To what extent were Yoder's affirmations reducible to ethics, or perhaps other fields (e.g., sociology) or conceptualities (e.g., historicism) whose terms refer exclusively to human (and/or sub-human) characteristics, activities, relationships and potentialities? To what extent did Yoder's affirmations incorporate a reality transcending these? And if some did, in what ways? I will not regard references to God or transcendence as genuine affirmations unless they assert, or at least strongly imply, something specific enough about transcendent reality that it cannot be sufficiently expressed in terms of human (and/or subhuman) realities.[9]

I will not be able to state Yoder's position definitively. Not only did he author several hundred works; Yoder also stressed that all knowledge is situated, and criticized efforts to set forth general positions as attempts to start from a vacuum.[10] Yoder instead unfolded different aspects of his thought in various ways in response to particular issues. If he had "a logical system of thought," as Carter claims, I will not have space to extract it.[11]

Nonetheless, I propose that Yoder's orientation toward the reductionism issue can be determined with reasonable adequacy from four works spanning much of his career: (1) His seminal contribution to believers church theology, *Preface to Theology*, comprising class materials from the 1960s and 1970s, focusing on Christology; (2) Yoder's most influential work, *The Politics of Jesus*, from 1972, slightly revised in 1994; (3) a brief essay focusing on *pluralism/relativism*, "But We Do See Jesus," published in 1984; (4) the short volume, *Body Politics*, from 1992.[12]

PREFACE TO THEOLOGY:
CHRISTOLOGY AND THEOLOGICAL METHOD

What role should *Preface* play in interpreting Yoder? This is somewhat unclear. Yoder never published *Preface*. Much of it derives from the 1960s, and the latest 1981 revision was hardly thorough. Yet Yoder addressed classical Christology in far greater detail here than anywhere else. *Preface*, then provides invaluable insight into what his other remarks on the subject meant, even if not every word can be pressed. Due to Yoder's complex treatment of this complex issue, I must consider *Preface* at far greater length than my other three sources.

To illustrate how believers church *systematic theology* might be done, Yoder traced various ways in which early Christians reflected on Jesus' significance in different settings. For Yoder this theologizing had a norm and starting-point: the Jesus-story climaxing in his resurrection to cosmic Lordship. *Lord* was the language of deity, and "Jesus Christ is Lord" was, as Oscar Cullman said, "the center of the earliest confession. . . ."[13] Yoder found this narrative outlined in what C. H. Dodd called the early *kerygma* (55-57), and filled out by what Yoder named the *primitive* or *uncritical* New Testament writings: Synoptic gospels, Peter, James, Jude, probably Revelation and the Didache (2002: 61-63).

Yoder distinguished these *uncritical* writings from those of the three New Testament *theologians*: Paul, John and Hebrews' author.[14] He sought to show how these used different languages to bring out various implications of the Jesus-narrative as it entered diverse, Hellenistic settings.[15] Take John's employment of *logos*. Yoder viewed logos as a Gnostic concept: a link in a chain connecting the highest divine being with earthly reality (154, 185). He showed how John not only used this Gnostic chain, but also broke it apart. For while the logos, for Gnostics, was neither God nor human, John pushed logos in both directions, and affirmed "an identity at both ends."[16]

Yoder considered John's language of the Word becoming flesh, like similar "high" Christological concepts in Hebrews 1 and Colossians 1, a valid "key to faithfulness" to the Jesus story.[17] Earlier Christians had spoken of Jesus being "adopted" or "exalted" to express his transcendent side. But since Jewish monotheism could not really accommodate a man being made God, "the only alternative" became "for God to take the initiative and become a man. . . . "[18] To be sure, these "high" Christologies were "saying more than [had] been clearly said"; yet not "something that wasn't believed before."[19]

But what exactly did these Christologies assert? Clearly, that Jesus was a complete, historical human being. And something too about transcendent reality? While Yoder considered kerygmatic language basically historical, he called the language toward the start of John, Colossians and Hebrews "ontological" or "cosmological." For Yoder, however, these writers went beyond ontological affirmations. Whereas Hellenistic cosmology was concerned with origins, the biblical authors, in his view, placed Jesus before these. Whereas Hellenists were concerned about mystical reality, Colossians declared all invisible beings subject to Christ. Yoder further styled cosmological assertions as "divinely revealed information. . . . revealed for its own sake." In contrast, biblical "affirmations of pre-existence and creation" were not "new information." They exemplified instead "the normal, appropriate missionary way to state the priority of Christ over the [cosmological] preoccupation of pagan faith."[20]

Yoder seemed to be saying that when biblical writers appropriated Hellenistic conceptualities, they did not refashion these to express new transcendent content, but, in effect, dismantled their transcendent reference. These writers, moreover, apparently disavowed the very intent of such schemas, which was to communicate mere "information . . . for its own sake." Yoder was evidently employing the common Neo-orthodox dichotomy between authentic revelatory language, which must always be "I-Thou," and language with cognitive content, which is always "I-it," or mere information. Now it might seem that declarations about Jesus being before cosmic origins would imply something about transcendent reality, material reality, and their interconnections. However, if such declarations emptied cosmological language wholly of its contents and intent, they could hardly affirm anything about the nature of God and the cosmos themselves.

Let us follow Yoder on to Nicea. He represented the general problem as finding a way to affirm both monotheism and Jesus' full humanity.[21] As he reviewed pre-Nicene Christologies, Yoder frequently enlisted the New Testament notions of monotheism, pre-existence, and Jesus' distinctness from the Father as criteria which they needed, but in some way failed, to meet.[22]

Yoder critiqued Nicea's political context (197-199). Yet he interpreted the Creed's content, except for its anathemas, as the product not of these factors, but of the legitimate Christological trajectory passed on from the New Testament. Yoder concluded that the creed "safeguard[ed] the New Testament content with at least a degree of success. . . . " and was "not strange or foreign to the substance of the Bible. . . . "[23] At the same time, he noted that the prior discussions, with their increasingly ontological vocabularies, had moved "*in form*. . . . farther and farther away from the gospel story" so that by Nicea "one recognizes no narrative to it anymore" (202). Yoder also denied that the creed revealed "information about deity" which one must believe for salvation. "That there is God the Father . . . the Son . . . the Spirit—and that these three are the same—" these were in the Bible, though not as "information." But Nicene, or trinitarian, doctrine is "the solution to an intellectual difficulty that arises if we accept the statements of the Bible" (204).

Yoder found the creed's thought-forms so "foreign" to biblical and modern thinking, and its political circumstances so dubious, that we must challenge whether it "does us much good" today (204). The "believers church tradition" should only claim that it "provided the best answer to an intellectual problem" (205). Still, Yoder maintained that Christians will always have this problem—Jesus' normativity and its relation to God's uniqueness—if they are biblical.[24]

Yoder was far more negative about Chalcedon. This arose largely from his portrait of Alexandrian Christology (erroneous, in my view). Yoder treated it as logically equivalent to Apollinarianism, which denied Jesus a human mind or soul (2002: 214), even though Alexandrians after Apollinarus considered it heretical. Yoder portrayed Alexandrian soteriology as *deification*: shedding one's humanity and literally becoming God.[25] Accordingly, Alexandrians taught that Jesus' deity swallowed up his humanity. Despite verbal affirmation of two natures, they, like their Eastern Orthodox heirs today, were really monophysites (218). For all these, Yoder continued, salvation occurred "fundamentally" at Bethlehem (213) where the Logos took on generic humanity before absorbing it. Jesus' life, death, and resurrection contributed little; it hardly mattered what kind of human he was.[26] Yoder considered the politics surrounding Chalcedon mostly as machination against Nestorius, who stressed Jesus' humanity more, but was declared heretical (216-217).

Yoder conceded that Chalcedon still sought, like Nicea, to "safeguard what a Christian has to say to be faithful to Jesus and still say it in terms of the culture. . . " (219). These two provided "fruitful definition of the . . . problem." They are helpful as "a fence," telling us what not to say, though "not as a faith" (221). Still, by Chalcedon the church had traveled so far from biblical narrative into ontology that it often raised the wrong questions (219). Yoder concluded that today's radical Anabaptists should probably not concentrate on affirming or fighting for the creeds—but still less should they fight against them (223).

Let us return to the major question. *Preface to Theology* contains Yoder's most detailed appraisal of Christology by far. What can it tell us about the extent to which his own theological affirmations were reducible to, or transcended, those of ethics (or any conceptuality limited to the human and/or subhuman realm)?

I do not find Yoder clearly attributing transcendent content to the christologies of John, Colossians, or Hebrews. I do not find him saying that when they employed cosmological concepts, they were expressing, or even hinting at, a different cosmological outlook. He did say that they were subverting all such efforts.[27] Yoder did propose, however, that Nicea's *homoousios* affirmed that God, in Jesus, was truly working in the world, and truly loves the world, in contrast to Arius' distant, uninvolved God. Further, this concept enabled Nicea to say, "in the language of ontology," that this love is *agape*: that God is not bound to the world, and does not need the world, but "that God's being among us is pure grace" (2002: 202).

Was Yoder himself affirming that Jesus' work as agape entails an ontological distinction, in the general sense of some actual, conceptualizable, difference between God's reality and the cosmos'? Or was he simply showing how ontology, in the sense of Hellenistic cosmology, might speak of agape, without implying that this carried ontological meaning in the first sense (from here on, I will normally use *ontology* in the first sense).

Preface's subsequent discussion of eschatology perhaps provides an answer. After describing biblical expectations of a new heaven and earth, Yoder proposed, as I have above, that systematic theology's task is to "relate this kind of expectation to the rest of reality" to what we learn through science, history, and other channels (254, cf. 263). Now most people today, Yoder continued, view the cosmos as a closed causal system. They find divine intervention, so prominent in biblical eschatology, troublesome.

What should theology do? Challenge the current view, and argue that interventions are possible? This route, Yoder granted, "has some logic in its favor" (258). Yoder did not directly affirm closed causality, and perhaps obliquely critiqued it.[28] Yet he insisted that Christian witness, and theological reflection on it, should not stress this issue. Why?

Because the New Testament had "no intention . . . to set up one worldview over against the other and tell you which one is right." It simply "spoke to its neighbors in their ordinary language" and "did not tell them their worldview was wrong" (257-258). When the New Testament, for instance, pictured Jesus returning from the sky, it simply employed the language of its culture. For Yoder, however, eschatology's "real content" was different: that "a unity of divine will acts consistently"; that God "does not want us to honor other gods"; that God wants to make "us a people of fellowship with God. . . . "[29] Consequently, if theologians or ordinary Christians opposed the "scientific" worldview, they would miss this real point. They would "depreciate, for the purposes of further conversation, the reality of the ordinary world in which our neighbors are living" (258).

Nevertheless, the New Testament apparently carried some implications about the cosmos as a whole for Yoder. For since "the resurrection is testified to as in some sense a real event . . . the culmination of God's purposes must also be really historic." Eternity cannot be a-temporal; even God cannot be either—though God may be "hyper-temporal," meaning "more temporal than we. . . " (276). Further, because millennial eschatologies "take time seriously" they "seem more fitting in one way."[30] Finally, Yoder rejected predestination and emphatically affirmed free choice in ways that, given his stress on historicity, he apparently meant to refer to the way things really are (2002: 280).

In fact, as Reimer maintains, Yoder may have spelled out such a view once in *Preface*: "We are aware of history as a process," Yoder remarked, as earlier ages were not. "History is the only reality we know, we do not think about essences anymore, about substances and *hypostases*, about realities `out there' having their being in themselves. We think of reality as happening in personal relationships, in institutional relationships, and in the passage of time."[31] Yoder acknowledged that he was describing historicism, and called it a "philosophical stance." This implied, I think, that he did not wholly endorse any one version of it. He apparently implied something similar in declining to affirm, and perhaps briefly critiquing, closed universal causality (258, 277). Nonetheless, Yoder found historicism "congruent with the Bible" and today (306).

Yoder valued both Hellenistic cosmology/ontology and modern historicism for their missionary potential—for expressing the New Testament *kerygma* in different cultures. As far as I can see, he never regarded Hellenistic ontology as capable of affirming anything about transcendent reality. Yet while he seemingly did not endorse historicism entirely, Yoder appears to have thought it able to get at the way things are (ontologically) better at least than other conceptualities. Moreover, in passing Yoder seemingly implied something about the transcendent—in remarks about resurrection and history's culmination. More directly, he apparently denied predestination and affirmed something about eternity's and God's temporality, and perhaps a real distinction between God and the cosmos. *Preface to Theology* perhaps pointed weakly toward an historical kind of ontology, even if not all the way to reductive historicism.

THE POLITICS OF JESUS

Following our trek through *Preface to Theology*, consideration of Yoder's most popular book will seem brief. So far, I have found Yoder affirming the ontological reality (in the broad sense of the term) of the historical man Jesus and, more generally, of the historical process. I have unearthed no clear indication that any kind of language could refer ontologically to transcendent reality, for him.

Politics aimed to present Jesus as "the bearer of a new possibility of human, social, and therefore political relationships," and his cross as "the culmination of that new regime. . . . " Yoder added that "*At this one point*"—the cross—"there is no difference between . . . Christ as God and Jesus as man."[32]

Yoder claimed that while certain understandings of Jesus were often treated as incompatible in contemporary Christology, in his approach they were not. No longer, he insisted, do we need to *"choose between the Jesus of history and the Jesus of dogma,"* for "The Jesus of history is the Christ of Faith."[33] In fact, Yoder continued, as he would in his subsequent career, his view was "more radically Nicene and Chalcedonian than other views." For he was urging that "the implications of what the church has always said about Jesus as the Word of the Father, as true God and true Man, be taken more seriously . . . than ever before."[34]

In enlisting classical Christology, however, Yoder's main aim was to affirm Jesus' ethical, or anthropological, normativity. What, he asked rhetorically, "becomes the meaning of incarnation if Jesus is not normative man?"[35] For Yoder, the original point of incarnation was that "God broke through the borders of man's definition of what is human, and gave a new, formative definition."[36]

Did Yoder also mean to affirm the transcendent claims associated with the creeds? He did refer to "the claim to preexistence and cosmic preeminence for the divine Son or Word" in John, Hebrews, and Colossians. But he only mentioned, much as in *Preface*, their function of affirming "the exclusivity of the revelation claim they were making for Jesus."[37] Yoder considered carefully Colossians' Jesus, the one in whom "all things in heaven and on earth were created, things visible and invisible," and in whom "all things subsist" (1:15-17). Yet Yoder's sole aim was to show how Colossians' powers language could be translated "into the concepts of modern social science."[38] He did add that this concern "need not imply rejection" of more "literal" understandings of the demonic.[39] Yoder also affirmed the Trinity, but simply to deny that it legitimated any ethics of the Father and/or Spirit which would dilute the Son's. For the Trinity originally meant that the one God "is most adequately and bindingly known in Jesus."[40]

Overall, Yoder surely intended to affirm the creeds in *Politics*, hardly to trash them as Constantinian. As in *Preface*, he enlisted classical Christology to endorse Jesus' ethical and anthropological normativity. Yet I find no clear indication that Yoder affirmed this Christology's transcendent intentions. He did, however, explain in footnotes that his social interpretations of not only demonic powers, but also justification, were not meant to deny more traditional readings—and he reiterated this in later years.[41]

By 1972, classical Christology was taking on a meaningful role for Yoder, though not the centrality Carter claims. Yoder was unpacking some of its social-ethical implications, but hardly those transcendent ones Carter also finds "absolutely essential to the logic of his overall position."[42] Perhaps, as Carter suggests, Yoder stressed the first because his intended, mostly evangelical audience did not, and neglected the second because this audience assumed its importance.[43] Yoder, however, was still lecturing on *Preface*. If pressed, he likely would also have critiqued the creeds, and sounded ambiguous about their continuing transcendent (ontological) import.

"BUT WE DO SEE JESUS"

As postmodernity arrived, Yoder adopted much of its language, including its relativistic bent. Systematic theology, then, can ask this: How much a relativist had he been all along? Had transcendent Christology, for him, always been culturally bound to Hellenism, lacking commonalities with conceptualities relative to our culture?

In 1984 Yoder addressed what he called "pluralism/relativism" at some length. If we understand relativism in a strictly epistemological sense, he sometimes appeared to endorse it. Yoder insisted, for instance, that "To ask, 'Shall we talk in pluralist/relativist terms?' would be as silly as to ask in Greece, 'Shall we talk Greek?'" We should not, moreover, seek to shed "our own pluralist/ relativist skins," for within them we must "restate whatever our claims are."[44]

Yoder reviewed, and praised, the New Testament strategies discussed in *Preface* for affirming Jesus' ultimacy in different thought-worlds.[45] Yet "the last thing we should do," he concluded, would be to translate its notions (such as pre-existence) into our time. That would be like trying, with the bases loaded, to kick a field goal (1984: 56). Was he implying that Hellenism and our pluralistic/relativistic outlook are wholly incommensurable?

Yoder was actually using pluralism/relativism quite loosely. He meant it to indicate the process through which people whose beliefs rest on particular claims (such as early Christians, or believers churches) move into a wider world, and find these apparently relativized by that world's conflicting truth-claims and/or assertions of more universal truths (47-48). In endorsing pluralism/relativism, Yoder was advocating not an epistemology, but a strategy for resisting that wider world's dismissal of Christian beliefs—and also for presenting it with these beliefs.

How did this strategy operate? First, employ pluralism/relativism itself to deconstruct other claims to universal truth. For pluralism/relativism emerged from the church's challenge to absolutist pretentions of empires and kings (60). And so, when people critique Christian faith from an allegedly superior or more universal perspective, show that their position is no "less particular, more credible, less the product of [their own] social location" (46).

Second, pluralism/relativism denies any absolute standpoint beyond our historical world for judging truth. It views this world as an immanent, self-contained process (57), which Yoder called "historical" (59); in *Preface* he called it "historicism." Much as in *Preface*, Yoder recommended that Christians communicate their beliefs within this framework.

This was not because Yoder regarded historicism as necessarily true. He acknowledged that Christians might address pluralism/relativism by challenging it (58-59), much as, in *Preface*, he conceded the plausibility of disputing whether the cosmos was a closed, causal system. Yoder was simply encouraging Christians to become "tactical allies of the pluralist/relativist deconstruction," not to embrace it as a philosophical "monism" (61). In fact, he wanted "the message of Jesus" to actually collide "with our pluralist/relativist world." (56) Still, as in *Preface*, Yoder thought this would most likely occur if Christians articulated their message within their neighbors' everyday worldview, rather than discrediting it.

Yoder thought that Jesus' normativity, or universality, could be expressed in such historicist, pluralist/relativist terms: "We report an event which occurred in our listeners' own world and ask them to respond to it. What could be more universal than that?" (59). "For our world it will be in [Jesus'] ordinariness as villager, rabbi, as king on a donkey . . . " that we shall express what the apostles expressed "in the language of preexistence. . . ." Pluralism/relativism/historicism will enable us "to enter any world in which people eat bread and pursue debtors, hope for power and execute subversives." (62)

What does this article contribute to questions about Yoder's reductionism? Once again, historical claims were the ones to stress. Traditional transcendent claims were too culture-bound to merit translation into our culture, at least for practical purposes. It seems that Yoder did not embrace epistemological relativism, though at points he appeared to. Yet something quite close (pluralism/relativism) provided an excellent vehicle for communication, as did historicism, which could even affirm Jesus' universality. Perhaps this was consistent with some kind of historical ontology, though I do not find Yoder hinting at this here.

Yoder did not explicitly deny a transcendent ontological dimension (in the broad sense of the term). Perhaps he even accepted it. Several sermons published the next year suggest that he might have, for these treated pre-existence in traditional terms.[46] Still, I do not find Yoder even touching the issue of transcendence theologically. I cannot, with Carter, regard this essay as a chief expression of his high Christology.[47]

BODY POLITICS

To detect Yoder's perspective on transcendent reality, I have chiefly probed his Christology. Other clues emerge from his relatively late treatment of an activity where people often claim to encounter transcendence: worship.

Yoder began *Body Politics* by challenging "the vast qualitative distance" often thought to separate worship and church from ordinary life and politics.[48] Again one senses his strong desire that Christians live and communicate their faith through "concrete historical presence, among their neighbors. . . " (75, cf. 44). To encourage this linkage, Yoder considered five practices central enough to church life to perhaps be called "sacraments."

Yoder stressed, however, that these are simply "ordinary human behavior." They are "not mysterious." We do not need a theology of the sacraments, for they can be thoroughly studied by sociology (144, cf. 46, 72, 77). In discussing what he called "breaking bread together," Yoder denied that the New Testament could shed "*any* light on . . . much later eucharistic controversies" (1992: 15, italics Yoder's). More broadly, Yoder defined the church as a "'community held together by commitment to important values.'"[49]

Yoder began with *binding and loosing*—those procedures, outlined in Matthew 18, for what is often called church discipline. As Yoder described it, this was "not very different" from the "social science" of Conflict Resolution (11). He listed eight close parallels between the two (12).

Second, turning to *breaking bread together*, Yoder claimed that the practice initiated by Jesus at the Last Supper was simply the disciples' "*ordinary* partaking together of food for the body" (16, italics Yoder's). Every meal should be a eucharist, or act of thanksgiving (19). Yoder did not connect breaking bread with any formal ceremony.

Third, the "concrete, social-functional meaning" of *baptism* was incorporation into a new community, transcending all former social distinctions.[50] With a literalism oddly resembling transubstantiation, Yoder insisted that "breaking bread together *is* an economic act . . . baptism *is* the formation of a new people. . . " (33, italics Yoder's). Open housing is as much "'real presence'" as baptism (27).

Did these practices involve any transcendent, divine dimension? Employing traditional language, Yoder claimed that God was acting "'in, with and under'" the human acts.[51] Yet did this G-word add anything to Yoder's sociological descriptions? While it usually did not, it occasionally did, especially in his fourth practice, *the fullness of Christ*. Here each member in a group exercises a distinct, "divinely validated and empowered role" (47). Yoder clearly distinguished such roles from individual abilities and from "commercial and industrial models of cooperation. . . " (49). Further, when Yoder affirmed that any such role was "given by the Spirit," he meant that it was "dependent or derivative, not a reason for pride."[52]

In a few other places Yoder mentioned a practice being bestowed without merit, by grace (42, 55, cf. 57). He traced these practices ultimately to Jesus' ministry, or to "the intervention into history" called "incarnation."[53] Yoder did seem to think that in the communal gatherings he described, God's Spirit would guide in ways not wholly reducible to human interaction[54].

In *Body Politics*, Yoder turned his sharply focused ethical glasses on church practices to render them "public, accessible beyond the faith community." (44). Though he very often depicted them as "ordinary human behavior" (id.), this is the one work where I find him clearly referring to a transcendent dimension. Several references to the Spirit's guidance affirm something specific about transcendent reality that cannot be sufficiently expressed in terms of human (and/or subhuman) realities.[55]

CONCLUSIONS

(1) As Yoder's prestige increases, it will be tempting to support one's viewpoint by simply quoting him, or invoking his name. This may be appropriate in reference to those few themes where Yoder enunciated a straightforward position, such as that Jesus was "the bearer of a new possibility of human, social, and therefore political relationships" (*Politics*, 63). Yet most of his statements, especially on the topic of this essay, were probes, experiments, prods to consider things

in fresh ways. Variously combined, they can appear to endorse quite different positions. But using them this way is not only misuse, but avoidance of the challenges he raised.

(2) Can we maintain, with Carter, that "protecting, declaring, and unpacking the claims of classical Christology is what Yoder is about" (17)? If this means that Yoder carefully analyzed this Christology and explained how people today can understand those features, including the transcendent references, which seem problematic, I answer in the negative. Even if Yoder assumed some such references, he often gave the impression that they, or at least their familiar expressions, were culturally conditioned products of a bygone era.[56]

(3) Can we maintain, in contrast, that Yoder regarded the creeds mainly as Constantinian excrescences, largely incompatible with believers church Christology? No. Despite the creeds' lamentable omission of Jesus' life and teachings, he found their significance entailed in creedal affirmation of Jesus' full and normative humanity. Yoder clearly knew, and critiqued, the political factors attending creedal formulation. Had he thought that these irretrievably tainted the creeds, he could hardly have called all churches to take them more seriously.

(4) If one finds the creeds consistent with Jesus' way of peace, might one enlist Yoder in general support of this perspective? Certainly, for Yoder promoted it. He did not expect this to replace the radical Jesus with a bland ecumenical one but to hopefully lead toward ecumenical embrace of the radical Jesus. Yet one should cite Yoder only for pointing this direction, not for following it through in detailed theological fashion.

(5) To what extent were Yoder's affirmations reducible to ethics, or perhaps other fields or conceptualities whose terms refer exclusively to human (and/or subhuman) characteristics, activities, relationships and potentialities? The great majority of his affirmations provide no intrinsic reason to refer to anything beyond these domains. Yoder often treated historicist categories as adequate. Yet he did not endorse historicism as a comprehensive metaphysic. His very way of theologizing was incompatible with fully accepting any *-ism* or ontology, including a fully historicist one.

To what extent did Yoder's affirmations incorporate a reality transcending these? and if some did, in what ways? Yoder, particularly in *Preface to Theology*, seems to have denied predestination and affirmed something about the historicity of Jesus' resurrection and the eschaton, about temporal aspects of God and eternity, and perhaps a real distinction between God and the universe. Yet even if these assertions pointed weakly toward an historical (not historicist) ontology, I know of no real evidence that he maintained any of them later on. I have discovered no clear affirmation of, or even strong implication concerning, any transcendent dimension of Christology—that is, any reference specific enough that it cannot be sufficiently expressed in terms of human (and/or subhuman) realities. This, of course does not entail that Yoder denied any such reference. I have, however, found one kind of transcendent affirmation: to the Holy Spirit's activity in genuine Christian communities (in *Body Politics*).

(6) Yoder did explicitly endorse historicism—as a tool of missionary communication (as he did pluralism/relativism). He assumed that people of his day were so conditioned by this outlook that talk of realities transcending it would impede the gospel. I am proposing, however, that interest in transcendent reality is strong today, and that inability to speak of it will often hinder mission. To enhance the missions and lives of believers churches, I am encouraging their theologians to articulate biblical language about spiritual and transcendent reality in light of contemporary conceptualities—without instinctively assuming that these are incommensurable, or immediately reducing the former for fear of losing the social-ethical. Believers church theologians can do so with gratitude for Yoder, and perhaps his blessing. But he gave us very little specific help in this task. We will need to break our own paths.

NOTES

1. Gordon Kaufman, *In Face of Mystery* (Cambridge, Mass.: Harvard 1993), 4.

2. This, of course, is my own understanding of systematic or constructive theology. Some may disagree, such as theologians who do not analyze contemporary conceptualities explicitly, and/or reject efforts to find points of contact with them (e.g., Karl Barth). I suggest, however, that the above features will appear somewhere in their work.

3. Not all theologians will conclude that a transcendent or spiritual realm exists. Kaufman, for instance, argues that theology should "refrain from postulating an . . . 'other world' at all," but instead "construct conceptions . . . of humanity, the world, and God . . . only in terms of *this world*" (1993: 325-326). *Christ*, for instance, refers to not a pre-existent, divine Son, but the story of Jesus and his earliest followers: to this "whole complex transformative reality" of announcing God's kingdom, healing, forgiving, loving enemies and championing the poor (383). This Christ reveals the overall direction of *bio-history*, which includes a mysterious dimension that can be called God the *Fa-*

ther (415-416). Yet this Father, transcendence, and bio-history exist nowhere but in the realm of *matter-energy*. Kaufman, that is, consistently *reduces* "God" and "Christ" to that realm.

Other believers church theologians speak of a distinctly spiritual dimension. James McClendon begins Christology with "the Risen One who confronts us here and now, today" in worship, work and witness. This awareness of Jesus' risen "Presence opens up the way for the understanding of the Person." *Systematic Theology: Doctrine* (Nashville, Tenn.: Abingdon, 1994), 239. McClendon's ethic is patterned after Jesus, much like Kaufman's. Yet it can be actualized only in company with the Risen One "who works in, with, and through our own working." *Systematic Theology: Ethics* (Nashville, Tenn.: Abingdon 1986), 243.

4. A. James Reimer, *Mennonites and Classical Theology* (Kitchener, Ontario: Pandora Press, 2001), 296.

5. Ibid., esp. 168-173. I will be using *historicism* in the reductive sense that Reimer apparently intends, where history, whose agents never transcend the human sphere, is "the categorical matrix for all meaning and value" and allows "no room for events with transcendent causes or foundations." This is J. Alexander Sider's formulation in his review of Reimer's *Mennonites and Classical Theology* in *Mennonite Quarterly Review* 76:1 (January 2002), 138.

6. Craig Carter, *The Politics of the Cross* (Grand Rapids: Brazos, 2001), 127.

7. Yoder sometimes applied this term to his efforts in *Preface to Theology.* Perhaps most precisely stated, he saw himself "beginning in the historical mode and moving toward the systematic." John Howard Yoder, *Preface to Theology* (Grand Rapids: Brazos, 2002), 35.

8. Carter, op. cit. 17; "I argue not only that Yoder affirms classical orthodox Christology, rather than reducing theology to ethics and spirituality to politics, but also that such a catholic affirmation is absolutely essential to the logic of his overall position (27, cf. 23).

9. Chris Huebner points out that using categories like these in interpreting Yoder can obscure the specific, *ad hoc* character of what he meant to say. Yoder often responded to issues by deconstructing the terms in which they were phrased and suggesting a different vantage-point. "Globalization, Theory and Dialogical Vulnerability: John Howard Yoder and the Possibility of a Pacifist Epistemology," *Mennonite Quarterly Review* 76:1 (2002), esp. 56-58.

I am phrasing my questions like this, first, because these are often asked of Yoder, although he did not put them this way, and I find them important. Second, theology can ask, from its broad horizon, whether a theologian actually operated in a certain manner, even if that theologian denied it. Third, and most important, I will use these questions as *hypotheses*, to provide an initial framework for approaching Yoder. They could well be revised as we proceed, which would amount to rephrasing the questions (showing that they were not really the best).

By searching for affirmations with specifiable content, I am not implying that such language is the only, or even the best, for theology. Language has many functions. This does not discredit, but rather encourages, examining one particular function, so long as one does not uncritically assume its priority.

10. See esp. "Walk and Word: Alternatives to Methodologism" in *Theology Without Foundations*, ed. Stanley Hauerwas, Nancey Murphy, and Mark Thiessen Nation (Nashville, Tenn.: Abingdon, 1994), 77-90; also Yoder, *The Priestly Kingdom* (Notre Dame, Ind.: Notre Dame, 1984) 7, 71, 114, 127.

11. Carter, op. cit. 225. From extensive reading of Yoder's work, Carter finds him "a very systematic and logical thinker" (18). It is "undeniable" that Yoder "has a system;" he probably pushed his "critique of `methodologism. too far" (235). One "cannot evade the systematic questions by refusing to write a systematic book" (235). Carter believes that by avoiding the systematic challenge, "Mennonite/Anabaptist (or Radical Reformation or believers church)" people magnify the common impression that it is too sectarian to be "a viable option for mainstream Christianity" (19, cf. 235). I am neither affirming nor denying Carter's claim about Yoder, but simply indicating that the issue is too complex for this essay.

12. I have not examined Yoder's treatment of Jesus' resurrection and Lordship in detail, though I have begun to (cf. n.15 below). This was central to Yoder's theology, and clearly entailed the ultimacy of Jesus' life and teachings in social-ethical matters (cf. Carter 145-150, 157-164). My question might be further pursued by asking whether Yoder clearly ascribed some transcendent meaning to it.

13. Yoder, *Preface to Theology*, 73, cf. 125. (Following page references in the body of this essay are to this source.)

14. Yoder often claimed that they were not at the center of Christian life in the first two centuries (Preface, 62, 93, etc) Yet he did not want to drive a wedge between them and the Synoptic gospels (95-96, 141).

15. Paul, for instance, when confronted in Corinth with denial of the bodily resurrection, expounded on it at length and showed that rejecting it entailed rejecting the entire kerygma. Though such theologizing had not been done at the *primitive* or *uncritical* level, Yoder regarded it as necessary, Spirit-directed and consistent with the Jesus story. *Preface to Theology*, 97-99.

It would seem that Yoder was regarding Jesus' resurrection as an historical, physical event. Later on he seemed to favor its plausibility (172-173). He affirmed that the "virgin birth" was "First of all a question of history . . . about what really happened" (168). Yet Yoder did not specifically affirm either (164-173). Under eschatology, Yoder stressed the importance of bodily resurrection in Scripture (e.g., 252-253, 276). Yet regarding its ultimate meaning, "It is not the purpose of our preface course to give answers" (275). See my discussion of this eschatology below. Carter, who promotes Yoder's orthodoxy, cites only one Yoderian affirmation of Jesus' bodily resurrection (Carter , op. cit., 70, n.42).

16. Yoder, *Preface to Theology*, 186. Yoder also claimed that Hebrews extended the concept Son "in two directions," to "identity with the Father" and to "being identified with humankind. . . " (117).

17. Ibid., 121. Precisely, it guarded against "denial that the Word became flesh"; it affirmed *incarnation*, or "the making visible of God in our life."

18. Ibid., 124. Moreover, Jesus, in "the early story is too unexplainable, too unique . . . to have been only another human like others from the beginning." It was "not enough to explain what he did" (124, cf. 182-183, 186).

19. Ibid., 134; the early church could speak of Jesus in terms normally reserved for God (182).

20. Ibid., 130. Whereas the pagan world would fit Jesus within the cosmos, these apostles "put Jesus *above it*" (italics Yoder's).

21. Ibid., 186; or to affirm "the New Testament concept. . . . that Jesus, the Word in Jesus, is genuinely of the character of deity and genuinely human, and that his work is the work of God and yet the work of a man" (138). Jesus must be "equal to God (sharing God's capacity to save us) and different from God. . . " (201).

22. E.g. Ibid., 191. Among other criteria were the distinct character and quality of the *logos* independently of the cosmos and before Jesus (190), and avoidance of subordination of the *logos* to the Father (191-192). Yoder affirmed, however, that the full incarnation of a *Logos*/Wisdom equal to God was unproblematic from a Jewish standpoint. The problem only arose from the Greek notion of a "metaphysical" or "philosophical absolute" difficult to combine with the humanity of Jesus (183).

23. Ibid., 201, 202; Nicea "provided the best answer to an intellectual problem" (205).

24. The Trinity provides "a test of whether your commitments to Jesus and to God are biblical enough that you have the problem the doctrine of the Trinity solves." Ibid., 204. Yoder could critique satisfaction theories of atonement for being "counter to the meaning of the doctrine of the Trinity" (304).

25. Rather than *divinization*, or "being made somehow Godlike," Ibid., 213, "by obedience, by faith, by accepting the gift of the Spirit. . . " (215), which Yoder apparently affirmed.

26. Yoder, like many critics of Chalcedon, faulted it mainly for overstressing Christ's deity at the expense of his humanity (e.g. McClendon, *Systematic Theology: Doctrine*, 256-257). But this is to employ Chalcedon's own criterion: that the humanity and deity should be equally balanced. Chalcedon's *intent* seems to function as a crucial Christological norm precisely in such efforts to critique its formulation and/or impact.

27. At one point on his path to Nicea, in discussing *patripassianism*, Yoder proposed that identifying God's works directly with Jesus' work led toward

identifying all of God's works with God, and hence to *pantheism*. On the other hand, separating God too sharply from Jesus led toward *deism*. Yoder was contrasting valid Christian affirmations from these two philosophies. Was he also least implying something ontological about the God-world relationship? Perhaps. Yet he prefaced these remarks by cautioning "we are talking about the documents, without committing ourselves to specific systematic-philosophical concerns." *Preface to Theology*, 188.

28. Yoder could say that "The assumptions that the universe is closed, that we know where its edges run and nothing is ever going to come in over those edges, do not fit the biblical understandings of creation and providence;" however, he immediately added, "at least as we could normally read them." Ibid., 277.

29. Ibid., 256. Yoder included that God "intervenes in history for our sake. . . " (256). Yet the next paragraph began the discussion of "'divine intervention'" that I am reporting. Yoder concluded by comparing his recommendation of closed causal conceptuality for *missionary* purposes with the New Testament's development of *pre-existence* for the same purpose (258).

30. Ibid., 276; yet Yoder also emphasized the realized dimension of eschatology (277-278).

31. Yoder 2002: 306. Reimer (171) quotes this passage and remarks, "Here Yoder shows his true colours."

32. Yoder, *The Politics of Jesus* (Grand Rapids, Eerdmans: 1972, 2nd. ed. 1994), 63.

33. Ibid., 106, 107.

34. Ibid., 105; later on he would call his main emphasis "compatible with the classic confession of the true humanity of Christ (i.e., the *core meaning* of *'incarnation'*)"; to regard Jesus as exemplary was a "necessary correlate of . . . divine sonship (the other side of *'incarnation'*)" so that those who minimize his example become ebionitic (1984: 9).

35. Yoder, *Politics of Jesus* 1972, 22; *Politics* 1994 (2nd. ed.), 10.

36. Yoder, *Politics* 1972, 101.

37. Ibid.

38. Ibid., 140.

39. Even though these were "quite distinct" from his sociological readings, as noted in Yoder, *Politics* 1972, 141-142 n.3. Yoder also denied that Colossians envisioned a cosmic Christ different enough from the historic Jesus that He sanctioned "general acceptance by God of the nature and structures of this world," and thereby "an ethic of world-affirmation" at odds with Jesus' teachings (102).

40. Yoder, *Politics* 1972, 101, cf. 103-104. Interestingly, somewhat as Yoder granted some validity to the *divinization* in *Preface*, in *Politics* he could call "Sharing the divine nature" one "definition of Christian existence" (118). He also affirmed the theme of being "in Christ" (120-121), noting that biblical *imi-*

tation language is "perhaps mystical," though he described it more precisely as affirming "an inner or formal parallelism of character and intent. . . " (117).

41. Yoder, *Politics* 1972, 232, *Politics* 1994, 226: Yoder added that this paragraph should perhaps have been placed more prominently (1994, 227); cf. 1972, 218-219, 141-142. See also Yoder, *For the Nations* (Grand Rapids: Eerdmans, 1997), 138, esp. n.26; and Carter's comments on these passages in *The Politics of the Cross*, 130.

42. Ibid., 27, cf. 17.

43. Ibid., 128-129. For Carter's overall treatment of the reductionism issue, see 113-136.

44. Yoder, "But We Do See Jesus," *The Priestly Kingdom*, 56 (following page references in the body of this essay are to this source). We should not ask whether Christianity could be supported in some universal way, or be "kept dry above the waves of relativity" (57).

45. John, Hebrews, Colossians, and also Revelation 4:1-5:4 and Philippians 2; Yoder, *The Priestly Kingdom*, 48-54.

46. Yoder, *He Came Preaching Peace* (Scottdale, Pa.: Herald, 1985), 72-88.

47. Carter, 65-66. I do find Yoder making several strong relativist claims: e.g. alleged universal truths on the far side of *Lessing's Ditch* are simply "not there . . . the less narrow truth over there is still also provincial" (*The Priestly Kingdom*, 59); there is no place "less particular . . . less the product of one's own social location" than another (46); "There is no road" to the "universality of the good" but Yoder's "low road" of particularity (62). Yet I do not find him convincing. From what vantage-point could he know that *all* thought-worlds are particular? As far as I can see, only a universal one. Yoder seems to be tacitly presupposing such a vantage-point, which entails the self-contradiction of all relativism: the affirmation that all perspectives are relative is itself an absolute statement.

I also do not agree with Yoder's claim that universality can be found within an immanent historicist framework. For by its very nature, everything therein is conditioned by and relative to everything else. Perhaps Yoder sought to avoid this by being a "thoroughgoing" historicist at every point *but* the incarnation, as Carter claims (113; cf. *The Priestly Kingdom*, 62): "The truth has come to our side of the ditch." But how convincing will this exception sound to people drawn into conversation by the common assumption of a shared historicist commitment? That raises questions about historicism's viability as a language for mission.

48. Yoder, *Body Politics* (Nashville, Tenn: Discipleship Resources, 1992) vi-vii, cf. 14, 75 (following page references in the body of this essay are to this source).

49. Yoder, *Body Politics*, 81 n.4. Elsewhere he defined worship as "communal cultivation of an alternative construction of society and of history." (1984: 43) In *Body Politics* Yoder seemed to be debunking common affective understandings of worship (vii). Yet he characterized his five practices as doxology,

celebratory and mandatory (72). In his 1985 sermons, Yoder acknowledged the reality of faith's inward side (*He Came Preaching Peace,* 103) and the divine initiative (105). His early work, *The Christian Witness to the State* (Newton, Kan.: Faith and Life Press, 1965) affirmed the divine initiative (9) along with personal salvation (11)

50. Yoder, *Body Politics,* 28 cf. 32-33. Yoder added that this new kind of belonging "provokes subjective faith" and apparently called this being "born again" (30). The apostles called that change in identity and behavior which baptism celebrates *repentance,* but "whether people feel guilt may not be so important" (42).

51. Ibid., 1, 48, 71. "The community's action is God's action" (3; cf. 6, 13, 44).

52. Ibid., 51. Paul taught that this *fullness* had not functioned previously, but was "achieved by Christ" (49). Nevertheless, it could "be translated into terms outsiders could understand to deal with role relationships in" other groups (50). Yoder also mentioned the Spirit's leading in his fifth practice, *the rule of Paul,* where each member contributes to group meetings (61-63), though I do not find the Spirit's role there clearly trans-human. He connected peoples 'ability to practice this with George Fox' "'that of God in every person'" (68).

53. Ibid., 77. A "closeness to Jesus" was brought about by the cross, which "does not do without" the Spirit and Father (45). This seems to imply some distinct transcendent dimension.

54. "The point at which the divine empowerment is crucial" is "trusting the Spirit's leading in contextual application." Through this we can be "guided and enabled by God's own presence." (9) In the fifth practice, *the rule of Paul,* anarchy will be avoided by any group which "yields sovereignty to the direction of [Jesus'] spirit [sic]. . . " (70).

55. The statement mentioned in note 53 strongly implies something distinctly transcendent. Carter (204) stresses the Spirit's role in *Body Politics,* and a "weak occasionalism" in Yoder's overall social theology. Carter defends Yoder against reductionistic charges, while acknowledging that this treatment was incomplete (196-201). Carter's case involves the claim that Yoder was assuming a Barthian outlook without stating it (194 n.51, cf. 202). I find this somewhat plausible, but am reluctant to affirm it without more evidence from Yoder's writings. Carter adds that Yoder's social theology was based on "justification by grace through faith" (204).

56. Carter, 17.

Select Bibliography of the Writings of John Howard Yoder

"Adjusting to the Changing Shape of the Debate on Infant Baptism." In *Oecumennisme: Essays in Honor of Dr. Henk Kossen*, ed. Arie Lambo, 210-214. Amsterdam: Algemene Doopsgezinde Societeit, 1989.

"Anabaptist Vision and Mennonite Reality." In *Consultation on Anabaptist-Mennonite Theology: Papers Read at the 1969 Aspen Conference*, ed. A. J. Klassen, 1-46. Fresno, Calif.: Council of Mennonite Seminaries, 1970.

"Armaments and Eschatology." *Studies in Christian Ethics* 1 (1988), 43-61.

"Body Politics: Five Practices of the Christian Community before the Watching World. Nashville, Tenn.: Discipleship Resources, 1992.

"Christian Attitudes to War, Peace and Revolution: A Companion to Bainton. Elkhart, Ind.: Co-op Bookstore, 1983. (Available in photocopied form from Cokesbury Book Store, Duke Divinity School, Duke University, Durham, N.C.)

"Confessing Jesus in Mission." Unpublished English version, "Jezus belijden in de zending," *Wereld en Zending* 25 (1996), 13-21. *Unpublished, Out-of-Print and Hard-To-Find Writings of John Howard Yoder*, ed. Martha Yoder Maust. N.D. Ind., Notre Dame U. Oct. 31, 2003. http://www.nd.edu/~theo/jhy/writings/christology/confessing.htm.

"Exodus and Exile: Two Faces of Liberation." *Crosscurrents* (Fall 1973): 279-309.

For the Nations: Essays Public and Evangelical. Grand Rapids, Mich.: Wm B. Eerdmans, 1997.

He Came Preaching Peace. Scottdale, Pa.: Herald Press, 1985.

"How H. Richard Niebuhr Reasons: A Critique of Christ and Culture." In *Authentic Transformation: A New Vision of Christ and Culture,* ed. Glen H. Stassen, 31-89. Nashville, Tenn.: Abingdon, 1996.

"How Many Ways Are There to Think Morally About War?" *Journal of Law and Religion* 11.1 (1994), 83-107.

"Meaning After Babble: With Jeffrey Stout Beyond Relativism." *Journal of Religious Ethics* 24 (Spring 1996) 125-139.

Nevertheless: The Varieties and Shortcomings of Religious Pacifism. Rev. ed. Scottdale, Pa.: Herald Press, 1992.

"Noah's Covenant and the Purpose of Punishment." In *Readings in Christian Ethics,* Vol. 2: *Issues and Applications,* ed. David K. Clark and Robert V. Rakestraw, 471-481. Grand Rapids, Mich.: Baker Book House, 1996.

"On Not Being Ashamed of the Gospel: Particularity, Pluralism, and Validation." *Faith and Philosophy* 9 (July 1992), 285-300.

"On Not Being in Charge." In *War and Its Discontents: Pacifism and Quietism in the Abrahamic Traditions,* ed. J. Patout Burns, 74-90. Washington, D.C.: Georgetown University Press, 1996.

"Patience as Method in Moral Reasoning: Is an Ethic of Discipleship 'Absolute'?" In *Wisdom of the Cross: Essays in Honor of John Howard Yoder,* ed. Stanley Hauerwas, et. al. Grand Rapids: Eerdmans, 1999.

Preface to Theology: Christology and Theological Method. Grand Rapids: Brazos, 2002.

"Reinhold Niebuhr and Christian Pacifism. " *Mennonite Quarterly Review* 29 (April 1955), 101-117.

"The Case for Punishment." Unpublished, 1995. *Unpublished, Out-of-Print and Hard-To-Find Writings of John Howard Yoder,* ed. Martha Yoder Maust. N.D. Notre Dame University. October 31, 2003. http://www.nd.edu/~theo/jhy/writings/home/ind-punish.htm>. Available also as "You Have It Coming: Good Punishment. The Legitimate Social Function of Punitive Behavior." Notre Dame, Ind.: Shalom Desktop Publishing, 1995.

The Christian Witness to the State. Wipf and Stock Publishers, 1997. Originally published by Newton, Kan.: Faith and Life Press, 1964/1977.

"The Ecumenical Movement and the Faithful Church." Focal Pamphlet No. 3. Scottdale, Pa.: Herald Press, 1958.

The Jewish-Christian Schism Revisited, ed. Michael Cartwright and Peter Ochs. Grand Rapids: Eerdmans, 2003. Originally *The Jewish-Christian Schism Revisited: A Bundle of Old Essays.* Elkhart, Ind.: Shalom Desktop Publications, 1996.

The Original Revolution: Essays on Christian Pacifism. Scottdale, Pa.: Herald Press, 1971.

The Politics of Jesus: Vicit Agnus Noster. Rev. 2nd ed. Grand Rapids, Mich.: Wm. B. Eerdmans, 1994.

The Priestly Kingdom: Social Ethics As Gospel. Notre Dame, Ind.: University of Notre Dame Press, 1984.

The Royal Priesthood: Essays Ecclesiological and Ecumenical, ed. Michael G. Cartwright. Grand Rapids, Mich.: Wm. B. Eerdmans, 1994.

To Hear the Word. Eugene, Ore.: Wipf and Stock, 2001.

"Walk and Word: The Alternatives to Methodologism." In *Theology Without Foundations: Religious Practice and The Future of Theological Truth,* ed. Stanley Hauerwas, Nancey Murphy and Mark T. Nation. Nashville, Tenn.: Abingdon Press, 1994.

"War as a Moral Problem in the Early Church: The Historian's Hermeneutical Assumptions." In *The Pacifist Impulse in Historical Perspective,* ed. Harvey L. Dyck, 90-110. Toronto, Ont.: University of Toronto Press, 1996.

When War Is Unjust: Being Honest in Just War Thinking. Rev. ed. Maryknoll, N.Y.: Orbis Books, 1996.

The Index

A

Abu-Sitta, Salman, 172
Acculturation of early church, 130
Acts and Luke, civil authorities in, 262-267
Adorno, Theodor, 170-171, 177
Allison, Dale C., Jr., 260
Anabaptists, 17. *See also* Mennonites, believers church, historic peace churches
  contemporary, 40-41, 194-195, 262, 324
  early, 92, 250, 307
  and Postmodernity Conference, 40
Anselm's Satisfaction theory, 302-316
  arguments for and against, 304-309, 313, 315
  humanitarian objections to, 308
  Reesor-Taylor's defense of, 312-315
Anti-Semitism, 251
Antonine Constitution (Roman Empire), 130-131
Apocalyptic theology, 275-278
Apollinarianism, 323-324
Aquinas, Thomas, 40, 247, 254
Arianism, 104, 133-135, 324
Aristotelian view of institutions, 247, 254
Associated Mennonite Biblical Seminary, 296-297
Atonement, 278, 281, 303-315. *See also* Anselm's Satisfaction theory
Audience as element of rhetoric, 43
Augustine of Hippo, 15, 30, 46, 52, 132, 247, 284
  on benefits of state church, 97

City of God, 128, 223-237
  ecclesiology of, 223-224
  persecution of heretics, 110-111
  political thought of, 222-227
  view of institutions, 254
  witness, 221-237
  and Yoder compared, 232-235
Aulen, Gustaf, 304

B

Babel, Tower of, 153-154, 164, 251
Baptism, 48-51, 149, 194,196, 216, 331
  believers church, 106, 113, 192
  in Christendom, 101, 189
  of Constantine, 129
  of Jesus, 289
Barnes, T. D., 134
Barns, Ian, 189
Barth, Karl, 26, 39, 42, 58, 166, 249, 252, 284
Barton, Stephen, 296
Baudrillard, Jean, 60
Beker, J. Christiaan, 275
Believers church. See also baptism
  Believers Church Conference, 194
  ecclesiology, 48-50, 248, 251-252
  features in common with Jewish Diaspora, 146-151
  language of transcendence in, 333
  systematic theology in, 318, 320, 321
Bender, H. S., 249
Berkhof, Hendrik, 133
Beskow, Per, 133
Bethel College, 145, 147, 149
Bienenberg Consultation, 126-127
Biesecker-Mast, Gerald, 16
Bluffton College, 40
Blum, Peter C., 13-14
Bonhoeffer, Dietrich, 248

Boniface, Count, 226
Boyle, Nicholas, 210
Brandon, S. G. F., 288, 293
Burckhardt, Jacob, 129, 132

C
Calvin, John, 197, 284
Canon, NT, development of, 254-255
Canonical interpretation, 256-259
Capital punishment, 310
Caracalla's edict, 130
Carter, Craig, 44-45, 188, 205, 320-321, 328-332
Cartwright, Michael, 41-42, 48, 50, 188, 190, 197-198, 213
Cassidy, Richard, 293
Chalcedonian Creed, 45, 323-324, 327
Christendom, 89, 113, 116, 146, 211, 280
    Jewish critique of, 165-166
    priesthood within, 106-107
    as vision of *shalom*, 115
Christian Century, 236
Christocentrism, 251
Christology, 41, 96, 134, 235, 281, 321-333
    Alexandrian, 323-324
    classical, 321-322, 327, 332
    as rhetoric, 42-47
Church. *See also* believers church; historic peace churches
    as alternative community, 215-217, 248
    as basis of knowledge, 26-26, 33
    Constantinian, 28-29, 99-100, 104-108, 113-114
    as interpretive community, 33-34, 188
    invisibility of, 29, 128, 189, 223. of
    as new social order, 277-278
    practices of, 195, 213-215, 330-331
    pre-Constantinian, 104, 115-116
    reform of, 112
    transcendence within, 333
    visibility of, 41, 62, 64, 86,104, 113

and world, 94, 102, 188-191, 217-218. *See also* witness; mission of the church
    duality of, 231-232
    Hauerwas on, 208-209
City of God. See Augustine of Hippo
Civil institutions, theology of, 15, 245-271
Coercion, 48, 110-111
Coles, Romand, 12
Collins, John J., 268
Colonization, 61
Colossians, 307, 322, 324, 327
Communication, 43, 46-49, 59, 84, 212
Community, Christian. *See* church
Concern Group, 250, 252
Confession, freedom of, 192
Connolly, William, 63-64
Conscience, public, minorities as, 110-113
Constantine, Roman emperor, 92, 132
    at Nicea, 93, 103-104
    praised by Eusebius, 97-98
    as symbol and legend, 128-129
Constantinian shift, 92-93, 99-107. *See also* Constantinianism
    Hauerwas's commentary on, 189
    impact of, on order of canon, 255
    motivations for, 96-102
    sociological changes of, 104-105
    Yoder's analysis of, 128-134, 138
Constantinianism, 15, 84, 89-116. *See also* Constantinian shift
    compared to Virilio's Pure War, 61-62
    defined and described, 92, 108, 128, 189
    ecclesiology of, 109, 127-128
    and ethics, 101, 135, 153, 156
    and instrumental reasoning, 154-155
    methodological, 28-31, 69
    in modernity, 95, 207-211
        neo-Constantinianism, 92, 103, 107

neo-neo-Constantinianism, 207
overemphasis on, 156
as paradigm for civilization, 102-103
terminology of, 89, 92, 94, 113-115,156
Continuity
of Hebrew and Christian Scriptures, 250-255
of Jesus with Torah, 260
Conversion, 216, 218
Conzelmann, Hans, 293
Cosmology, Hellenistic, 322-326
Courts of law, secular, 267
Creation, theology of, 235, 254
Creeds, ecumenical, 41-46, 50, 134, 324, 327-328, 332. *See also* Nicene Creed, Chalcedonian Creed
Cullman, Oscar, 293, 321
Cultural engagement, Jewish, 228
Cur Deus Homo. See Anselm's Satisfaction theory
Cyprian, 130

D
D'Costa, Gavin, 268
Daniel, book of, 149, 227, 253, 282
Darwish, Mahmoud, 161-162, 172-173
Davies, W. D., 260
Decius, Roman emperor, 131
Deconstructionism, 77, 153
Deleuze, Gilles, 61
Demonic powers, 327, 113, 297
Denck, Hans, 83, 307
Derrida, Jacques, 13-14, 76-86
Descartes, René, 26, 27, 79
Deuteronomic problem, 15, 84, 114, 116. *See also* Schlabach, Gerald, living rightly in the land
Deuteronomy, 164, 173, 290
Diaspora. *See* Judaism, Diaspora
Differance, 80. See also Derrida, Jacques
Digeser, Elizabeth DePalma, 130-131

Diocletian, Roman emperor, 98, 131, 132
Diognetus, Epistle to, 148
Dissent, 103, 110-111
Divine speech, 43, 46-47
Dodd, C. H., 321
Doerksen, Paul, 16
Donfried, Karl, 277
Drake, H. A. (Hal), 98, 135
Driver, John, 303-304, 309, 310
Dualism of church and world, 155, 208-209, 231-232

E
Ecclesiology, 28, 92-95, 109, 130, 136-139, 229
Augustine's, 223-224, 230
Constantinian, 109, 127-128, 114, 129,
diaspora, 64-65, 145, 151
exile as formative for, 162-166
free church, 194, 251-252
nonviolent, 42, 48-50, 64-65, 166, 188-189
Pauline, 284
Ecumenical councils. *See* Chalcedonian Creed; creeds, ecumenical; Nicea, Council of; Nicene Creed;
Ecumenical dialogue, 52, 126, 139. *See also* unity, Christian
Edict of Milan, 98, 128
Edict of toleration, 98
Effectiveness, 32, 61-62, 70-71, 110, 248
Eliot, T. S., 76
Eller, Vernard, 27
Elliott, Neil, 277
Ellis, Marc, 176-178
Emeritus, Augustine's letters to, 97
Enlightenment, 95-96, 115, 130, 153, 175, 212
and Constantinianism, 207-209
methodologies, 25-29
view of civil institutions, 254
Epistemology

crisis of, 216-217
of peace, 23, 35, 44, 66-67, 82, 111
violent, 25
Eschatology, 27, 102, 114, 223, 229-231, 275-277, 325
Esther, book of, 149, 282
Eucharist, 50, 196-197, 214, 265, 296, 330
Eusebius, 97, 100, 101, 105, 128-129, 132
Evangelism, 297. *See also* mission of the church
Evil, 85, 297
Exile, 161-179 *See also* homelessness; peace of the city
    Babylonian, 163-164, 221
    as dependence on YHWH, 164
    destructiveness of, 168-169
    Diaspora as, 165
    as metaphor, 170
    as opportunity, 163-165, 171-172, 228
    and nonviolence, 165
    return from, 162, 172-177, 282
    as vision for the church, 163-164
Exodus, book of, 164, 269
Ezra-Nehemiah, 253-255, 282

F
Faith and faithfulness in Pauline theology of, 278-281
Finger, Thomas, 16
First principles, 26, 69
Fodor, James, 42
Foucault, Michel, 14, 61, 78, 82
Foundationalism, 27, 33, 153, 188, 208. *See also* methodologism
Francis of Assisi, 102
Free church. *See* believers church
Freedom of religion, 48, 128. See also voluntarism.
Friesen, Duane K., 15, 96, 102

G
Gadamer, Hans-Georg, 137-138
Galatians, 275-279

Galerius, Roman emperor, 98, 132
Garrett, Susan, 290, 295
Genesis, 253, 257. *See aso* Babel, Tower of
Gemara, 150
Georgi, Dieter, 277
Gibson, Jeffrey, 290
Gift
    Christian life as, 34-36
    truthfulness as, 66
    witness as, 70-72
Gilman, Sander, 174
Grace. *See* gift
Greek philosophy, ancient 90, 100. *See also* Socrates; Stoicism
Gustafson, James, 212

H
Habiby, Emile, 177
Harink, Douglas, 15, 205
Harnack, Adolf von, 304, 313
Hauerwas, Stanley, 16-17, 48, 186-198, 205-218, 259
    on Constantinianism, 93-96, 101
    on spirituality of peaceableness, 236-237
    on theology of witness, 39-43
Hays, Richard B., 260-262, 278-280, 296
Hebrew Scriptures, 250-259
Hebrews, book of, 107, 307, 311, 322, 324, 327
Hegel, Georg Wilhelm Friedrich, 27, 28
Heidegger, Martin, 78
Heilke, Thomas, 15
Herbert the Snail, 75, 85
Historic peace churches, 126-127, 139, 246-247. *See also* Mennonites
Historicism, 326, 329, 332
Historiography, 15, 128, 135-139
History, meaning of, 130, 146-147, 232, 254
Hobbes, Thomas, 91
Homelessness, 145-157, 170-171

vs. landedness, 174
Horsley, Richard, 277
Hovey, Craig R., 16
Hubmaier, Balthasar, 83
Huebner, Chris K., 11, 14, 44, 154
Huebner, Harry, 16
Human agency, relinquishing of, 32
Hume, David, 91
Hunter, Carol M., 147
Husserl, Edmund, 78

I
Imitation of Christ, 280
Imperial expansion, 97
Incarnation, 26, 46, 137, 152, 223, 314, 327, 331
Inclusion of Christians in Roman Empire, 98
Individualism, 49, 108, 168, 192-194
Infowar (information in warfare), 59-60
Institutions, theology of, 247-248
Instrumental reasoning, 155, 197
Interreligious dialogue, 46, 268
Irenaeus, 254
Isaiah, 252, 288, 290-293
Israel
    God's election of, 283-284
    modern state of, 147, 167. *See also* Zionism

J
James, William, 39
Janzen, Waldemar, 252, 256-259, 262
Jeremiah 29:7 (word to exiles). *See* peace of the city.
Jesus, Yoder's portrait of, 288-291
    evidence supporting, 293-294
    exegetical weaknesses, 289-293
    missing aspects, 294-296
Jewish-Christian relations, 283-284
John, Gospel of, 47, 262, 307, 322, 324, 327
John Paul II, Pope, 40, 52
Johnsson, William G., 292
Jouvenel, Bertrand de, 108

Joyce, James, 169
Jubilee, 15, 178, 252, 288-297
Judaism, 14, 15. *See also* Zionism; Israel; Jewish-Christian Relations
    assimilation of, in U. S., 176
    Diaspora, 145-151
        and cultural engagement, 228
        and mission, 65, 149, 228
        as model for church, 64-66, 148-151, 251-252, 281-284
        reversal of, 175
        second-temple, as prototype for world order, 252-255
Juhnke, James C., 147
"Just Peacemaking (study paper, Historic Peace Churches," 127
Just war tradition, 67-68, 230, 247
Justice and pacifism, 127
Justification, Pauline concept of, 278-280

K
Kant, Immanuel, 29, 91, 108
Käsemann, Ernst, 275
Kautz, Jacob, 307
Kierkegaard, Søren, 27, 78
King, Martin Luther, Jr., 248, 269
Kraus, C. Norman, 310
Kroeker, Travis, 193-194, 197

L
Lactantius, 98-101
Lakatos, Imre, 78
Language,
    meaning implicit in, 79
    translatability of, 153, 211-215, 206
Lash, Nicholas, 296
Law, 245-271. *See also* natural law; Torah.
    Jewish, as prototype for Western civil law, 270-271
    relationship to gospel, 259
    secular courts of, 267
Lessing, Gotthold, 25, 26, 91

Levenson, Jon D., 267-269
Levinas, Emmanuel, 47, 81
Leviticus, 258, 290
Liberalism, 91, 97, 116, 166, 217, 268, 275
    defined, 207
    Hauerwas's opposition to, 192-194, 207-214
Liberation theology, 36, 268
Licinius, Roman Emperor, 98
Liestal, Switzerland, 126
Liturgy: see worship.
Locke, John, 91
Logic of violence, 61-64
Lordship of Jesus Christ, 70, 104, 109-113, 209, 321
Lukacs, Georg, 170
Luke-Acts, 262-267, 288-297. *See also* Jubilee; release
Luther, Martin, 259, 278

M
MacIntyre, Alasdair, 138, 211, 216, 217, 296
Marcellinus, 226
Marcion, 45, 251, 254, 256
Mark, Gospel of, 258, 263, 290, 292, 296, 307
Marty, Martin, 100
Martyn, J. Louis, 275-276
Marxism, 268
Matthew, Gospel of, 250, 291-292, 296, 307, 330. *See also* Sermon on the Mount
McClendon, James, 93, 95, 194
Meeks, Wayne, 296
Menno Simons Lectures, 147
Mennonite Economic Development Agency (MEDA), 250
Mennonites, 12, 17, 77, 198, 249, 267. See also Anabaptists
    and liberalism, 217
    and Old Testament, 255-256
    pacifism of, 245-247, 267
    parallels with Judaism, 259
    rejection of Anselm, 310

social ethics of, 248
stance toward civil institutions, 250, 258, 267
voluntarism of, 191-194
and witness to the world, 40, 259
and worship, 197
Yoder's influence on, 296-297
Methodists, 197-198
Methodologism, 25-28, 30, 162, 188, 217. *See also* foundationalism
Methodology, 24-25, 34
    Constantinian and non-Constantinian, 28-31
    relationship to discipleship, 23-25, 34-36
Middle axioms, 211-213, 234
Middle East, 161-178, 268
Milan, Edict of, 98, 128
Milbank, John, 42, 193
Mille, J. S., 91
Millenarian movements, 102
Miller, John W., 45, 151-152, 250, 252-255
Minorities, 29, 189, 210-211
    early Christians as, 135, 146, 266, 282
    Mennonites as, 259, 267
    power of, 109-110, 224
Mishnah, 150, 260
Mission of the church, 70-71, 233, 297, 333. *See also* witness
Missionary communities, 148-149
Monasticism, 102
Monophysitism, 104, 324
Moral agenda, public, 111-113
Mott, Stephen Charles, 289-290
Murphy, Nancey, 77
Music Machine, 75

N
Nabokov, Vladimir, 169
Nation, Mark Thiessen, 197
Nationalism and sin of pride, 233
Nations, 188-191, 253, 281. *See also* church and world
Natural law, 111, 235, 268

Natural theology. *See* creation, theology of
Nehemiah, 253-255, 282
Neo-Constantinianism. *See* Constantinianism in modernity
Neo-Platonism, 152-153
Nestorianism, 104, 134, 324
Nicea, Council of, 93, 103, 129, 133-134, 323-324
Nicene Creed, 40, 323, 324, 327
Niebuhr, H. Richard, 188, 236-237
Niebuhr, Reinhold, 39, 85, 109, 110, 188, 248-249
    debate with H. Richard Niebuhr, 236-237,
    Yoder's attention to, 228-231
Nietzsche, Friedrich, 78, 82
Non-Constantinian epistemology. *See* epistemology of peace.
Non-Constantinian identity, 147-148
Nonviolence, 48, 58, 151. *See also* ecclesiology, nonviolent; exile and nonviolence; pacifism
    and Anselmian atonement, 312
    and ecumenical dialogue, 41, 126, 127
    and effectiveness, 248
    Jewish, 147
    and just war tradition, 68
    and realism, 29
Nonviolent
    discourse, 85
    epistemology. *See* epistemology of peace
    method, 36, 56

O
O'Donovan, Oliver, 48, 94, 95, 193-194, 257
Obedience, 31
Old Testament, 250-259
Ollenburger, Ben, 290
Ordering of society, Christian, 156
Origen, 130

P
Pacifism, 30-31, 44, 58. *See also* nonviolence
    and Augustine, 235-237
    critiqued by Virilio, 57
    and just war theory, 69
    and justice, 127
    of Mennonites, 245-247
    and policing, 267
    vocational, 255
Paine, Thomas, 91
Palestinian experience, 161, 167-168, 172-177. See also exile.
Particularity, 52, 217, 267-270, 151-154
Patience, 67, 82-84
    Christian life as, 34-36
    of Jesus, 47
    as method, 56, 64, 66
    and pacifism, 62, 71, 110-111
    (song title), 75, 85
    and uncertainty, 86
Paul and civil authorities, 262-267
Pauline theology, 274-284
Peace narrative, 146-147
Peace of the city (Jeremiah 29:7), 65, 148-149, 162-164, 221-222
    Augustine on, 227
    and Christian witness, 153, 233
    and pacifism, 235
    as salvation of culture, 228
Peaceableness, 42-44, 236
People of God, 65, 162-178, 281
Performance, 42, 46-53, 296-297
Persecution, 97, 110-111, 132
Persuasion vs. coercion, 110-111
Peters, John Durham, 46-47
Peterson, Erik, 133-134
Philo of Alexandria, 254, 267
Pietism, 197
Plato, 46, 90, 225, 254
Pluralism, 209-211, 268, 328-329
Policing, 267
Postmodernism, 210
Power structures, 109-110
Practices. *See* witness, practices of;

church, practices of; worship, practices of.
Pride of nation states, 232
Priesthood of all believers, 106-107
Primitive New Testament writings, 321-322
Principalities and powers, 258, 276-277, 327
"Protection of Endangered Populations" (WCC study paper), 127
Protestant tradition, 278
Punishment, role of, 310
Pure War (per Virilio), 56, 60-61

Q
Qumran, 260, 294

R
Rationality. *See* liberalism.
Rawls, John, 268
Raz-Krakotzkin, Amnon, 175-178
Reames, Kent, 205
Redekop, Calvin, 250
Reesor-Taylor, Rachel, 16
Reign of God, 258
Reimer, A. James, 15, 42, 319-320, 326
    and Constantinianism, 92, 114,
    devaluing of the transcendent, 41, 45, 197, 320
    particularity and. universality, 146, 151-154
    voluntarism in believers church, 194
Reiser, Konrad, 126
Relativism, 25-27, 82, 153, 209, 328
Release, meaning of, in Luke, 290, 295-296
Resistance (per Virilio), 62-64
Restitutionist view of history, 136-137
Restorative justice, 313
Resurrection, logic of, 30-33
Revelation, book of, 94-95, 251, 254, 307, 322
Roman empire, 126-139
    Augustine's critique of, 223-225,

    232
Christian symbols in, 100-101
    political changes in, under Constantine, 97-98, 130-134
    sociological changes in, under Constantine, 104-105
Ruhbach, Gerhard, 134

S
Sacerdotalism, 106
Sacraments, 306, 330. *See also* baptism; church, practices of; Eucharist;
    worship, practices of
    role of, in Christendom, 101-102, 189
    as social witness, 50-51, 330
    theology of, 40-42, 48-51, 101, 196-197
Sacrifice and punishment, 313
Said, Edward, 14, 162-178
Sartre, Jean-Paul, 85
Satan, 295, 297
Satisfaction theory of atonement. *See* Anselm's Satisfaction theory
Sattler, Michael, 307
Saussure, Ferdinand de, 79
Schism, Jewish/Christian, 282
Schlabach, Gerald W., 15, 40
    and Constantinianism, 113-114, 128, 156-157
    living rightly in the land, 84, 156-157, 173-174
Schweitzer, Albert, 275
Scripture as central symbol for Jews and Christians, 150
Sectarianism, 77, 153, 190, 228
Secularization, 207
Seek the peace of the city: *See* peace of the city.
Serendipitous induction, 33
Sermon on the Mount, 245-246, 260-263. *See also* Matthew, Gospel of
Shalom, as manifested in Christendom, 115

Shavit, Ari, 177
Shipwreck symbolism in Acts, 265-266
Sider, J. Alexander, 15
Siemens, Mark, 127
Signs, meaning implicit in, 79
Siker, Jeffrey, 195-196
Silberstein, Laurence, 174-176
Smith, Adam, 91
Social location influence on Yoder's thought, 249-250
Society. *See also* church and world. ordering of, 156
Sociopolitical context of Jesus and Paul, 274
Socrates, 90-91, 108-109
Southern, R. W., 99
Speech. *See* divine speech
Speed, relationship of, to violence, 57, 59, 63, 67
Spirituality of peaceableness, 236-237
Stoicism, 101, 227
Stout, Jeffrey, 154, 208, 210
Supercessionism, 251-256, 262, 267, 283-284
Swartley, Willard M., 15
Swartzentruber, A. Orley, 250
Synagogue, 150, 250-252
System within Yoder's theology, 77-78
    lack of, 13, 82, 230, 304, 321
Systematic theology, 318-321, 306

T
Talmud, 150-151
Tannehill, Robert C., 260, 263-267
Technology, as component of warfare, 59-61
Temptations of Jesus, 289-290
Terrorism, 59
Tertullian, 130, 131
Theodosius, Roman emperor, 99, 131
Theological writers of the NT, 322
Toleration, edict of, 98

Tolstoy, Leo, 110
Tool (rock band), 75, 85
Toole, David, 14
Torah, 150, 252, 259-260, 269-270
    Matthean view of, 260-262
Tradition of Roman Catholic church, 197
Transcendence, 90, 150-151, 320, 328-333
Translatability, 153, 206, 211-215
Trocmé, André, 288
Troeltsch, Ernst, 26, 106
Truth claims, 82-83, 235, 267-268, 328
Truthfulness, 84

U
Uncritical writings of New Testament, 321-322
United Nations, 253
United States, 147, 189, 249
Unity, Christian, 41-42, 52, 97. *See also* ecumenical dialogue.
Universality, 26, 151, 210, 217, 265-268, 329

V
Valerian, Roman emperor, 131
Van Beeck, Franz Josef, 45
Violence
    in Western culture, 57, 59-61
    unavoidability of, 81, 85
Virilio, Paul, 14, 56-64, 71
Voluntarism, 48-49, 100, 188, 191-194
Vulnerability as outcome of peacemaking, 31

W
War, 56, 59-61, 216. *See also* just war tradition
Wealth, relationship of, to violence, 59
Weaver, Alain Epp, 14, 45, 315
Weaver, J. Denny, 46, 303-304, 309-310
Welker, Michael, 270
Wesley, John, 197

Western culture, 48-49, 56
Wheaton College, 193
Williams, George Hunston, 133
Williams, Rowan, 296
Willimon, William, 93-95, 101
Witness, 40-42, 52, 206, 221-237. *See also* mission of the church; church and world
    as disruptive, 216
    non-Constantinian, 70-71, 115-116
    practices of, 213-215
    to those in power, 115-116, 211-213, 231, 233
    world's response to, 215-217
Wittgenstein, Ludwig, 12-13, 212, 217
Women in Gospel of Luke, 294
Word and deed, connection of, 50
World Council of Churches, 126-127
Worldview, 147-148, 312, 320, 325, 329
Worship
    and ethics, 195-197, 213
    instrumentalist view of 197
    practices of, 217
    Yoder's definition of, 195
Wright, N. T., 277, 283
Wycliff, John, 102

X
Xenophon, 90

Y
Yale University, 217
Yoder, John Howard,
    impact of, 12, 296-297
    social location of, 249-250
    writings of,
      "Adjusting to the Changing Shape of the Debate on Infant Baptism," 51
      "Anabaptism and History," 136-137
      Body Politics, 50, 105, 191, 213, 321, 330-333
      "But We Do See Jesus," 43, 328

"Christian Case for Democracy," 213
Christian Witness to the State, 156, 211, 230, 249
"Confessing Christ in Mission," 46
Exodus and Exile: Two Faces of Liberation, 162
For the Nations, 145, 188, 190, 206, 228
"Hermeneutics of Peoplehood," 34, 155, 191-192
"Methodological Miscellany," 82
"On Not Being Ashamed of the Gospel," 43
"Patience as Method in Moral Reasoning," 23-36
"Paul: Jewish Missionary," 149
"Peace Without Eschatology," 128
Politics of Jesus, 103, 134, 152, 155, 280, 297, 311, 315, 321
    and Jubilee in Luke's Gospel, 288-292
    and Pauline theology, 274-277, 280
    and transcendence, 326-328
Preface to Theology, 309, 311, 321-329, 332
Priestly Kingdom, 155, 189, 191
Reinhold Niebuhr and Christian Pacifism, 229
"See How They Go With Their Face to the Sun," 145, 281
"Walk and Word: The Alternatives to Methodologism," 23-36
When War is Unjust, 247
Yoder, Perry, 310
Young, Frances, 296

Z
Zehr, Howard, 313
Zionism, 147, 166, 173-177
Zweig, Stephan, 145

The Contributors

Gerald Biesecker-Mast is Associate Professor of Communication at Bluffton College, Bluffton, Ohio. He is a graduate of Malone College and received his Ph.D. in rhetoric and communication from the University of Pittsburgh in 1995. He has published numerous articles on Anabaptist-Mennonite persuasion and is the co-editor of two volumes of essays: *Anabaptists and Postmodernity* (Pandora Press U.S., 2000) and *Teaching Peace: Nonviolence and the Liberal Arts* (Rowan and Littlefield, 2003).

Peter C. Blum is Associate Professor of Sociology and Social Thought at Hillsdale College, Hillsdale, Michigan, where he has taught since 1992. Originally from Ohio, he received his B.A. from Goshen College, Goshen, Indiana in 1985 and holds graduate degrees in sociology and philosophy from the University of Notre Dame. He is the author of several recent and forthcoming essays on contemporary social theory and Anabaptist thought.

Paul Doerksen teaches Christian Studies and history at Mennonite Brethren Collegiate in Winnipeg, Manitoba. He received his Master of Theological Studies from Conrad Grebel University College, Waterloo, Ontario and is in a Ph.D. program at McMaster University, Waterloo, Ontario. He and his wife Julie, a choral conductor, are the parents of three daughters—Cecely, Hannah, and Greta.

Alain Epp Weaver lives in East Jerusalem where he directs the relief, development and peacebuilding work of Mennonite Central Committee in Palestine/Israel. In addition to co-authoring a history of Mennonite Central Committee's work with Palestinians and editing a *Festschrift* for Mennonite theologian Gordon Kaufman, Alain has published articles in such journals as *The Review of Politics, the Journal of Religious Ethics, the Mennonite Quarterly Review,* and *Christian Century*.

Thomas Finger is an independent scholar living in Evanston, Illinois, where he is adjunct professor at Garrett-Evangelical Theological Seminary. He received his Ph.D. in Philosophy of Religion and Systematic Theology from Claremont Graduate School in 1975. During 2002

Finger was a Fellow of the Young Center for the Study of Anabaptist and Pietist Groups at Elizabethtown College in Pennsylvania. His most recent publication is *A Constructive Theology in Anabaptist Perspective: biblical, Historical, Contemporary* (InterVarsity Press, forthcoming). He has published in numerous journals such as *The Mennonite Quarterly Review*, *Ecumenical Trends* and *Perspectives in Religious Studies*, and has long been active in national and international ecumenical circles.

Duane K. Friesen is Professor of Bible and Religion at Bethel College, North Newton, Kansas. He also is on the faculty of Associated Mennonite Biblical Seminary: Great Plains, in Kansas. Friesen is a graduate of Bethel College and Mennonite Biblical Seminary, Elkhart, Indiana, and received his Th.D. in Social Ethics from Harvard Divinity School in 1972. He is the author of numerous articles and several books, most recently of *Artists, Citizens, Philosophers: Seeking the Peace of the City* (Herald Press, 2000).

Douglas Harink is Associate Professor of Theology at The King's University College in Edmonton, Alberta. He recently served as president of the Canadian Theological Society and of the Canadian Evangelical Theological Association. Harink is the author of several journal articles and, most recently, *Paul Among the Postliberals: Pauline Theology Beyond Christendom and Modernity* (Brazos Press, 2003). He is currently writing a theological commentary on 1 and 2 Peter for Brazos Press.

Thomas Heilke is Interim Associate Dean of International Programs and Associate Professor of Political Science at the University of Kansas, where he teaches classes on the history of political philosophy, politics and religion, and international relations. He received his Ph.D. from Duke University in 1990. He is the author or editor of numerous books, articles, and chapters on a variety of topics, including Anabaptist political thought.

Craig R. Hovey is at Trinity Hall, Cambridge, England, where he is a Ph.D. student in the Faculty of Divinity at the University of Cambridge. He is the author of various articles and reviews.

Chris K. Huebner is Assistant Professor of Theology and Ethics at Canadian Mennonite University, Winnipeg, Manitoba . He has published several journal articles on the theological intersection of knowledge and politics, most recently, "Globalization, Theory and Dialogical Vulnerability: John Howard Yoder and the Possibility of a Pacifist Epistemology," *Mennonite Quarterly Review* 76:1 (2002): 49-62. He received his Ph.D. from Duke University in 2002.

Harry Huebner is Vice President and Academic Dean at Canadian Mennonite University, Winnipeg, Manitoba, Canada where he is also Professor of Philosophy and Theology. He received his Ph.D. from the

University of St. Michael's College, Toronto, in 1981. Huebner is co-author with David Schroeder of *Church as Parable: Whatever Happened to Ethics?* (CMBC Publications, 1993), the editor of several volumes, and author of several journal articles.

A. James Reimer teaches theology at Conrad Grebel University College, University of Waterloo, Ontario, and Toronto School of Theology (TST), University of Toronto. He is Director of Toronto Mennonite Theological Center, a graduate teaching and research center at TST, and is active in teaching and preaching within the Mennonite community. Reimer has written many articles and a number of books, the most recent being *Mennonites and Classical Theology: Dogmatic Foundations for Christian Ethics* (Pandora, 2001), and *The Dogmatic Imagination: The Dynamics of Christian Faith* (Herald, 2003).

Rachel Reesor-Taylor is Assistant Professor of Religion at Bluffton College, Bluffton, Ohio. She received an M.A. from McGill University, Montreal, Quebec, and is still working to complete her Ph.D. from McGill. Before arriving in Bluffton, she spent one semester at Associated Mennonite Biblical Seminary as the recipient of the Women's Lectureship Stipend, and taught at Queen's Theological College, Kingston, Ontario. She has prepared numerous papers for conferences and/or publication on the topics of atonement, Anselm and contemporary Mennonite theology.

Gerald W. Schlabach is Associate Professor of Theology at the University of St. Thomas in Minnesota. He has also taught at Bluffton College in Ohio and served in Central America with Mennonite Central Committee. He received his Ph.D. from the University of Notre Dame in 1996. His most recent book is *For the Joy Set Before Us: Augustine and Self-Denying Love.*

J. Alexander Sider is a theology and ethics doctoral candidate in the Graduate Program in Religion at Duke University, Durham, North Carolina. He is a graduate of Messiah College, Grantham, Pennsylvania, and Duke University Divinity School.

Willard Swartley is professor of New Testament at the Associated Mennonite Biblical Seminary where he also served as director of the Institute of Mennonite Studies. He holds a Ph.D. from Princeton Theological Seminary (1973). Swartley is New Testament editor of the Believers Church Bible Commentary Series. He has edited numerous books and has authored many articles and books, among which are *Slavery, Sabbath, War and Women: Case Issues in Biblical Interpretation* (Herald Press, 1983); *Israel's Scripture Traditions and the Synoptic Gospels: Story Shaping Story* (Hendrickson Publishers, 1994); and *Homosexuality: Biblical Interpretation and Moral Discernment* (Herald Press, 2003).

The Editors

Ben C. Ollenburger is Professor of Biblical Theology at the Associated Mennonite Biblical Seminary. He was previously Instructor in Religious Studies and Philosophy at Tabor College, Hillsoboro, Kansas and Assistant Professor of Old Testament at Princeton Theological Seminary. Among his publications are the commentary on Zechariah in the *New Interpreter's Bible* (Abingdon, 1996) and *Old Testament Theology: Flowering and Future* (Eisenbrauns, 2003).

Gayle Gerber Koontz is Professor of Theology and Ethics at the Associated Mennonite Biblical Seminary in Elkhart, Indiana, where she has taught and served in administrative roles since 1982. Her doctoral thesis (Boston University, 1985) examined religious pluralism in relation to the work of John H. Yoder and H. Richard Niebuhr. She has taught theology in Mennonite Central Committee assignments in the Philippines, Rwanda and Burundi. Koontz is author of various journal articles and is developing a longer manuscript with the tentative title, "Geography of the Spirit: Toward a Theology and Ethics of Place."